The Ingenious YANKEES

By Joseph Gies

Bridges and Men
Adventure Underground
Wonders of the Modern World

By Joseph and Frances Gies

Life in a Medieval City
Leonard of Pisa and the
    New Mathematics of the
    Middle Ages
Merchants and Moneymen
Life in a Medieval Castle
The Ingenious Yankees

With Melvin Kranzberg

By the Sweat of Thy Brow

The Ingenious
YANKEES

Joseph and Frances Gies

Thomas Y. Crowell Company

NEW YORK   ESTABLISHED 1834

Designed by Ingrid Beckman

Manufactured in the United States of America

Library of Congress Cataloging in Publication Data

Gies, Joseph.
    The ingenious Yankees.

    Bibliography: p.
    Includes index.
    1. Technology—History—United States. 2. Inventors—United States—Biography. I. Gies, Frances, joint author. II. Title.
T21.G5   609'.73   76-10239
ISBN 0-690-01150-4

1 2 3 4 5 6 7 8 9 10

ACKNOWLEDGMENTS

THIS BOOK WAS RESEARCHED at the Northwestern University Library, the McKeldin Library of the University of Maryland, and the Library of Congress, as well as at museums, restorations, and historic sites: Batsto Early Iron Village, the Cyrus McCormick Memorial Museum, Greenfield Village, the Hagley Museum, Harper's Ferry National Historical Park, the Henry Ford Museum, Historic Salem, Hopewell Village National Historic Site, the John Deere Historic Site, the Merrimack Valley Textile Museum, Mystic Seaport, Old Sturbridge Village, the Pennsylvania Farm Museum, the Saugus Ironworks Restoration, the Shelburne Museum, the Slater Mill Historic Site, the Smithsonian Institution's Museum of History and Technology, the Thomas A. Edison birthplace, and Williamsburg.

The authors wish to express their gratitude to several scholarly authorities who read portions of the manuscript and offered suggestions, criticisms, and corrections: Richard Sanders Allen, covered-bridge expert; Edwin A. Battison, Curator of the Smithsonian's Department of Mechanical Engineering; Grace Rogers Cooper, the Smithsonian's Curator of Textiles; Craddock Goins, Curator of the Division of Military History of the Smithsonian; James J. Hughes, Vice-President of the American Iron and Steel Institute; Lewis T. Karabatsos of the Lowell Historical Society; Gary Kulik, Curator of the Slater Mill Historic Site; Cecil R. Norman, Archivist of the Goodyear Rubber Company; Paul Rivard, Director of the Rockwell-Corning Museum; Donald R. Woodford of the American Telephone and Telegraph Company; and Richard N. Wright, Secretary-treasurer of the Canal Society of New York State.

We also owe thanks to a number of persons and institutions in connection with the illustrations. Richard Sanders Allen generously lent us covered-bridge pictures from his collection. The American Iron and Steel Institute, the American Telephone and Telegraph Company, the Edison National Historic Site in Orange, New Jersey, the Goodyear Tire and Rubber Company, John Deere and Company, the Pennsylvania Historical and Museum Commission, the Singer Company, the Slater Mill Historic Site, and Sperry Remington all contributed photographs. We are also grateful to the Buffalo and Erie County Historical Society, the Canal Society of New York, the Eleutherian Mills Historical Library, the Free Library of Philadelphia, Greenfield Village and the Henry Ford Museum, Harper's Ferry National Historical Park, the Library of Congress, the Museum of the City of New York, the National Archives, the New York State Historical Association in Cooperstown, the New York Historical Society in New York City, the Philadelphia Museum of Art, the Rhode Island Historical Society, and the University of Michigan's Engineering-Transportation Library. Our special thanks to Carol Forsyth of the Smithsonian's Museum of History and Technology for her help in our picture research.

CONTENTS

PHILADELPHIA 1876

Philadelphia 1876

ON THE MORNING of May 10, 1876, Chestnut, Market, Walnut, all the streets of downtown Philadelphia, were decked with flags and thronged with traffic—horsecar, steam car, carriage, omnibus, foot. Visitors from the old cities of the East Coast, from the farms and new cities of the Middle West, from the war-scarred South, from California, mingled with a sprinkling of Europeans in a cavalcade headed for Fairmount Park, scene of America's first great International Exhibition. Philadelphia had won the honor of playing host to the nation's Centennial celebration after a fierce battle with jealous rivals, mainly Boston and New York, and both the city and the state of Pennsylvania had contributed generously, even rashly, to make the show a success.

Long before the opening hour of 9 A.M. a huge crowd had collected on Elm Avenue before the Main Gate, with the stream from the city joined by crowds from the new hotels on Lancaster Avenue built especially for the Exhibition, and from the Pennsylvania Railroad's Centennial Depot, directly opposite the fairgrounds. Elm Avenue was lined with peanut stands, pie stalls, cake-and-lemonade stands, itinerant apple-men, apple-women, Bologna sausage vendors, ice cream parlors, beer gardens, and shows—the Museum, starring P. T. Barnum's Wild Man of Borneo, a full-scale model of a Pennsylvania oil well, and a section of a California "Big Tree." However the visitors arrived, or wherever they came from, they all gaped at the immensity of the Exhibition. The Main Building covered twenty-one acres of ground, dwarfing every other building in America, and in fact exceed-

3

Opening day at the Philadelphia Centennial Exhibition, May 10, 1876, in front of the Main Hall. (Philadelphia Free Library)

ing anything ever built before in the world with the sole exception of the exhibition hall Paris had built on the Champs de Mars for its own Exhibition of 1867. But the Paris hall had housed the entire exhibition, while Philadelphia's Main Building was only the largest of five huge halls and scores of "pavilions."

When the gate opened at nine o'clock, the crush poured into the grounds to find two platforms erected in front of Memorial Hall, north of the Main Building, one for President Ulysses S. Grant, visiting Emperor Pedro II of Brazil and a crowd of lesser dignitaries, the other for a chorus of a thousand voices. The orchestra struck up an overture of national anthems, and followed it with a "Centennial Inauguration March" composed by Richard Wagner. After the invocation, the chorus sang the "Centennial Hymn," by the venerable John Greenleaf Whittier, beginning:

> Our fathers' God! from out whose hand
> The centuries fall like grains of sand,
> We meet today, united, free,
> And loyal to our land and thee,
> To thank thee for the era done,
> And trust thee for the opening one.

Main Hall. (American Telephone and Telegraph)

After speeches and more music, at noon the flags were raised on all the buildings, and a hundred-gun salute thundered. Then President Grant and the emperor led the way down the length of the cavernous Main Building, out the far end, and past one of the Exhibition's many fountains, to another immense new building, Machinery Hall.

Here George H. Corliss, wealthy Providence industrialist and Centennial Commissioner for Rhode Island, waited on another platform. Behind him towered his personal gift to the Exhibition, the Corliss Double Walking-Beam Steam Engine, whose 30-foot, 56-ton flywheel was designed to supply the power for all the machinery exhibited in Machinery Hall. With deferential pride, Corliss showed the president and the emperor how to turn a pair of wheels and, when as much of the crowd as could squeeze in was in place, gave a hand signal. The two heads of state obediently turned their wheels, and overhead the twin walking beams began to rock, stirring the mighty flywheel into silent motion. Throughout the vast hall belts began to move and wheels to spin, and in a few moments hundreds of machines were humming and clacking. Spontaneously, the crowd burst into a long, delighted round of applause.

The tableau was perfect. Those who had come to Philadelphia bemused with images of Betsy Ross and the Liberty Bell were awakened at a stroke to the reality of America's first century—the transformation of the country from a scattering of seaboard towns and farms on the edge of a continental wilderness to an industrial colossus, bestriding North America and rivaling, or rather surpassing, the old European powers.

Machinery Hall was the true heart of the Exhibition. Understandably, Great Britain and the continental European nations were limited in their contributions by the expense of shipping, but it was not short of amazing that three-fourths of the whole mighty display was American.

Lathes, presses, power looms, steam hammers, milling machines, pumps—the variety and profusion were impressive without the numerous superlatives attached to them. The steam-hydraulic cotton press of the Taylor Iron Works of South Carolina was "the most powerful in the world." The section of wire cable for John A. Roebling's famous Niagara suspension bridge was the largest in the world, and about to be surpassed by that for the new Brooklyn Bridge, whose 1,595-foot main span dwarfed all the bridges of Europe. As a sort of analogue to the Corliss engine, a 7,000-pound pendulum clock by Seth Thomas acted as electrical master to twenty-six slave clocks around the building.

The central aisle was crowded with the latest models of one of America's most valued inventions, the sewing machine, a portrait of whose chief inventor, Massachusetts's Elias Howe, gazed benevolently down on visitors to the exhibit. Several other makes of sewing machine were also represented, but the largest manufacturer, Isaac Singer, had so many new models that he had built his own pavilion elsewhere on the grounds.

An array of locomotives and equipment included George Westinghouse's revolutionary air brake, just introduced on the Pennsylvania Railroad. Christopher Sholes's new "type-writer," manufactured by the Remington Arms Company, astonished visitors by printing neat and legible characters at the touch of the op-

Hoe rotary press in Machinery Hall, which turned out copies of the *New York Herald* and *Philadelphia Times*. From *Harper's Weekly*, December 9, 1876. (Library of Congress)

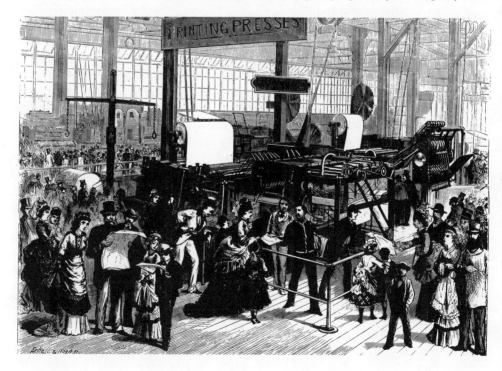

erator's fingers. Massive rotary presses of the Bullock and Hoe companies demonstrated their prowess by turning out thousands of copies of the *New York Herald* and the *Philadelphia Times*. A group of machines exploiting the invention of the late Charles Goodyear fashioned "India rubber" boots and shoes for visitors.

To the connoisseur of technology, perhaps the most telling display in Machinery Hall was in the area containing the products of William Sellers & Company of Philadelphia and Pratt & Whitney of Hartford, Connecticut, America's foremost manufacturers of machine tools—the machines that make machines. Sober black iron monsters whose varying steel edges could cut, chip, stamp, mold, grind, and otherwise shape metal, they had made possible the world-famous "American System of Manufacture," meaning high-speed mass production with interchangeable parts. In the separate U.S. Government Building nearby, workers and machines from the Springfield Arsenal demonstrated the system itself by assembling rifles from identical parts machined to a thousandth of an inch tolerance.

Between the Sellers and Pratt & Whitney displays the Midvale Steel Works of Philadelphia showed off its largest axles, shafts, and chilled-steel bars, demonstrating a sophisticated American capability with this once-exotic metal whose quantity production had first been achieved by an American. Steel's birth as a structural material was the subject of another display, a model showing how the steel arches of Captain James Eads's mighty St. Louis Bridge had been formed and joined.

Baffling to the layman, but nonetheless impressive, was an 8-foot-long mechanism mounted on a pair of trestle legs and looking like the insides of a thousand-keyed piano. This was George B. Grant's "Calculating Machine," an American version of Charles Babbage's much-talked-about British calculator. Grant's creation was considered an improvement on Babbage's, though certainly less original, but it suffered from the same inherent defect, the unsuitability of mechanical components to perform the lightning-swift operations that only electronics would permit. No one guessed the future relationship of the perforated paper rolls that programmed the twelve-piece "Electro-Magnetic Orchestra" in Horticultural Hall with the Babbage-Grant machines.

The discovery of radio waves had not yet brought the word *electronics* into the language in 1876. Yet the practical application of electricity to communications initiated by Joseph Henry and Samuel Morse was the object of an ingenious modification by twenty-nine-year-old Thomas Edison, a "multiplex" telegraph capable of sending several messages at once over the same wire. That, however, was a small wonder compared to another offshoot of the telegraph that had not yet arrived in Philadelphia on May 10. When a few weeks after the opening Alexander Graham Bell demonstrated his telephone, it became the invention the Centennial Exhibition was remembered by.

In the Main Hall, devoted to products rather than the means of producing them, American genius shone less brightly in competition with fine porcelains, silver and gold ware, bronzes, tiles, furniture, lamps, candelabra, and other art objects from the craftsmen of the Old World. In his speech President Grant had touched with un-American deprecation on the mediocrity of the nation's contributions to the fine arts, referring to "older and more advanced nations" and apologizing that "whilst proud of what we have done, we regret that we have not done more."

Even among the art objects were some American triumphs, but characteristically they tended to be technological: two immense steam-driven pipe organs, and the pianos of Steinway, Weber, Knabe, and Chickering.

Also in the Main Hall were the famous Yale locks of Stamford, Connecticut, acknowledged the best in the world, and an American military arsenal featuring the Gatling gun, the world's first machine gun, and heavy breech-loading Parrott guns that rivaled the German Empire's exhibit of the Krupp cannon that had bombarded Paris.

The third largest building in the Exhibition was Agricultural Hall, an innovation in international exhibitions, in which American technology predominated even more than in Machinery Hall. The world-famous McCormick Reaper was displayed in its latest model fitted with an automatic binder; the Adams Power Corn Sheller; Slosser's self-loading excavator; the Union Corn Planter; the Buckeye Mower and Reaper; the Sweepstakes Thresher; and an array of grain drills, horse rakes, hay loaders, fruit dryers, gang plows, portable steam engines, and steam road rollers that would have bewildered an American farmer of 1776. A separate Wagon Annex housed another famous line of American products—farm wagons, milk carts, and ice wagons renowned for their lightness, strength, and durability. No one yet foresaw the union of American wagon-and-carriage manufacture, centered in southern Michigan, with a new European invention, the internal combustion engine, one version of which was displayed by Langen & Otto of Germany.

Qualitatively, American food products did not compete with European any better than did American art—the new California wine made no pretension of rivaling French. But again American technology supplied a masterpiece: Gail Borden's condensed milk, invented twenty years earlier but only just becoming an important consumer product.

Even the Women's Pavilion had a strongly technological atmosphere, displaying in addition to art by women (a head of Iolanthe carved in butter by "Mrs. Brooks of Arkansas" was much admired), industrial machinery typically operated by women and inventions made by women. The machinery was mostly for spinning and weaving, and was powered by a steam engine run by a young lady from Iowa, who, it was noted, kept her engine and engine room in a spic-and-span state of tidiness that male engineers rarely achieved. The inventions were uniformly aimed at lightening household tasks: a mangling machine, self-fitting patterns, a blanket washer, a lockable flour-barrel cover, gas-heated smoothing irons, a curtain stretcher, a dish washer and dryer, a traveling bag that doubled as a chair.

General Joseph R. Hawley, closing the Exhibition on November 10 after a satisfying numerical triumph for the American record book (ten million attendance, eight million paid, beating the Paris Exposition of 1867), was well justified in summarizing: "The United States have been advertised to an immense extent. The world knows a great deal more about us than it ever did before."

He might have added that America now knew a great deal more about itself than it had before. The overflowing technological abundance of the Exhibition swelled native hearts with pride, and provoked little if any carping dissent. Yet amid the self-congratulation there was perhaps a tiny note of regret. In the art exhibit in Memorial Hall one of the most popular paintings proved to be Jerome Thompson's *The Old Oaken Bucket,* nostalgic image of a rustic past, and the New England appliance manufacturer who built a 1776 log cabin to contrast with his latest model stove and washer was surprised to find the log cabin, with its authentic Pilgrim Father spinning wheel, outdrawing the modern kitchen.

The country had come so far so fast it found itself a little taken aback. No nation had ever before undergone an experience like America's first hundred years, and the more one looked back at 1776, the more the question seemed in order: how did it all happen?

PART I

1

America 1776

OF THE TWO AND A HALF MILLION PEOPLE who, with varying degrees of enthusiasm or reluctance (or awareness of what was going on) declared the British colonies they inhabited along the North Atlantic seaboard to be free and independent states, about two and a quarter million lived on farms or in small villages. Most were full-time farmers, the rest blacksmiths, carpenters, storekeepers, and ministers, many of whom farmed part time. However they felt, the event surprised few. Before a shot was fired at Lexington a British visitor recorded: "The colonies we have planted in America have arisen to such a height of populousness, power and wealth that an idea of their future independency starts into the mind of almost every man on the very mention of them in conversation: some assert the period near at hand."

The typical American farm had no more than ten to twenty acres devoted to cultivation, and produced only modest and precarious surpluses. Wheat was the favored crop in the northern states, but in many places such as rocky New Hampshire, only rye or barley could be successfully cultivated, and the farm family ate black bread. Oats, buckwheat, peas, beans, turnips, clover, hemp, and flax were also grown in limited amounts, mostly for the farm family's own consumption. Besides these seed crops brought from Europe, created out of millennia of observation and experimentation from the Tigris-Euphrates to the British Isles, American farmers cultivated three valuable plants developed by the native "Indian" peoples of the Western Hemisphere—corn (maize), tobacco, and potatoes.

The American eighteenth-century landscape: a Pennsylvania farm. From *Columbian Magazine*, 1788. (Library of Congress)

The American farmer's tools were those of contemporary European agricultural technology. Wooden plows with wrought-iron shares scratched the soil to a depth of two or three inches at great cost in human and animal labor, partly because the iron cutting edge, or share, was too narrow to cut well, and the wooden mold-board, meant to turn the earth over, was shaped so that much of the earth fell back into the furrow. Harrows were crudely fashioned of brushwood armed with iron or often wooden teeth. Sickles and scythes were also made, either by the farmer himself or by the village blacksmith, according to the designs handed down through the centuries in western and Mediterranean Europe.

"Worse ploughing is nowhere to be seen," wrote the anonymous author of *American Husbandry,* published in London just before the Revolution, because in soil-rich America "very bad tilling . . . will yield excellent crops. . . . They depend on this plenty of land as a substitute for all industry and good management." Threshing was by jointed hand flails much like those invented in Gaul in the fourth century. Potatoes and other root crops were dug with wooden spades, tipped or sometimes covered with iron. Cattle were few, scrawny and random-bred, pigs were skinny half-wild "razorbacks." Unplanned crop succession and grazing rapidly depleted the soil, forcing most farmers to move after a few years, sometimes before fields were entirely cleared. Clearing was a laborious process accomplished by girdling trees to kill them, waiting for them to fall, dragging them off, and either digging out stumps or simply guiding the plow horse around them. The same English observer was shocked by the wastage—"which utterly destroys woods of trees which require an hundred years to come to perfection. . . ." In the 1790s another visitor, Isaac Weld, commented, "The Americans . . . seem to be totally dead to the beauties of nature." The sight of a wheat field or cabbage garden was far more admired than "the most romantic woodland views." He commented, "They have an unconquerable aversion to trees. I have heard of Americans landing on barren parts of the northwest coast of Ireland and evincing the greatest surprise and pleasure at the beauty and improved state of the country, 'so clear of trees.' "

The farmhouse was a one-story, low-ceilinged, rough timber structure, held together by "trunnels"—treenails, i.e., wooden pegs—the chinks in its plank walls plastered up with mud, and either painted red or left unpainted. Cooking was done in the fireplace, as in the Middle Ages, in an iron pot made, like the other cooking utensils, by the blacksmith. Meat was generally game, sausage, bacon, ham, salt pork, or chicken, with fresh pork, beef, or mutton an occasional treat. Bread was made from the grain grown on the farm, converted to flour by the local miller, who, as from time immemorial, kept as his payment a portion that might vary from a sixth to a sixteenth. Sugar, salt, molasses, and other luxuries were traded for at the village store. Farmers handled little cash.

Stockings were knitted in long evenings before the log fire. Beds were wooden frames, with straps to support a straw tick, or if the household was a prosperous one, a hair mattress and featherbed.

Children worked, if they survived infancy, and women worked as long as they survived childbirth. Few farm families ever saw a doctor, many never even a midwife. The frequent funerals were often without the services of a minister, and the mechanics of coffin and burial were performed by family or neighbors. Literacy, however, was widespread, especially in New England and Pennsylvania, though spelling tended to be picturesque.

On the frontier—upper New England, western New York and Pennsylvania, the Appalachians—life was rougher. The original habitation of the frontier farmer was a brushwood shelter, which only slowed the wind down, with perhaps a bearskin rug to roll up in on the earth floor. By the second winter, there was a log cabin, a medieval invention imported from forested Sweden. The chimney was mud and sticks, the furniture homemade wooden benches, table, and bed frame. Instead of straw the tick was stuffed with grass, moss, or corn shucks. After a first winter of surviving on venison, wild turkey, squirrel, and rabbit, often without salt, the new season's vegetables—turnips, cabbages, peas, beans—were greedily welcomed. So was bread, made from rye, wheat, or corn, cultivated perhaps with no more than a fork fashioned from a tree branch. A pioneer cash crop was potash, obtained by burning some of the girdled trees, pouring water on the ashes, and boiling, used for making soap and glass.

In the whole settled region, there were only a handful of towns—Boston, Providence, Newport, Albany, New York, Philadelphia, Baltimore, Charleston, Savannah—and no cities. The lack of a large urban center was perhaps the most striking difference between this New World nation and its European parents. It was a peculiar source of strength in the war against the British army, which could hardly find any place worth capturing. Philadelphia, the largest town, numbered about 30,000, a twentieth the size of London or Paris. Its streets were narrow and unpaved, the close-set red-brick shops and houses of its craftsmen and merchants of modest proportions. There was no structure of imposing size in Philadelphia or any other town. The Schuylkill was bridged by a crude pontoon span clumsily opened to let boats through. There was only one theater, relegated by Quaker morality to just outside city limits. Boston was equally devoid of theaters, though a British officer in 1775 sarcastically noted that Puritan strictness did not bar prostitution, a height neighboring Beacon Hill being named Mount Whoredom.

Philadelphia also boasted a small college for training clergymen, a library, and, its special pride, a "Philosophical Society" for scientific discussion, an offshoot of the European Enlightenment. Apart from shipbuilding, an industry that operated on a European scale in Philadelphia, Boston, New York, and several other coastal towns, American manufacturing enterprise was local and strictly handicraft. Philadelphia and New York manufactured some fifty or sixty products—iron implements, harness and leather goods, candles, pewterware, and other necessities of household and barn—for the benefit of farmers within the town's circle. Local raw materials were used, mainly wood, for tool handles, gunstocks, wagons, furniture.

Neither Philadelphia, New York, Boston, nor Baltimore had a municipal sewage or garbage system beyond the private wagoners who dumped their loads immediately outside town. Their services were limited to the middle-class quarter; the working-class alleys were filthy. Water supply was by spring or well, and a source of cholera. New York still depended on well water that was actually rain water filtered through the city's streets, graveyards, and other empty spaces to Manhattan's granite substructure, and tasted so bad that travelers' horses sometimes refused it. Lack of a water-supply system was a serious handicap in fighting the chronic fires, and in 1774 an ambitious plan had been set afoot for construction of a reservoir and log-pipe distribution system. The war and British occupation intervened, and in September 1776, a fire destroyed everything between Whitehall Street and Broadway, including Trinity Church. Thanks to Benjamin Franklin, Philadelphia had a volunteer fire department; most other towns fought fires with ad hoc bucket brigades.

City street lighting had been accomplished for several decades by assigning every seventh householder on each principal street the responsibility of hanging out a whale-oil lamp; the lamplighter's six neighbors contributed to the cost of maintenance. Philadelphia had progressed in 1752 to public streetlights.

The police function was in the hands of paid watchmen. Philadelphia's watch was praised by English visitors as "well-regulated," but that of Boston was often embroiled with the occupying Redcoats. Penal technology included, besides the town jail, a gallows usually located just outside town (in Boston on the narrow Neck, so that anyone entering the city passed it), a red-painted whipping post, and a pillory.

Boston was the most strictly commercial town. Long Wharf, jutting into Town Cove, was an extension of King Street (modern State Street), lined with docks and warehouses, world famous among sailors. Andrew Faneuil's warehouse, property of the son of Huguenot merchant Peter Faneuil, one of Boston's great benefactors, stood opposite the Bunch-of-Grapes Tavern at the corner of King Street and Mackrell Lane (now Kilby Street), renowned on both sides of the Atlantic for its punch. The most prominent feature of Boston's terrain was Beacon Hill, whose signal fire had beckoned to ships for well over a hundred years. Ropewalks, cordage and canvas shops further advertised the town's maritime character. The ordinary crafts—butchers, candlemakers, soapmakers, brewers—were limited in number in Boston, where they served only the town itself, in contrast to New York and Philadelphia, whose handicraft industry supplied whole regions.

For the mass of city dwellers, as for the farm families, working life was a dawn-to-dusk-or-later drudgery, with small and uncertain rewards and unavoidable hazards. The war merely heightened hardship and danger for part of the population.

The condition of life for the various classes was very similar to that prevailing in contemporary Western Europe, and not widely different from that of the previous several centuries. A merchant or sailor from Columbus's Genoa would have had no particular difficulty finding his way around the Boston waterfront. A citizen of fifteenth-century Florence or Bruges would not have encountered many surprises in Philadelphia, as its daily life was pictured in letters home by Philip Mackenzie, a twenty-four-year-old planter from South Carolina who visited the city in the spring of 1776:

> Philadelphia is a Town of Bright Colors. The Shop fronts are most of them painted Red, Blue, Green or Yellow. The big swinging Signs are like Joseph's Coat of many colors. The Carriages—there are not Many of them [fewer than a hundred, in fact]—are colored too, or I should say many of them are. And the greater part of the Men wear Red or Green Coats, and the Ladies have Dresses of all colors of the Rainbow. . . .
>
> I am staying at a Boarding House that is on Front Street near Race . . . pretty nearly in the center of Things. . . .
>
> The House is large with big Rooms. My Room and Board cost Two Pounds Ten Shillings a week. . . .
>
> Several members of Congress are among [the guests]. . . . Dinner is always at Four O'clock. The rule is four meals a Daye. Coffee or Tea and a Roll when you Rise, say round Seven O'clock, Breakfast or Lunch, call it what you will, at Eleven, then dinner at Four, and Supper about bedtime.
>
> My Room is Very Pleasant. Has a Fireplace in it and plenty of Closets. The Walls are not Painted but Papered. . . .
>
> Miss Graydon has White Servants. No Blacks. It got me sort of Flustered at first, I mean Telling a Nice-looking White Woman in a neat Gray Dress to bring me so-and-so. . . .

In another letter he described a visit to Benjamin Franklin, America's only international celebrity:

> The Maid who met me at the Door conducted me to the library, a very Large Room with a high Ceiling. Dr. Franklin was sitting there with a number of his friends. As it was a Cold Daye a plesant Fire was burning in the Fireplace or Franklin Stove. . . .
>
> Three of the men present were Members of Congress: Robert Morris, of Pennsylvania, and Richard Henry Lee, from Virginia were Two. The other man's name I did not Catch. . . .
>
> Tea was served and wine too besides Cakes. Franklin drinks Madeira wine, but remarked in the Course of Conversation that he had never used Tobacco in any way. . . .
>
> He says we in the South ought to have Conestoga Wagons on our Roads. . . . They are long, covered Wagons shaped in such a fashion that the Front and Back ends Rise higher than the Middle. The Body of the Wagon is rounded something

like a Boat. This keeps the freight from sliding around on a rough road. . . . The wheels are Six feet High, and the Iron Tires are Seven and Eight inches Wide. Compare this with our flat-bottomed Wagons which, if you are Carrying a Heavy Load, are Likely to turn over on a bad road. . . .

There was . . . quite a lot of Conversation about Thomas Paine. Robert Morris remarked that Paine's book Common Sense had already sold 120,000 Copies, and it has been Published only Three Months. . . .

Among the well-to-do class Mackenzie observed "a vast amount of Bad Taste, Vulgarity and Ostentashous Behavior. . . ." Visiting the home of wealthy Quakers, he was struck above all by the conspicuous consumption at dinner, where "they had Fourteen Difrent Courses besides a lot of little Nick-Nacks. Among the meats were Hams, Chickens, Ducks, Roast Beef and Meat Pies made of Lamb, I think. Also they had Soup, Oysters and the Lord knows how many Vegetable Dishes and Desserts, such as Sillabub, Jellies, Sweet creamy dishes, Custards and Floating Island. For Beverages they served Punch, Wine, and finally Coffee. . . ." A local specialty to which Mackenzie took a fancy was the fried-pork-and-cornmeal dish already famous as Philadelphia scrapple—"I like it, and have it every Morning for Breakfast."

Returning home by way of New York, the young Southerner was able to sample the "Stage Wagon" that ran thrice weekly between the two towns. "It is a Large Wagon with a canvass top and Sides. The Seats are Benches without any backs. They make the Trip in a little less than Two Dayes. The Stage Wagon leaves Philadelphia Monday morning at Eight o'clock and Reeches New York Tuesday afternoon late. We spend the Night at some Inn on the Road. The Fare is Twenty Shillings [a month's wages for most Americans]." The stage carried no mail; the national postal service Franklin had organized the year before was limited to a thrice-weekly post-rider link between Philadelphia and Cambridge, to keep Congress in touch with Washington's army besieging Boston.

Two days from Philadelphia to New York, a distance of 100 miles, was excellent road time. In South Carolina a wagon took four days to do the 80 miles between Charleston and Mackenzie's sister's home in Orangeburg. In the whole country there were few bridges over small streams and none over large ones—fords and ferries provided the crossings, with numerous delays and accidents. Equipped with neither springs nor suspension straps, the stage wagon was scarcely more comfortable than an ordinary farm wagon. Two passengers sat on either side of the driver, taking their places after the rest had clambered back to the rear benches. Town carriages were a little more comfortable but not much, and Benjamin Franklin was one of many who preferred a sedan chair.

In 1776 American scientific and technical contributions to civilization's progress scarcely weighed in the scale against the benefits America had drawn from the Old World. The most talked-about American invention was Franklin's stove, which Philip Mackenzie admired, and whose inspiration Franklin explained to him: "'I saw that most of the Heat from fires in our Fireplace went up the big Chimney. You could sit ten feet from a fire and be cold. . . .' That started the Dr. to Thinking of ways to Throw the heated Air back in the room. So, he said, I made a Stove or Fireplace that draws in the Cold Air, heats it and sends it out again, not up the Chimney but into the Room. . . . He did not Seem to Think it an important invention, but it Certainly is very Ingenyus to say the Least." It was indeed. The "Pennsylvania Fireplace" represented the first significant improvement in heating since the invention of the fireplace itself in medieval Europe. To accomplish its effect Franklin constructed a flue that wrapped around an iron "air-box" before entering the chimney, heating the air in the box, which was then released into the room by shutters at the side of the stove, to be replaced with cold air through a vent at the bottom.

To the Franklin stove may be added Franklin's lightning rod, the practical fruit of his scientific experiments with electricity; the Conestoga wagon that pleased Philip Mackenzie; and three other American inventions—the flatboat, the keelboat, and the Pennsylvania (or Kentucky) rifle.

The flatboat, originally developed by Germans on the Delaware, proved extremely valuable on the Western rivers, down which it drifted while the huge sweeps at its sides and stern held it in the current and helped it avoid snags, on which it nevertheless frequently caught. A partial roof covered a cabin of sorts, a cargo hold, and stables for animals. Navigating a flatboat upstream was a virtual impossibility. The more sophisticated keelboat, on the other hand, could be made to ascend a river, though barely. One leading version, called the Durham boat, after its Delaware River inventor, Robert Durham, resembled a giant canoe (itself a valuable technological acquisition from the Indians), with a heavy timber running the length of its bottom to protect—somewhat—against snags and rocks. Narrow running boards along the sides provided platforms for polemen who, by the most strenuous labors, could shove the craft forward against a current.

The Pennsylvania rifle was also a contribution of German immigrants, gunsmiths who settled around Lancaster. The principle of rifling, that is, incising long, gently spiral grooves inside a gun barrel to give the ball a stabilizing spin, had been invented in Europe some two hundred years earlier, but the necessity for loading through the muzzle had made its application difficult. European gunsmiths first solved the problem, not very satisfactorily, by making the ball slightly larger than the rifle bore and providing the soldier—or rather the hunter, for whom rifles were chiefly made—with a ramrod and mallet to ram the oversize but soft piece of lead down the barrel. The Lancaster Germans either invented or brought with them from Europe a better way. They made the ball smaller than the bore and taught their purchasers to provide themselves with small greased patches. Each ball was half wrapped in the patch, then easily rammed home, cleaning the barrel of powder residue. On firing, the patch nicely took the rifling grooves. Given a long barrel and small gauge, the Pennsylvania rifle saved on ammunition weight and gave extraordinary range and accuracy—250 yards or more, compared with 80 to 100 for a smoothbore.

Yet though it was employed by sharpshooters, rangers, and Western irregulars with good effect in the war, the rifle was by no means the standard American military small arm. Washington's line regiments were armed with smoothbore muskets, the best (and most numerous) of which was the French 1763 Charleville, supplied by America's chief European ally. Without 20,000 of these shipped in secret convoy by the playwright-secret agent Caron de Beaumarchais, along with 200 cannon and a large quantity of ammunition and other supplies, the decisive battle of Saratoga could hardly have been fought. By the end of the war some 100,000 muskets (not all Charlevilles) had been provided from France.

One reason for the poverty of American technology was that the British government, out of short-sighted mercantilism, discouraged American manufacture. Britain began importing American iron ore from Jamestown in 1607, but American forests offered unlimited charcoal for smelting, and iron works were soon established in Massachusetts, Connecticut, Rhode Island, and New Jersey. The industry spread southward. George Washington's father helped found the first iron-works in Maryland in 1715, and by 1776 Pennsylvania had more than fifty forges and furnaces.

The furnaces' appetite for charcoal dictated sites deep in the forest for most of the "iron plantations." The furnace, a truncated pyramid of stone, was built next to a small hill, with a kind of covered bridge from the hilltop to the stack, over which the charge of ore, charcoal, and limestone was trundled to the furnace top. The bellows that produced the air blast was squeezed by a large waterwheel. Inside the casting house, at one side of the furnace, the molten iron ran off into sand molds. If the works had a forge, where the cast "pig iron" was refined and hammered into blooms or bars of wrought iron, its bellows too was operated by water-power. Nearby stood the house of the ironmaster, feudal lord of the community, amid the workmen's cottages of stone, logs, or clapboard, the blacksmith's shop, the barns and stables, and the company store. When the furnace was in blast, the roar resounded through the countryside, and at night its flames and sparks lighted the sky for miles.

But English iron manufacturers bitterly protested the competition from the colonies, and by the Iron Act of 1750 Parliament forbade Americans to build forges or rolling and slitting mills. The colonists were thus permitted to make "pigs," raw material of the industry, to export to Britain, where the British iron-masters could work them into bars and rods of wrought iron to be forged into horseshoes, plowshares, and nails to be sold back to underdeveloped America. Even liberal William Pitt, who had little inkling of what his namesake city on the Allegheny was going to become, pronounced himself "opposed to allowing the colonists to make even a hobnail for themselves." A Boston newspaper in 1765 acidly commented, "A colonist cannot make a button, a horse shoe, nor a hobnail, but some sooty ironmonger or respectable buttonmaker in Britain shall bawl and squall that his honor's worship is most egregiously maltreated, injured, cheated, and robbed by the rascally American Republicans." The British policy of restricting American manufacture extended to many other industries, making prices for numerous manufactured articles artificially high, and irritating American farmers as well as businessmen. The farmers had another prohibition to resent: the Proclamation of 1763, which forbade them to cross the mountains and carve free farms out of the Indians' wilderness.

By the eve of the Revolution, Parliament's restrictions were being truculently challenged by American lawbreakers. An English observer reported home in 1774 that "the inhabitants in the Colonies . . . do make many things, and export several manufactures, to the exclusion of English manufactures of the same kinds. The New England people import . . . very large quantities of cotton, which they spin and work up with linen yarn into a stuff, like that made in Manchester. . . . Hats are manufactured in Carolina, Pennsylvania and in other Colonies. Soap and candles, and all kinds of wood-work, are made in the Northern Colonies and exported to the Southern. Coaches, chariots, chaises, and chairs, are also made. . . . Coach harness, and many other kinds of leather manufactures, are likewise made . . . and large quantities of shoes have lately been exported . . . to the West India Islands. Linens are made to a great amount in Pennsylvania and cordage and other hemp manufactures are carried on in many places with great success; and foundry ware, axes, and other iron tools and utensils are also become articles of commerce, with which the Southern Colonies are supplied from the Northern."

Ironmasters and other metallurgical tradesmen played a conspicuous role in the Revolution. Four ironmasters (George Taylor, James Smith, George Ross, and

Hopewell Village, Pennsylvania, restoration of iron furnace of 1770. The charcoal house, extreme right, was built on the brow of a hill known as the furnace bank. Wagons, such as the one that stands in the foreground, delivered charcoal here, to be carried in baskets or carts, along with the iron ore and limestone that made up the "charge," over a covered bridge that spanned the gap between the bank and the furnace, and dumped into the furnace head. The waterwheel that operated the blast machinery is on the other side of the furnace; the casting house, where molten iron was drawn off into molds in beds of sand, is in the foreground. (Authors' photograph)

Stephen Hopkins) signed the Declaration of Independence, and several other pa-triot leaders, including Ethan Allen, Nathanael Greene, Paul Revere, and Rufus Putnam, were involved in the metal trades. Once the break with the mother coun-try was made, American industry was not only freed but spurred. Ironworks switched from illegally casting pots, stove plates, mill hardware, and sash weights to cannon, cannonballs, and fittings for caissons, wagons, and ships. A Tory spy at Batsto Furnace in the New Jersey pine barrens dispatched intelligence reports to the British governor:

> Shott supplied by John Cox from Batsto Furnace in New Jersey—sent in four waggons—
> first load . . . 650
> 2nd . . . 400
> 3rd . . . 1128
> 4 . . . 445
> Weight—½ of them 6 and the other 9 pounders. Send to Philadelphia for ships of armed Privateers fitted out from that Port.

Connecticut offered bounties for gunlocks and complete guns, and other states similarly stimulated arms manufacture. In 1778 the Continental Congress author-ized an iron foundry in Springfield, Massachusetts, for casting of cannon, a works that in 1792 became the famous Springfield Armory, or Arsenal. In Pennsylvania the war saw twenty-one black-powder mills in operation. By the war's end, such efforts valuably supplemented the supply of ammunition and weapons from Euro-pean sources.

The native textile industry also made a patriotic surge. Most of the production was homemade for close-to-home consumption, but in Philadelphia the germ of a factory system appeared in the grouping of a number of weavers under one roof. In 1777 Connecticut lent Nathaniel Niles of Norwich £300 to make wire for the teeth of wool cards (combs), and Massachusetts the same year promised £100 for the first 1,000 pounds of "good merchantable card wire" produced in a water-powered mill from American iron.

The war also inspired invention. A remarkable American military innovation passed nearly unnoticed and afterward remained long forgotten: nothing less than the world's first combat submarine, invented by a young Yale man named David Bushnell. Bushnell's *Turtle* was 7½ feet long and 6 feet tall, just large enough to accommodate a one-man crew. Propulsion was provided by a hand-cranked screw propeller, the first screw propeller, so far as is known, ever to be used in naviga-tion. Against all odds Sergeant Ezra Lee of Washington's army made a torpedo at-tack in the *Turtle* on the British warship *Eagle* in New York harbor, and was only prevented from a spectacular success by a single failure in Bushnell's otherwise accurate calculations. The *Turtle*'s torpedo was a waterproofed keg of black pow-der with a clockwork-governed gunhammer fuse. Bushnell had designed it to be affixed to the enemy hull by a screw bit turned from inside the submarine. The tiny *Turtle* lacked the mass to provide adequate pressure for Sergeant Lee's deter-mined effort to screw the explosive to the *Eagle*'s hull, and in the end he had to give up. Withdrawing, he was threatened by a boatful of British soldiers from

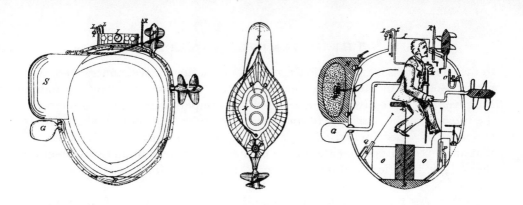

David Bushnell's submarine, the *Turtle*, propelled by a hand-cranked screw propeller, the first screw propeller known to be used in navigation, made the world's first torpedo attack in 1776, against the British warship *Eagle* in New York harbor. The attack failed, but caused the *Eagle* to retreat up the bay. (Smithsonian Photograph No. 34,346)

Governor's Island, and cutting his torpedo loose with the clockwork going, he produced an explosive fountain that not only drove off the soldiers' boat but caused the *Eagle* to weigh anchor and retreat up the bay. Bushnell later pioneered naval mines (which is what his "torpedo" really was), and actually destroyed at least one enemy ship.

True, the military course of the war painfully reflected America's industrial backwardness. The British Army won most of the battles, captured New York, Philadelphia, Savannah, and Charleston with little difficulty, and suffered its only serious defeats, at Saratoga and Yorktown, through rashness and the French intervention. Nevertheless, American strength grew with the fighting. Washington's army, though forming only a fraction of the allied power at Yorktown, had by 1781 achieved a qualitative level comparable to the British and French. The improvement reflected experience, French assistance, and the country's war-stimulated economy.

The shipbuilding industry, its regular market shut down by the British blockade, found a splendid new one. No fewer than two thousand privateers were commissioned, their service proving so lucrative that almost as many American men served on board them as were drafted into the army. Salem privateers alone captured and sold 445 prizes, making Elias Hasket Derby, the town's chief shipowner, probably the first American millionaire.

Agriculture also profited from the war, both directly and indirectly. Farmers sold to the American army, when it could afford to pay for their produce, to the rich French allies at doubled prices, and to the British enemy. More significantly for the agricultural future, the Proclamation of 1763 was overruled and the mountain gates opened to the Conestoga wagons. By the close of the war the flood of farmer-pioneers implied major change in the national economic geography. When the decision of Yorktown confirmed the seizure of the West, it only remained to oust the native Indian population, a procedure about which the pioneers on the spot shared none of the compunctions of the government back East.

The optimism born of independence already conceived of technical solutions to the tremendous transportation problems of the huge little country. New York patriot Gouverneur Morris, on a mission to General Schuyler's army confronting Burgoyne in 1777, enlivened the headquarters campfire with a glowing forecast of the progress of the "useful arts" in America now that the country was free. "He announced," a Continental officer recalled later, "in language highly poetic . . . that at no very distant day the waters of the great western inland seas would, by the aid of man, break through their barriers and mingle with those of the Hudson."

Farther west there remained an awkward obstacle in the form of Spanish political control of the lower Mississippi and the territory to the west, but the pioneers of the 1780s and 1790s had plenty of room in the rich Ohio valley and the other trans-Appalachian forest land. They were hardly affected by the postwar depression that afflicted the East, partly as a result of the dislocation of old trade patterns by the new relationship with Britain. The Eastern townspeople, starved for British manufactures during the war, invited a flood immediately after it, whose results were summarized by Elbridge Garry: "The scarcity of money in consequence of our excessive and extravagant importations of British frippery has occasioned stagnation of trade."

Yet at that very moment the western farmers were beginning to float their livestock, corn, wheat, flour, whiskey, and lumber down the Mississippi for sale to the Spaniards of Louisiana and West Florida or for export to the West Indies or southern Europe. It remained nearly impossible to navigate the Western rivers upstream, but here was the germ of a national pattern of immense promise.

In *The Federalist*, Alexander Hamilton proposed a program: "Let the Thirteen States, bound together in a strict indissoluble Union, concur in erecting one great American system superior to the control of all trans-Atlantic force or influence, and able to dictate the terms of the connection between the old and the new world!" Hamilton was thinking of action on the political and economic planes, but the idea also called for new technology, without which the basic problems could not be solved. The country had fabulous resources, and among them was its share of able young men, many of whom were already thinking about the problems.

2

The Adventures of John Fitch

ONE APRIL SUNDAY IN 1785, John Fitch was returning with a friend from a church service in Neshaminy, in Bucks County, Pennsylvania, an unusual event since, by his own account, Fitch "never troubled churches much." This time he regretted doing it, because he was suddenly attacked by a painful rheumatism in one of his long Yankee legs. Hobbling homeward, he was passed by a rich townsman in horse and buggy. Fitch owned a horse himself, but was renting it out at the moment. Suddenly it occurred to him that one might run a buggy without any horse by the power of steam. Reaching his home in Warminster, he set to work designing a steam engine that could be harnessed to wheels. A week's study led him to the conclusion that the state of American roads made a steam vehicle impractical. He then turned his attention to steam navigation.

A few days later Fitch walked to Neshaminy to show drawings of an engine to an educated acquaintance named Nathaniel Irwin. Irwin turned to his bookcase, lifted down a heavy reference book called *Philosophia Britannica,* and leafing through it showed Fitch a description of the Newcomen atmospheric pressure steam engine. Fitch recorded his reaction in his memoir: He was "considerably chagrianed" to learn that somebody else had—seventy-three years earlier—thought of the idea of a steam engine.

That one of America's most gifted inventors should, at the age of forty-one, have had absolutely no knowledge of the work of Denis Papin, Thomas Savery, Thomas Newcomen, and James Watt (whose original patent in England was al-

Newcomen atmospheric steam engine, c. 1760, earliest surviving example of the prime mover invented by Thomas Newcomen in 1712. Left arm of the rocking beam is connected to a lift pump, right to a piston in a vertical cylinder. Low-pressure steam is admitted into the cylinder; the cylinder is suddenly cooled by a spray of cold water, the interior condensation causing a partial vacuum. The atmosphere above then forces the piston down in the cylinder, causing the pump to rise at the other end. In John Fitch's day there was only one steam engine operating in America, a Newcomen pump at the Schuyler Copper Mines in New Jersey. (Collections of Greenfield Village and the Henry Ford Museum, Dearborn, Michigan)

ready sixteen years old) says something about eighteenth-century America and about John Fitch. The sequel perhaps says even more. However "chagrianed" he might be to find that another had anticipated his idea, he saw that Newcomen's seventy-three-year-old pumping device at least proved that steam power could indeed be harnessed, and so he determined to go ahead and build a steamboat. The conclusion is compelling: if the steam engine had not already been invented, John Fitch would then and there have invented it.

Cranky, quirky, obstinate, independent, John Fitch was a born character. By the time he arrived at his steamboat resolution, he had already had a lifetime of adventure. Son of a rugged Presbyterian farmer of Windsor, Connecticut, who "never spent five shillings at a Tavern in his life," and would not permit his children to pick apples on the Sabbath, John, like nearly every child of Revolutionary America, learned his letters from the New England Primer. When he was five he burned his hands putting out a fire in the kitchen. His brother Augustus, instead of sympathizing, punished him, apparently thinking the fire was John's fault. "This," he wrote later, ". . . being what I may call the first act of my life, seemed to forebode the future rewards I was to receive for my labors through life. . . ."

Brilliant, and avid for knowledge, he mastered his father's worn copy of Hodder's *Arithmetic* and at nine figured how many minutes old he would be at ten. At eleven he husbanded his brief time off from farm work to cultivate a potato patch and raise enough potatoes to sell for ten shillings and buy Salmon's *Geography* from a local merchant who sent away to New York for it.

A Connecticut boy of John Fitch's bent had a natural career in sight: clockmaking. But though he got himself apprenticed to Benjamin Cheney, a clock-maker in East Hartford, he did not learn the craft because his churlish master, jealous of his professional secrets, refused to teach him or even let him learn by himself, as he was very capable of doing. Obtuse Cheney used the boy as a drudge. Fitch's spirited protests won him at least some rudiments of brassmaking and finally a transfer to the care of Cheney's brother Timothy who treated him just the same, teaching brasswork but guarding the secrets of clockmaking. Fitch finished his apprenticeship, set up in Windsor as a brassmaker, and at the first opportunity volunteered to fix a brass clock that ran badly. Taking it apart, he studied its works, repaired it, and put it back together. Very soon he knew clocks as well as the surly Cheneys.

His memoir, written late in life, gives a tantalizingly enigmatic account of his thirteen-month marriage to a girl from Simsbury, Connecticut, named Lucy Roberts. "I cannot say I ever was passionately fond of the Woman," he wrote, "but for the sake of some Promises I determined to marry her." According to Fitch she was an insufferable nag, but Fitch himself was not the easiest of men to get along with. From the wedding day on, "there was some Intestine Broils." Whoever was to blame, Fitch abandoned her in 1769, when he was twenty-six years old, despite Lucy's pregnancy, their infant son, and her eleventh-hour pleas and promises. A venture in partnership in potash-making had failed, and with seven or eight dollars in his pocket he left Lucy standing in the dooryard, the child in her arms, and set out on foot, heading north to Massachusetts. He wrote in self-justification: "I know nothing so perplexing and vexatious to a man of fealings as a turbulent Wife and Steamboat building. . . . For one man to be teised with Both, must be looked on as the most unfortunate man of the world."

After some wanderings he arrived in Trenton, New Jersey, where he found a tinsmith who needed several hundred brass buttons. Fitch had never made a brass button, but he accepted the order without hesitation and filled it to satisfaction. He had up to then never handled a pocket watch, but he seized an opportunity to clean that of his tinsmith acquaintance, taking it apart and reassembling it after "much difficulty." From a drunken silversmith he acquired first, knowledgeability, and second, valuable tools; he set up his own shop, and was soon thriving. Adopting Franklin's recommendation that honesty was sound policy—a fairly radical suggestion in a world of small businessmen and sharp dealing—he proved an adept salesman as well as craftsman and in five years was worth 800 pounds.

At the beginning of the trouble with Britain, Fitch first worked as a gunsmith for the local Committee of Safety, then obtained a commission in the militia. But after he was passed over for promotion, his prickly sense of injustice made him quit the army. When Washington retreated to Trenton, pursued by Cornwallis, Fitch fled to Bucks County, Pennsylvania, with a wagonload of stock and tools, leaving shop and furnishings to be looted by the British. The next winter (1777–78), while the New Jersey militia was threatening him with court-martial for desertion, Fitch profiteered off the army at Valley Forge by selling beer and whiskey to the army sutlers. To avoid any stigma, he joined the local Pennsylvania militia for a few forays against the Tories.

His real problem proved to be not the New Jersey militia or the British, but the depreciating Continental currency, which along with the theft of some silver coin he had buried left him nearly penniless by 1780. He hit on a fresh expedient. Trading his otherwise almost worthless currency for Virginia land warrants—titles to western lands that could be claimed upon surveying—he hiked across the mountains to Fort Pitt and joined a convoy of flatboats and barges bound down the Allegheny to the Ohio. Fitch had never seen a river convoy before, and knew of the Indians only by hearsay, but he gave his more experienced companions a sensible suggestion—lash all the boats together for travel on the Ohio. After an ambush that wounded several men and captured one boat, they took his advice. Reaching Kentucky, Fitch struck up an acquaintance with an impoverished minister named Barnard and enlisted him as a partner in the surveying operation. The two built a cabin in the wilderness and spent the summer laying warrants on selected land. An early winter prevented Fitch from returning east till spring.

The next year (1782) Fitch again undertook a western enterprise, this time with nearly fatal results. Having become aware of the burgeoning down-river trade, he resolved to buy flour in Fort Pitt and take it to New Orleans for sale. In Fort Pitt he heard the news of "Williamson's Massacre" of a hundred inoffensive Delaware Indians, an event likely to provoke retaliation, but joining a well-armed flatboat party he set out on March 18. The boat ran aground in the Ohio, and was only gotten off by strenuous efforts. "Exceedingly fateaged," the boatmen tied up for the night, ignoring Fitch's proposals that they post a sentry and load their guns. An Indian attack in the morning caught them unprepared, enjoying "a hot buttered dram," and though Fitch made a desperate attempt to cut the boat loose with an axe, the Indians captured the whole party after shooting and scalping two.

Rather to their surprise, the prisoners were not immediately put to death, but taken on a twelve-day march to the Indian village, where they were forced to run the gauntlet while squaws beat them with clubs. Two or three white men—British agents or traders—studied their papers and told the Indians the captives were not warriors, thereby saving them from the stake. Instead they were designated for sale to the British authorities at Detroit, whither they headed by a hard weeks-long march. At one point a party of Delawares from Detroit met them, got drunk, and would have slaughtered the captives except for the intervention of their captors. During the journey Fitch became estranged from his companions, first as the result of his typically forthright criticism of their cowardice at the time of capture, and second by his refusal to join in their harebrained escape plans.

Finally safe in the British stockade at Detroit, the prisoners found that they were the bearers to this remote outpost of the news of Cornwallis's surrender at Yorktown the previous year. The commandant first refused to believe it, and then tried to suppress the news, but the delighted prisoners shouted through the guard-house window, "Cornwallis with his whole army is taken!"

The captives were presently marched to Prison Island in the St. Lawrence, where they joined a large batch of more conventional prisoners of war. Fitch's companions told the others that Fitch was "the Damdest Tory that remained un-hung," but Fitch soon made himself popular by aiding the bolder spirits in their incessant escape attempts. He had kept one tool, his graver, and used it to earn a little money graving objects for the British soldiers, and with some trading and cajoling soon acquired materials to make more tools. These he lent for the escape attempts in between their employment to make buttons and other objects, marketing them so successfully that he actually protested when orders came for the prisoners' exchange. En route home he managed to offend both the American colonel and the British Navy captain on board his ship, the latter by borrowing a scale and dividers from a sailor and accurately figuring the ship's distance from New York and Philadelphia. Even on being exchanged, irrepressible, irascible Fitch made trouble over the fact that he was not given a written parole.

Undaunted by his experiences, Fitch undertook new expeditions to Kentucky in the next two years. His companions on the first trip supplied money but left all the work to Fitch, who walked back East after finishing the job, overtaking en route his mounted ex-companions who had had several days' start. He thought nothing of doing thirty or even forty miles a day on Indian trails and mud roads, through rain, cold, and snow. On the second trip he and another party surveyed 250,000 acres, then had to resurvey most of it to meet a new congressional requirement on land awards. With large land speculators busy buying up most of the West, there was a demand for government land surveyors, and Fitch applied for a job. His usual luck held, and he failed to get it. That winter (1784–85), back in Bucks County, he drew, engraved, and printed—with a borrowed cider press—a new map of the Northwest Territory, based on the existing Hutchins and Mc-Murray map but updated and corrected with his own firsthand knowledge. It was while he was doing the printing that he had his sudden inspiration about steam propulsion on the way home from church.

The Newcomen engine that Fitch's friend Nathaniel Irwin showed him in the pages of *Philosophia Britannica* introduced steam in the bottom of a piston chamber to push the piston up. The steam was then condensed by a jet of cold water, creating a partial vacuum; and atmospheric pressure, aided a little by gravity, drove the piston down. Steam was reintroduced to shove the piston up for the next stroke. Repairing a Newcomen engine in 1769, James Watt had hit on the idea of drawing the steam off into a separate condensing chamber so that the piston chamber could be kept hot, an alteration that brought a radical improvement in efficiency and fuel savings.

Fitch knew nothing of all this. How he came to think of steam power at all remains a mystery. Steam was hardly talked about in America, even in Philadelphia. There was only one actual steam engine in existence in the country, a Newcomen pump operating at the Schuyler Copper Mines in New Jersey. *Why* he thought of it, however, is no mystery at all. His experience on the Western rivers had taught him the most important fact in American economic geography—that boats going down the Ohio and Mississippi had only to overcome such problems as Indians, river pirates, rapids, snags, floods, and storms, but boats coming up had to fight a 12-foot-a-second current. Despite muscular rowing and poling, occasional stretches where animal towing or sails were practicable, bushwhacking (grabbing shore underbrush and pulling the boat forward), and snubbing with a line around a tree up ahead, the task of moving a boat back up the river from New Orleans was difficult bordering on impossible. Most boatmen sold their boats for lumber and walked back, turning an old Indian trail into the storied Natchez Trace. The result was that upstream cargoes amounted to only one-tenth of downstream, an economic anomaly that begged for a technological solution.

Addressing himself to the mechanics of steam propulsion, Fitch devised a row of paddles driven by a chain on a pair of sprockets on the side of a skiff. Operated manually, the contraption worked, and Fitch went off to Philadelphia for the double purpose of peddling his new maps and soliciting backing for his steamboat. According to Nathaniel Boileau, a young friend home for vacation from Princeton, Fitch also designed a paddle wheel—if so, he once more hit on an idea that Europeans had had before him.

In Philadelphia, Fitch called on Dr. John Ewing, provost of the university, in his house on sedate South Third Street, and won the scholar's written endorsement of his steamboat model. Proceeding to New York, where the Continental Congress still sat, selling maps as he went, he tried to get a congressional appropriation for development of his invention. Many Eastern congressmen had little interest in the development of the West, and besides, Congress had more debts than money; Fitch got no help from his government. A foreign government did express interest; the Spanish minister, Don Diego de Gardoqui, offered financial support in return for exclusive Spanish rights to the invention. Fitch patriotically refused, but regretted it later: "God forbid that I should ever be in like error again. . . . The Strange ideas I had at that time of serving my Country, without the least suspicion that my only reward would be nothing but contempt and opprobrious names, has taught me a mighty lesson in mankind."

Returning to Philadelphia, he called on Dr. Franklin, who listened attentively amid his litter of electrical instruments, musical glasses, and scientific knicknacks and gave Fitch's project his blessing, but offered only a few dollars in financial support. Fitch refused and wished later that he had "treated the insult with the indignity which he merited, and stomped the poltry Ore under my feet." He suspected Franklin of a desire to steal his idea—unjustly, because Franklin was seduced by a quite different and less practical steam-propulsion technique, one he had picked up in Europe from Swiss mathematician Daniel Bernoulli, a water version of jet propulsion. The principle was theoretically valid, and in fact boats embodying it have actually been built, but it could not compete in efficiency even with Fitch's crude paddle-oar chain.

En route home Fitch learned for the first time, from William Henry, a friend in Lancaster, Pennsylvania, that steam navigation was not a new idea. Henry said that he himself had thought of it years before, but could not claim priority because Tom Paine had talked about it in 1778, and had probably had the idea much earlier. Neither Henry nor Paine had ever tried to work the idea out on paper, as Fitch had done. A little later, at Fredericktown, Fitch heard that James Rumsey, a tavern keeper in Bath, back in eastern Pennsylvania, had built some kind of a boat to run against the current, though, according to his informant, Thomas Johnson, former governor of the state, it did not use steam but a contraption turned by the current. Johnson, however, only knew of the boat at secondhand. He suggested that Fitch go see a man who had actually watched the craft in operation while staying at Rumsey's inn. This eyewitness was General George Washington.

Fitch turned his indefatigable footsteps toward the Potomac, took the ferry to Mount Vernon, and dropped in on the Father of his Country. Washington received him, as he received all kinds of callers—ex-soldiers, widows, favor seekers, admirers—but at mention of Rumsey's boat grew taciturn, scrupulous to protect an inventor's secret. When Fitch, not to be evaded, asked the direct question, did the boat run by steam, the general abruptly left the room. Dogged Fitch stayed put. Finally Washington returned and stated that the model he had seen had not used steam, but that Rumsey had said something to him about steam—what exactly, he did not sufficiently "attend to," and so could not recollect.

As long as he was in Virginia, Fitch thought he might as well try the Virginia legislature for help, since the Kentucky territory, with its Ohio River steamboat potential, belonged to Virginia. Walking to Richmond, he interviewed John Edwards, the representative of the Kentucky district, who urged him to petition the assembly. Doing so, he won the eloquence of Assemblyman James Madison to his cause as well as the support of Governor Patrick Henry, but the assembly, improvident as all the other legislatures, voted no money. A scheme of Fitch's to raise money by getting the assemblymen to help sell his maps foundered on the legislators' apathy.

Giving up on Virginia, Fitch tried the state capitals in Maryland, Delaware, Pennsylvania, and New Jersey, and finally, in New Jersey, won an important concession—exclusive rights to building and operating steamboats in state waters for fourteen years. Before leaving the state he dropped in on Tom Paine. Paine bought a map and wished Fitch well; he himself was busy at the moment with another daring technical innovation, building a model of an iron arch bridge.

In April 1786 Fitch hit on a means of raising some capital, organizing a joint stock company with forty shares, of which he kept twenty for himself and peddled the others for $20 apiece, a price that small Philadelphia merchants—the grocer, the hatter, the tavern keeper—could afford. When he had collected $300 he called on the best mechanic he could find, a German clockmaker named Henry Voight who was known to be interested in steamboating. Voight's interest had been captured by the Franklin-Bernoulli jet-propulsion scheme, but Fitch easily talked him into his chain-drive design.

The two set to work, and in a few weeks built a model boat with a homemade steam engine geared to Fitch's paddle chain. It worked so poorly that it had to be written off as a failure, even though the experiment gave Fitch a remarkable insight, that a steam engine should admit steam at both ends of the piston instead of only one as in the old Newcomen engine. This was a principle James Watt had published in 1782, and which Watt was now perfecting.

Voight was discouraged by the failure and ready to give up. Fitch took the more imaginative course of going to the grog shop and cheering himself up with "West India produce," lurching out late at night with the bottle in his hand to drink himself to sleep. Next day he stayed in bed all day. But at midnight he suddenly got the idea of using cranks instead of the unsatisfactory chain to drive his paddles. As the watchman outside called, "One o'clock!" he jumped out of bed, found a candle, and began drawing. At dawn he pulled off his nightcap, pulled on breeches and jacket, and ran to Voight's clockmaker's shop calling, "Harry!"

Plan of Mr Fitch's Steam Boat.

John Fitch's paddle-propelled steamboat. From *Columbian Magazine,* 1786. (Library of Congress)

By the end of July a reequipped skiff was in the Delaware, and to the astonishment of riverside onlookers and the immense satisfaction of its two-man crew, the little boat chugged sturdily upstream against the current.

Thus was born just ten years after the Declaration of Independence out of the brain of a thorny, individualistic Connecticut Yankee, a remarkable and historically decisive invention: The American steamboat.

Fitch assumed that it was also the world's first steamboat, but in this he was mistaken. An inventive French nobleman, the Marquis Jouffroy d'Abbans, had designed, built, and navigated a small steam craft on the Saône River in Burgundy in 1783, three years earlier. Little is known of Jouffroy's boat, and his experiment drew scarcely any attention even in France. The marquis evidently had no thought of commercializing his invention, for which there was little demand in Europe.

Fitch, on the contrary, set to work at once to raise money for a commercial boat, to obtain a monopoly privilege on the Delaware, and to help Voight build a bigger steam engine. In 1787 he gave free rides to delegates to the Constitutional Convention.

Next year, with a new, larger boat in the river, Fitch fought a pamphlet battle with James Rumsey, who claimed to have built a steam-powered boat (on the Franklin-Bernoulli principle) in 1785. Fitch claimed Rumsey was back-dating his invention by two years, and the efforts of Rumsey's friends to get Fitch's patents repealed failed. Rumsey's boat never got anywhere, the tavern keeper eventually dying of apoplexy in London, where he was vainly seeking financial support.

Voight meantime was getting edgy about the patents, in which he thought he should have a share. Temporarily, the testy German quit the project, and his

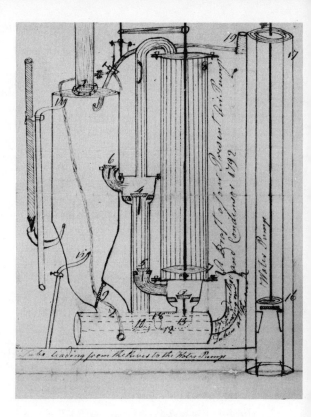

John Fitch's drawing of his 1792 steam engine pump and condenser. From the Fitch papers. (Library of Congress)

place was taken unsatisfactorily by Dr. William Thornton, the architect-tinkerer who later designed the national Capitol. The new condenser Thornton built did not work, and neither did one Voight built, but Fitch finally contrived one that did. "We reigned Lord High Admirals of the Delaware," he exulted. "No boat in the River could hold its way with us," though several, both sail and oar, raced them.

By 1790 Fitch, Voight, and Thornton were ready to begin commercial service (Thornton's main contribution being the design of an "elegant cabin"). After a time trial in which the newest boat did a measured mile in 7½ minutes, the company placed an ad in the Philadelphia papers:

"The Steamboat is now ready to take passengers, and is intended to set off from Arch Street Ferry, in Philadelphia, every Monday, Wednesday and Friday for Burlington, Bristol, Bordentown and Trenton, to return on Tuesdays, Thursdays and Saturdays. Price for passengers 2/6 to Burlington and Bristol, 3/9 to Bordentown, 5 shillings to Trenton." On Sundays the boat was to ply back and forth in the opposite direction, down the Delaware to Chester.

From mid-May to the end of August the first commercial steamboat service in the world ran a regular schedule. Many passengers used it, and there were no accidents and no technical problems of consequence. But the venture was an artistic success and commercial failure. Basically, the volume of traffic was not large enough, and the run not long enough. The stage, though more expensive, could reach Trenton faster, the road being straighter than the river. Sailboats were not so much slower that it mattered greatly in a run of less than a day, and sailboats were appreciably cheaper to operate.

Fitch was not blind to the economic sense of the steamboat question. He knew very well that the right river for the steamboat was not the Delaware but the Mississippi-Ohio. He calculated that four men could navigate a steamboat of 50 tons up the Ohio at 60 miles per day, "much the cheapest transportation that could be used." But his persistent efforts to get financial backing for a Western enterprise failed. Henry Voight took a job in the new United States Mint, where Fitch applied too but was turned down. To his further exasperation, Thomas Jefferson, Henry Knox, and Edmund Randolph, after lengthy deliberations, decided to give federal patents to both Fitch and Rumsey, adding insult to injury by describing Rumsey's boat rather than Fitch's ("for applying the force of steam to trunk or trunks, for drawing water in at the Bow of a boat or vessel," etc.). But fresh financial support from Thornton and a word of encouragement from the governor of Louisiana sent him back to work on his newest boat, the *Perseverance.*

Fitch was managing to live largely thanks to the kindness of a tavern-keeping widow named Mary Kraft, who let him run up bills. Henry Voight came over to the tavern nightly to talk steamboats and deism—both he and Fitch shocked friends by denying the divinity of Jesus Christ—and took to remaining after Fitch had gone to bed. Presently Mary became pregnant, and since Voight was married, Fitch offered to marry her himself "and Pledge my word of honor never to bed with her." To this solution Mary objected, and Fitch instead helped arrange for the child to be born in "an obscure house." But when Mary got pregnant again she left town, gave her name at her new address as "Mary Fitch," and had Fitch sent for at her confinement. Fitch accepted the role, but this time Voight had the nerve to object, coming and yelling at the window that the child was his and making Fitch wish "that the Devil had me rather than to have been so entangled. . . . On the Whole I acknowledge that I have far exceeded Quixot in relieving Distressed Ladies. . . . All I can say of the matter is this: I think this is a dam wicked world and when I get clear of it never wish to come back to it any more. I have frequently been apt to conclude it is a place where they transport souls to from other Planets that is not fit to live in them, the same as Great Britain used to send Convicts to Virginia. . . ."

His backers, along with Voight, soon gave up on the *Perseverance,* but a gleam of hope arose unexpectedly from abroad. Aaron Vail, U.S. consul at Lorient, France, had seen Fitch's boats on the Delaware, took out a French patent in Fitch's name, and sent for the inventor. Fitch sailed from New York in early 1793, and landed in France just in time for the Reign of Terror. He witnessed the Revolution in Paris and Nantes, though he was so preoccupied with his steamboat that he almost overlooked it. The civil war in Brittany finally discouraged him and he sailed to England, en route inventing a "Ready Reckoner" to simplify keeping track of a ship's course. Sailing captains who had learned navigation through long apprenticeships did not want the art simplified, and Fitch's sensible improvement died.

Although Aaron Vail had given him a letter of credit to pay for his passage home, he returned by steerage-indenture, landing in Boston and working off his indenture on the waterfront while trying to promote his Reckoner and a new design for a waterwheel. Despite all disappointments, he was oddly serene: "The

Posthumous portrait of John Fitch.
(Smithsonian Photograph No. 3,474-A)

JOHN FITCH.

happiest days of my life is since I came to Boston. My labour is an amusement and affords me a moderate sustinence, and my accommodations are modest and agreeable, and I live retired and unknown . . . no cumber of business on my hands, no vilenous acts to disturbe my repose at night." In a bit of doggerel written at this time he rued the fact that

> For full the scope of seven years
> Steam Boats exited hopes & fears
> In me, but now I see it plain
> All further progress is in vain
> And am resolved to quit a Scheming
> And be no longer of pattents dreaming
> As for my partners *Dam them all* . . .

In 1795 he paid a visit to his sister Sarah and her husband at Windsor, Connecticut, and the following year (or possibly the year after) he journeyed to Kentucky to check up on his land warrants. The Kentucky wilderness was blooming with squatters' farms, and Fitch hired a lawyer to prosecute his claims, which he thought should be worth a sizable sum. But his health was poor; he did not feel up to much, and thought death was probably near. He made a deal with a tavern keeper in Bardstown to supply board, lodging, and a pint of whiskey a day in return for a bequest at his death of 150 acres of land. He had already made his will, asking to be buried "on some public highway or place of the greatest resort of the living . . . some Public House that I could hear the Song of the Brown jug on the first day of February every year." He thoughtfully enclosed a copy of the "Song of the Brown Jug" with the will:

> With my Jug in one hand and my pipe in the other
> I'll Drink to my Neighbor and Friend,

All my cares in a whiff of Tobacco I'll smother,
My Life I know Shortly must End. . . .

I'll ne'er trouble myself with the cares of my Nation,
I've Enough of my own for to mind.
All we see in this World is but Grief and Vexation,
To Death I am shortly Resigned.

So we'll Laugh, Drink, and smoke and leave nothing to care
And Drop like a Pair Ripe and Mellow,
When Cold in my Coffin, I'll leave them to Say
"He's gone, what a True hearted Fellow."

He did not want to be buried "on or near any Christian burying ground." He requested that his debts be paid from money due him, that his New England property go to his two children there, and that seven or eight pounds he had in the Masons' funds go to "give everyone present [at his funeral] a good Drink so as to make them feel Glad they are alive. . . ." He directed that his memoirs not be edited to modify his antireligious expressions or his strictures on the officers of government.

He lived on in the Bardstown inn for a year, drinking his daily pint of whiskey, playing games with Squire Rowan's little granddaughter and building a model steamboat three feet long in the blacksmith shop. His invention, he was confident, was "one of the greatest and most useful arts that has ever been introduced into the world; and although the world and my country does not thank me for it, yet it gives me heartfelt satisfaction."

One morning he told his innkeeper that he was not dying fast enough, and pledged another 150 acres to double his whiskey allotment. In the spring of 1798 he was in constant pain. The doctor prescribed opium, and after making a new will Fitch saved up a dozen opium pills, washed them down with whiskey, and went to sleep. George Weller, the village carpenter, recalled later: "I made Mr. Fitch's coffin. It is of cherry and fastened with screws. It was long, for he was a tall man."

By the time the first Western steamboat paddled past Bardstown in 1811 Fitch's grave was forgotten, but in 1844 it was rediscovered and given a headstone. In 1926 Congress appropriated $15,000 for a monument at Bardstown, and the remains of a thorny, difficult, intemperate, but gifted and gallant American original were reburied in Court Square.

3

Oliver Evans Invents
the Automated Factory

SOME INVENTIONS COME INTO BEING as designed responses to clearly articulated demands. Birmingham button manufacturer Matthew Boulton encouraged Watt to go ahead with his steam engine because the British industrial community, equipped with new mass-production textile machinery but without a suitable power source, was "steam-mill mad." In other cases a need is visible but does not translate into economic demand because the capital for development is lacking. Such was the case with John Fitch's steamboat, which the American West needed but could not at the moment pay for. In still other cases an inspired response to an immediate problem proves to have value for a future time beyond contemporary conception. This last was the case with the automatic flour mill, patented by Oliver Evans in the same year (1786) that John Fitch triumphantly steam-paddled up the Delaware; the automatic flour mill came to be recognized a century and a half later as the world's first automated factory.

Not content with one historic innovation, Evans simultaneously recorded another by asking the legislature of Pennsylvania for the exclusive right to operate "steam wagons" on the state's roads—the first patent application for an American automobile.

Oliver Evans came from a background a cut above John Fitch's. Born in Newport, New Castle County, Delaware, southeast of Wilmington, in 1755, he was the fifth of twelve children of Charles Evans, a "cordwainer," or shoemaker. The elder Evans' occupational station was not as humble as it may sound to a later day—

handmade leather boots and shoes classed as luxury goods, requiring capital, tools, and skill. In 1757 Charles Evans bought a farm in Mill Creek Hundred, and here Oliver grew up. Though nothing is known of his boyhood, it is evident from his writings that he had a good education—paid for by his parents, since there were no free public schools in Delaware.

In 1771, at the age of sixteen, Oliver was apprenticed to a wheelwright, a choice congenial to a youth whose mechanical bent already was coupled with a deeper scientific interest. The next year one of his brothers told him about an experiment he and the blacksmith's boy had carried out: Stopping up the touch hole of a musket barrel, they had put in a gill of water, rammed wadding down on top to seal it, and laid the breech end of the gun in the smith's fire. The result was an explosion as gratifying as if the weapon had been loaded with gunpowder. "It immediately occurred to me," Oliver wrote later, "that there was a power capable of propelling any waggon, provided that I could apply it; and I set myself to work to find out the means of doing so."

Soon after, Evans, like Fitch, encountered a book that described the Newcomen engine (probably a different book, perhaps Desaugliers' *A Course of Experimental Philosophy,* whose second edition was published in 1744). Unlike Fitch, Evans was aware of the Newcomen engine, but was surprised to learn that "they had so far erred" as to use only atmospheric pressure to drive the piston, and steam merely to create a vacuum rather than as a force of its own. Fitch had made the same observation without knowing of Watt's new design, but Fitch's thought occurred in 1786, while Evans had the idea in 1772, only three years after Watt's patent of 1769, of which Evans was entirely ignorant. Evans was equally ignorant of the steam-powered military vehicle that had actually been built and demonstrated by Captain Nicolas Cugnot in Paris in 1769.

For the time being he was distracted from steam-engine thoughts by a more pressing problem. The colonies' tense relations with Britain were creating a shortage of wool-combing cards, or more precisely, of the wire teeth needed to arm the leather-bound blocks. To his family and friends Oliver Evans suggested a hand-cranked machine that could cut and bend the wire teeth into the proper configuration. He encountered the first shock of the young inventor, ridicule, but when an injury to his foot gave him time to carve a model, a friend named George Latimer saw its merit. With the aid of some Jamaica rum, Latimer persuaded a skeptical blacksmith to translate the model into iron. The resulting mechanism produced wire teeth so successfully that, as Evans related later, "They all changed their language, and nothing could surpass the ingenuity of Oliver."

He applied to the Delaware legislature for $500 to build a factory to produce his machine, and like John Fitch found legislators sympathetic but impecunious. Reverting to private enterprise, he contracted with a Wilmington textile manufacturer to make a machine that would turn out 500 card teeth per minute, and made one that actually produced 3,000. Not satisfied with this success, he designed a new machine that pricked holes in the leather and set the teeth in place by the single motion of a hand crank, and turned out 300 complete wool cards a day. He now experienced the second shock of the inventor; his invention was pirated from Philadelphia to Boston and thousands of wool cards were produced without a cent of royalties or a word of credit to Oliver Evans.

In 1778 Oliver and two of his brothers were enrolled in Captain William Robeson's Pennsylvania militia company, but the British soon abandoned Philadelphia and the Evans boys apparently saw no action. Oliver and Joseph Evans bought a village store at Nine Bridge, on Tuckahoe Creek, in the Maryland part of the Delmarva Peninsula. It was here that Oliver first had the opportunity of observing the inefficiency of eighteenth-century flour mills.

The little stone or log buildings were sited on every stream. Many were of the most primitive type, the Greek or Norse mill, with no gearing, the revolving "runner" or upper millstone being attached by a vertical shaft directly to a slow-moving horizontal waterwheel in the stream below. The coarse brown meal that was produced was bolted (sifted), as for centuries past, by a hand-cranked bolting wheel, or by a hand sieve. Even the largest mills, equipped with the more sophisticated vertical wheels geared to the drive shaft, employed a procedure that was not only wasteful of labor, but, as Evans noted in a description years later, distinctly unsanitary:

> If the grain be brought to the Mill by land carriage, the Miller took it on his back, a sack generally three bushels, carried it up one story by stair steps, emptied it in a tub holding four bushels. [The tub] was hoisted by a jack . . . which required one man below and another above . . . [and] was moved by hand to the granary, and emptied. All this required strong men. From the granary it was moved by hand to the hopper of the rolling screen, from the rolling screen by hand to the Millstone hopper, and as [it was] ground it fell in a large trough, retaining its moisture; from thence it was with shovels put into the hoist tubs which

Oliver Evans. (Smithsonian Photograph No. 32,825-T)

employed two men to attend, one below, the other above. . . . [It] was emptied in large heaps on the Meal loft, and spread by shovels, and raked with rakes, to dry and cool it, but this necessary operation could not be done effectually, by all this heavy labour. It was then heaped over the bolting hopper, which required constant attendance, day and night, and which would be frequently overfed, and cause the flour to pass off with the bran, at other times let run empty, when the specks of fine bran passed through the cloth. . . . The great quantity of dirt constantly mixing with the meal from the dirty feet of every one who trampled in it, trailing it over the whole Mill and wasting much, caused great part to be condemned, for people did not even then like to eat dirt, if they could see it. . . . It required much labor to mix the richest and poorest parts together, to form the standard quality, this lazy millers would always neglect, and the great part would be scrapped or condemned. . . .

While he was turning over the mill problem in his mind, Oliver courted and married Sarah Tomlinson, daughter of a Delaware farmer, the wedding taking place in Old Swedes Church in Wilmington on April 22, 1783. After the marriage the couple returned to Tuckahoe, where Oliver spent his honeymoon completing a paper model of the flour mill he had conceived. A chief concern was the elimination of the hopper boy, whose function was to spread the newly ground meal for cooling on the upper floor (meal loft) of the mill with a rake, and then to rake it into a chute by which it dropped into the bolting hopper. Oliver designed a revolving rake in the form of a broad strip of wood 12 feet long, armed on the bottom with wooden teeth, mounted at the base of one of the mill's vertical drive shafts. Adjustable for height, the rake swept in a circle to spread and stir the meal for cooling and drying. The new device took the name of the hopper boy, whose task it performed. To his automatic "hopper boy," Evans added or adapted several mechanisms already known but never before assembled into a systematic whole; many had never before been used in milling.

He conceived a wholly automatic process by which the incoming grain would be lifted by an endless chain of buckets, powered via pulleys by the same waterwheel that ran the vertical shaft. At the top of the mill, the elevator would deposit the grain in a machine equipped with a fan for cleaning. Thence it would pass to a hopper feeding the millstones. After grinding, another elevator would lift the meal to the hopper boy on an upper floor, whence it would pass by broad gravity-powered belts to the bolting machine on an intermediate floor to be sifted, and then to barrels below for packing. Horizontal movement, he figured, could be accomplished by a conveyer consisting either of an endless screw, or a "drill," an endless band of wooden rakes housed in a wooden trough, powered, via gearing, from the mill's waterwheel. The three types of conveyors—bucket, belt, and screw—used in the process remained the basic conveyors of nineteenth- and twentieth-century factories.

By 1785 Evans was ready to construct his mill on a property he and his brothers had bought three years earlier from their father, on Red Clay Creek in Mill Creek Hundred, on the site of the ruins of an old stone mill. That September the mill was completed. Nothing like it had ever been seen before in Europe or America—grain delivered by wagon to the ground floor, rising to the top by waterpower, descending by gravity, while all the steps of drying, milling, spreading, cooling, and sorting were accomplished with self-acting rakes, troughs, conveyors, and chutes. Evans's mill turned out twenty-one barrels of superfine flour for every hundred bushels of wheat, with only one man in charge, compared with a miller and two assistants in an old-fashioned mill that produced only seventeen barrels per hundred bushels.

Amazing though the new establishment was, it did not stampede the milling profession. Many millers were skeptical, telling Evans, "You cannot make water run uphill, you cannot make wooden millers." Even some millers who saw his mill in operation reported that "the whole contrivance was a set of rattle traps unworthy the attention of men of common sense." More to the point, most of the little mills that lined the rivers and creeks were family enterprises or partnerships

Oliver Evans's automated flour mill, engraving from *The Young Millwright and Miller's Guide.* Bucket elevators (39, 27, 5) carry the grain and flour vertically; screw devices carry it horizontally (37, 21, 31, 15, 45); the automatic hopper boy (to spread and dry the meal) is pictured at 25. (Library of Congress)

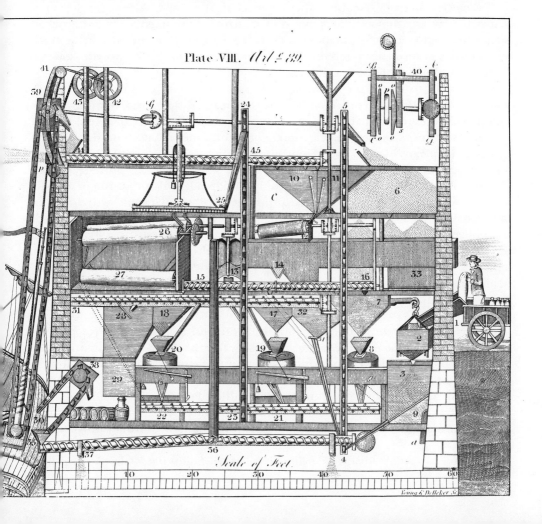

in which laborsaving was only a theoretical consideration. Nevertheless, Evans was able to get five leading millers of New Castle County to submit a petition supporting his patent application to the Delaware legislature. Both Delaware and Pennsylvania legislatures acted favorably, as later did Maryland and New Hampshire. And in 1787, when Evans returned to the steam-wagon project he had shelved five years before, Maryland further distinguished itself by becoming the first state to acquiesce in his request for patent privilege for his "New Plan of applying [steam] to Propelling land Carriages to travel with heavie Burdens up and Down hills without the aid of Animal fource with such Velocity as may be Convenient, and be guided by a person sitting therein Secure from the Inclemency of the weather. . . ." The Pennsylvania legislature, appealed to earlier, had simply passed over the steam wagon without comment.

Others did comment, generally in terms ranging from incredulity to sarcasm. While Evans was explaining his concept to one group of gentlemen, a hearer waggishly inquired how he would manage to get his ponderous vehicle out of the way of other wagons. "Why Sir," said Evans, "were you the waggoner, and did not give room for me to pass, I would crush you and your waggon to the earth." According to Evans the jokester remained silent and civil afterward. A few years later a somewhat similar dialogue took place in a British Parliamentary hearing when someone asked George Stephenson what would happen if a cow got on the track in front of his steam locomotive. "That," said Stephenson in his North Country burr, "would be verra bad fra the coo."

Evans stuck to the steam-wagon idea even though aware of the road problems that had caused Fitch to abandon it. One reason for Evans's perseverance was his gentlemanly judgment that Fitch and James Rumsey, the inventive tavern keeper, had a clear priority in steam navigation. The significance of steam on the Western rivers by no means escaped him. He made a prediction that startled Philadelphia, that "men now living" would see the Western waters covered with steamboats and that a child already born would travel from Philadelphia to Boston in a single day. "The time will come," he boldly prophesied, "when people will travel in stages moved by steam engines, from one city to another, almost as fast as birds fly, fifteen or twenty miles an hour. . . . A carriage will set out from Washington in the morning, the passengers will breakfast at Baltimore, dine at Philadelphia, and sup at New York the same day. . . . And," adding an inventor's curse, "it shall come to pass, that the memory of these sordid and wicked wretches who opposed such improvements, will be execrated, by every good man, as they ought to be now."

Returning to his automatic flour mill, Evans furnished his brother Joseph with the large sum of $100 expense money for a sales tour of the Middle Atlantic states with the object of enlisting local millers as county agents for the new machinery. Although he offered rights to the new system free to the first miller in each county to adopt it, Joseph failed to sign up a single miller. Particularly discouraging was the fact that most of the millers of the nearby Brandywine, a milling aristocracy famous throughout the country, temporized until the new mill had proved itself elsewhere.

In 1790 Evans took advantage of the first United States patent law to acquire a fourteen-year patent that superseded his state privileges (Patent No. 3). The patent gave him the right to charge $40 for the use of his invention by a mill with one pair of stones. He soon had agents out selling, but found it difficult to make money —the millers either stuck to the old way or built his machinery without paying him anything.

One of the few honest men to take advantage of Evans's invention was George Washington, who became one of the first licensees. Touring the country in 1791, the new president made a point of calling at the flour mills of Joseph Tatnall on the Brandywine. Tatnall, whom Washington wished to thank for sticking to his mill in the Revolution's dark days and grinding meal for the Continental Army, was an exception among the Brandywine millers, an enthusiastic (and paying) proponent of the Evans system, which he had installed the year before. Washington took Tatnall's advice and adopted it for his Dogue Creek Mill at Mount Vernon, his secretary corresponding with Evans about the construction and the hiring of a miller. But the majority of the Brandywine millers maintained their obstinacy to such a degree that, according to Evans, the mills of the district "lost their preeminence in the United States, and have descended to the second grade."

In 1791 Evans sold his store in Maryland and moved to Wilmington; the following year he liquidated his Delaware property, selling the Red Clay Creek mill to a partner, and transferred his household to Philadelphia, temporarily the national capital, where he hoped to find better scope for his ambitions. In the Philadelphia directory of 1793 he was listed as "Oliver Evans—constructor of mills— 437 N. 2nd Street." A notice in the *General Advertiser* revealed his new location "To those concerned in Mills in the United States," and announced that he would "thankfully receive any applications for the use of his Patent Improvements on Mills, and the art of manufacturing Flour," furnishing drawings and descriptions, and was also ready to sell "boulting cloths and mill stones of the first quality, at the lowest prices. . . . Orders by post, or otherwise, will be as punctually attended to as if the parties were present."

The money from his mill business he invested in what was more and more becoming his true infatuation, the steam engine. By now he had familiarized himself with Watt's engine. Watt, he found, had radically improved the old Newcomen engine by three major changes: a separate condenser, which permitted the steam to be drawn off for condensation after each piston stroke without cooling the piston chamber; the double-acting principle, which introduced steam at either end of the piston instead of relying on atmospheric pressure for the down stroke; and an ingenious flyball governor that made the engine self-regulating, and therefore suitable for use in factories where the number of machines drawing power caused constantly fluctuating demand. The Watt engine was admirably adapted for Britain's great need, an industrial power source. But American industry had little need for an independent power source for the present (and for many years hence) because of the profusion of rapidly falling streams. What America had a need for was an engine powerful enough to drive a steamboat up the Mississippi and Ohio. For that purpose, Evans perceived, the Watt engine would not suffice because it did not produce a high enough steam pressure.

The high-pressure steam engine amounted to an entirely different concept from the low-pressure developed by Watt, creating quite different problems and leading to different results. In Evans's engine the steam was not condensed, but discharged into the atmosphere. This resulted in a slight wastage of pressure, but in an engine designed to operate at high pressure the consideration had no significance. There were other technical reasons for having a condenser, and eventually condensers were restored to high-pressure engines, but in the absence of theory, Evans simply gained an economy in materials and manufacture by eliminating Watt's condenser.

Evans was not the first to conceive of the advantages of using steam at high pressure or even, a little more surprisingly, the first to build such an engine. The double-piston engine Captain Cugnot built for his French army vehicle in 1769 was high-pressure, as indeed it had to be to move a land vehicle. Afloat, a low-pressure engine sufficed, at least in the absence of a strong current, and its extra weight, owing to its larger piston diameter and consequently larger chamber and boiler, could be carried without inconvenience. But Evans was thinking first of a road vehicle and second of a boat for the Mississippi.

Like Watt, he planned to introduce steam alternately at either end of his chamber, but under a pressure of 25 to 30 pounds per square inch compared with Watt's 3 to 5. The resulting piston stroke would be correspondingly powerful, at the expense of considerable strain on the copper boiler. To strengthen his boiler Evans proposed girdling it with 3-inch-thick wood staves tightly encircled by welded iron bands, not a very satisfactory answer to pressures above 25 pounds per square inch. Evans knew his boiler needed iron plating, but in the 1790s American ironmasters could not yet make plate iron.

Because of its smaller piston, chamber, and boiler, the high-pressure engine economized on metal, expensive in America, and its greater appetite for fuel was no great disadvantage because of the abundance of wood.

In 1794–95 Evans sent drawings and specifications of his engine to England to try to get a patent, but his emissary failed to obtain one before dying in London in 1798. By that time a gifted Cornishman, Richard Trevithick, was at work on a high-pressure engine and eventually used it to power the world's first practical locomotive. Watt steadfastly opposed high-pressure engines as dangerous and unnecessary, which they were for the industrial applications Boulton & Watt were satisfying.

At the same time that he was trying for a British steam-engine patent, Evans was angling through another emissary for a British patent on his flour mill. This messenger, a Philadelphia clockmaker named Robert Leslie who was in London to patent some improvements in watch construction, reported back that milling in England was done entirely by wind-driven mills too small to make use of Evans's machinery. In England the path toward Evans's conception of more efficient milling lay through steam power, which was presently applied in the Albion Mills constructed in London by Watt's fellow Scotsman John Rennie, later the builder of New London Bridge.

During the 1790s, Evans devoted his spare time to writing *The Young Millwright and Miller's Guide,* which he hoped to finance by subscription. As the book grew and added more and more copperplate illustrations, it became increasingly expensive, and in 1794 he vainly petitioned the Pennsylvania legislature for financial aid. His deficit was finally made up by a $1,000 loan from John Nicholson, the Comptroller General of the state. With the ups and downs of his business, in 1797 Evans was unable to pay off the debt and had difficulty in raising $50 to pay Nicholson on account. A few years later his creditor, ruined by one of the mercurial turns in business fortune normal to the times, was in debtor's prison. When Evans learned of Nicholson's misfortune, he hastened to pay in full what remained of the $1,000 debt, and allowed the prisoner to draw on him for more, reversing their relationship.

In 1800 or 1801, Evans finally set to work to build his steam wagon, but got sidetracked by a new idea, and his first high-pressure engine was designed to grind gypsum into plaster of Paris, much in demand as fertilizer and as cement to join burr stones for flour mills. Before he was finished, the little (6-inch diameter, 18-inch stroke) engine cost him $3,700, practically his whole capital, but it ran beautifully, grinding twelve tons of plaster of Paris in twenty-four hours and serving as a prototype for larger engines. Within a few years, Evans's high-pressure engines were widely known in a dozen applications. Among improvements over Watt's engine, a significant one was aimed at economizing on the size and strength of the working beam, which in the Watt engine transmitted power from the piston under one end to the crankshaft under the other. Evans positioned the crankshaft and piston on the same side, an arrangement that created a problem of linkage, since the piston rod was no longer directly under the beam. He solved the problem with a device that became world-renowned as the Evans straight-line linkage.

Where Evans got his parts machined is not known; at that time there were few lathes capable of boring and turning cylinders with accuracy. The probability is strong that they were fabricated in Nicholas Roosevelt's new Soho Works, on the Passaic River near Newark, New Jersey, named after Watt's famous Birmingham plant. If hardly on the scale of its namesake, the Soho Works was impressive by American standards, with waterwheel-powered lathes and boring machines, wooden bellows, forges, furnaces for melting and refining copper.

In preparing drawings for his parts suppliers, Evans always drew components full size, because he had no confidence in American mechanical labor's working to scale. He used a two-foot rule, a straight edge, a T-square, and a pair of compasses. When he had occasion to exhibit his drawings, he had them reduced in scale by copperplate engravers.

Also in 1801 Evans received a call from a stranger from the West armed with an imaginative idea. Louis Valcourt was a French émigré who had settled in New Orleans where, together with a Captain James McEver, he had conceived the idea of building a steamboat for the Mississippi. Hearing of Evans, Valcourt journeyed to Philadelphia to commission an engine. Evans designed a powerful engine with a cylinder of 9-inch diameter and a 36-inch stroke. By the end of 1802 his engine and boiler arrived in New Orleans by sea, and were soon installed, by two mechanics sent by Evans from Philadelphia, in a hull prepared in advance by Captain McEver. By the spring of 1803 the boat was ready.

The bold and skillfully prepared enterprise deserved a better fate than it suffered. A sudden flood of the temperamental river swept the boat half a mile inland

and grounded it beyond recovery. McEver and Valcourt cleverly extricated themselves financially by selling the engine to a local sawmill, where it proved sturdy and powerful, sawing 3,000 feet of board ($150 worth) in a twelve-hour day. Local sawyers, seeing themselves displaced, made three attempts to burn down the mill and on the third try succeeded.

On February 14, 1804, Evans obtained a new patent for a high-pressure steam engine and boiler. In his specifications he pointed out the key principle: "as the heat of water is increased in arithmetical progression the elastic power of steam is increased in geometrical progression . . . doubling the heat . . . increases the power of the steam about one hundred times. . . ." That was an overoptimistic guess, but the general idea was right.

That year he found another opportunity to build a steamboat. The motivating force was not commerce but garbage, a mass of which had accumulated in front of the Water Street wharves on the Schuylkill. A scow with a hand-operated windlass and scoop had proved inadequate in doing the job, so the new Philadelphia Board of Health was persuaded to try steam.

The engine to power the digging machinery, Evans thought, might as well power the boat itself. Further, it might as well power it en route to the water. As a result, though Evans's *Orukter Amphibolos* (Amphibious Digger) had several predecessors in steam navigation, it scored a first—the first American powered land vehicle (Captain Cugnot's steam tricycle of 1769 was the world's first). *Orukter* consisted, in Evans's own description, of "a heavy flat-bottomed boat, 30 feet long and 12 feet broad, with a chain of buckets to bring up the mud, and hooks to clear away sticks, stones and other obstacles. These buckets are wrought by a small steam engine" (which also supplied motive power). Because his shop was a mile and a half from the Schuylkill, Evans fitted *Orukter* with ground traction wheels in addition to her stern paddle wheel for the water, and drove her down Market Street to Center Square, where for several days she circled the new Water Works building. In an advertisement in the *Philadelphia Gazette,* Evans invited the citizens to view the marvel, which was on display "at the expense of the workmen, who expect 25 cents from every generous person who may come to see its operation; but all are invited to come and view it, as well those who cannot as those who can conveniently spare the money." Finally she was run down the sloping riverbank at low tide, and her paddlewheel fixed to her stern, with a belt connection to the engine shaft. As the tide rose, the scow floated off the frame that held the axle and wheels, and steered by a long stern oar, steamed down the river. On her trial run *Orukter* turned into the Delaware with the tide, steamed up to Dunk's Ferry, sixteen miles above Philadelphia, and returned.

While busy with the steam engine projects, Evans embarked on a companion book to *The Young Mill-wright and Miller's Guide—The Young Steam Engineer's Guide.* The financial problems of the earlier publication were compounded by further difficulties—debts incurred in his patent battles, and, worst of all, the failure of Congress to renew his patent of 1791 for the flour mill improvements. "I was left in poverty at the age of 50," Evans wrote, "with a large family of children and an amiable wife to support, for I had expended my last dollar in putting my 'Columbian' steam engine into operation, and in publishing the 'Steam Engi-

Orukter amphibolos. This representation of Oliver Evans's steam carriage appeared on the cover of *The Mechanic,* 1834. (Alba B. Johnson Collection)

neer's Guide,' a work still more difficult and abstruse than the 'Millwright's Guide.' . . . It brought on gray hairs again, and the use of spectacles, and greatly injured my constitution and health a second time, but which I soon regained upon quitting intense study, and resuming active bodily exercise but the gray hairs and the use of spectacles I could never get rid of." In a spirit of bitterness, he changed the title of the book to *The Abortion of the Young Steam Engineer's Guide.*

The new *Guide* contained another idea that was before its time: artificial refrigeration. Evans observed: "If an open glass be filled with ether and set in water under vacuo, the ether will boil rapidly and rob the water of its latent heat till it freezes. . . ." He proposed a powerful vacuum pump driven by a steam engine to volatilize ether, thus taking heat from the water around it, while a second pump recompressed the ether within a barrel immersed in water, changing the ether to vapor again. Thus he imagined refrigerating the reservoirs containing the drinking water of American cities—concluding the description, however, by likening himself "lest I be thought extravagant" to Watt's forerunner, the Marquess of Worcester, whose ideas were flouted by his contemporaries.

A year later, in 1806, he was once more expanding his horizons. He bought a building a few blocks from his previous workshop and turned it into a foundry to do his own casting and molding. In this new establishment Evans developed a new bellows technique for forcing a blast of air into the furnace that brought him and his foundryman to the verge of the later malleable iron process, and within hailing distance of the Kelly-Bessemer process. He also experimented with anthracite coal in place of charcoal for smelting. The location of his "Mars Works," as he named it despite its being devoted exclusively to peaceful purposes, had a drawback, which became evident with the arrival of summer heat—its proximity to Pegg's Run, used by Philadelphia's slaughterhouses, tanners, and glue-makers to dispose of offal. By the end of August, Evans was moved to write the city commissioners protesting "the air contaminated by the noxious effluvia," and stating that if he were doomed to breathe such polluted air, as he had done for the past month, for the entire period of his occupation of the property, "I would rather cho[o]se to set fire to the whole, and as the saying is, run away by the light of the conflagration." He got no satisfaction from the municipal government.

The pollution was less exasperating than the patent problem, but early in 1808, three years' persistent lobbying was rewarded by a new grant from Congress extending his mill machinery patent for another fourteen years. Evans notified infringers who had built mills in the interval when his patent was in abeyance, and got prompt satisfaction from at least one—President Jefferson, who paid $89.60 to Evans's Virginia agent. Evans wrote a grateful reply: "Mr. Moody has sent me a copy of your answer to his application which I hope will induce others to follow your generous and Patriotic example. I am sensible that the law did not require of you or any who erected and used my improvements during the interval of my patents such payments. . . ."

Yet even Jefferson was doubtful that inventions should be "a subject of property," and so widespread was the resistance to patent royalties that Evans, normally an even-tempered genius, was plunged by an adverse court ruling (1809) into an uncharacteristic and costly fit of despair. Philadelphia district court judge Bushrod Washington, a nephew of the former president, had already aggrieved Evans in the case of an infringing western Pennsylvania miller. Now he delivered a preliminary opinion in another case, to the effect that a patentee was a violator of public rights. Evans summoned his family and in a melodramatic scene threw into the blazing fire his bundle of drawings and specifications for inventions, including his plans for steamboat navigation of the Mississippi. "Such doctrine from such authority," he wrote, "determined me that patent rights were property too untenable to be worthy of the pursuit of any prudent man. That it was highly dangerous to leave my papers to lead any of my children or grand children into the same road to ruin, that had subjected me to insult, to abuse and robbery all my life."

Judge Washington's opinion proved an empty threat, and Evans recovered his composure. Soon he was engaged in new enterprises. Aware of the rapid growth of Pittsburgh, he invested capital and brains in a steam flour mill, shipping some of the engine components by wagon and flatboat from Philadelphia, making others in Pittsburgh. Three years earlier (1806), a young Kentuckian named Luther Stephens, reading Evans's *Steam Engineer's Guide,* had walked to Philadelphia to show him a better way to solve the problem of admitting steam alternately to either end of the cylinder. Stephens's rotary valve at once became part of Evans's engine designs, paid for with a full 25 percent of the basic patent, and Evans rewarded the young man with a partnership with Evans's son George in running the new Pittsburgh plant.

By 1814 Evans had twenty-eight steam engines in operation or under manufacture, grinding grain, sawing lumber, drawing wire, rolling and slitting iron, grinding lead, spinning cotton, manufacturing cloth, and powering boats. By 1815 high-pressure engines were in such demand in the West that a pair of Pittsburgh pirates, Daniel French and Thomas Copeland, shamelessly copied Evans's design in a cheap version and undersold him.

Despite pirates and hostile judges, Evans did very well with his engines. The largest he built was a hundred-horsepower model for the Fairmount Water Works in Philadelphia. The Fairmount Works had installed a Boulton & Watt low-pressure engine with a similar pump diameter some years earlier, and no little interest attached to the head-to-head competition of the two engines under a single roof. The result was controversial. The Boulton & Watt engine burned only seven cords of wood in twenty-four hours to the Evans's thirteen, but pumped only 1,733,632 gallons to the Evans's 3,072,656. The fuel factor would have been decisive in England, but in Philadelphia it was canceled out by the better performance. In the West, where wood was cheap, the high-pressure engine's fuel appetite was scarcely even a consideration.

At sixty, feeling the weight of years, Oliver Evans sat down and penned his own epitaph:

> This stone and sod, combine, to hold
> A Wreck'd volcanic engine; old
> Which steady wrought on, sixty years
> Then faulter'd, and did need repairs
> The fire at times, would scarcely burn
> The boiler fail, and leak'd in turn
> Motions grew slower every hour
> At ——, lost all its power
> Nor can all Artists, in the nation
> Repair it, or revive its motion
> Here is the end of Oliver, he died —— day of ——
> Where has the active spirit flown
> Who formed opinions, of its own?
> Did disregard the laugh of fools
> The Claims of things, the pomp of schools
> Spirits, Hobgoblins and Ghosts
> Satan and Hell, the work of Priests
> Took his full share of this short life
> With a beautious virtuous loving wife
> As he wished others do to him
> Just so, he strove to do to them
> In this straight course, his Bark did steer
> And never felt a pang of fear.

A year later, in 1816, his wife of thirty-three years died. Suffering from a liver complaint, he continued to fight infringements. In 1818 he was contemplating remarriage. "Evan [his bachelor younger brother] and I are both looking out but make poor progress among the Maids and Widows," he wrote a business associate. But the second Mrs. Evans soon appeared in the person of young Hetty Ward, daughter of an innkeeper with an establishment on the Bowery in New York.

A year after the marriage, at his new father-in-law's home, Evans was stricken with pneumonia. He was gravely ill when the painful news reached him that his Mars Works had been destroyed by fire, and he died on April 15, 1819.

The *Pittsburgh Gazette* spoke for the West in mourning: "The Eastern papers announce the death of that celebrated and most useful citizen, OLIVER EVANS. . . . A few men such as Franklin, Rumford, Davy and Evans, who bend the highest and most abstract principles of science to the use of man, in facilitating the common operations of life, will be remembered by a nation's gratitude, when the comparatively insignificant herd of metaphysicians and conquerors shall have passed into total oblivion."

Not long after, the translator of the French edition of *The Young Steam Engineer's Guide* penned a European appreciation of its author: "Few men have been as useful to society as Oliver Evans. Very few have displayed an equal perseverance in rendering these services to their fellow men, that is, in spite of their fellow men. His contemporaries never appreciated him at his true value; but an understanding posterity will place his name among those who are most truly distinguished for their eminent services rendered to their country and to humanity."

The Pittsburgh editor and the French translator would be equally surprised to know that a century and a half later Oliver Evans still lacks a popular biography, and that his name is hardly known to his countrymen. May their forecasts yet come true, and "an understanding posterity" accord America's greatest early inventor "a nation's gratitude."

4

Sam Slater
Discovers America

WHILE JOHN FITCH AND OLIVER EVANS were taking the first giant steps toward the steamboat that would liberate the powerful economic forces gathering in the West, two other young men were busy with contrivances that would revolutionize the economies of the two other major sections of the country, the East and the South. The second of the two, Eli Whitney, was a New England Yankee. The first was an immigrant of a special type little celebrated in traditional American history, with its emphasis on political and religious freedom and economic opportunity for the underprivileged. Samuel Slater was not underprivileged. What he represented in the history of American immigration was talent in search of a field of action.

Holly House, in Derbyshire, England, where Samuel Slater was born in 1768, was a large stone farmhouse surrounded by pastures in which flocks of long-wooled sheep grazed. Samuel was the fifth child and second son of William Slater, a prosperous farmer whose profits allowed him to invest in real estate and timber. Samuel's childhood in the Midlands, the seedbed of Britain's Industrial Revolution, paralleled the early development of the textile industry. He was one year old when Richard Arkwright patented his machinery to prepare and spin cotton; before he was two, Arkwright's first mill, at Hockley, was in operation. As he grew up, the neighboring River Derwent powered an increasing number of cotton mills, including one in the Slaters' own town of Belper.

William Slater's roots were in the rural past, but his commercial activities

formed a bridge to the industrial future. Acting as an agent for Arkwright's partner Jedediah Strutt, he arranged for the purchase of land and water privileges
for a mill in nearby Milford, a commission that led to an offer of apprenticeship
for one of Slater's sons. Strutt suggested the eldest, William, but the father thought
William better fitted to succeed him on the farm, and recommended instead four-
teen-year-old Samuel, who had distinguished himself at the local school and who
"writes well and is good at figures." Samuel had also demonstrated mechanical
aptitude; to facilitate one of his household chores, that of winding worsted for his
mother's spinning, he had made a polished steel spindle.

Spinning had first been mechanized in England with the invention of a machine patented by Lewis Paul in 1738, used in mills in London and the Midlands
in the 1740s. The first really effective mechanization came with James Hargreaves'
jenny, a hand-powered machine that could operate several spindles at once, patented in 1770. Richard Arkwright was a mechanic-entrepreneur who conceived
and carried through the application of waterpower to the carding and spinning
processes. Because the flow of materials through a succession of machines had to
be meticulously adjusted, not only the machinery but the management was of
first importance in the Arkwright system.

Samuel Slater went to work in Jedediah Strutt's Belper mill, not as a laborer,
but as a management trainee, living at Strutt's house and serving as his right-
hand man. Before the indenture was signed, William Slater was fatally injured in
a fall from a load of hay; on his deathbed, he told his son, "You must do that
business [the indenture] yourself, Samuel, I have so much to do, and so little time
to do it."

On January 8, 1783, Samuel signed his own indenture, guaranteeing him "Meat
Drink washing and Lodging" along with training in the "Art of Cotton Spinning."
The new life soon absorbed him to the exclusion of everything else. Though the
Strutt house in Milford was within an easy walk of his home, the boy did not visit
his widowed mother for the first six months of his service, preferring to spend his
Sundays studying the machinery in the mill.

In the typical Arkwright mill, the waterwheel was located adjacent to or beneath the building. Its rotary motion was increased in speed and transformed in
direction by gearing, and transferred by a system of vertical and horizontal shafts
to every machine in the mill. Until the invention of "picking" machines that later
did the preliminary cleaning, cotton had to be prepared by hand, usually in the
houses of families near the mill, who spread the fibers on a "flake," a surface
woven out of taut cords, beat them, and picked out foreign matter. At the mill,
the cleaned cotton was graded and sorted before beginning the four-step mechanical process, copied directly from the centuries-old hand process, essentially consisting of repeated stretchings and twistings. First the carding machine's revolving
cylinders covered with steel-wire bristles combed the fluffy mass into parallel fibers, ejecting it in a thick soft rope called a sliver. Second, a series of drawing
machines attenuated the sliver, stretching it by passing it through several pairs
of turning rollers, the first pair turning slowly, the last much faster. Third, a
series of roving machines, equipped with similar rollers, stretched the attenuated
sliver further and imparted a slight twist, to help hold it together. The product of

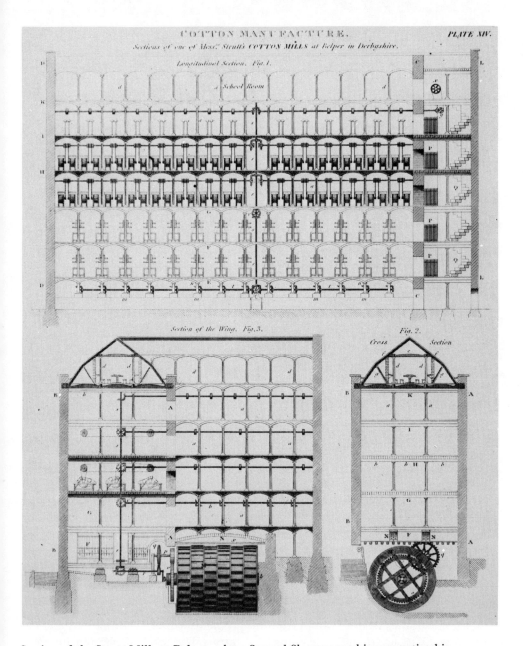

Sections of one of Mess.r Strutt's COTTON MILLS at Belper in Derbyshire.

Longitudinal Section. Fig.1.

School Room

Section of the Wing. Fig.3.

Cross   Section   Fig.2.

Section of the Strutt Mills at Belper, where Samuel Slater spent his apprenticeship.

these machines was a uniform strand of cotton fiber which could be fed to the spinning machine, equipped like the drawing and roving machines with rollers that further reduced the strand, but also with spindles holding rapidly revolving bobbins and flyers that gave the yarn a final twist so that it could not be further stretched.

By the standards of a generation later, the early Arkwright machinery, with its ill-fitting gears and rope drives, was clumsy and subject to chronic breakdown.

Iron was used only where indispensable; even cogwheels were of wood. One annoyance was the failure of the spun yarn to distribute itself properly on the spindles. Samuel Slater solved the problem with an improved heart-motion cam, for which Strutt rewarded him with a guinea. In Slater's own account of his apprenticeship he wrote (referring to himself in the third person), "During four or five of the late years [at Belper], his time was solely devoted to the factory as general overseer, both as respected making machinery and the manufacturing department." Frequent patent suits and controversies further educated him in the important legal side of the business. In 1789, as the end of his seven-year apprenticeship drew near, he asked Strutt to give him the "oversight" of the building and management of new works at Milford, to enlarge his experience.

Already he was meditating emigration. The rush of Midlands manufacturers to install Arkwright machinery threatened an overexpansion of the British textile industry. Slater asked Strutt whether he considered it a "permanent business." "It is not probable, Samuel," replied the older man, "that it will always be as good as it is now, but I have no doubt it will always be a *fair* business, if it be well managed."

Shortly after, Slater made his final decision, and with a discretion that characterized him throughout life, kept it to himself. Britain's manufacturers had successfully pressured Parliament to forbid the export of Arkwright machinery, drawings, specifications, or workmen. The edict proved as unenforceable as the old prohibition against American manufactures. A Hargreaves jenny operated in Philadelphia during the war, and immediately afterward several state legislatures boldly solicited defectors from Britain's Industrial Revolution. In 1786, two Scottish brothers, the Barrs, emigrated to Massachusetts where in return for a £200 subsidy from the state's general assembly they produced an Arkwright carding machine and a spinning machine. A second model of the spinning machine was acquired by the state from another emigrant, Thomas Somers, for £20. Other British mechanics meantime carried the new technology to nearby continental Europe.

Thus Samuel Slater had predecessors when a Philadelphia newspaper came to his attention with the story of a £100 reward granted by the Pennsylvania legislature to a person who had built a carding machine, and a report that a society had been authorized by the legislature to promote manufacture.

Slater may have guessed that application of the borrowed technology on the western side of the Atlantic would run into problems. Circumventing Parliament's edict proved easier than overcoming the intractable mechanical difficulties of fabricating workable machinery in a nonindustrial country. The Hargreaves jenny built in Philadelphia during the Revolution had had such poor success that its owner, a contractor for Continental Army uniforms, had reverted to handspun thread. A cotton mill at Beverly, Massachusetts, built in 1787, was struggling with the Barr and Somers machines, but achieving little success. Even in England the new machinery demanded frequent mechanical attention, and in America there were few skilled mechanics and no sources for machine parts.

There were, however, numerous forges and blacksmith shops, as well as flour mills and sawmills that required mechanical skill, as did shipbuilding, with its demand for anchors, fittings, and navigational instruments. A town that united shipbuilding with waterpowered mills was Pawtucket, Rhode Island, a few miles inland from the Narragansett Bay port of Providence, at a point where in the course of a hundred yards the Blackstone River fell over twenty feet. For more than a century the swiftly coursing water had powered wheels for flour mills and forges. Since 1718 a full dam harnessed the river, with a trench at one side to provide a fishway.

Pawtucket was by American standards a technologically advanced community. Among its outstanding citizens was Oziel Wilkinson, a Quaker blacksmith whose specialty was forging anchors. In 1789 Wilkinson's help was enlisted by a carpenter named Joshua Lindley to build a carding machine copied from that on display in Bridgewater, Massachusetts (two other mechanics, Daniel Anthony of Providence and John Reynolds of East Greenwich, were simultaneously employed by Rhode Island merchants to copy the Bridgewater spinning machine).

Assisting Oziel Wilkinson's work on the carding machine was his eighteen-year-old son David, who decades later recalled that when his father had completed the machine it was put on display for a time in the Market House in Providence where it was hand-cranked "by a colored man named Prince Hopkins, who had lost one leg, and I think one arm, in Sullivan's expedition at Newport, a few years before." The cotton was taken from the carding machine in rolls about eighteen inches long and carried to the shop of Providence merchant Moses Brown, also a Quaker, where it was drawn by hand into long ropes for spinning.

David Wilkinson had actually witnessed the first stirrings of the American textile industry thirteen years earlier, in 1775, when he was a fascinated spectator as a fellow smith of his father's named Eleazer Smith constructed a machine that may have been a pirated version of Oliver Evans's invention for setting teeth into leather hand cards. "I was then about five years old," David recalled in his memoir, "'and my curiosity was so great to see the work going on, that my father sat me on Mr. Smith's bench, to look on, while he worked. And at this time, seventy years afterwards, I could make a likeness of nearly every piece of that machine, so durable are the first impressions on the mind of youth." More recently David had "forged and ground spindles" for a jenny built by John Reynolds, the East Greenwich mechanic who copied the models at Bridgewater. "I made a small machine to grind with, which had a roller of wood to roll on the stone, which turned the spindle against the stone, and so ground the steel spindles perfectly. . . ." David also helped Daniel Anthony and his son in "finishing and keeping in order their machine."

Yet none of these textile machines was giving satisfactory service when in early 1789 Moses Brown made the decision to expand and mechanize his business. Buying up Anthony's and Reynolds's spinning machines and Lindley's carding machine, as well as several jennies, he transferred them to rented space in Ezekiel Carpenter's fulling (textile-finishing) mill in Pawtucket, where the fishway had been converted into a millrace for what Moses Brown intended to make the site of the first successful waterpowered cotton-spinning mill in America.

To manage the mill, Moses Brown chose his son-in-law William Almy and his nephew Smith Brown, establishing the firm of Almy and Brown to make and sell cloth, the yarn spun on the jennies and spinning machines providing the material for weaving cotton cloth by hand loom in the neighboring houses. But mechanical spinning again proved frustrating. The machines were too heavy to be run by a hand crank, and too imperfect to be run by waterpower. Moses Brown blamed the failure partly on the workmen, mostly Irish immigrants, who were "of the most transient kind, and on whom little dependence could be placed." Both he and his younger partners believed that their problems could be solved if they could find a mechanic experienced in the operation of the machines.

Thus was the stage set for the arrival in the New World of Samuel Slater. On September 1, 1789, twenty-one-year-old Samuel went home to Holly House to bid his mother good-bye, still without confiding his plans. "I am going by stage to London, and have come to put together my clothes for the trip," is all he said. He never saw her again, although she lived to a ripe old age and survived, according to her own account, "three good husbands"; nor did he see his old master, his boyhood friends, the old mill, or Holly House; but he remembered them all vividly, and according to his friend and biographer George S. White, "These early remembrances would cause the tear to escape, even in his old age." He left behind, too, the property he had inherited from his father, perhaps as a hedge against possible failure in America: two houses in Belper, a nail store, and another building.

The excellent Manchester stage probably carried him the 134 miles to London in three days, if the weather was fine. In London he made contact with an America-bound captain, then did the sightseeing—Westminster Abbey, St. Paul's Cathedral, the Tower—while waiting for the captain to complete his cargo and passenger list. Like many a country boy, he was victimized by a petty crook who sold him silk stockings that, as he discovered on returning to his lodging, lacked feet—an incident which he said later "sharpened his eye teeth." Only when the captain was ready to sail, on September 13, did Slater write his mother revealing his destination.

Early accounts described Slater as slipping on board ship in disguise in order to foil the law, but such measures were not really necessary in 1789. The very fact that those forbidden to emigrate belonged to certain specified occupations made it easy to deceive the port official, who merely scanned the passenger list of each outgoing ship, and found only merchants, farmers, and laborers sailing. No mechanics or manufacturers were ever listed, since these two classes were forbidden to leave Britain. Even when an occasional zealous official learned that a passenger had misrepresented his occupation, the offender was usually simply put ashore.

Searches of baggage, however, were routine, and anyone found trying to smuggle manufacturing models of machinery, or drawings and specifications, was liable to imprisonment. Slater, shipping as a "farm laborer," carried no models, drawings, or notes. What he carried instead (besides his indenture, concealed, as a letter of introduction to the New World) was an extraordinary grasp of mechanical principles, an excellent memory, and the results of a very careful study of the Arkwright machinery and its management at the Belper mill.

Sixty-six days later (November 18) he landed in New York. His original plan had been to go to Philadelphia, where he might have met Oliver Evans, John

Fitch, and Benjamin Franklin, but a few days after arriving, he obtained a job with a small textile firm, the New York Manufacturing Company, on Vesey Street. He soon found that Manhattan was not the place for the American Industrial Revolution to begin, for the simple reason that it had practically no waterpower.

There was plenty of waterpower a day's sail to the northeast. From a Captain Brown whose sailing packet ran between New York and Providence, Slater heard about Moses Brown, no relation of the captain's, who was seeking help in mechanizing his textile operation. To Captain Brown, Slater entrusted a letter addressed to the Quaker merchant:

> New York, Dec. 2, 1789
>
> Sir,—A few days ago I was informed that you wanted a manager of *cotton spinning* &c., in which business I flatter myself that I can give the greatest satisfaction, in making machinery, making good yarn, either for *stockings* or *twist,* as any that is made in England; as I have had opportunity, and oversight, of Sir Richard Arkwright's works, and in Mr. Strutt's mill upwards of eight years. . . .

He mentioned his New York connection, but expressed the opinion that its machinery was "not worth using," and added, "My intention is to erect a *perpetual card and spinning.*"

The letter drew a prompt reply:

> Providence, 10th 12th month, 1789
>
> Friend,—I received thine of 2nd inst. and observe its contents. I, or rather Almy & Brown, who has the business in the cotton line, which I began, one being my son-in-law, and the other a kinsman, want the assistance of a person skilled in the frame or water spinning. An experiment has been made, which has failed, no person being acquainted with the business, and the frames imperfect. . . . As the frame we have is the first attempt of the kind that has been made in America, it is too imperfect to afford much encouragement; we hardly know what to say to thee, but if thou couldst perfect and conduct them to profit, if thou wilt come and do it, thou shalt have all the profits made of them over and above the interest of the money they cost, and the wear and tear of them. We will find stock and be repaid in yarn as we may agree, for six months. . . . If thy present situation does not come up to what thou wishest, and, from thy knowledge of the business, can be ascertained of the advantages of the mills so as to induce thee to come and work ours, and have the *credit* as well as advantage of perfecting the first water-mill in America, we should be glad to engage thy care so long as they can be made profitable to both, and we can agree. I am, for myself and Almy & Brown, thy friend,
>
> Moses Brown.

"Frame" was eighteenth-century for machine, and water spinning meant waterpowered spinning.

In January Slater took Captain Brown's packet to Providence, where Moses Brown met him with Quaker courtesy, escorted him to the fulling mill in Pawtucket, and introduced him to Sylvanus Brown, a mechanic skilled with woodworking machines. "Sylvanus," he said, "I have brought to thee a young man who says he knows how to spin cotton; I want thee to keep him tonight and talk to him, and see what he can do." Next day Sylvanus reported that Slater seemed to know

Samuel Slater in the 1830s. (Library of Congress)   Moses Brown. (Rhode Island Historical Society)

his business. But as far as the existing machinery was concerned, the young Englishman shook his head. "These will not do; they are good for nothing in their
present condition, nor can they be made to answer."

Moses Brown was dismayed, and probably suspicious. What he had envisioned
was the acquisition of a capable mechanic to make the Anthony machines work.
What his young English visitor wanted was a contractual partnership in return
for building spinning machinery from scratch.

The two intelligently hardheaded men, Yankee and English, businessman and
mechanic, worked out a compromise. Slater would put in a ten-week effort at the
not-quite-nominal wage of a dollar a day to build a spinning machine, using such
parts of the old machines as he could. Moving into Oziel Wilkinson's house on
Quaker Lane for board and room, he set to work and in ten weeks succeeded in a
way that satisfied both men, producing from the Anthony machinery a twenty-
four-spindle spinning machine that worked.

The demonstration convinced Moses Brown that Slater could make him the
machinery he wanted. He had a contract drawn up by which the old machinery
was to be modified, cannibalized, or replaced, and a complete set of Arkwright
machinery—two carding machines, drawing and roving frames, spinning machinery carrying one hundred spindles—built and installed.

Slater signed in a spirit of triumphant exhilaration. "If I do not make as good
yarn as they do in England," he declared, "I will have nothing for my services,
but will throw the whole of what I have attempted over the bridge."

He once more set to work in Sylvanus Brown's shop, an ex-woodworking establishment that had been converted to metalwork. He had two helpers, an elderly black man named Jenks, apparently a slave freed by Moses Brown when Brown joined the Society of Friends, and young David Wilkinson. David undertook to forge all the iron parts for the machinery. "All the turning was done with hand tools," Wilkinson wrote later, "and by hand power, with crank wheels. When the card rims and wheels were wanting, I went with Slater to Mansfield, Massachusetts, to a furnace owned by a French gentleman named Dauby, who came I think with Lafayette's army. . . ." There were problems with the iron, which Slater said shrank more than English iron, but Wilkinson devised a rim that did not break under stress.

Slater enlisted a Quaker hand-cardmaker named Pliny Earle, of nearby Leicester, Massachusetts, to make two sets of cards for the machine, one for the revolving cylinder and one as an upper, stationary set. Pliny had trouble executing the novel order, and Slater, working day and night, made sketches and devised tools for him and for David Wilkinson. Gradually the carding machinery took shape along with the Arkwright spinning machinery. Slater used iron sparingly, as in Strutt's factory, for the shafts of the spindles and for the rollers. No milling machine existing in America, the lower of each pair of rollers had to be milled (grooved) by hand to grip the yarn firmly against the leather surface of the upper.

Slater's version of the Arkwright machinery was set up in Ezekiel Carpenter's fulling mill. With everything nearly ready, a maddening problem developed. One of the two carding machines began rolling up fibers into a massive tangle instead of delivering them in a roll for the drawing and roving machines. The Wilkinson family heard their boarder, sitting by the fireplace, "utter deep sighs, and frequently saw the tears roll from his eyes." Mrs. Wilkinson asked, "Art thou sick, Samuel?"

He explained his problem, adding, "If I am frustrated in my carding machine, they will think me an imposter." The trouble was that Pliny Earle's experience was with hand cards, and he did not fully realize that a different technique was necessary for machines. The available leather would not hold the wire bristles firmly, and the teeth slipped out of position. In the end Earle had to build a special machine to set the teeth.

Once the carding machine was completed, in December 1790, the mill began operation. It was a modest enterprise in comparison with Josiah Strutt's mills, and the first two years were lost in learning and testing. Besides his mechanical difficulties, Slater found that he had to educate his partners in the philosophy of mass production. In eighteenth-century America, cloth was made strictly for custom. A cloth merchant received an order, put his hand spinners and weavers to work, and delivered it. Such a system—really pre-medieval—was unthinkably wasteful in a mechanized mill, whose efficiency depended on continuous operation. Slater conceived his own role as that of supervising manufacture of as much cotton yarn as he could turn out with his machinery, while his partners busied themselves with developing the markets.

The day the mill opened, December 20, 1790, Slater hired four boys, and a few days later three more boys and two girls. Ranging in age from seven to twelve

Replica of Slater's 1792 carding machine.
(Old Slater Mill Museum)

years, the nine children constituted the labor force of America's first successful factory. No one in the community questioned the employment of children (or even Slater's disciplinary techniques, which included occasional canings). Children always worked on the farm or in the home as soon as they were able, often at spinning. Having them work at machines under a factory roof was merely a novelty. The boys and girls toiled twelve hours a day, six days a week, victims not of capitalism, much less of technology, but like all the children of the age, of a low-energy, low-production economy, in short, of a lack of technology.

The child operatives were not drawn primarily from the lower classes; several of the original nine belonged to prominent Pawtucket families. Ten-year-old Smith Wilkinson was the youngest of the five sons of Oziel Wilkinson—Abraham, Isaac, David, Daniel, and Smith. Put to work tending Slater's carding machine, Smith rose to a management role, and eventually to owning his own mill.

The children's hours were long, but Slater's were longer. He arrived well before daybreak to spend two hours chopping the waterwheel free of ice. "The inhabitants of Pawtucket . . . saw Slater labouring day and night," wrote George S. White, "and sometimes beheld him loaded with a bale of cotton on his back."

When, on his first day in Pawtucket, Moses Brown had brought Slater to the Wilkinson house in Quaker Lane, the three Wilkinson daughters had shyly fled. But sixteen-year-old Hannah had lingered behind a door to peep at the stranger, and Samuel, catching a glimpse of her, fell in love. His few free hours he spent regaling her and her two sisters with stories of his childhood, his home, and his family. The Wilkinsons treated him like a son—up to a point. In a day when religion was taken seriously, the gap between ritual-free, democratic Quakerism and conservative, liturgical Church of England was formidable, and when he learned Slater's intentions, Hannah's father threatened to send her away to school. Ardent Samuel swore to "follow her to the ends of the earth," and the old Quaker relented.

They were married on October 2, 1791. In due course Hannah presented her husband with six boys, and between pregnancies produced an outstanding contribution of her own to the Industrial Revolution in the shape of cotton thread for sewing. Heretofore, sewing thread had been made of flax; one day when spinning some Sea Island cotton, Hannah noticed the evenness and attractiveness of the yarn and wondered if, doubled and twisted, it would make good sewing thread. She experimented and discovered that the resulting thread was actually stronger than linen. Cotton sewing thread became an important new product not only in America but in England, where during Napoleon's blockade it replaced silk for the heddle strings of looms, and where it was manufactured by the Strutt and Arkwright mills—a very fair repayment for the machinery Slater had plagiarized.

By the end of 1792 the Almy, Brown, and Slater enterprise was prospering to a point that dictated plant expansion. Abandoning Ezekiel Carpenter's little ex-fulling mill, the partners picked a site just upstream to erect a traditional box-shaped, two-and-a-half-story building of plastered and whitewashed plank walls on a frame of oak posts and beams that became the first successful cotton mill on American soil. Despite the high fire hazard of candles, oil drippings, and masses of cotton fiber, the new structure survived to become known as "The Old Slater Mill" and to be permanently preserved, in the form of a museum, as a New England landmark.

To power the new waterwheel, which Slater took care to enclose in a shed to protect it from ice, Oziel Wilkinson was set to work building a dam and flume. The new dam short-circuited the old one, provoking protests and then lawsuits,

Textile machinery in the Slater mill, from George White, *Memoir of Samuel Slater*. Carding machines (left) equipped with revolving cylinders covered with steel wire bristles comb the cotton into parallel fibers, ejecting it in a ropelike "sliver"; drawing machines (right) attentuate the sliver. (Library of Congress)

but the partners paid no attention to either and got away with their effrontery. Machinery brought from Carpenter's mill was supplemented by new, and in July 1793 the bell in the cupola clanged reveille for the mill children at the new site. Women were also employed, especially to help with the bleaching, which was accomplished by spreading the new yarn out in the meadow north of the mill and moistening it with watering cans for four weeks while the sun did the bleaching.

As the new mill multiplied yarn production, a sudden demand for hand weavers was created that could only be filled from abroad, mainly from England. Thus Samuel Slater became the Moses of an army of immigrants from his native land. The English weavers' drinking habits proved out of keeping with the austere customs of New England, but despite friction, the newcomers played a vital role in the growth of the infant American industry.

Slater compensated for his countrymen's dissoluteness by introducing Pawtucket's, and probably Rhode Island's (and possibly America's) first Sunday school, copied after those of Strutt and Arkwright in England, with the doubly commendable aim of teaching the Scriptures and supplying the children with the three R's that their work week denied them. The school was equipped with three New Testaments and five Noah Webster spelling books. At first Slater taught the children himself, but soon hired a theology student from Rhode Island College (later Brown University) after overcoming the young man's scruples against profaning the Sabbath.

Moses Brown had intended to produce a variety of finished cloths rivaling those imported from England. Under Slater's astute guidance, the firm pursued a nar-

Slater spinning frame. (Smithsonian Photograph No. 41,151)

rower, more farsighted vision: wholesale production of a small range of basic cotton yarns in large quantity for a wide market, with factory production concentrating on warp yarns for weaving and stocking yarns for knitting.

Slater had established the basics of the new British factory system in New England: control of machines and production, management of supplies, division of labor. But the conservatism of his partners continued to frustrate him. Even though they accepted his broad dictates, they were timid about mass production, and Slater chafed under too slow or too small deliveries of raw material and equipment. His letters to his partners were filled with complaints: "A number of the frames are stopped for want of rollers," he wrote in one letter, and in another, "I shall have to leave off work every night [for want of candles]." In 1797 he decided to open his own mill, taking his father-in-law and the husbands of Hannah's sisters as partners. The "New Mill," also known as the "White Mill," built on the eastern bank of the river, directly across from the Old Slater Mill, was much larger and gave Slater scope to follow his bold policy of maximized production promoted by widespread advertising.

Following the opening of the White Mill, cotton mills suddenly began to spring up all over. Some of Slater's hands left for Cumberland, a few miles north, to start their own mill; later these same men and their associates started mills in other areas. Smith Wilkinson wrote, "I believe nearly all the cotton factories in this country, from 1791 to 1805, were built under the direction of men who had learned the art or skill of building in Mr. Slater's employ."

Not only cotton manufacturing but American manufacturing in general was profiting from Slater's example. In 1791 Alexander Hamilton's historic *Report on Manufactures* had alluded to the scarcity of skilled mechanics and the shortage of capital in the form of machinery as the great handicaps faced by American industry in achieving large-scale production. As an example of what could be accomplished when these handicaps were overcome, Hamilton pointed to the "Manufactory at Providence" (he meant Pawtucket) of Samuel Slater. By the mid-'90s, in addition to the new cotton mills, large glass factories had been built in Boston and in Frederick, Maryland; a hat factory in Danbury, Connecticut, engaged in the export trade; and a sailcloth factory in Boston employed three hundred persons.

The factory system spread from cotton to wool. The process of finishing wool cloth was mechanized first—cleaning, shrinking, shearing, and dyeing—in fulling mills (like Ezekiel Carpenter's) in the 1790s. In 1793, three years after Samuel Slater built his cotton carding machines for the Pawtucket mill, John and Arthur Scholfield emigrated from England to build wool-carding machines in a barn in Newburyport, Massachusetts. From the fulling and carding mills, complete factories that spun wool yarn and wove wool cloth (still on hand looms) developed gradually in the early 1800s.

As industry grew, British mechanics followed British weavers across the Atlantic, nearly always heading straight for Slater's mill. Slater not only steered them to employment, but often lent them money. One who arrived in 1803 took him by surprise—it was his younger brother, John, who was delivered to Pawtucket by a Providence acquaintance with the words, "I have brought one of your country-

Mule spinning, from George White, *Memoir of Samuel Slater*. A combination of jenny and water spinning machine, the mule operated by moving the carriage, mounted on wheels, outward from the spools that held the rovings, stretching and twisting the fibers. Shortly before the carriage reached its outer limit, the rollers through which the rovings passed stopped turning, giving the yarn an extra stretch, which made it possible to produce fine yarns. (Library of Congress)

men to see you, and can you find anything for him to do?" Failing to recognize his grown-up brother, Slater interrogated him like any newcomer: Where did he come from? Derbyshire. What part? Belper. His name? John Slater. The Providence acquaintance likened the ensuing scene to "Joseph's seeing his brother Benjamin."

John Slater brought news of an important development in English spinning: the Crompton mule, a combination of jenny and water frame, which could spin fine yarn for muslins. Samuel was planning another new mill, and John was dispatched by pack-horse trails along the Blackstone River to search out a site. He chose a spot in the wilderness twelve miles from Pawtucket, where the Monhegan (now Branch) River fell forty feet, and ponds upstream provided reservoirs. By the spring of 1807 the new mill was in operation, with John as superintendent, and a village sprang up that was christened Slatersville.

In the succeeding decade, scores of other mill villages dotted the wilderness streams of southern New England. Built from scratch wherever a rapid fall of water was available, often remote from a labor force, the mill towns included amenities designed to attract workers. Cottages lined grid-pattern streets hemming in the mill, fronting on river and millpond. The owners sought to hire whole families, but also provided boarding houses for single workers, and usually a church, a school, a company store, sometimes a library. Shade trees were planted along the streets and in the mill yards. Waterpower kept the mills and villages small, and the air unpolluted. A mill owner wrote, in 1836, "We can have no Manchesters on this side the Atlantic, while our thousand rivers and streams afford an inexhaustible supply of unimproved power."

In 1812 Hannah Slater died, at the age of thirty-seven, following the birth of her sixth child. Five years later Samuel married Esther Parkinson, a widow who had been Hannah's close friend. His proposal by mail has survived:

> North Providence, R.I., Sept. 23, 1817
>
> Dear madam,—As the wise disposer of all events has seen fit in his wisdom to place you and me in a single state—notwithstanding, I presume none of his decrees have gone forth which compels either of us to remain in a state of widowhood. Therefore, under these and other circumstances, I now take the liberty to address you on a momentous subject. I have been inclined for some time past to change my situation in life. . . . Now if you are under no obligation to anyone, and on weighing the subject fully, you should think that you can spend the remainder of your days with me, I hope you will not feel reluctant, in writing me soon to that effect. . . . I have six sons to comfort you with, the oldest is about fifteen years . . . the youngest is in his sixth year, I believe they are all compos mentis, and they are as active as any six boys, although they are mine. . . . Probably you consider me rather blunt in this business, hope you will attribute that to the country

Workers' cottages in Harrisville, New Hampshire, a surviving mid–nineteenth century mill village. (Authors' photo)

that gave me birth. I consider myself a plain candid Englishman, and hope and trust, you will be candid enough to write me a short answer. . . . I am, dear madam, your well wisher,

Samuel Slater.

Characteristic discretion made him add: "N.B.—Hope you are a freemason as respects keeping secrets."

Always careful with his money—his favorite proverb was, "Do not keep more cats than catch mice"—Slater was now a wealthy man. He inventoried his estate in 1817:

> I own the house, &c., in which I live in Pawtucket, one other house, and six house lots, one house and land in Seekonk, and third part of the old factory, so called, counting fifteen hundred spindles, water privilege, stores, and five dwelling houses; and one third part of three farms in Attleborough and Saybrook. One house and lots near Hartford, also one quarter part of several buildings and lots in Providence. One quarter of a brick house in Boston, one quarter of the estate in Smithfield [Slatersville], containing two cotton factories, with between five and six thousand spindles, together with three water privileges, about thirty-five good houses, and twelve hundred acres of land. My estate in Oxford, Mass., consisting of one cotton factory of two thousand spindles, one woollen establishment, grist and saw mill, sixteen dwelling houses, and seven hundred acres of land. Also one handsome farm in Pelham, and a right in six mortgaged estates, to the amount of ten thousand dollars. . . .

Slater's business went on growing until the panic of 1829, and included a mill in Amoskeag, New Hampshire, acquired by foreclosure in 1825, that became famous as having more spindles than any mill in the world; the Jewett City Cotton Manufacturing Company, near the Rhode Island border in Connecticut; an iron foundry in Providence. In 1827 he helped build in Providence one of the first cotton mills in America to use steam power. But in 1829 responsibility for the debts of his brothers-in-law and others, amounting to $300,000, forced him to sell William Almy his third share of the "Old Mill" in Pawtucket and his fourth of the Slatersville property. Slater weathered the depression, and by 1831 had an additional seven mills in Webster, Massachusetts, though he was increasingly tormented by rheumatism. "I am now rather creeping up hill, and make out with the assistance of my crutches to hobble about my room two or three times a day," he wrote a business associate.

He was confined to his Pawtucket house when President Andrew Jackson visited him in 1833 to address him as "the Father of American manufacturing." "I understand you taught us how to spin, so as to rival Great Britain in her manufactures," the president remarked. Slater replied, "Yes, sir, I suppose that I gave out the psalm, and they have been singing to the tune ever since." As he prepared to leave, Jackson observed that Slater must be happy to see prosperity and progress around him; "I am told cotton cloth is lower than was ever known before." Slater replied that cotton cloth was rather too low for profit. "But I suppose it is as good as raising corn for fifty cents per bushel, so that we must not complain."

On his deathbed in Webster, Massachusetts, in 1835, Slater's last word to his wife was a characteristically terse, "Farewell." America's first industrial capitalist was gone, but not before founding, on a secure technological and marketing base, America's first manufacturing industry.

5

Eli Whitney: the Cotton Gin and Interchangeable Parts

AT THE MOMENT when Samuel Slater's mill machinery was suddenly enlarging the demand for raw cotton, the tobacco, rice, and indigo planters of the South were encountering marketing difficulties that made them eager to turn to cotton as a staple. Unfortunately, there was a problem. Of the two great cotton-plant varieties, long-staple and short-staple, the first resisted cultivation and the second resisted cleaning. Only at Sea Island, Georgia (which gave its name to the variety in the United States), and along the Georgia-Carolina coast as far as Charleston did the long-staple plant flourish. The short-staple grew in more or less any warm, moist climate, but its seeds stuck like glue to the lint, from which they had to be torn or cut by hand. It took one person a day to clean a pound of the stuff.

The smooth seeds of Sea Island cotton were removed mechanically. The lint was run through a pair of wooden rollers, grooved lengthwise, and turned by a hand crank in opposite directions, like a clothes wringer. The cleaning device was neither an American nor a European invention, but a product of India, where for hundreds of years it had been known as a churka. In 1790 Dr. Joseph Eve of the Bahamas and Augusta, Georgia, fitted up the churka with accessories that permitted it to be powered by a horse or waterwheel, but though Dr. Eve and others who tinkered with it claimed that their improvements made it effective with short-staple cotton, they vastly exaggerated. The obstinate short-staple seeds either passed through or clung and broke between the cylinders, scattering fragments throughout the cotton.

Portrait of Eli Whitney, by Samuel F. B. Morse; painted c. 1822. (Yale University Art Gallery)

Yet the churka supplied a basic starting point, and Carolina planters felt with a sort of gambler's prescience that an improvement was due any moment. In 1793 many actually raised short-staple cotton in the hope that someone would invent an effective gin ("gin" in the sense of trap) in time for the crop.

Throughout the planting country, people were talking about such a machine. Consequently, it was not surprising that three planters gathered at Mulberry Grove, Georgia, in the winter of 1792–93 fell to discussing it. Retired army officers, Majors Bremen, Forsyth, and Pendleton, they were paying a call on Catherine Greene, widow of their old commanding officer, General Nathanael Greene. Nathanael and Catherine were originally Rhode Islanders, and had settled in the South as a direct result of Greene's famous Southern campaign against Cornwallis in 1780–81 that had led to Yorktown. Mulberry Grove, the property of a Tory lieutenant governor, was a gift of the state of Georgia to the general for his services.

Captivating Catherine Greene was one of the most prominent and popular ladies in the South, famed for her charm as a hostess and remembered for her courageous spirit at Valley Forge. Listening to her guests, she had a sudden inspiration. "Gentlemen," she said, "apply to my young friend Mr. Whitney—he can make anything." She displayed an embroidery frame that the mysterious Mr. Whitney had made for her needlework, and several toys he had made or repaired. The gentlemen expressed a desire to meet the young mechanic, and Whitney himself was produced. He proved to be a handsome young fellow with a Yankee beak, luminous dark eyes, a firm chin, and a well-proportioned figure.

Although fresh out of Yale College, Eli Whitney was twenty-seven years old.

Like Samuel Slater and Oliver Evans, he was the son of a prosperous farmer. On his farm in Westborough, Massachusetts, the elder Whitney had a workshop equipped with a lathe and other tools to make and repair household furnishings and farm implements. As a boy, Eli showed the mechanical curiosity and aptitude of Slater, Evans, and John Fitch, once feigning illness and staying home from church to take apart and reassemble his father's watch. At twelve he fashioned a violin that made, he recalled, "tolerable good musick." The oldest of four children, he was a reliable performer of chores, watering sixty head of cattle every morning. According to his sister, he was "remarkable for thinking and acting for himself." At fourteen he installed a forge in his father's workshop to make nails, in demand because the war had shut off the British supply, while the American industry had been handicapped by the old Parliamentary restraints. So successful was his nailmaking that he hired an assistant, and when the war's end brought a flood of British nails on the market, he switched his production to hatpins and walking sticks.

In 1783, at the age of seventeen, when an American boy's schooling was normally over, he suddenly decided he wanted some higher education. Answering an advertisement for a schoolmaster in nearby Grafton, he got the appointment and, by studying nights to stay ahead of his pupils, earned enough salary—$7 a month, poor pay even for 1783—to finance a summer term at Leicester Academy. For three years he taught winters and learned summers, until he had enough arithmetic, Latin, and Greek to qualify "to keep a Grammar School." It was also enough to win admittance to college, and Whitney had decided he wanted to go to Yale. Harvard was nearer, but the head of Leicester Academy was a Yale graduate, and may have told him about the scientific apparatus recently acquired by Yale's progressive president, Ezra Stiles, who read the French *Encyclopédie* volume by volume as it came out and corresponded with Franklin. At any rate Whitney bade farewell to his little red schoolhouse where he had been a popular master; closing-day ceremony was well attended by parents as well as pupils, and "not an Eye in the house but was moistened."

His academy pay hardly sufficed to finance Yale, but his father, impressed by his scholarship and determination, advanced him money, not without risk and sacrifice. Whitney, Sr., a large corpulent man who often held town office and served as justice of the peace, drove his son to Brookfield, whence he could get the stage to New Haven. He "payd all expense—left me the Dollars and bid me goodby," recorded Eli.

Yale consisted of a dormitory (Connecticut Hall), houses for President Stiles and the one other professor, a refectory, and the chapel, which doubled as repository for the library and the "philosophical apparatus," i.e., scientific equipment. To the college collection, consisting of a set of the basic machine components (lever, wheel and axle, cord and pulley, toothed gear wheels, plane, wedge, screw), a quadrant, a theodolite, an air pump, and a variety of natural curiosities such as mammoth tusks and snakeskins, Dr. Stiles had personally added a three-foot telescope, a micrometer, and an orrery—a model for demonstrating the motions of the planets. Stiles and Professor Josiah Meigs conducted all lectures, while three tutors drilled students in grammar and composition, history and geography, disputation and theology. Because the jail was next door in crowded College Square, recitations and prayers were often accompanied by the audible groans, curses, and screams of the jail's mixed population of debtors, felons, and lunatics.

The library boasted 3,000 books, most of them comprising a gift dating from 1733, but including a copy of Newton's *Principia* donated by Newton himself, a volume that may have enlightened Whitney about the failure of a perpetual-motion machine he had once invented. Despite the cost of college—nearly $400 a year including bed and bedding, board, candles, fuel, laundry, and books, of which his father apparently paid half or more—Yale was not only a great experience but promised to provide him with a substantial reward in the shape of a legal career. At the graduation exercises in September 1792, marked by a fireworks display to celebrate the state's forgiveness of the college's back taxes ($40,000), Eli appeared in new store-bought clothes—pants, coat, waistcoat, cotton shirt, slippers, and silk hose. Following commencement, he received a disappointment that proved one of destiny's silver-lined clouds—a teaching post Dr. Stiles had lined up for him in New York to provide for him while he studied law had evaporated. Something vaguer and much farther off, a tutoring job in South Carolina, had turned up to replace it. The intermediary for the tutoring job was a recent Yale alumnus named Phineas Miller, who though only a year older than Whitney was manager of the estate of the late General Nathanael Greene. At the moment Miller was in New Haven, and suggested that Whitney accompany him, Mrs. Greene, and the children, who were summering at Newport, back to Mulberry Grove, across the Savannah River from the household that was seeking the tutor.

The trip South started off with multiple disasters. En route to New York, Whitney was seasick and the party shipwrecked on the rocks below Hell Gate. Everyone clambered ashore safely on upper Manhattan and hired wagons to get down to New York. Hardly arrived, Whitney ran into an acquaintance on the street, shook hands, and discovered that the acquaintance "was broke out full with the small-Pox." At the recommendation of Miller and Mrs. Greene he took advantage of an ancient Asian invention, recently accepted by the American medical establishment, and still called "variolation," by which a doctor punctured his skin with a needle to give him a mild case—"with only a dozen pock."

The week-long voyage to Savannah left him not fully recovered, and Whitney accepted Mrs. Greene's invitation to convalesce another week at Mulberry Grove before going on to his tutoring post. The plantation, whose once famous trees no longer supported silkworm culture, and which produced corn, rice, and potatoes only with immense labor, was sunk in debt, but the Greene household lived a life of leisure and even luxury, with plenty of food, domestic slaves, a spacious house, and gardens. By this time Whitney had become aware that Phineas Miller was something more than an estate manager to thirty-nine-year-old Catherine Greene— "I find myself in a new natural world," he wrote home, "and as for the moral world I believe it does not exist so far South." Because of his inoculation, Mrs. Greene had white flags hoisted at the river landing and along the avenue leading to the plantation house, and Whitney thought of a way to justify prolonging his stay—he procured the smallpox virus and vaccinated, or variolated, all fifty of the plantation's slaves.

Exactly when General Greene's ex-officers introduced Whitney to the cotton-seed problem is not clear from his account, written almost a year later, except that it was shortly after his arrival at Mulberry Grove in November 1792. His response was a modest disclaimer to the effect that he had never seen either cotton or cottonseed in his life. But he promised to study the problem, and soon after went to Savannah, brought back a parcel of cotton, and talked the problem over with Phineas Miller, who strongly urged him to try. His tutorial post had meantime disappointed him by promising only fifty guineas instead of the hundred he had anticipated. He soon "struck out a plan of a machine," and communicated it to Miller, who enthusiastically offered funds and a room in the basement for a workshop. "In about ten days I made a little model, for which I was offered, if I would give up all right and title to it, a Hundred Guineas. . . ." Putting Miller off, he returned to work, surrounded by the inquisitive Greene children, and produced a full-scale machine that one man could operate to clean "ten times as much cotton as he can in any other way before known and also clean it much better than in the usual mode. This machine may be turned by water or with a horse . . . and one man and a horse will do more than fifty men with the old machines."

Essentially Whitney approached the problem of separating seeds from cotton from the reverse side, designing a machine that pulled the cotton from the seeds rather than the seeds from the cotton. The principal element in his gin was a horizontal cylinder set in a frame and (like the churka) turned by a crank, armed with iron spikes or teeth that matched the slots in an iron guard on the face of the lint box, positioned directly in front of the cylinder. The spikes speared the cotton and yanked it through the slots with such force that the lint was torn from the seeds, leaving the seeds in the box. No plate iron was available, so he made his teeth from a coil of iron wire that "one of the Miss Greenes had bought . . . to make a bird cage."

The full-size machine (its cylinder was 26 inches long and 6 inches in diameter) gave scope for a full-size trial, and a problem immediately developed. The fibers caught by the teeth rolled up around the cylinder, clogging it and preventing it from turning. A popular story, origins unknown but not confirmed by Whitney, had it that Catherine Greene suggested the solution by picking up a stiff-bristled hearth brush and asking him why he did not try that. What Whitney actually did was to add a small supplementary cylinder, set with bristles, attaching it to the crankshaft by means of a belt that caused it to turn in the opposite direction to the main cylinder. It worked—the bristles pulled the lint free of the teeth.

Catherine Greene invited the neighbors in to admire the new invention. Their exclamations began to make clear the dimensions of its value and even the dangers. Though they urged Whitney to take advantage of the new United States patent law, their excitement was a warning of potential piracy. Shortly after, on May 27, 1793, Whitney and Phineas Miller signed an agreement to share profits on the cotton gin while Miller continued to pay for the work of development. Whitney then sailed for the North.

Their idea was to establish a factory in New Haven to manufacture cotton gins. The first gins would be set up in Mulberry Grove to gin the district's 1794 cotton crop, whose planting Miller would stimulate by appropriate advertising. After

Patent model of Whitney's cotton gin.
(Smithsonian Photograph No. 73–11289)

that, they would gradually extend their operation into the Carolinas. It seemed a reasonable plan, but they entirely underestimated the demand for the gin.

Landing in New York, Whitney proceeded first to Philadelphia by stage, filing a patent application with Secretary of State Jefferson. En route to New Haven he stopped off in New York to witness an examination of cotton ginned by his machine at Mulberry Grove; the cotton was declared of good quality and sold at auction at "the highest price." At New Haven he set to work with energy and ingenuity, building a wire-drawing block, a lathe, and special turning tools. After waiting vainly for the yellow fever epidemic that had driven the government from Philadelphia to subside, he sent his full patent description to Jefferson on October 15 (1793). The application was destroyed by the Patent Office fire of 1836, but a "True Copy" Whitney made a few months later survives to provide evidence of what the final version of the original cotton gin was like:

"The cotton is put into the Hopper, carried thro' the Breastwork, brushed off from the teeth by the Clearer and flies off from the Clearer with the assistance of the air, by its own centrifugal force. The machine is turned by water, horses, or in any other way as is most convenient.

"There are several modes of making the various parts of this machine, which together with their particular shape and formation, are pointed out and explained in a description with Drawings." Jefferson assured Whitney of his patent as soon as he sent in a model, and expressed great interest in the invention.

At New Haven that winter Whitney had to battle serious difficulties. Determined to make his new gins as large as possible, he repeatedly cracked the wooden cylinders with the hundreds of iron wire teeth driven into them. To solve the problem, he built another machine, one for cutting wire teeth uniformly. By February of 1794 he had completed six large gins to take to Georgia and a miniature for the Patent Office. On March 14 Edmund Randolph, the new Secretary of State, granted the patent.

Two weeks earlier Miller published his announcement in the Georgia *Gazette,* stating that he would gin any amount of green-seed cotton on the basis of one pound of cleaned cotton for every five pounds delivered. Since it normally took three pounds of raw cotton to produce one pound of clean, Miller proposed to keep two-thirds of a pound for each five pounds cleaned, or two-fifths of the cleaned cotton. Such payment in kind was the time-honored arrangement for millers, fullers, sawyers, and other processers. Miller's proposition may have been a little too greedy, but the terms were not really the problem. Planters did bring their cotton, in large quantities. Whitney crated his disassembled gins in New Haven, two gins to three large boxes, and Miller set them up in pairs, each pair turnable by a horse or waterwheel. Miller was successfully expanding the business in Georgia and had established one operation in South Carolina when in the spring of 1795 a fire destroyed Whitney's New Haven shop, with tools, materials, and twenty unfinished gins. At the same time Miller, trying for a quick fortune in another direction, lost heavily in the Yazoo land speculation that exploded in a scandal over bribes to the Georgia legislature. Catherine Greene came to his rescue by putting her resources, consisting of several plantations, at Miller's disposal, an arrangement formalized by their marriage in 1796.

Fire and scandal were remediable disasters. A worse catastrophe building for the firm of Whitney, Miller, and Greene was not. Using Miller's high charges as an excuse, and the mechanical simplicity of the gin as a means, the planters of Georgia and Carolina industriously set to work copying it. One pirate, Edward Lyon, not only stole the design through espionage but fabricated and sold gins that he brazenly declared to be "improved models." Another, Hodgen Holmes, actually did improve the gin by using teeth cut from sheet iron, Whitney's original preference, and won a patent from the federal government, even though he had actually copied Whitney's device from drawings. Dr. Eve and others who had made the earlier churka-type gins "improved" their models by adding all Whitney's features. Injury was compounded by insult as the swarm of imitators launched an incredibly malicious propaganda campaign in England to persuade British manufacturers that Whitney's original gin damaged cotton fibers, and for a time Whitney and Miller were unable to sell cotton in England. Miller sued Georgia trespassers only to have the local jury impertinently sustain the planters, using a loophole provided by faulty wording of the Patent Act, which read, "If any person shall make, devise, *and* use . . ." where it should have read *"or* use." Even the South's slave code helped protect pirates. Slaves, barred from testifying in court, could operate a cotton gin in a loft, where no white witness ever saw it. Whitney later wrote Robert Fulton about an occasion on which the rattle of three nearby pirate gins could be heard on the steps of the Georgia courthouse in which Whitney was vainly trying to prove that the machine had been used in Georgia. By 1800 Whitney succeeded in getting the Patent Law reworded, and eventually Miller and Whitney won substantial awards from the legislatures of South and North Carolina. A licensing arrangement, suggested by a Yale classmate of Miller's, also brought in revenues. By that time Miller and Catherine Greene had had to sell Mulberry Grove, and Miller died shortly after, a victim of fever. The awards and licensing fees mostly disappeared in litigation costs, and Whitney bitterly concluded that "An invention can be so valuable as to be worthless to the inventor." As he described the situation to Fulton, "The use of this Machine being immensely profitable to almost every individual in the Country all were interested in trespassing & each justified & kept the other in countenance."

Whitney of course was right, but what he could scarcely be expected to see was the degree of justice on the planters' side. An invention that the whole community badly needed had to be made available to it, if possible on terms favorable to the inventor, otherwise on terms unfavorable to him. Watt's steam engine was pirated; Samuel Slater and others plagiarized Arkwright's textile machinery; Oliver Evans's automatic flour mill was freely copied; and many other nineteenth-century inventors suffered similarly. The fatal characteristic of Eli Whitney's cotton gin was that it was so wonderfully simple. Given a good look at it, or a good drawing, any carpenter or smith could make one, in any size, to suit the pirate's needs and purse.

If Whitney got little profit, he at least got much honor. Yale awarded him a Master of Arts degree in 1795, when the gin's national importance was already apparent. Ultimately the economic benefit conferred on the South, and on the United States, was beyond anyone's most optimistic calculation. The 2 to 3 million pounds of green-seed cotton that a few upland planters in South Carolina and Georgia had grown hopefully in 1793 spread by 1820 to a cotton belt far expanded west and north that produced 80 million pounds, nearly a third of an immensely increased world supply. By this time a large part of the crop was going to the factories lining the New England river valleys, where copies of Samuel Slater's machinery, driven by the splashing waterwheels and tended by ex-farm women and children, were turning out cotton thread. That same year the Missouri Compromise signaled one of the major effects of the gin—the formal, fatal division of the United States over slavery, a result produced, strangely enough, by the economic partnership created between North and South by Samuel Slater and Eli Whitney.

The legal war over the cotton gin was not only costly but exasperating and frustrating. Shortly before Miller's death, Whitney wrote his partner:

> The extreme embarrassments which have been for a long time accumulating upon me are now become so great that it will be impossible for me to struggle against them many days longer. . . . I have labored hard against the strong current of Disappointment which has been threatening to carry us down the Cataract of distruction—but I have labored with a shattered oar and struggled in vain unless some speedy relief is obtained. . . . I am now quite far enough advanced to think seriously of settling in life. I have ever looked forward with pleasure to a connection with an amiable & virtuous companion of the other sex. . . . I would not be understood that I have, or have ever had any *particular* person in view—pointed attachment of this kind I have studiously avoided, because I have never been in circumstances that would allow me to enter into such a connection. . . . Life is too short at best and six or seven years out of the midst of it is to him who makes it, an immense sacrafice. My most unremitted attention has been directed to our business. I have sacraficed to it other objects from which, before this time, I certainly might have realized 20, or 30, Thousand Dollars.

Miller himself was married and a man of property, "and, tho' you are under some temporary embarrassments, you are enjoying life;" in contrast, "Toil, anxiety and Disappointment have broken me down. My situation makes me perfectly miserable. . . . I had rather be out of Debt and out of business without a shilling than be in a situation half so much embarrassing as my present one."

Chance had led Whitney to his first invention; need drove him to his second, of an entirely different order, but of a significance fully comparable to that of the cotton gin. The John Adams administration's quarrel with revolutionary France in 1798 disclosed the national weakness in arms manufacture. The new Springfield (Massachusetts) Armory had turned out scarcely a thousand muskets in three years, and the newer Harper's Ferry (Virginia) none at all in two. The government turned frantically to private gunsmiths, appropriating the huge sum of $800,000. But the few skilled gunsmiths in the country, fabricating weapons one at a time, lock, stock, and barrel, would take years to equip an army.

In a letter to Oliver Wolcott, Secretary of the Treasury, written May 1, 1798, Whitney put forward a remarkable proposal: "I am persuaded that Machinery moved by water adapted to this business would greatly diminish the labor and facilitate the manufacture of this article—machines for forging, rolling, floating, boreing, grinding, polishing, etc. may all be made of use to advantage.

"Cartridge or Cartouch Boxes is an article which I can manufacture. I have a machine for boreing wood of my Invention which is admirably adapted to this purpose. The making of swords, hangers, Pistols etc. I could perform."

Whitney proposed to make 10,000 "stand of arms"—musket, bayonet, ramrod, wiper, and screw-driver, the complete arms needed to equip a soldier—for $134,000, or $13.40 apiece, not a particularly low price since in 1795 the government had imported muskets for $9 apiece. But with the French Revolutionary War peaking in intensity, imports could no longer be had, and Congress jumped at Whitney's offer. A contract was signed in Philadelphia after just three weeks' negotiations, including correspondence with Whitney's lawyer in New Haven. The government would supply a model, the French Charleville 1763, of Saratoga-Yorktown fame, and would furnish black walnut gunstocks at 25 cents apiece. Four thousand muskets with bayonets and ramrods were to be delivered by September 30, 1799, the remaining 6,000 by the following September. A $5,000 advance permitted Whitney to pay off pressing debts.

Implicit in Whitney's proposal to use "Machines for forging, rolling" and other operations was the momentous idea of interchangeable parts. With his water-powered machines—which remained to be created—Whitney meant to manufacture rapidly large numbers of each part of a musket, then assemble the muskets. For Whitney, the beauty of the plan lay less in the speed with which powered machinery could turn out the parts than in the elimination of scarce, expensive skilled labor.

As in the case of John Fitch and Oliver Evans, Whitney had European forerunners of whom he apparently knew nothing. As early as the 1720s, Christopher Polhem, a Swedish scientist and engineer, built a mechanized factory that employed the principle of interchangeable parts to produce clocks, padlocks, knives, forks, scissors, files, and nails. In 1722 a French gunsmith, name unknown, undertook to apply interchangeability to musket manufacture; the idea was taken up again by Honoré Blanc, superintendent of the Royal Manufactory of Arms at St. Etienne, who established a special factory to produce musket locks in 1778. In 1785 Blanc demonstrated his method to Thomas Jefferson, then American ambassador to France, who wrote, "I put several [musket locks] together myself,

Eli Whitney Gun Factory at Mill River, New Haven, painted by William Giles Munson. (From the Mabel Brady Garvan Collection, Yale University Art Gallery)

taking pieces at hazard, as they came to hand, and they fitted in the most perfect manner. . . . He effects [interchangeability] by tools of his own contrivance, which at the same time abridge the work, so that he thinks he shall be able to furnish the musket two livres cheaper than the common price." Jefferson vainly "attempted to remove this Artist to the United States."

Jefferson's acquaintance with Blanc's work was of benefit to Eli Whitney when unforeseen difficulties plagued his enterprise. He had trouble acquiring a good mill site, and when he found one, at Mill Rock, on Mill River near New Haven, early winter stopped construction, Philadelphia's yellow fever epidemic delayed delivery of his gunstocks, and Connecticut floods prevented his Canaan machine-part contractors from fulfilling their contract. Despite his $5,000 advance, he could not work out credit arrangements that would permit buying in quantity. Finally, he had problems with his labor, and had to ask for an extension of his own contract deadline. He wrote Oliver Wolcott on July 30, 1799, "I must . . . candidly acknowledge that much more time must necessarily be taken up in the first establishment of the business than I had at first any conception of . . . I must not only tell the workmen but must show them how every part is to be done."

Wolcott sent Captain Decius Wadsworth, the army's inspector of muskets, to Mill Rock to determine if Whitney's excuses were valid. Captain Wadsworth was a Yale classmate of Phineas Miller who knew Whitney's cotton gin well and brought a sympathetic understanding to Mill Rock. On his recommendation, Wolcott granted Whitney's request for a reprieve from the contract, writing sensibly, "I should consider a *real improvement* in machinery for manufacturing arms as a great acquisition to the United States." Wolcott enclosed a letter of credit on the Collector of the port of New Haven for $1,500 to ease Whitney's financial problems.

The first batch of muskets was not in fact delivered until September 1801, two years after the original contract date, and numbering only 500 instead of 4,000. Twenty-six other contractors had delivered only about a thousand muskets (so it was just as well that the French war threat had passed) but Whitney felt he should make an explanation in person, and as a result a memorable incident took place. Setting out for the new capital on the banks of the Potomac, where Jefferson had now assumed office as president, Whitney took along one complete musket and the parts for several locks. At either the White House, the War Department, or possibly at the incomplete Capitol building, he deposited the lock components on a large table, then choosing parts at random, assembled a lock. He invited the officials present (who included Jefferson and new Secretary of War Henry Dearborn) to do the same. They were all delighted with the result—the parts were so uniform that a musket lock could be assembled from any appropriate group.

The demonstration was decisive as far as the government was concerned, Whitney was given further extensions and more money, and Jefferson wrote James Monroe, the governor of Virginia:

"Mr. Whitney . . . has invented moulds and machines for making all the pieces of his locks so exactly equal, that take 100 locks to pieces and mingle their parts and the hundred locks may be put together as well by taking the first pieces which come to hand . . . Leblanc, in France, had invented a similar process in 1788 & had extended it to the barrel, mounting & stock. . . ."

The machinery by which Whitney achieved his delayed but impressive performance in production remains obscure because, perhaps out of exasperation with his cotton-gin experience, he took out no patents. All we know is a description written by ten-year-old nephew Philos Blake to Blake's sister: "There is a drilling machine and a bouring machine to bour berels [barrels] and a screw machine and too great large buildings, one nother shop to stocking guns in, a blacksmith shop and a trip hammer shop. . . ."

Whitney set down the theory of his machine organization in a letter to Wolcott:

"One of my primary objects is to form the tools so the tools themselves shall fashion the work and give to every part its just proportion—which when once accomplished will give expedition, uniformity and exactness to the whole. . . . In short, the tools which I contemplate are similar to an engraving on copper plate from which may be taken a great number of impressions exactly alike."

For all his enlightened enthusiasm, Jefferson did not really grasp the significance of interchangeable parts in manufacture. In his letter to Monroe, he laid stress on the value of interchangeability in musket repair—"out of ten locks, e.g. disabled for the want of different pieces, 9 good locks may be put together without employing a smith." That advantage seems modest. After a battle, the army left in possession of the field might perhaps do such repair work, but would be more likely to salvage whole muskets from the casualties. Whitney himself was inclined to stress the economy of dispensing with skilled labor, a point of great importance to any manufacturing operation and especially valuable in early America. Blanc in France actually grasped the advantages of interchangeability better than did Whitney. The true economic sense of mass production, the dramatic lowering of unit costs, was as yet difficult to perceive.

Even in his limited aim, Whitney gained only a qualified success. The handicraft technique survived and for a while was credited with better results in the sense of more reliable weapons. Wood and iron machines could not yet attain—or maintain—the precision necessary for a really satisfactory mass-production operation, and standard gauges did not yet exist. Whitney's impressive demonstration for Jefferson was probably partly rigged by a careful selection of parts. His normal procedure was apparently to do some hand-finishing on parts at the moment of assembly. Whether he ever achieved genuine interchangeability remains in doubt.

Yet Whitney had started something and he had started it in fertile soil. In France Honoré Blanc and his successors made many thousands of muskets by interchangeable-parts manufacture, but French industry, dedicated to old-fashioned handicraft production of fine goods, made no attempt to adapt the technique. In Britain a French émigré engineer, Marc Brunel, manufactured pulley blocks for the British navy by a well-thought-out system of interchangeable parts production in which he made use of the gifted British machine-tool expert, Henry Maudslay. But though the experiment was technically a brilliant success, the Brunel-Maudslay system was no more copied by British industry than was the Blanc system by French.

Only in America did the idea take hold. Whitney had an imitator almost at once (possibly even a coinventor) in Simeon North, a gunsmith of nearby Berlin, Connecticut, who made pistols under government contract. Of far more significance was the adoption of the technique by the New England clock industry, whose craftsmen had always followed the European tradition of hand-fabricating their wheels and gears with compasses, saws, and files. In 1806 Eli Terry of Plymouth, Connecticut, built a waterpowered factory, installed lathes and other machinery, and by 1807 was astounding his competitors by turning out 200 wooden-movement clocks a year, a figure that ultimately rose to thousands, with movements of brass as well as wood. Any debt owed by Terry to Whitney remains conjectural, despite an assertion by Terry's one-time partner and later rival Seth Thomas that the Plymouth factory's machinery "was hinted to him by Eli Whitney."

Whitney's system had an important implication for the development of another basic component of American industry: machine tools. To make machinery, metal-working machines were needed. Britain was at this moment in the midst of creating these basic tools, adapting some from the lathes, planes, bits, augers, awls, chisels, and gouges of woodworking, and inventing others. Henry Maudslay was the leader in the development. Maudslay has generally received credit for originating the important "slide-rest lathe," in which the cutting tool was carried on a sliding carriage, advanced by a long screw that ran parallel to the axis of the workpiece.

But Samuel Slater's young friend, brother-in-law, and mechanic, David Wilkinson, invented a lathe very similar to Maudslay's in 1796, at least a year earlier than Maudslay, and it was Wilkinson's lathe that diffused in America (and in many other places in the world). In 1786–87 Wilkinson's father had started making large iron drive screws for paper-manufacturing presses, sending young David to Hope Furnace, in Scituate, Massachusetts, to cast the screws in clay molds, David then finishing them by hand in Pawtucket. The Wilkinsons expanded to making drive screws for clothiers' presses and oil mills. "But they were imperfect," David wrote," and I told my father I wanted to make a machine to cut screws on centers [in other words, on a lathe], which would make them more perfect."

The project took several years and was interrupted by David's other activities— helping Samuel Slater, building lock machinery for the Middlesex Canal, even an early steamboat. In 1794 Oziel Wilkinson built a rolling and slitting mill in Pawtucket, and here David put into operation his new machine "on the principle of the gauge or sliding lathe now in every workshop almost throughout the world. . . . I cut screws of all dimensions by this machine, and did them perfectly."

Wilkinson was especially proud of the rocklike stability of his device. In 1797, he journeyed to Philadelphia to apply for a patent, returning home to find that the well-known ironmaster Jacob Perkins had come to see his machine, and had been so delighted with it that he had "laughed out, and remarked that he could do his engraving on cast steel for Bank Note plates with that machine,—that he could make a hair stroke with [it], for it would never tremble. . . ." Another visitor, a master machinist from England, had quite a different reaction: He "advised me as a friend to abandon my new machine, for said he, 'you can *ner* do it, for we have tried it out and out at *ome,* and given it up; and don't you think we should have been doing it at *ome* if it could have been done?' "

Wilkinson made patterns for his lathe and had it cast, "and it worked to a charm." He sold the patterns for ten dollars to Richard and William Anthony, sons of the Daniel Anthony for whom he had helped build a model of the Arkwright spinning frame in 1789—"And this is all I ever received for so valuable an invention." It was all he received up to the time of writing his memoir in 1846, but two years later, when he was almost seventy-eight years old, he was the recipient of a significant as well as gratifying award of $10,000 by resolution of Congress "for the benefits accruing to the public service [i.e., the arsenals] from the use of the principle of the gauge and sliding lathe of which he is the inventor."

As for Eli Whitney, through the early years of the new century his life continued to be full of hard work, anxiety, and frustration. He wrote a friend:

"You will find me a solitary Being, without a companion & almost without a friend . . . living on plain fare in a humble cottage. . . . If I had a house, a wife & a home—." He referred to himself as "Old Bachelor." The fact seems to be that he had fallen in love with the magnetic Catherine Greene, but never to have dared tell her so. Twice-widowed Catherine would have been receptive to an offer from Whitney. Her letters were transparent. "I wish to god my dear friend you were married," she wrote. ". . . I am prepared to love any woman who would make you happy." And again, "Never—Never shall I Cease Considering you My Son—and never never Cease lamenting that you were not born so," a gross exaggeration of their twelve-year age difference. And, "I wish also to whisper other secrets in your Ear—which I certainly should do if you were seting by me. . . . I comfort myself sometimes in looking at your picture and mentally conversing with it—and sometimes in the Lover stile give it a kiss." And, "You see how little I can do without you—and I can see how much I could do—if I had your advice and assistance for a month . . . Save my life in saving your own—for I find I can not comfortably be in this world if you are not of it." And, "Your picture ornaments my toilet table—It is every day looked at and some times kissed—that is to say when you are sick." But Whitney, diffident, obtuse, or distracted by a large government contract resulting from the outbreak of the War of 1812, let Catherine die in 1814 without ever seeing her again.

Two years later he married, at the age of fifty-two. His bride, Henrietta Edwards, whom he had known since she was a little girl, was twenty years younger, not renowned for her beauty, and on the verge of becoming a spinster. Yet they were evidently happy in their eight years of married life. Whitney's death in 1825 left three children (another had died), of whom Eli Whitney, Jr., grew up to take over his father's arms business.

Despite the cataclysmic effect of his cotton gin on the South, Whitney never took any interest in politics, and the word *slavery* is not even mentioned in his correspondence. The indifference was mutual. The gin-created cotton kingdom, driven to expand to escape exhausted soil, took slavery with it westward, and created fatal conflict with the wheat and corn farmers of the old Northwest over the trans-Mississippi territories. Press and pulpit of the whole country debated slavery and bandied secession, but the man whose invention had loosed the whirlwind was largely forgotten.

In 1832 a South Carolinian published an article about Whitney with the avowed aim of rescuing the South's benefactor from oblivion, but it was not till the end of the century that American schoolchildren learned that "Eli Whitney invented the cotton gin in 1793."

Even longer delayed was recognition of his role in the history of mass production, partly perhaps because of his casual failure to patent machinery, but mostly because the significance of mass production was so tardily appreciated.

PART II

PART II

6

America 1801

THE TWENTY-FIFTH ANNIVERSARY of the young Republic coincided with the opening year of the new century, and also, as Jefferson and his followers assumed office, with the renewal of democratic political revolution. Though the careers of Samuel Slater, Oliver Evans, and Eli Whitney reached well beyond 1801, most of their important innovations were at least conceived by 1801 (and unlucky John Fitch had died in 1798). The year 1801 may thus serve as a convenient point in the gathering technological revolution to stop and survey the country's changes.

Philadelphia and the other seaboard cities were filling in their waterfronts with new warehouses, adding new shops to their downtown streets (a few of which were paved), and laying out new street grids on their outskirts to accommodate clusters of houses for increasing numbers of craftsmen and laborers. The grid pattern for New York stirred environmental outcries against the violence threatened to Manhattan's natural contours of wooded hills and valleys, but the opposition was trampled and New York avenues decreed forever north-south and its streets east-west.

Stately new houses appeared in favored residential districts, and civic structures, some of impressive size, added a metropolitan touch to scruffy downtown streets, brightened by new theaters and concert halls. In 1801 portraitist Charles Willson Peale's museum, enlivening Philadelphia's Independence Hall with a miscellany of the owner's paintings, stuffed animals, and technological gadgetry, scored a scientific coup by exhibiting a mastodon skeleton discovered on a New York farm.

Boston's bridge over the Charles was pronounced by an English visitor to be "a most prodigious work for so infant a country . . . worthy of the Roman Empire."

That was ignorant exaggeration—a simple timber trestle, even one 1,800 feet long and costing £24,000, bore no engineering comparison with the mighty stone arch bridges of Rome (except that Boston's bridge had a draw span over the channel, a medieval European invention unknown to the Romans). New York was even planning a City Hall with a marble façade on the south side, though freestone on the north, implying no very daring optimism about future growth. A few wealthy New Yorkers built country houses as far out as the upper Bowery or beyond, such as the mansion shipping magnate Archibald Gracie built on the East River. The litter and pollution of Europe's larger cities was already a New York problem, though hardly comparable with the old, recurrent plagues of cholera and yellow fever. The poor quarters, where garbage was flung in the street for the goats and pigs, had vastly expanded since 1776 without changing their old customs, and the leather tanners congregated in Nassau and nearby streets were turning the Collect Pond, where John Fitch may possibly have demonstrated one of his steamboat models, into a giant cesspool. Water from the city's two principal sources, the fifty-year-old "tea-water pump" in Chatham Street and Aaron Burr's new Manhattan Company (ancestor of the Chase Manhattan Bank) was becoming suspect.

Problems of growth notwithstanding, America's infant cities were unmistakably prosperous in the first years of the new century. Their prosperity was matched, or exceeded, by the prosperity of the great sprawling countryside, spilling across the Allegheny Mountains in a hundred streams of ox-drawn Conestoga wagons. The

Broadway and City Hall, New York, 1819; watercolor by Baron Axel Klinckowstrom. (Museum of the City of New York)

The broad-wheeled, low-bellied Conestoga Wagon, hauled by four- or six-ox teams, carried settlers over the Alleghenies in the 1790s and 1800s. (Collections of Greenfield Village and the Henry Ford Museum, Dearborn, Michigan)

rising value of farm land brought a phenomenon unknown to the Old World. The first wave of agricultural frontiersmen, who cut, girdled, and burned away the wilderness, built cabins, put in a quick crop of corn, and sold their holdings at a profit to successors who set to work cutting, building, fencing, and stump-pulling to turn the place into a replica of the farms they had left behind in Vermont or New York. Within a few years the second-wave settler was likely to move on to escape the exhaustion of the soil, but he prospered while he stayed. Farm laborers commanded high wages—twenty-five to thirty cents a day. "It is peculiarly difficult for a man of property to hire a laborer," wrote an English Unitarian minister visiting Kentucky. "He must humor him a good deal and make him sit at the same table with him."

Wheat, corn, rye, and other Northern cereal crop acreages grew rapidly, though their progress was eclipsed by that of the South's new wonder crop, short-staple cotton, now invading the western Carolinas, western Georgia and even the Alabama-Tennessee wilderness. Farther west a French planter from the West Indies named Etienne de Bore proved that sugar cane could be grown profitably in the vicinity of New Orleans. That tropical port was also enriched by the flatboats and keelboats floating down the river loaded with grain, livestock, rice, indigo, tobacco, wood, potash, and pitch. In the opposite direction streams of skinny hogs and cattle were driven over the Appalachian trails to Lancaster, York, and other receiving centers where they were sold to Eastern farmers for fattening.

The abundance of the rural American table impressed foreign visitors. An Englishman who asked his landlady in western Pennsylvania for breakfast had to stop her in the act of wringing the necks of a pair of chickens. His protest that he only wanted a boiled egg, bread, and tea embarrassed the good woman: "Shall I fry some ham for you along with the eggs? . . . Well, will you take a little stewed pork?" In the end, she placed on the table "a profusion of ham, eggs, fritters, bread, butter and some excellent tea." He ate only bread, tea, and egg, and paid a quarter, which the landlady accepted with reluctance, since what he had eaten was, in her words, "hardly worth anything."

Retail goods were also plentiful in western Pennsylvania, though they had to be carried over the mountains. A traveler observed that the stock of a country store included "a needle and an anchor, a tin pot and a large copper boiler, a child's whistle and a pianoforte, a ring [sun] dial and a clock, a skein of thread and trimmings of lace, a check frock and a muslin gown, a frieze coat and a superfine cloth, a glass of whiskey and a barrel of brandy, a gill of vinegar and a hogs-head of Madeira wine." Country storekeepers still dealt mainly by barter with the farmers, who came in once a year to settle up.

But convincing as the picture of American success seemed, it was largely an artificial phenomenon. The great European war, or series of wars, begun with the French Revolution and continued with Napoleon, was giving a tremendous impetus to expansive young America. Not only did American farmers suddenly find rich markets abroad, but American shipping, the country's one mature industry, inherited a magnificent windfall in the carrying trade as the British fleet blockaded European ports and French privateers harried British shipping. The Far East trade proved especially profitable to American enterprise, ships sometimes earning their entire cost in a single voyage. Philadelphia's Stephen Girard acquired a shipping fortune sufficient to found a bank with a capital of $1,250,000. American shipbuilders (and by consequence American shippers) enjoyed the advantage over their European rivals of huge reserves of excellent ship timber. American oak, cedar, and live oak sold for less than the European fir, pine, and larch which they far outlasted.

The atmosphere of war prosperity contributed to the federal government's exceeding its own conception of its powers in 1803 with the Louisiana Purchase, by which to the still empty expanses of Maine, western New York State, western Pennsylvania, the Ohio-Great Lakes country and the Tennessee-Alabama wilderness was added a realm whose very boundaries were uncertain. The immediate stimulus for the purchase was the demand of the Ohio Valley frontier-farmers for a secure hold on New Orleans, but the readiness of Thomas Jefferson, Robert Livingston, and James Monroe to buy all Louisiana reflected the tripling of the nation's population and its rapid spillage westward in the quarter-century since 1776.

The question was, what would happen when war prosperity ran out? What were the country's real prospects in a normal world? Could it fill those inconceivably immense western spaces, or even hold onto them? Could it defend New Orleans now that it had it? Aaron Burr's conspiratorial scheme of 1805–06 for detaching the West and forming a new nation, a scheme into which one of the leading generals of the United States Army, James Wilkinson, enthusiastically entered, showed how precarious was the union between the seaboard-dominated East and the river-oriented West.

Behind the façade of agricultural prosperity lay a technology whose backwardness continued to astonish European visitors. The fabulous land was plundered rather than cultivated, successive crops of wheat, corn, cotton, or tobacco ruthlessly robbing it of its vitality. "The aim of the farmers in this country (if they can be called farmers)," George Washington had written with asperity, "is not to make the most they can from the land, which is . . . cheap, but the most of labor, which is dear; the consequence of which has been, much ground has been *scratched over* and none cultivated or improved as it ought to have been; whereas a farmer in England, where land is dear, and labor cheap, finds it in his interest to improve and cultivate highly, that he may reap large crops from a small quantity of ground."

Pennsylvania plow, late eighteenth century, with wooden moldboard. (Collections of Greenfield Village and the Henry Ford Museum, Dearborn, Michigan)

In reality, the American farmer did not even make the most of labor, dear though it was. Plows were still ill-designed, both the old scratch plows of the eastern seaboard and the turning plows used for breaking the western grasslands and for deep plowing. These latter, which sometimes had the moldboard (the turning element) sheeted with iron to reduce friction, required two or more yoke of oxen, managed by a boy leading and a man to hold the plow handles, just as in Piers Plowman's time. A second plowing, at right angles, was commonly necessary, followed by harrowing with an implement that had advanced only slightly from the older clump of brush into a homemade wooden frame. Grain and hay were still cut with scythes; flax, hemp, and rice with sickles. The largest farms increasingly used animals for threshing, but in the most primitive way, by trampling the grain on a treading floor, as in prehistoric times.

As long as there was plenty of land, and as long as the land yielded good crops to bad farming, American farmers cared little for improvements in their equipment. Thomas Jefferson among others gave attention to the problem of plow design, and in 1793 made what has been called the first attempt at scientific design. In 1797 Charles Newbold of New Jersey built a plow of cast iron except for the handles and beam, and Robert and Joseph Smith of Pennsylvania soon after made an all-iron plow. But while iron plows were in wide use in England, they were regarded with suspicion by American farmers, who thought the iron poisoned the soil they were busy ruining.

Jethro Tull's seed drill and similar planting devices, used in England for decades, were also rejected by American farmers, in favor of the ancient method of broadcast sowing of small grains and hand dropping of other seeds in hills or rows. The British-invented fanning mill for cleaning threshed grain won some acceptance, but most farmers stuck to the technique of ancient Babylon, in which the grain was tossed in the wind to blow the lighter chaff away from the kernels. A horse-drawn mower-reaper was patented in the United States as early as 1803, but like similar inventions on the other side of the Atlantic only served to demonstrate how tantalizingly difficult that problem was going to be.

Philadelphia's savants, heirs of the Benjamin Franklin tradition, sought to improve farming methods through the Philadelphia Society for Promoting Agriculture, which vainly contrasted the "American Method" of "unproductive fallows" with the "English Method" of manuring and planting "fallow crop"—turnips, potatoes, beans, followed by grain crop and clover—and went so far as to offer a suitably inscribed silver plate and gold and silver medals for the best experiment with the English rotation method and other improvements.

More immediate success attended another line of agricultural enlightenment. George Washington Parke Custis sponsored some sheep shearings on his Arlington, Virginia, farm in 1803 and the germ of the fair was born. Elkanah Watson, a progress-minded York State Yankee who moved to Massachusetts, in 1807 imported the first Merino sheep from Spain. He exhibited them "under the great elm tree" in the town square of Pittsfield, attracting so much attention that he organized the Berkshire Agricultural Society to sponsor an annual livestock show. The next year he introduced a short-legged, grass-fed pig and a prize English bull, and in the winter of 1809, rather surprisingly, the pickerel. Agricultural societies, began to proliferate throughout New England.

Yet as the new century began, America remained by European and especially British standards a backward country. Of the individually impressive contributions of John Fitch, Oliver Evans, Samuel Slater, and Eli Whitney, only Whitney's cotton gin had had dramatic impact.

Although much American iron was of good quality and easily extracted, a large proportion of the iron used by forges—some 9,000 tons a year—came from England, Sweden, and Russia. Further, the best edged tools and wrought-iron products still came from Europe. The many waterpowered smithies and small foundries that covered the country tended to discourage the development of larger establishments, with a negative effect on technical progress. Henry Cort's valuable innovation of shaping iron by rolling instead of trip-hammering, introduced in England in 1784, was not tried in America till 1816.

Despite Samuel Slater, not only did New England's textile machinery lag behind Britain's, but the gap between the large and the small industrial rivals was widening. While hundreds of copies of Edmund Cartwright's power loom turned out wool and cotton cloth in the English Midlands, not a single such machine operated in the United States, where yarn was still woven into cloth by men and women working in their village homes and farms, exactly as in the European Middle Ages. The cotton gin, instead of tying South to North, seemed to be having the opposite effect of tying the South to Great Britain. And while in Britain the steam engine and the textile machinery were creating, through the push-pull, industry-market combination of technological-economic forces, powerful offshoots in metallurgy and mechanical engineering, America's commercial prosperity seemed scarcely to need or to encourage technological growth. Few industrial enterprises represented capital investments of as much as $50,000; most of the mills—cotton, woolen, flour, paper, sugar, lumber, fulling, flax, iron, and gunpowder—were worth far less, as were the narrow ropewalks, the one-story distilleries and breweries, the tanneries, brick kilns, and glass factories, and even the mines and quarries. And these represented only a minor segment of a manufacturing industry that remained mostly in the hands of individual craftsmen applying their specialized skills in their own tiny shops—blacksmiths, shoemakers, hatters, tailors, bakers, coopers, carpenters, cabinetmakers, clockmakers, button makers, tinsmiths, potters, weavers, printers, masons, chandlers, soapmakers, saddlers, silversmiths, jewelers, wheelwrights, coppersmiths, locksmiths, broom and brushmakers—most of them using tools and materials that would have been familiar to their medieval ancestors.

The ship-modeling technique developed by Orlando Merrill of Newburyport, Massachusetts, providing for the first time a scientific basis for naval architecture through experimentation with scale models, was a noteworthy exception. But despite all happy present indications, America's technological-economic future did not really lie in ocean commerce.

It lay, rather, inside North America. America had a vast capacity for enriching itself, for creating and trading the products of its own wealth.

Extracting the wealth from the earth and converting it into viable commodities was not enough. What was needed was a system for cheaply moving the riches—raw, semifinished, refined, or perfected—from one part of the country to another. As a start on such a system, America had important assets—numerous natural coastal harbors, tremendous rivers and lakes, expanses of flat and gently rolling country, an abundance of critical raw materials, above all timber, which had the advantage of being, in its natural state, readily utilizable.

Three lines of solution to the transportation problems were under discussion in the opening decade of the nineteenth century: first, improvement of river transportation, with canals to connect the natural waterways into an economically rational system; second, hard-surfaced roads to take wheeled vehicles where water transport was impossible, especially across the Allegheny Mountains; and third, bridges to overcome the obstacles that the rivers presented in one direction while serving as arteries in another.

Improving river transportation meant dealing effectively with current, snags, seasonal low and high water, and certain other difficulties, some peculiarly American. In Cincinnati, packet keelboats, that is, keelboats carrying passengers on a more or less regular schedule, advertised themselves as comfortable and safe, and equipped with bullet-proof cabins, excellent portholes for shooting at river pirates, and one-pounder cannon. In its one-month trip to New Orleans, the packet was accompanied by an escort vessel with an armed crew. No serious defensive measures were considered against the snags of the Ohio and Mississippi, though a canal to short-circuit the Ohio rapids at Louisville was under discussion. In the 1790s and early 1800s, Massachusetts built the 27-mile Middlesex Canal, joining Boston Harbor with the nearest bend of the Merrimack River. In New York a similar work bypassed the Little Falls of the Mohawk. A much more ambitious work, a canal linking the Mohawk with the Hudson at Cohoes Falls, was started but soon given up. Elkanah Watson, the agriculturally innovative upstate New Yorker who was the moving spirit of the operation, admitted frankly that the work was handicapped by American incompetence: "We were all novices. . . . Indeed we were so extremely deficient in knowledge of the science of constructing locks and canals, that we found it expedient to send a committee of respectable mechanics, to examine the imperfect works then constructing on the Potowmac. . . . We had no other resource but from books." The "Potowmac" works were a total failure.

Nevertheless, despite the admitted ignorance, and despite all obstacles, natural, financial and technical, some New Yorkers continued to dream of a hydraulic engineering work to dwarf all these canals, finished and unfinished, a waterway linking the Great Lakes with the Hudson. Gouverneur Morris, who had regaled General Schuyler's staff around the campfire in 1777 with his canal vision, had lost none of his enthusiasm. In 1801 he wrote that for a tenth the cost of Britain's last unsuccessful campaign in Europe a waterway could be built to take "ships from London through Hudson's River into *Lake Erie.*" To the objections of a friend with whom he argued at a Schenectady inn in 1803, he replied with a quotation from Vergil: *Labor omnia vincit improbus,* "Hard work conquers everything." A canal 360 miles long through country with only six inhabitants per square mile nevertheless seemed to border on fantasy.

If the West could not be tied to the East by water, what about by land? Some progress had been made: by the turn of the century the Post Office reported that "scarcely a village, court house or public place of any importance but is accommodated with the mail," via 16,000 miles of post roads. On the better roads stagecoaches carried the mail, and on the frontier, post riders made 35 to 40 miles a day. But "the post road," wrote a visitor to Maine, "is so bad that you cannot find it without a guide in the woods. What is understood by making a road in a new country is merely cutting down and removing the large trees, leaving the stumps and small wood. The breadth varies from three to four and twenty feet." Maine's post roads were no worse than those of the West. Wilderness Road through Cumberland Gap and Braddock's Road to the headwaters of the Ohio were well-worn and capable of taking wheeled vehicles, but even these presented formidable difficulties in bad weather, and few of the other mountain crossings were more than trails for pack trains. Zane's Trace, built by Ebenezer Zane of Wheeling to connect Wheeling with Limestone (later Maysville), Kentucky, consisted in 1801 of a path through the forest made by cutting down the small trees and avoiding the large ones. By similar trails Zane's Trace connected with the ancient moccasin-worn Natchez Trace to the lower Mississippi, used by the riverboatmen, which became a post route by act of Congress in 1800.

Roads in the older part of the country were little better. One visitor from Ireland in the 1790s who braved both East and West pronounced Maryland's roads the worst in the Union. He continued:

> Indeed so very bad are they that on going from Elkton to the Susquehannah ferry, the driver frequently had to call to the passengers in the stage, to lean out of the carriage first at one side, then at the other, to prevent it from oversetting in the deep ruts with which the road abounds: "Now gentlemen, to the right;" upon which the passengers all stretched their bodies half way out of the carriage to balance it on that side; "Now gentlemen, to the left," and so on. . . . If the road runs contiguous to a wood, then, instead of mending it where it is bad, they open a new passage through the trees, which they call making a road. It is very common in Maryland to see six or seven different roads branching out from one, which all lead to the same place. . . . The dexterity with which the drivers of the stages guide their horses along these new roads, which are full of stumps of trees, is astonishing. . . .

Pennsylvania was a leader in road building as in much else. In 1792 a group of businessmen won from the legislature a concession of incorporation for the purpose of building a turnpike from Philadelphia to Lancaster, birthplace of the Pennsylvania rifle and the Conestoga wagon, and jump-off point to the West. Raising $300,000 by sale of stock they applied an excellent if expensive road-building technique developed in the eighteenth century by Pierre Trésaguet in

France and Scotsman John Loudon McAdam in Britain, a durable, well-drained stone-and-gravel roadbed with a good flat-stone surface. The Lancaster Pike was an instant success, stimulating a flood of followers, if not imitators. Few built as good roads as the Lancaster, most companies preferring to improve existing dirt roads by digging drainage ditches and humping the roadway. The routes to the West left plenty to be desired, after the 70-mile stretch of even, stone-paved highway from Philadelphia, but the broad-wheeled, low-bellied Conestoga wagons, painted blue underneath and red on top, hauled by four- or six-ox teams, crawled picturesquely over the Alleghenies.

The first "national road," that is, built by federal funds, was the Cumberland or National Pike, only authorized by Congress in 1805, and hardly started before the War of 1812 halted construction.

The "macadam" technique supplied a ready-to-hand means of building roads. Bridges were another matter. The beautiful elliptical stone arches that carried European highways across rivers and streams were an impractical extravagance in America where cutting and dressing stone called for expensive (and hardly existent) labor. What was needed in America was a cheap—meaning wooden—bridge, and one that could be built by a minimum amount of semiskilled labor.

More important even than roads and bridges was John Fitch's steamboat, still waiting three years after its inventor's death for appreciation and exploitation. But interest was growing rapidly; not many more years could pass before this indispensable key to unlock America's future would be used.

7

The Steamboat Race

JOHN FITCH, OLIVER EVANS, AND ELI WHITNEY were farmers' sons, no handicap to a career in technology for a mechanically gifted American boy of their era. David Wilkinson was the son of a blacksmith, an even more advantageous heritage. New Yorker John Stevens, after Evans the most undeservedly obscure of the early inventors, also had a helpful family background. His parents were rich. His father and uncle operated a fleet of merchantmen, and his maternal grandfather was James Alexander, a distinguished lawyer. The Stevenses lived at No. 7 Broadway, facing Bowling Green, in a block of mansions whose owners included the Livingstons and the Van Cortlandts. The famous No. 1 Broadway was occupied by Archibald Kennedy, Collector of the Port of New York, and in the war served successively as headquarters for Washington, Cornwallis, Howe, and Clinton.

John Stevens was educated at private school and graduated from King's College (Columbia) in 1768, when he was nineteen. Among his classmates were Gouverneur Morris and Broadway neighbor Robert R. Livingston, who in 1771 married Stevens's sister Mary. The Stevenses were politically moderate, only joining the rebel cause on the eve of the Revolution. John Stevens's brother-in-law Livingston was more forward, serving in both Continental Congresses, helping Thomas Jefferson draft the Declaration of Independence, and in 1777 becoming Chancellor (chief judge) of New York State. Through his maternal uncle William Alexander, who claimed the title Lord Stirling while commanding a division in

LEFT Portrait of Robert Fulton, c. 1806, by Benjamin West. (New York State Historical Association, Cooperstown)

RIGHT John Stevens. (Smithsonian Photograph No. 644A)

Washington's army, Stevens obtained a commission that permitted him to spend the war comfortably as a staff officer and emerge with the lifetime rank of colonel. During the war he met and married Rachel Cox, a renowned New Jersey beauty, and, looking for a suitable residence in the country outside New York, discovered a ruined ex-Tory estate across the Hudson called Hoboken. Baron von Steuben also had an eye on Hoboken, but could offer the state only his military laurels, whereas Colonel Stevens was able to put up £18,000 in a public auction.

Hoboken originally consisted of 564 acres, to which the colonel later added another 125 while building a handsome new house, completed in 1787, the year of the Constitutional Convention in Philadelphia. Stevens's brother-in-law Livingston, who had largely written New York's constitution, played a conspicuous role in Philadelphia, and was doubtless among the delegates who rode on John Fitch's boat in the Delaware. He probably described it to Colonel Stevens, who also became aware of steam navigation through the rival pamphlets of Fitch and James Rumsey.

Stevens developed an immediate interest. He did not suffer from Fitch's poverty of reference resources; he had a fine library and the money to procure more books. Quickly perceiving that the weight and bulk of the conventional iron boiler imposed a severe handicap in the application of steam to navigation, Stevens wrote Rumsey a letter with some suggestions, perhaps with the hope of winning an invitation to participate in Rumsey's project. If so, he was rebuffed, and shortly after was using his influence with Livingston, Van Cortlandt, and others to try to block both Rumsey and Fitch from New York State patents in order to get one for himself.

When the Albany legislative committee granted Rumsey his patent on the basis of prior application, Stevens turned to the new federal government, whose first president had just moved back into the Kennedy house on Broadway, and whose first Congress was sitting in City Hall. Invoking the Constitution's provision for the "encouragement of science and the useful arts," Stevens appealed to Congress to grant him patents covering a boiler design he had conceived and a "method of propelling a boat by steam." Implicit was a call for a national patent law. In favor of steamboats Stevens waxed rhapsodic: once they were practical, commerce both domestic and international would profit to such an extent that "the earth would . . . be everywhere stimulated to bring forth with its utmost vigor; civilization and the arts would spread rapidly over the face of the globe; then, and not till then, might it be said that man was really the master of this world, with everything in it subservient to his will." His appeal won immediate support, and following a spirited debate the U.S. Patent Law was adopted in April of 1790, a month before Fitch, Voight, and Thornton began their summer-long commercial service on the Delaware. The law placed the patent responsibility in the hands of the secretary of state, at the moment Thomas Jefferson. Jefferson entrusted the patent applications already received to his secretary, Henry Remsen, but called in the secretary of war and the attorney-general (Henry Knox and Edmund Randolph) to study the rival steam patent applications by Rumsey, Fitch, and Stevens.

Jefferson's committee would have had still a fourth contender to consider if Elijah Ormsbee of Providence and David Wilkinson, Samuel Slater's young assistant and brother-in-law, had filed an application for the small steamboat they assembled that summer (1791) at Cranston, Rhode Island. Ormsbee read of John Fitch's boat and asked David if he could make an engine suitable for a steamboat. David "went home and made my patterns, cast and bored the cylinder, and made the wrought iron work." The two men ran their boat briefly in the Seekonk River at Providence just to show that they could do it, then "being short of funds, we hauled the boat up and gave it over."

Meantime the first U.S. patents were issued. Patent No. 1, July 31, 1790, went to Samuel Hopkins, for an improvement in "the making of Potash and Pearl ash by a new apparatus and Process." The second was to Joseph Simpson for the manufacture of candles, the third, as we have seen, to Oliver Evans for his automated flour mill. The next several were for making punches for type-founding, for an improved method of distilling, for a pile-driving method for bridge foundations, for threshing grain, for cutting and polishing marble, for raising nap on cloth, for breaking hemp, for making nails, for a new bedstead, and for a treadmill device for propelling boats by cattle. On August 26, 1791, the steamboat question was settled by the Solomonlike judgment of issuing patents to all three inventors—Fitch, Rumsey, and John Stevens.

It was already evident that examining all patent applications was a laborious process, and a new Patent Act of 1793 routinely granted patents to citizens upon an oath of originality and payment of a fee. In case of conflict, it was left to the inventors to settle in court.

By the time Stevens acquired his patent, his old friend and Broadway neighbor Chancellor Livingston had become infatuated with steamboats. Like many able and strong-minded persons, Livingston underestimated his own ignorance in an unfamiliar field, and tried to persuade Stevens and others of the merits of the Franklin-Bernoulli jet-propulsion principle. Had Livingston been less dogmatic, he might have given his valuable backing to a New Haven merchant seaman named Captain Samuel Morey who after five years of experimentation in 1795 obtained a United States patent for a steam-propelled stern-wheeler in which, the following year, he gave Stevens and Livingston a ride in the Hudson. Livingston refused to be interested, and Stevens was intent on his own design.

Stevens enlisted able technical help in the person of Nicholas Roosevelt, whose Soho Works on the Passaic River had built parts for Oliver Evans' steam engines. Before agreeing to back Stevens' design, Livingston insisted on Roosevelt's showing a sketch of the Franklin-Bernoulli engine to one of his English workmen, Charles Stoudenger. Stoudenger said he could make the necessary drawings all right, but "don't blame me if it don't work."

Livingston finally came off his jet scheme, and after a brief insistence on another impracticality, a horizontal wheel under the keel, gave in and let Stevens design the boat. Returning to his more congenial field, the New York legislature, Livingston got a bill passed repealing Fitch's grant that still had three years to run, and giving himself a twelve-month monopoly to build a 20-ton boat that would navigate at 4 miles per hour. Stevens and Roosevelt set to work fashioning a steam engine, but ran into such difficulty boring the cylinder with their inadequately equipped plant that Livingston tried to buy an engine, or at least a piston and cylinder, from Boulton & Watt. The British government, still trying to contain the bursting Industrial Revolution, refused a permit, and Stevens and Roosevelt finally got their engine finished in the summer of 1802. It was no mere copy of Watt's. Seeking to overcome the vibration effect of the alternating piston strokes on a light hull, Stevens had conceived a small brass cylinder aligned horizontally in the bottom of the boat; steam was admitted to alternately strike two wings attached to an axial shaft, causing the shaft to spin; passing out of the cylinder through packing, the shaft was terminated outside the boat in a device described as having small windmill-like arms, evidently a screw propeller, the first to be used in a conventional surface vessel (David Bushnell's *Turtle* had a screw propeller).

The little boat, the *Polacca,* with Stevens at the helm, chugged south through Upper New York Bay, and via Newark Bay into the Passaic as far as Belleville and back. Its speed was disappointing—3½ miles per hour—but the performance was good enough to enable Livingston to talk the Albany legislature into an extension of his monopoly. Roosevelt's Soho Works was set to work on a larger, conventional engine, with a 16-inch-diameter cylinder; once more the boat ran, but the vibration was terrific, and Stevens concluded, "Scrap her and build another."

Stevens had been struck by the discovery of a French scientist, M. Belamour, that "the elasticity of steam is nearly doubled by every addition to the temperature of thirty degrees Fahrenheit"—one of the first instances of an engineer learning something from a scientist. This was the principle of the high-pressure engine Oliver Evans had already patented, but Stevens had the further idea of lessening the hazard by a "multitubular boiler," that is, one in which the water was boiled in several separate one-inch-thick copper tubes instead of in one large boiler-tank. He obtained a patent on April 11, 1803.

Chancellor Livingston meantime had been sent to France by President Jefferson as United States Minister (en route making a vain attempt to induce the British government to part with a Boulton & Watt engine). The same April day in 1803 that Stevens obtained his patent, Livingston had an extraordinary experience. Foreign Minister Talleyrand called him in and asked him how he would like to buy the Louisiana Territory.

It was not surprising that Livingston and special envoy James Monroe jumped at the bargain that nearly doubled the size of the United States. But Livingston, with his steam navigation interest and information (not to mention his New York monopoly), saw something more in the deal than mere statesmanship might conceive. United States acquisition of the western shore of the Mississippi River and, most important, of its mouth, made intensive exploitation of the fabulous western empire an immediate possibility.

By an uncanny coincidence, Livingston had just made the acquaintance of a personable, technically knowledgeable, and highly enterprising American in Paris who was certain he could build a steamboat for either the Hudson or the Mississippi.

Robert Fulton was a Pennsylvanian who had already done amazingly well on a capital of a farming background, three-R's schooling, good looks, charm, self-confidence, artistic talent, and an aptitude for mechanical devices. Like Livingston, Fulton had been in Philadelphia in 1786–87 and had doubtless witnessed John Fitch's demonstrations on the Delaware. Wealthy Philadelphians thought enough of his miniature portraits—the commercial art of the day—to finance his passage to England to study technique. Despite the help of Benjamin West and others, Fulton's painting career did not prosper in London, and he was soon reduced to financial straits. "Pondering how to make funds to support me," he turned to technology. Canals were under intensive promotion in Britain, and Fulton suggested several improvements and innovations, including an impractical, but world's-first-conceived excavating machine. He also proposed steam navigation, not a new idea in Britain.

The social-minded industrialist Robert Owen advanced him money, which was never fully repaid, the philanthropic Owen merely commenting later that "I consider the little aid . . . I gave to enable him to [eventually] bestow so great advantage on his country and the world as money most fortunately expended." Fulton also made friends with Edmund Cartwright, the ex-clergyman who had invented the power loom, and who was at the moment experimenting with an internal combustion engine—an idea which a little later seized Colonel John Stevens in Hoboken.

Fulton's schemes in England came to nothing, and he crossed the Channel to France, where from canal digging he soon switched to a rope-making machine (plagiarized from Cartwright), a profitable "Panorama" mural in Montmartre representing the most recent burning of Moscow, and—evidently inspired by a published description of David Bushnell's *Turtle,* a submarine. Despite considerable opposition inside the French government on the grounds that such a weapon would be barbarous, Fulton succeeded in getting enough support to carry out remarkable experiments. In July 1800, his *Nautilus*—a name destined for lasting fame—submerged in the Seine and cruised for an hour, propelled, like the *Turtle,* by a hand-cranked screw. The same year he sank a hulk in the harbor at Brest by means of a Bushnell-type spar torpedo. Full of mettle, he boldly attempted to sink two British brigs off the coast, but they easily evaded his slow approach.

By the time Livingston arrived in Paris, Fulton's charm had made a firm friend of Livingston's ministerial predecessor, Joel Barlow (in fact of the whole Barlow family), and naturally enough he got acquainted with the new minister. They hit it off at once—everyone did with Fulton—and when Livingston introduced the subject of steamboats Fulton brimmed with confident enthusiasm. In the summer of 1802, with Livingston's backing, he got a French mechanic to build a three-foot-long model boat propelled by a set of paddles powered by clock springs, after a sketch he had titled in his notebook, "The Steam Boat from New York to Albany in 12 Hours." To experiment with it he dammed up a brook at Plombières, a resort in the Vosges whither he had accompanied Mrs. Barlow, creating an early version of a hydraulic research center. In October he and Livingston signed a formal partnership agreement whose stated object was the construction of a steamboat 120 feet long to carry sixty passengers between New York and Albany at a speed of 8 miles an hour. Livingston advanced £500 for an experimental boat to be built on the Seine, and Fulton borrowed a French engine, got a boiler made, and built a 75-foot boat with huge 12-foot paddle wheels on either side. A storm capsized the craft and only by strenuous efforts was he able to rescue the machinery, but in midsummer 1803, three months after the Louisiana Purchase, he made a successful run that drew a notice in the official *Journal des Débats:*

"At six o'clock in the evening, assisted by three persons only, [Fulton] put his boat in motion . . . and for an hour and a half afforded the curious spectacle of a boat moved by wheels like a cart, these wheels being provided with paddles or flat plates and being moved by a fire engine."

The editors of the *Journal* said, and apparently knew, nothing of Jouffroy d'Abbans's steamboat on the Saône of twenty years earlier, or even of a French patent of the year before that covered all the features of Fulton's Seine craft, making it impossible for him to seek a patent.

Livingston enthusiastically wrote home to Stevens about "Mr. Fulton, with whom you will be much pleased. He is a man of science and embued with the best of principles. . . ."

It is difficult to believe that Stevens was "much pleased" to hear that his chief financial backer had been seduced in Paris. At home he was striving mightily to perfect a high-pressure engine, and suffering the vast annoyance of discovering that somebody else was competing with him and very possibly ahead of him. An article about Oliver Evans's steam-engine experiments in the *Philadelphia Aurora* had come to his attention, and he feared a patent collision.

Stevens's wife had a brother-in-law in Philadelphia, Dr. John R. Coxe. At Stevens's entreaty Dr. Coxe called on Evans with a series of written questions, to which Evans responded with gracious equanimity while Coxe carefully wrote down the answers:

"With what weight on the square inch is the safety valve loaded?" "30 pounds, 56 pounds expected."

"With what material is the piston packed?" "Hemp."

"Is the piston rod attached to the balance beam?" "To the crank of a flywheel."

"What is the length of the stroke of the piston and how many strokes up and down are made per minute?" "Ten inches stroke, 30 strokes up and down."

Evans later wrote Stevens offering to build him an engine that would outperform a Boulton & Watt. By this time he had no fewer than twenty engines in use or under construction, and suggested that Stevens go up to Middletown, Connecticut, to inspect his twenty-four-horsepower engine there, asserting that if needed he could build one twice as powerful.

Both Stevens and Evans made progress in their development of high-pressure engines through the winter of 1803–04, and both registered their advances in the spring, when Evans secured his patent. In May, Stevens launched his new boat, the *Little Juliana*. The *Polacca* had attracted scant attention, but *Juliana* caused some excitement, according to Professor James Renwick of Columbia, recalling the event some years later:

> A crowd [was] running toward the river. On inquiring the cause, we were informed that "Jack" Stevens [one of Colonel Stevens's two sons] was going over to Hoboken in a queer sort of boat. On reaching the bulkhead by which the Battery was then bounded, we saw lying against it a vessel about the size of a Whitehall rowboat, in which there was a small engine *but no visible means of propulsion.* The vessel was speedily underway, my late much-valued friend, Commodore Stevens [John Cox Stevens] acting as coxwain, and I presume the smutty-looking personage who fulfilled the duties of engineer, fireman, and crew, was his more practical brother, Robert L. Stevens.

Professor Renwick's identification of the crew was accurate, and his emphasis on the absence of a visible propelling component very much to the point. *Little Juliana* was propelled by twin screws, not apparently to increase power (both were driven by the same engine) but to overcome a tendency in *Polacca* to veer. Her engine was high-pressure and reciprocating, the "rotatory" engine of *Polacca* having proved a disappointment apart from the fact that the packing around the shaft leaked steam. To prevent strain on the hull, Stevens had had the cylinder rigidly connected to the base of the supports holding the cog wheels on either side. The two 16-inch-diameter cylinders Stevens bored in his own little workshop in Hoboken. The *Little Juliana* made several trips at good speeds, but her high-pressure boiler finally blew up, by good luck without injuring either of the young Stevenses.

John Stevens's screw-propeller steamboat of 1804. (Smithsonian Photograph No. 36,229)

Stevens still insisted the true formula for steam navigation was "a multitubular boiler which would stay tight and produce high-pressure steam; a quick-moving engine, directly connected to the propeller shaft; short, four-bladed propellers; and twin screws," a forecast of remarkable prescience, though not completely fulfilled for decades. He sent young John Cox Stevens to England to try to get Boulton & Watt to build him a strong enough boiler, but Matthew Boulton's son, now in charge of the famous plant, refused even to look at the model of Colonel Stevens's engine—"high Steam," he stated peremptorily, "was entirely out of the question." John Cox was further exasperated by the exactions of English landlords, restaurateurs, servants, and coachmen—"the greatest set of rascals in the world . . . if I give them a guinea to change, they are certain to return me all bad shillings, and, perhaps, a pocket-piece instead of half a guinea." After having his watch stolen, he sat all night "with my hands upon my money."

Throughout 1805 Colonel Stevens was tied up with other projects—a proposed floating bridge for the Hudson, a tunnel under the river (totally unfeasible until Marc Brunel invented the tunneling shield twenty years later), a steam-powered fireboat, and floating batteries for New York Harbor. To raise money for his experiments he decided to sell off a piece of his estate fronting on the river, and laid out a town plot that became the city of Hoboken.

He did not return to his concept of a large passenger steamer for the Hudson (though he built a small ferryboat that made regular crossings at 3½ miles an hour) until the summer of 1806, just as Robert Fulton arrived from England, bringing with him a Boulton & Watt engine and boiler.

By 1806 nobody in America really needed a Watt engine. Nevertheless, it was a source of wonder that an American had been allowed to import one. The explanation lay in the realm of cloak and dagger. When war had broken out again between Britain and France in 1803, the British Admiralty had turned an apprehensive eye toward the inventive American in Paris. His submarine and torpedo weapons might conceivably nullify Britain's naval advantage enough to permit Napoleon's army, concentrating at Boulogne, to cross the Channel. A secret message was sent inviting Fulton to meet "Mr. Smith," a British agent, in Amsterdam. Fulton agreed to the rendezvous, whose results he summarized cryptically in his notebook: "I agreed on certain conditions and Mr. Smith set off for London to give in my terms." "Smith" returned with a counteroffer in December, and to a third and final meeting he brought a letter from Lord Hawkesbury, British foreign secretary, meeting all Fulton's demands; two months later Fulton was in England. In London he explained his spar torpedo to the Admiralty and set off for Birmingham to deliver his engine and boiler specifications. He found time for a flying visit to Scotland to inspect the *Charlotte Dundas,* a steam craft built to work on the Forth and Clyde Canal. Her creator, William Symington, had launched a steamboat as early as 1788, only two years after John Fitch's first success, and had for a time taken passengers on excursions in the Clyde (though not apparently attempting a regular service).

Fulton did not plagiarize any ideas from Symington, but perhaps should have; Symington gave his engine a horizontal beam that permitted it to work directly on the paddle wheel, whereas Fulton used a vertical beam that required gearing and a flywheel.

Early in 1805, Boulton & Watt notified him that "the Goods for your Engine were forwarded" to London, enclosing a bill for £548. The copper boiler, made by Cave & Son, came to a bit over £475. In Philadelphia Oliver Evans was offering high-pressure engines—in their nature more compact, with smaller cylinder diameters, and therefore cheaper—for only $886.60. Fulton, long away from home, had no idea of the progress made there in the past decade and was glad to pay the British price. For that matter, it seemed fair, since the Admiralty was paying him a retainer of £200 a month. He stood to profit much more if his spar torpedo sank anything, but several attempts against French ships in Boulogne failed, and in the summer Napoleon took his army off to the Danube to battle the Austrians and Russians in the Austerlitz campaign. When the French fleet was destroyed at Trafalgar and Pitt died, the torpedo project was abandoned by the Admiralty. Richer by a £15,000 payoff, and with the freedom to offer his invention elsewhere, Fulton took his steam engine and boiler and headed for home.

In New York he lost no time entrusting to Charles Browne, a leading East River shipbuilder, the hull design he had prepared. Here if nowhere else Fulton showed originality. A long, low, flat-bottomed, wall-sided, rectangular-sectioned box that more nearly resembled the future railroad freight car than any ship known to sailors, the design was the product of studies he had made of friction, a line of research that had distracted him from the matter of hull strength foremost in the minds of a hundred generations of naval architects. It was fortunate that

Fulton's boat was intended solely for the peaceful Hudson, yet his attempt to apply scientific principles, however unproductive the result, was noteworthy.

The most significant feature of Fulton's boat was its size. One hundred and fifty feet long, it was much the largest steam craft so far built. In the end, owing partly to minor difficulties that had to be overcome, such as giving the engine adequate framing support, the cost mounted to $20,000, exceeding Fulton's estimate and temporarily embarrassing even Livingston. But by now steam navigation had high credibility, and the two partners experienced no difficulty borrowing enough money to complete construction.

Colonel Stevens was finishing his own Hudson passenger boat, the *Phoenix,* two-thirds as long as Fulton's and equipped with a large multitube boiler (nineteen tubes instead of the twelve in his earlier boilers) and paddle wheels instead of screws. He wrote Livingston: Could they not combine to "avoid collision [and] contribute mutually toward bringing to perfection one of the greatest works for the benefit of mankind that had ever yet been effected"? The colonel hinted that by working together they could protect and prolong Livingston's monopoly on the Hudson, whereas if forced to compete they would open the door to "interlopers." More forcefully, if somewhat inconsistently, he expressed his conviction that monopoly was contrary to the "Spirit and Letter of the Federal Constitution" that Livingston had helped write, and finally threw in a claim that his new boat would outrun Fulton's.

Coming at the moment of financial difficulties, Stevens's letter suggested to Livingston an obvious solution. He invited his brother-in-law to buy into the Fulton boat for $5,000. That amounted to an insult to Stevens, who thought himself a better steam engineer than Fulton, had several patents to Fulton's none (a fact, however, of which Stevens was unaware), and had virtually originated the U.S. patent law. Though maintaining a lengthy argumentative correspondence with Livingston (interspersed with the friendliest personal interchanges, advice about family matters, and the like), Stevens declined to have anything to do with the severely shaped monster in the East River, sometimes called the *Clermont,* after Livingston's Hudson estate, but generally known as the *Steamboat* (though also equipped with two sails, a square sail in the bow and a fore-and-aft in the stern). On August 9, 1807, four years to the day after Fulton's experimental craft chugged along the Seine, twenty-one years after John Fitch's triumph on the Delaware, and twenty-four years after the Marquis Jouffroy's success on the Saône, the *Steamboat* had her first trial. Apparently because her paddle wheels were not yet firmly housed, speed was held to 2 miles per hour against a one-mile tide. The engine was also exposed, provoking a comment that she looked "like a backwoods sawmill mounted on a scow and set on fire." For an idea whose time had come, Fulton's creation commanded small attention from the New York press and public. When ten days later she prepared to cast off in earnest, Fulton heard "many sarcastic remarks," doubtless including the long-remembered epithet, "Fulton's Folly," coined during her construction.

Derision was silenced when at one P.M., with forty passengers aboard, most of them friends and relatives of Fulton and Livingston, the *Steamboat* quit her moorings in the Hudson and headed for Albany, 150 miles away. The wind was unfavorable, a factor that proved a publicity asset, because running solely on her Boulton & Watt low-pressure engine she passed one sailing vessel after another. At one P.M. next day she pulled up to the dock at Chancellor Livingston's Clermont estate, 110 miles from New York. At nine next morning the cruise was resumed and the remaining 40 miles to Albany done in eight hours. Next morning at nine the *Steamboat* headed south, arrived at Clermont at six P.M., started off at seven A.M., and was back in New York at four the following morning—total distance covered, 300 miles; total elapsed running time, 62 hours; problems and mishaps, none.

Fulton set to work at once arranging for passenger service. New York's twenty-odd newspapers still did not recognize the *Steamboat* as news, and Fulton had to buy advertising space and write letters (paying for their publication) to get newspaper publicity. Fare from New York was fixed at $2.50 to West Point, $3.50 to Poughkeepsie, and $7 to Albany, with numerous intermediate stops. Passengers could, in fact, be picked up or set ashore anywhere on the river, with a minimum charge of $1. Service was begun in September and though an early freeze put an end to operations in late November, the *Steamboat* had in three months earned $21,000, a thousand dollars more than her cost, a most auspicious beginning.

In the 1808 season, under a new name, the *North River*, she made over fifty trips to Albany. Livingston induced the legislature to renew the monopoly for five years for each additional boat the firm built, and in 1809, a nearly identical sister ship, the *Car of Neptune*, whose low-pressure engine was built by Nicholas Roosevelt's Soho Works, was launched. Subsequently two more flat-bottomed, wall-sided sisters, the *Paragon* and the *Washington*, doubled the company's fleet (the *North River* was finally given her historic name of *Clermont* in 1810).

Robert Fulton's *Steamboat*, later known as the *Clermont*, on its maiden voyage up the Hudson to Albany on August 9, 1807. (Library of Congress)

A slightly embarrassing moment occurred for Fulton when Colonel Stevens, demanding to see his patent, uncovered the fact that Fulton had none. Tardily he applied for one (January 1809) and in the light of his prestigious commercial success had no difficulty obtaining it, though his specifications were so abstract and theoretical, filled with references to "plus pressure," "minus pressure," hull resistance, proportion of engine to hull, that it was hardly clear what he was patenting.

The truth was, there was simply nothing left to patent. The low-pressure engine, the high-pressure engine, the paddle wheel, and the screw propeller were all invented. The original design features of the *Clermont* and her sisters—the weak hull configuration and the unnecessary flywheel—were blunders soon to be discarded. Nevertheless, it was Fulton's unoriginal and ill-designed boat that after a quarter century of technically successful experiments suddenly made steam navigation an economic reality.

More than a reality, it was a flamboyant success. In addition to their four Hudson boats, Fulton and Livingston soon had a pair of ferries operating to Jersey City and making money almost as fast as the Hudson line. Of the first boat to operate on the every-half-hour service (fifteen to twenty minutes per trip) Fulton wrote, "She has had in her at one time 8 four-wheeled carriages 29 horses and 100 passengers, and could have taken 300 more."

The thoroughfare between the ferry slips on the New York side was renamed Fulton Street.

Turning to Long Island Sound, another promising territory, Fulton built two new steamboats named for the two partners. The *Fulton* and the *Chancellor Livingston* were both given conventional ship-hull configurations, though the unnecessary flywheel was still retained. The *Livingston* registered an important advance, adopting coal as fuel, a change that required no technical alteration. The press gave more attention to the huge "dining saloon," along either side of which ran two tiers of curtained berths. The lavish *Livingston* ran well over $100,000, the costliest structure of any kind built in America. She rapidly paid for herself.

Success put an intolerable strain on the Livingston monopoly. Colonel Stevens had never given in to his brother-in-law's arguments (even when Livingston enlisted Rachel Stevens to reinforce them) but had been too gentlemanly to challenge them in the river and in court. His final offer, to run only one boat in the Hudson against the monopolists' two, and that only if his boat proved faster in a trial, was unceremoniously turned down, and Fulton went so far as to threaten to ruin the New Brunswick line Stevens was planning with cut-rate competition unless Stevens quit New York waters. Stevens gave in, and as a result scored a sensational first himself. His *Phoenix,* planned for the Hudson and completed only a month after the *Clermont,* had lain idle for nearly two years, when in June 1809, under the command of twenty-one-year-old Robert Livingston Stevens, she steamed out through New York Bay into the Atlantic to become the first steamboat to navigate the open sea. Anchoring inshore every night, young Stevens reached Philadelphia in eight days, tying up at the Market Street Wharf at nine P.M. on June 23. By fall the *Phoenix* was established on John Fitch's old Delaware route from Philadelphia to Trenton.

John Stevens's *Phoenix,* the first steamboat to navigate the open sea, sailing from New York to Philadelphia in June 1809. (Smithsonian Photograph No. 5,058-A)

But even safely outside New York, the *Phoenix* made Fulton and Livingston nervous, and besides, Stevens was by no means abandoning the lucrative New York-to-Hoboken ferry business. So the two monopolists approached the colonel again, and the result was an expansion of the monopoly to include Stevens and to cover all the commercially important waters of the United States. Stevens was assigned the Delaware, the Chesapeake, the Santee, Savannah, and Connecticut Rivers, and the "Providence run," while Fulton and Livingston took New York, including Lake Champlain, the New Brunswick run, and, the plum, the Ohio-Mississippi system. Livingston's brother Edward, who had gone to New Orleans immediately after the Louisiana Purchase, was in a position to help get them a legislative monopoly. Edward won them a sympathetic ear from Governor William Claiborne, possibly aided by Claiborne's pique with Oliver Evans, who had declined to become excited over a duck-foot paddle contraption invented by Claiborne's brother. In any case, the governor granted Livingston and Fulton a Western monopoly of far greater potential value than their Eastern one, which was now giving them trouble.

While Nicholas Roosevelt went to Pittsburgh to build their first Western steamboat, the monopolists found themselves confronted by illegal but efficient competition on the Hudson. Albany promoters formed the "New Hudson Company" with two boats equipped with Evans engines. The situation was full of irony—barred from the Western rivers where his high-pressure engines were needed (and where he had an operating iron foundry) Evans was now installing them in the Hudson where low pressure would do just as well, and where high pressure constituted an unnecessary hazard. The skippers of the two Evans-equipped boats, the *Hope* and the *Perseverance,* won the distinction of being the first steamboat captains to employ the technique of tying down safety valves to extract maximum power. Evans condemned them not only for rashness but stupidity: "These boats outsailed Fulton's, but . . . they used steam 80 lbs to the inch. . . . So that it appears they excelled by using my inventions in a most bungling and disadvantageous manner. I could with the same engine produce double the power by shutting the steam off at ¼ the stroke." In his newest engines he was effecting this economy, probably the most important advance made in the high-pressure engine and the one that contributed most to its ultimate triumph.

Fulton and Livingston retained a leading New York lawyer, Thomas Addis Emmet, brother of the Irish patriot Robert Emmet, and he won a case for them against a New Jersey infringer, but advised his clients privately that their monopoly would not hold up much longer. Everything else aside, the monopoly rested in part on the New York legislature's claim of jurisdiction over all waters up to the low-tide mark on the Jersey shore, a claim that ran contrary to common law as well as common sense. The fact that one of the infringers, Aaron Ogden, was elected governor of New Jersey in 1812 lent weight to Emmet's forecast, though the legal war continued for a dozen years, until Chief Justice John Marshall delivered a crushing antimonopolist, profederal government decision, vindicating John Stevens's arguments. Meantime Nicholas Roosevelt completed the *New Orleans* and took her from Pittsburgh down river to Louisville (October 1811), where he conducted trials against the current. But the *New Orleans* with her low-pressure engine was not designed to navigate the whole river system. Roosevelt took her to New Orleans where she operated between New Orleans and Natchez for two years before hitting a snag and sinking. Other boats soon followed the trailblazer. The *Enterprise,* powered by a high-pressure engine built by Daniel French, one of the Pittsburgh pirates of Oliver Evans's engine and multitube boiler, steamed upstream from New Orleans to Louisville in 25 days and cleared 40 percent of her initial cost in her first year, a showing that a Cincinnati newspaper observed, "speaks plain to every understanding."

On the outbreak of the War of 1812, all three of the leaders of steam navigation, Evans, Fulton, and Stevens, advocated steam-powered warships. Evans's conception, provoked by British Admiral George Cockburn's depredations in Chesapeake Bay, was a vessel with two heavy guns, an armored deck, and water tanks that would permit her to submerge most of her hull on the approach of the enemy. Fulton's idea also called for two heavy guns, mounted on a twin hull enclosing a paddle wheel and engine. Instead of armor he proposed a gun deck of five-foot-thick timber. Fulton's ship was actually built to protect New York harbor, completed after the war's end, and used as a naval depot for many years.

Colonel Stevens's boat was a more sophisticated conception than either Evans's or Fulton's, and was also eventually built, though only after interminable interruptions that delayed her completion till the brink of the Civil War.

The British Admiralty, too, thought of steam for the War of 1812, but the war ending, cautiously reconverted what would have been the first active steam warship to merely another sailing sloop. Yet a steamship did play a role in the war,

The American oceangoing steamer *Savannah*, which crossed the Atlantic in 1819. (Library of Congress)

and an important one. Andrew Jackson commandeered the *Enterprise* to carry supplies for his army for the battle of New Orleans. The *Enterprise*'s useful participation had powerful symbolism: the battle, though fought after the peace had been signed at Ghent, preserved New Orleans and the mouth of the Mississippi for the United States. If the young republic's arms did not particularly shine elsewhere in the war, she nevertheless showed surprising muscle in defending this key but distant part of her thinly populated territory against a Britain that was at the pinnacle of her "Mistress of the Seas" career.

A month after Jackson's victory, Robert Fulton was visiting his incomplete warship on the Jersey side of the North River while still convalescing from a severe cold. He suffered a setback that apparently amounted to pneumonia and died a few days later, not yet quite fifty years old.

His fame was secure, and perhaps excessive, though generous Oliver Evans, visiting New York in 1817 and admiring the *Chancellor Livingston* (the Chancellor himself had died at Clermont in 1813), wrote: "Fulton is adored here and deserves it."

The notion that "Robert Fulton invented the steamboat" arose in the later nineteenth century when such shorthand technological history was acquiring popularity. The error was not confined to the American public and American publications. Early editions of the *Encyclopédie Larousse* identified Fulton as the *mécanicien des Etats-Unis* who "first applied steam to navigation." As the history of the steamboat was rediscovered, Larousse and other reference works shifted to crediting Fulton only with having made the steamboat "practical." Larousse, interestingly enough, contained no entry for Jouffroy d'Abbans till well into the twentieth century, when after a period as "inventor of steam navigation," he was reduced to "one of the inventors of steam navigation."

The latest Larousse is right: no one man invented the steamboat (or, for that matter, anything else). Fulton himself publicly credited Jouffroy, probably partly out of a desire to move the invention outside the United States, where he was in the odd position of being embarrassed at having succeeded where others had failed. His attempts to patent superficial features of his boats, such as rigging them with sails, were a little pathetic and more than a little silly. Fulton's achievements are sufficient to support his lasting fame, but John Fitch and John Stevens, who save for the fortuitous Livingston-Fulton meeting in Paris would surely be credited with the invention of the steamboat, should not be forgotten. Neither, surely, should Oliver Evans.

In practice, if not in theory, Stevens gave up on the high-pressure engine. Evans stuck to it, even though several of his boilers exploded and in the East low-pressure rivals were able to exploit the public's fears and drive the high-pressure engine from the rivers. The fears were well-founded, though not totally allayed by the low-pressure engine, which also occasionally blew up. But in the West, the high-pressure engine triumphed despite explosions, which, for that matter, were only one of the hazards—along with snags, bars, flood, fires—that incessantly plagued Western steamboats.

Stevens was sixty-four when Fulton died and sixty-eight when Evans died, but he had a major contribution yet to make in his septuagenarian years, which must await a later chapter.

A last footnote may be added here to the story of the maturation of the steamboat, a process that continued for several decades. Two months after Oliver Evans's death (June 20, 1819) a small schooner was sighted off the Irish coast apparently in distress, a plume of black smoke visible over her hull. An Admiralty cutter sailed out from Cork to offer assistance and discovered the stranger to be the *Savannah,* captain Moses Rogers (former skipper of Stevens's *Phoenix*), and in no need of aid. The smoke came from a chimney between main and fore masts; amidships on either side a paddle wheel churned. The cheeky Americans had brought one of their steamboats across the Atlantic!

8

The Covered-Bridge Builders

WHEN BRITISH TRAVELER ISAAC WELD started his journey through the new "States of North America" from Philadelphia in 1795, his stage coach crossed the Schuylkill on one of three floating bridges made of tree trunks chained together with beams laid lengthwise and decked over with planks. A heavy carriage sank the bridge slightly beneath the surface of the water. In the channel a span could be unbolted and swung open to permit boats to pass. The bridges were so frequently damaged or carried away by floods that when a flood was anticipated the cables anchoring the spans in place were released and the bridge allowed to float downstream to wherever it came ashore, where it could be secured.

Weld crossed the Schuylkill's makeshift bridge without mishap, but he ran into problems a little later at the Susquehanna. There was no bridge, only a ferry, and at the moment the river was frozen over. Nevertheless, the boat was pushed into the water and three black men, armed with clubs, were stationed in the bow to break the ice while four others, with iron-headed poles, pushed the boat forward. At the end of half an hour "their hands, arms, faces and hats, were glazed over entirely with a thick coat of ice, formed from the water which was dashed up by the reiterated strokes of their clubs. Two hours elapsed before one half of the way was broken . . . the clubs were shivered to pieces; the men were quite exhausted; and having suffered the boat to remain stationary for a minute or two in a part where the ice was remarkably thick, it was frozen up, so that the utmost exertions of the crew and passengers united were unable to extricate it."

For his American travels, prudent Weld carried a brace of pistols, and a few shots in the air attracted the attention of people on shore. A "batteau," a flat-bottomed rowboat, was sent out to assist. The rowboat was slid up on the ice in front, and rocked until it cracked the ice. Its three-man crew crowded into the stern to raise the little craft's bow, hauled it up again on the ice by boathooks, and rocked it again. "In this manner we got on, and at the end of three hours and ten minutes found ourselves again upon dry land," the Englishman recorded.

Among other crossings Weld made were another fording of the Susquehanna between Lancaster and York where the Columbia rapids were negotiated by rowing up against the stream under the shore, then striking for the opposite side under the protection of some islands in the stream, and a bridge over the James at Richmond, half-pontoon and half on log casements filled with stones—"there is no railing, and the boards with which it is covered are so loose, that it is dangerous to ride a horse across it that is not accustomed to it." He had other adventures, but his bridge-and-ferry experiences alone might have explained the sentiment with which he closed his account of the American trip, pronouncing himself "well pleased at having seen as much of [America] as I have done; but I shall leave it without a sigh, and without entertaining the slightest wish to revisit it."

Bridges were badly needed all up and down the river-striped East coast, acutely in the coastal cities, and most acutely of all in Philadelphia, with its tree-trunk pontoons. The trouble was not so much that they often floated off completely, but that with river traffic on the Schuylkill growing heavier every year, the nuisance of opening the navigation span had grown intolerable. What Philadelphia needed was a high-level fixed bridge, or, as the High Street (modern Market Street) businessmen called it, a "permanent" bridge. As early as 1787 Philadelphia's *Columbian Magazine* had published a design for a bridge consisting of four 100-foot timber arches with two piers in the river. The design was presented anonymously, but may possibly have been the work of Tom Paine, whose mind was as rationally innovative in engineering as in politics. An arresting feature for most of *Columbian*'s readers was that the bridge was to be completely covered in, with roof and sides to protect structural members against weather. At about the same time Paine tried to sell Gouverneur Morris in New York on the idea of an iron bridge, to be operated as a private toll crossing over the Harlem River. Only one iron bridge had ever been built, the celebrated iron arch over the Severn at Coalbrookdale in England, erected by ironmasters John Wilkinson and Abraham Darby partly as a demonstration of their product (and preserved today as a British national monument). Morris shied away from an iron bridge on grounds of cost—no foundry in the United States could cast arch ribs of the size required—and when Philadelphia's city fathers did the same, Paine took his model to England. There it was eventually erected over the Wear River, the second metal bridge ever built.

Back home in Philadelphia, Charles Willson Peale, artist and proprietor of Peale's Museum, offered a design for the Schuylkill crossing. Peale sketched a gigantic wooden arch, 390 feet long, strengthened by heavy truss railings, and took out the first U.S. patent for a bridge design. He also wrote the first U.S. bridge-engineering treatise, "An Essay on Building Wooden Bridges," in which he erroneously argued against covering on the grounds that the rotting effect of alternate wet and dry could be countered by making tight joints and liberally applying tar. High Street's businessmen did not buy Peale's design, but it may have stirred them to organize the Schuylkill Permanent Bridge Company with Judge Richard Peters as president.

To most of the promoters, "Permanent Bridge" implied stone, and Judge Peters found a European engineer experienced in stone-arch bridges: William Weston, a Britisher who had been hired to build turnpikes in Pennsylvania. Weston's proposal of a three-span stone arch over the Schuylkill was approved, and work began on the requisite four foundations: two shore abutments and two heavy piers in the stream. All four proved to be arduous tasks, requiring the greater part of a year. The technology used was Roman-medieval, but new to America. One of the pier foundations involved building a cofferdam in the river, probably the first, and so far certainly the largest, cofferdam built in America, consisting of a tight circle of timbers driven into the river bottom to provide a pumped-out, shallow-water working space. Just outside the cofferdam was anchored a floating stage on which four horses turned a treadwheel lifting a quarter-ton oak ram, probably the largest piece of engineering equipment yet seen in America. With it the pier foundations were driven to bedrock at 41 feet below high water.

The laborious foundation work was completed with a cornerstone bearing a somewhat cryptic inscription:

TFCSOTSPBWL October xviii MDCCC

The stone mason entrusted with the cornerstone had found himself embarrassed for room to carve the entire message he had been given: "This first corner stone of the Schuylkill Permanent Bridge was laid October 18, 1800," and excused himself to a curious observer, "By the time they dig up this here stone, the people will be much more learned than you and I be." But the foundation work exhausted the capital Judge Peters had been able to gather for the whole work, and plans for stone arches had to be dropped. Weston had sailed home to England, whence he sent a plan for iron arches, but United States foundries were still not up to casting large iron members, and importing them from England remained prohibitive.

That left wood. Neither Paine's nor Peale's design would fit on the four foundations now standing. But Judge Peters had read about a new kind of wooden bridge built by a Massachusetts Yankee named Timothy Palmer, and journeyed north to inspect Palmer's work and interview the builder.

Palmer, a native of Newburyport, Massachusetts, proved to be a rawboned, fifty-two-year-old master carpenter and "bridge architect" with a big Roman nose and his hair in a queue. He had built a bridge over the Merrimack 3 miles above Newburyport, connecting Deer Island in the river with either shore, and had repeated his design over the Kennebec and Connecticut rivers, the Piscataqua Great Bay, and across the Little Falls of the Potomac at Georgetown. As a result of his interview with Judge Peters, Palmer appeared in Philadelphia in the summer of 1804 accompanied by his assistant, Samuel Carr, and four skilled New England workmen. Filling out his crew with local carpenters, he dazzled his employers with the rapidity of his construction. Temporarily supported by timber

Timothy Palmer. (Richard Sanders Allen Collection)

falsework in the river, his spans rapidly grew from the piers to the foundations and across the middle of the river till by January 1, 1805, the bridge was opened to traffic. With workmen still busy in the overhead structural members, the first wagons and carriages passed through.

The passers-through even more than the observers on shore were struck by the novelty of the bridge's design. Its basic support consisted predictably of three arches mounted on the four foundations William Weston had built, but the long, flat, elliptical arches (the center span measured 194 feet, 10 inches) were strengthened by a series of heavy vertical and diagonal timber members that rose from the arches to connect with an overhead horizontal "chord" that ran the length of the bridge on either side of the roadway. The two chords were joined by horizontal timbers, transverse and diagonal, over the roadway. Each span was thus an arch strengthened by a truss.

Thirteen years earlier, in his Merrimack River (Deer Island) Bridge, Palmer had built the first known arch-truss bridge in America. There were surprisingly few even in Europe, though the third edition of *Encyclopaedia Britannica,* published in Edinburgh in the 1790s and enthusiastically pirated in Philadelphia, showed the form. A truss is a structural element based on the triangle, and derives its value from the fact that unlike a square or polygon it cannot be distorted but only broken. Medieval European engineers had first exploited the truss for bridges, and Andrea Palladio's sixteenth-century *Treatise on Architecture,* translated into English in 1742, pictured four different types. Whether Palmer had ever read either Palladio or the *Britannica* is uncertain; the probability is that he simply invented his bridge by elaborating the ancient kingpost and queenpost forms used since time immemorial for short crossings. The kingpost consisted of a pair of right triangles sharing a common side in the form of a vertical post. A pair of such kingpost trusses could easily carry a roadway, or for that matter support a mill floor or barn, between them. The queenpost truss was a stretched-out version of the king in which the two triangles were separated by a square or rec-

113

Palmer's "Permanent Bridge" over the Schuylkill at Philadelphia, completed in 1805.
(Richard Sanders Allen Collection)

tangular panel, which the triangles at either end held rigidly in place. The queen-post could span a slightly broader stream than the king, but both were limited to very short crossings. To bridge wide rivers without planting many piers in the stream, European engineers, as represented by Palladio, had evolved the panel truss, a series of rectangles or squares with diagonals to give them the strength of the undistortable triangle. Yet European engineers had shown little confidence in the truss by itself, and favored using it to reinforce the ancient, dependable arch.

Two wooden bridges that may have been truss-strengthened were built in America before Timothy Palmer's patent application, one at Norwich, Connecticut, and one at Bellows Falls, Vermont. Little is known of the first, the Leffingwell Bridge, built in 1764 over the Shetucket River, other than the name of its builder, John Bliss, and the fact that it was 124 feet long, but the second, a toll venture on the Boston-Montreal road erected by Colonel Enoch Hale in 1785, is believed to have been supported by a complicated timber pier cantilevered out above a rock in midstream, with two clear spans of about 100 feet reaching the shore on either side.

Palmer's Deer Island bridge was unrelated to either of these designs. It consisted of two independent arches, the longer of 160 feet, meeting on the rocky island. Over the Great Bay of the Piscataqua in New Hampshire he built a 244-foot clear span, probably the longest in the world at the time.

Over the Schuylkill, in addition to his three trussed arches, Palmer built "wing walls," or approach trestles, of 750 feet, making the whole structure 1,300 feet long. Because the upper chord was straight (curving down, however, at either end toward the abutments), the truss panels varied in height over the three arches, from 20 feet deep at the arch crown (top) to 35 at the arch springing, directly over the pier or abutment. The bridge looked exactly like what it was—wood seeking to imitate stone in the traditional arch form.

The Permanent Bridge differed from Palmer's earlier designs in a significant way. His New England bridges had all taken the path of least resistance by allowing the roadway to hump with the rise of the arches, so that wagons had to climb

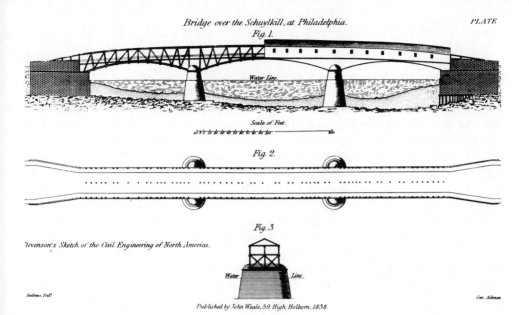

Bridge over the Schuylkill, at Philadelphia.
Fig. 1.

PLATE

Water Line.

Scale of Feet.

Fig. 2.

Fig. 3.

'tevenson's Sketch of the Civil Engineering of North America.

Water   Line

Andrews. Del!

Geo. Aikman

Published by John Weale, 59, High Holborn, 1838.

Drawings showing the structure of the Permanent Bridge, from David Stevenson, *Sketch of the Civil Engineering of North America,* 1838. (Richard Sanders Allen Collection)

uphill toward the bridge's midpoint. The much heavier traffic anticipated at Philadelphia brought more consideration of the roadway. In agreement with Judge Peters, who took closest interest in every stage of design and construction, Palmer built a broad, 42-foot-wide deck, divided down the middle to keep traffic separated, and nearly level, a condition achieved by spending a little more money and adding a little more timber.

Palmer intended to leave the Permanent uncovered, like his New England bridges, to showcase his novel structural system. But when Judge Peters pressed him on covering, the bluff Yankee readily admitted that the Permanent Bridge would last twice or three times as long—"perhaps forty years" as against ten or twelve—if given weatherboarding and roofing. Judge Peters personally drew sketches of the covering, which was entrusted to prominent Philadelphia builder Owen Biddle. Based on the very best aesthetic principles of 1804, the long, continuous main housing included simulated colonnades and forty-four oval windows decorated with shutters, while the eight lower panels (four on either side) directly over the piers and abutments were made to look like masonry, with fake stone blocks whose deception was ingeniously heightened by sprinkling stone dust on the fresh gray paint. William Rush, a locally noted "naval sculptor"—he had carved and painted the figureheads for the U.S.S. *Constellation*—was commissioned to create wooden statues representing Commerce and Agriculture for either end of the bridge. Finally, a stone obelisk on the eastern (Philadelphia) bank congratulated all "those who by enterprising, arduous, and persevering exertions achieved this extremely beneficial improvement."

That was meant chiefly for Judge Peters, whose exertions in favor of the bridge had indeed been enterprising, arduous, and persevering. For Timothy Palmer, whose contribution had been smooth, expert, and deceptively facile, a handsome silver tankard and tray were suitably inscribed, while his portrait was done by a visiting French miniaturist. Palmer appreciated Philadelphia's patrician generosity—the best he had done in New England by way of gratuity was a beaver hat. He had meantime started another Middle State commission, a two-arch span over the Delaware at Easton, Pennsylvania, which he planned from the start as a covered bridge and which proved to be his longest-lasting monument, its legend, "Erected 1805 T. Palmer" greeting wagoners for the next eighty years. After completing it Palmer retired from building bridges himself, though he continued to supply designs.

Not only did the covered bridge's covering fully vindicate Judge Peters's belief that it would protect the structural members against rain, snow, and excessive summer dryness, but it soon demonstrated many other advantages. It kept snow from accumulating on the roadway (though New England tollkeepers had to snow-pave their bridges in winter to accommodate sleighs). The barnlike siding and roof reassured horses and cattle, which often did not like to venture out over rushing water. When outdoor advertising arrived, the exterior provided space for religious and secular messages, promoting patent medicines and chewing tobacco along with quotations from the Bible. The dark interior provided a romantic setting for young lovers in wagons and buggies, and spectator sport for farm boys hidden in the roof rafters. Finally, it added a memorable touch to the American landscape, a long, weathered, gable-roofed shed hanging strangely over the river gorge, a tantalizing mystery with just a hint of its structural meaning in diagonal timbers glimpsed through a row of windows.

But most important, the covered bridge supplied a technical solution to one of the problems that blocked the young country's aspiring growth. The brilliance of the solution was not fully realized in Timothy Palmer's arch-truss design. Ultimate perfection lay not in addition but in subtraction.

The same year that Palmer built Philadelphia's Permanent Bridge, 1804, another self-taught New England engineer patented a radically improved bridge design. Theodore Burr, born in Torringford, Connecticut, in 1771, studied Palladio's designs and tried out a number of his own before hitting on a radical step forward: an arch supporting a structurally independent kingpost truss. Burr's truss assumed a role coequal, if not actually superior to the arch, an arrangement that brought cost savings because the arch did not need as much timber as in Palmer's design. It proved so successful that its inventor's name became a name for the bridge, often lower-cased and also often misspelled (bur, birr, bhurr). Economy alone was not responsible. Burr's truss-arch proved capable of an astounding reach. When the Pennsylvania legislature authorized four bridges in the 100-mile stretch of the Susquehanna between Northumberland and McCall's Ferry, Burr ambitiously went after all four contracts, and landed three. Adding two more jobs over the North Branch of the Susquehanna at Berwick, Pennsylvania, and over the Susquehanna in Tidewater Maryland, he found himself financially overextended. The legislature was paying him largely in stock shares of the bridges' future tolls, and he had trouble meeting payrolls with more than promises, especially when Pennsylvania merchants refused to accept the scrip

The Burr Arch-Truss Bridge. Patented by Theodore Burr in 1804, it is represented in a model built by the inventor. (Pennsylvania State Museum)

Burr borrowed from New York banks. "Gentlemen," he wrote a supply company, "your friend T. Burr is perplexed and vexed at least fifty times in one day." He kept his humor and somehow kept the loyalty of his irregularly paid work force.

At Northumberland an arch span came loose, sinking a construction gondola and floating off downstream. Burr retrieved the arch and had it back up in two weeks. A worse accident hit the McCall's Ferry job, where the broad Susquehanna is squeezed between high hills, creating a wild gorge some 360 feet wide and a stream 100 feet deep. Burr built his arches along the shore, swinging them out into the stream when complete. After battling rains, floods, and storms all fall, he had one arch ready to go in December 1814. Ice forming upstream cracked on the rocks and jammed the narrow pass. A thaw followed by a new freeze created a mountain of ice that threatened the floats and falsework (timber support) carrying the arch. Burr conceived a bold solution that courageous workmen carried out—cutting the arch in two, letting go the floats, and sliding the arch and false-work on the ice to get it into position. The workmen had to bridge an open space offshore, then chop away the peak of the ice mountain to make a level path. Waist-deep in icy slush, they managed to get wooden runners under the mass of timber with no other mishap than one man falling 50 feet into a patch of open water; rescued, he was back on the job a few days later. Eight capstans slewed the arch around to a transverse position, but hauling it upstream a few hundred feet proved more than the crew could manage. Resourceful Burr enlisted all the farmers in the neighborhood, reminding them of their stake in the great bridge. The county on one side of the river was Lancaster, on the other York, and Burr organized a new War of the Roses by pitting Lancaster against York in competition to get the two arch halves in place. Every day scores of farmers pushed and hauled, until late on the night of February 1, 1815, the final wedge locked the two halves together, and the last piece of falsework was knocked away. Illuminated by huge bonfires on either bank, the giant arch hung in the air. Burr supplied rum all around and everybody, regular work force and volunteers, stayed drunk for two days.

The McCall's Ferry Bridge had a clear span of 360 feet, four inches, the longest span of any bridge in the world in its day, and perhaps the longest wooden arch ever built, including modern laminated timber arches supporting sports arena roofs. Three years later, in the early spring of 1818, a tremendous ice jam ripped Burr's arches from their abutments, trusses and all, carried the whole covered bridge downstream and wrecked it beyond salvage. Burr's entire commission was in toll stock, and he was wiped out. Four years later he died broke and was apparently buried in potter's field—his grave has never been found.

With the destruction of the McCall's Ferry Bridge, the long-span championship reverted to Philadelphia, though not to Timothy Palmer. In the interim a non-Yankee engineer, Württemberg-born Lewis Wernwag, who had probably emigrated to America to avoid military service, and had become one of Philadelphia's best-known mechanics, turned to bridge building at the age of forty-one with spectacular results. His first construction was a drawbridge to carry the Frankford-Bristol Turnpike over Neshaminy Creek northeast of Philadelphia. His second was in response to the demand of the city's businessmen for an immediate second crossing of the Schuylkill, at Upper Ferry (such had been the success of Timothy Palmer's Permanent Bridge). Wernwag proposed a single arch-truss of 400 feet—five years before Theodore Burr's 360-foot McCall's Ferry span. The design scared his backers, who felt that a 340-foot span was daring enough. The reduced length dictated an abutment in deep water at the western side, and Wernwag had considerable trouble reaching bedrock. Even at the 340-foot length he had to arch his whole bridge, but he cleverly reduced the amount of hump in the roadway by mounting it atop its parallel supporting arches and giving it a larger radius (flatter curvature) than that of the arches. Roadway and arches were connected by long trusses running along either side and down the middle of the bridge.

Wernwag also used iron in an innovative way, holding his huge wooden structural members slightly apart with iron links and screw bolts that could be tightened if the timbers shrank, and which provided an easy way to replace individual beams.

On the day in 1812 scheduled for the removal of the pile-mounted falsework supporting the bridge, some of Wernwag's sponsors were a little worried by the widely voiced popular apprehension—when the supporting timbers were knocked out, would the bridge fall down? Wernwag picked the party up on the porch of Sheridan's Tavern and led them down to the bridge and out onto the scaffolding. He had them finger the blocks at the top of the falsework, immediately under the arches. "They're all loose!" Wernwag nodded. He had ordered them loosened the day before, and the bridge had been standing freely on its abutments for twenty-four hours.

To silence lingering skepticism, Wernwag loaded a wagon with twenty-two tons of stone and had it hauled across his bridge by sixteen horses.

The longest bridge in the world until McCall's Ferry was completed, Philadelphia's new marvel was immediately dubbed the "Colossus." A more descriptive phrase was found by visiting English actress Fanny Kemble. Wernwag had demonstrated an aesthetic as well as an engineering sense, and the graceful, windowed covering of his bridge, which completely enclosed the roadway and extended down to protect the lower arches, he painted white, giving the impression, in the actress's words, of "a white scarf thrown across the stream."

Wernwag built many more bridges and achieved the financial success that escaped Theodore Burr, but the main technical triumph was Burr's. Wernwag's patent was in fact a step backward, making the arch once more, as in Timothy Palmer's design, the principal element and assigning the truss merely the mission of evenly distributing an eccentric load. Burr's lighter arch was easier to build, and after his death his design was pirated far into the South and Midwest. Burr arch-trusses were built in profusion through the nineteenth and twentieth centuries (they lasted, too; many Burrs eighty and a hundred years old are in service today). No other timber bridge design ever achieved such long-run popularity, but it remained for another Connecticut Yankee to carry Burr's conception to its logical conclusion.

Ithiel Town was a New Haven church architect who built in New England and around the country. In place after place with a river-crossing problem, Town noted, there was plenty of wood in the surrounding forest, but skilled labor was beyond hiring. It was in North Carolina in 1820 that he had his inspiration. A significant difference between an arch and a truss was that the arch was hard to make and the truss easy. The Burr truss panels stood by themselves, but were not strong

Wernwag's Colossus, a single span over the Schuylkill at Upper Ferry, Philadelphia, with the Fairmount Water Works in the background. (Library of Congress)

enough to sustain live loading without the help of the arch. Why not simply make them stronger by adding more wood? Town sketched what must be the simplest civil-engineering innovation ever, got it patented, and made a fortune. His design was nothing more than a lattice of overlapping diagonals, and he named it the Town Lattice Mode.

This wonderful bridge could be put up in a few days by a single carpenter with a few unskilled helpers. Except for the horizontal chords at top and bottom there were no heavy structural members, only the light planks that made up the diagonals, pinned together with trunnels, the wooden pegs used by colonial farmers in building their houses. An admiring wag wrote that it could be built by the mile and cut off by the yard. Town fitted the Yankee image—not only an inventive genius, but a shrewd promoter. Instead of bothering to build his bridge himself, he advertised the design and kept a sharp eye out for pirates, whom he treated with genial lenience, charging them two dollars a foot instead of the one dollar he took from honest applicants.

In 1830 Town began receiving competition from the Long Truss, invented by Colonel Stephen H. Long, a West Pointer from Hopkinton, New Hampshire. The Long design was a series of box panels crossed by heavy diagonals, with added bracing underneath from the abutments and above in the form of a triangle crowning the truss at midspan. As in all truss-bridge designs, the two trusses making up a bridge were firmly joined over and under the roadway, creating a rigid cage.

The Long truss never achieved the popularity of the Town or Burr, but it probably inspired William Howe of Spencer, Massachusetts, to patent a similar design with a momentous alteration. Every structural member of a bridge is either in compression or in tension—either being pressed together or pulled apart by the weight of the bridge and the loading. Wood, though strong in compression, is weak in tension. It occurred to Howe that a much stronger bridge could be created if the vertical members of a Long-type truss panel, which were in tension, were made of iron. Howe's patent, dated 1840, came in response to the demands of an entirely new loading factor for bridges, the railroad, and led straight to the modern steel-truss railroad bridge.

Thus the old covered bridge of romantic legend made an invaluable contribution to a realm of technology not yet even born when Timothy Palmer spanned the Schuylkill.

9

Francis Cabot Lowell, Boston Pirate

In 1811 A THIRTY-SIX-YEAR-OLD AMERICAN of gentlemanly bearing and business knowledgeability arrived in Manchester, England, a town that had astounded the world in the past generation by a burst of vitality that had doubled, redoubled, and re-redoubled its size around a mushrooming nucleus of smoke-streaming textile mills. Francis Cabot Lowell of Boston was welcomed by Manchester's owners and superintendents and escorted through their whirring, pounding, shrieking factories whose looms were turning out cloth by the mile. Cabot owed his V.I.P. treatment in part to his own commanding but engaging presence, but mostly to his occupation, that of American merchant. American merchants bought Manchester cloth; Lowell was a customer.

What his British hosts did not know, and what gentlemanly Francis Cabot Lowell neglected to tell them, was that he had just quit being a merchant and was now in the first stage of embarking on a fresh career as their manufacturing competitor. Had they had an inkling of what was going through their affable guest's mind they would have escorted him right out of Manchester, possibly with tar and feathers.

Whether Lowell had come to England expressly for the purpose of industrial espionage is unknown. Until a few years before, his mercantile career, and indeed his whole life, had been a success story—not on the already beloved American up-from-poverty model, but in a more normal up-from-the-upper-middle fashion. His father and grandfather Lowell had been Boston ministers, but the Cabots on his

Francis Cabot Lowell, from *New England Magazine,* 1890. This silhouette is the only known portrait of the father of cloth manufacture. (Library of Congress)

mother's side were merchants, and though he went to Harvard like a church-intended scholar, he was rusticated for starting an unclerkly bonfire in the Yard, and earned his degree in 1793 after being tutored in mathematics in nearby Bridgewater. Entering commercial life under the wing of a Cabot uncle, he sailed as supercargo up and down the coast and on a voyage to France where he gave early evidence of his capacity for dissimulation by helping to fool boarding parties from blockading British cruisers. He was soon in business for himself on the Long Wharf, and forming commercial alliances with Boston's leading merchant-patricians: importer Nathan Appleton; Patrick Tracy Jackson, whose sister Hannah he married; and Uriah Cotting, whom he helped to finance a major Boston improvement—the India Wharf and Broad Street development, by which a congeries of little old colonial warehouses were replaced by stately five-story brick structures fronting on a handsome avenue. As the name India Wharf implied, Lowell and his business friends were trading profitably with the Far East, with Lowell especially active in the Canton branch.

Then came catastrophe from Washington. Britain and France, blockading and counterblockading each other, were treating neutral rights with scant ceremony, and the British Navy, short of men, had taken to impressing sailors from American merchant vessels under the pretext (and often the reality) of their being British subjects. President Jefferson, seeking a means of pressure on the belligerents, hit on the device of an embargo cutting off American trade. Unfortunately, the measure had little impact on Britain or France, but brought ruin to businessmen throughout New England and New York. Relaxed in 1809 and 1810, sending American exports to a record high, the embargo was restored again over vehement protests from the North, and ultimately followed up by a declaration of war (June 18, 1812) just as the British government decided to give in. Territorial greed of the American West and South (aimed at Canada and Florida) played as large a role as neutral rights in bringing on the war, against which congressmen from the Northeast voted almost unanimously, and during which New England even came to contemplate secession.

Yet one segment of New England business remained unruffled. Samuel Slater and his fellow cotton spinners had no objection whatsoever to the cutting off of trade with Britain, which left them as sole suppliers of machine-spun, hand-loomed cotton cloth to the American market. Francis Cabot Lowell, one of the brightest and boldest minds in Boston, may well have thought of switching from commerce to industry before sailing to England with his family in 1810 on what was labeled a vacation trip in the interest of his health (which was, it is true, frail). The fact that he settled not in the English Midlands but in Edinburgh lends support to the theory that he had arrived without a preconceived plan. On the other hand, despite the presence of many Tory Bostonian friends of the Lowells, Edinburgh seems an odd choice for a health spa, and an interest in Britain's now booming Industrial Revolution was evinced in a visit he made to Scotland's largest ironworks.

However the idea blossomed in his mind, when his friend Nathan Appleton visited Edinburgh late in 1811, he found Lowell on the point of departure for Manchester. To Appleton, Lowell freely confided his intention of learning everything he could about the English textile industry, above all the famed Cartwright power loom. The Reverend Edmund Cartwright, with whom Robert Fulton had talked steam and internal combustion engines, had perfected his loom in 1785, but it had not become widely used by the time of Samuel Slater's smuggling act of 1789, and in 1811 remained, rather surprisingly, a British monopoly. One reason probably was that demand for power weaving could only logically arise when power spinning had created a surplus of yarn. In England the surplus had been produced by about a decade of Arkwright's spinning machinery. Slater, Almy, and Brown had started their Pawtucket spinning operation in the 1790s, and though the smaller scale of their enterprises had had a somewhat slower effect, by the time Lowell sailed to Britain, the yarn from New England's 300 little spinning mills was piling up in the cottages of thousands of hand weavers, and some businessmen and mechanics were trying to build a power loom.

Through early 1812, Lowell sojourned in Manchester, visiting mills and shops, watching the machinery work with unflagging interest, plying operatives and management with unobtrusive questions. The mill owners may have been happy to talk about their machines to a congenial listener. Many people, hand weavers and their sympathizers, were bitterly hostile to the devices. During the past year, the masked nocturnal raiders who called themselves Luddites had attacked mills and destroyed machinery at Nottingham and elsewhere.

Lowell evidently did not consider his conduct to be a breach of ethics, doubtless rationalizing on grounds similar to those of the plantation owners who pirated Whitney's cotton gin. Besides, espionage and piracy were standard operating procedure in the British textile industry, whose owners had made their spectacular progress by tirelessly stealing and improving each other's mechanical advances.

In addition to the Manchester weaving machinery, Lowell seems to have borrowed another quite different British idea. Thirty miles from Edinburgh the utopian-minded businessman Robert Owen had established his New Lanark manufactory, and surrounded it with model housing for his workers. Mill owners in Lancashire, who recruited their labor from the local poorhouses, did not trouble themselves with such niceties. The poorhouse resource was not available to American manufacturers, and Lowell might well have perceived in Owen's altruistic design the material advantages of a factory-town environment that would attract workers.

. Sailing for home on the eve of war, Lowell and his family were captured along with their ship by a British frigate and taken to Halifax, where his baggage was thoroughly searched, so perhaps it was as well that he had made few notes or sketches of Manchester machinery. Back in Boston he made a bold pronouncement: American industry would soon compete in textile manufacturing with the British. He announced the organization of the "Boston Manufacturing Company," and invited family and close friends to participate, offering the first opportunity to his Cabot uncles. But the two old gentlemen, bred-and-born Boston merchant-venturers, would have nothing to do with manufacturing, a vocation neither socially approved nor financially proven. Lowell descended a generation and approached his brother-in-law Patrick Tracy Jackson, who proved as enthusiastic as Lowell himself, advancing $20,000 and agreeing to participate in management. Several other merchants then joined in with sums of five to ten thousand, and Lowell himself invested $15,000, bringing the company's starting capitalization to $100,000, an impressive sum indeed for a totally new enterprise. It reflected the combination of recent accumulation of shipping profits and present total stagnation of commerce thanks to Jefferson's pacifist embargo (continued under Madison), but also a remarkable confidence in Lowell's presentation of his project (even if his uncles refused to be impressed). Every investor was a personal friend.

Fundamental to the success of the Boston Manufacturing Company was Lowell's ability to reproduce the Cartwright loom, or a reasonable facsimile, and the necessary auxiliary equipment. Unlike Samuel Slater, Lowell had no experience with machinery, and despite high intelligence, a fair mechanical aptitude, and Patrick Jackson's energetic help, he slaved in a loft in Broad Street for a year without success. Frustrated but not defeated, he sought expert help. He first applied to Jacob Perkins, the Amesbury iron master who had admired David Wilkinson's lathe, and who had become known for a number of improvements in textile machinery. Perkins was interested in mechanized weaving, but he had ambitions of his own and declined Lowell's offer. He recommended a youthful, thirty-four-year-old friend and former employee, Paul Moody.

Moody was another of New England's gifted village mechanics. His background was even more clearly middle class than Whitney's or David Wilkinson's. All six of his brothers received a genteel education at Dummer Academy, an opportunity

Paul Moody passed up out of a preference for working with his hands. He had helped design and build a Slater-type mill (mechanical spinning, hand weaving) to turn out cotton satinet for a manufacturer at Amesbury. By 1814, when he joined Lowell's enterprise, Lowell had chosen the village of Waltham, up the Charles River from Boston, as his manufacturing site. Jackson had purchased the land, buildings, and water rights of a small paper mill. The two partners had fabricated two looms, neither of which worked, and the shareholders were beginning to fidget.

Moody commenced methodically by building and equipping a machine shop in Waltham. He then set to work to perfect Lowell's pirated loom, using every means that came to hand, buying some machine components and fabricating others. Together with Lowell, he checked out all the shops tinkering with textile machinery in New England, in New Jersey, in Maryland—borrowing, stealing, buying, trading. Finally, in the fall of 1814, partner Nathan Appleton was invited to drive out to Waltham to see the loom work.

"I well recollect the state of admiration and satisfaction with which we sat by the hour, watching the beautiful movement of this new and wonderful machine," wrote Appleton with fitting reverence, "destined as it evidently was, to change the character of the textile industry."

By this time Lowell had matured his plans. Logic alone governed his decision to introduce a radical advance over the British system of manufacture by concentrating all the stages of production—cleaning, carding, spinning, weaving, and finishing—in a single large building. To Paul Moody he entrusted the task of fitting all the machinery—new, old, bought, built, cannibalized—into the concept of totally integrated production.

Moody bought several metal lathes, undoubtedly copies of David Wilkinson's slide lathe, from a foundry in Easton, Massachusetts, and spent the winter of 1814–15 modifying the machinery and installing it in the huge brick mill Lowell had built fronting on the Charles. The building was architecturally simple, but attractive and thoroughly functional: four stories of working machinery surmounted by a clerestory (a row of windows set in the angle of two roof gables) and topped by a cupola. The floors and partitions were made up of 6,000 board feet of lumber sold to the company by stockholder Uriah Cotting. Jacob Perkins fabricated a waterwheel of his own patent design, and by February 1815 the Boston Manufacturing Company was ready to start turning out the first factory-made cloth in America.

No details are known of the original Waltham machinery. Appleton described the loom as "different" from the Cartwright, and it was evidently inferior to the newest British loom, the "Scotch," designed by William Horrocks in 1813, which made its appearance in Rhode Island in 1817 and eventually superseded the Moody machine in the Boston Company's mills as well as others. Yet the Moody loom, which Lowell and Jackson prudently patented in their own names, was a success and a spectacular one, when combined with the other Waltham machines. Besides improved versions of the Slater-Arkwright spinning machinery of two decades earlier, Moody created an innovative dressing machine for strengthening warp thread by sizing, preparatory to introducing it to the power loom. Lowell had brought back from England a drawing he had surreptitiously made of such a machine, but the rough sketch was of only slight help, and Moody encountered a difficult problem: the wooden rollers that carried the yarn into the sizing solution swelled from moisture. He tried to cover the rollers with pewter, but could not get satisfactory pewter shells from his foundry. Moody's brother David suggested trying soapstone molds for casting pewter, and it occurred to Moody that the rollers themselves might be made of soapstone. The idea worked, and the resulting "Waltham dresser," clearly superior to its British antecedent, served the American textile industry with little change till the Civil War. Moody's "double speeder," an improved version of British roving machinery for twisting the cotton slivers observed by Lowell, is said to have profited from Lowell's own contribution of mathematical calculations.

The quantity of cloth produced at Waltham in 1815 was small—only one loom was operating—but Lowell's concept of an integrated manufacturing operation from raw cotton to finished cloth was proved sound. The "Waltham System," destined to supply the basis for American textile-industry technique, was born.

A fundamental component of the Waltham System was one that proved an enduring principle in mass production—standardization of the product on lines of maximum simplicity. Fancy weaves, in which the British and French excelled, Lowell ruled out. Likewise the new British printed cottons, or "calicos." The Waltham product was a plain cotton sheeting, but stronger and more durable than the cheap sheeting long imported from India, and, as Lowell anticipated, highly marketable in the frontier West.

Lowell had given no thought to the actual mechanics of marketing, the only aspect of his scheme that he had not worked out in advance, and the first small quantities of cloth, given to Mrs. Isaac Bowers's shop in Cornhill Street, Boston, brought a disappointment. Mrs. Browers's customers were too status-conscious to buy any but imported goods. But Nathan Appleton had recently set up a commission house called the B. C. Ward Company, which sold goods through auctioneers. A trial by this route was an instant success, the auctioneer getting prompt sales at thirty cents a yard, five cents more than Lowell had estimated. Ward was made exclusive agent at a commission of 1 percent, later raised to 1¼ percent.

Nathan Appleton profited, and so did all the little band of original shareholders in the Boston Manufacturing Company. A 12½ percent dividend in 1817 was followed by semiannual dividends of 8 to 13 percent; by 1822 the shareholders had received 104½ percent on their investments. Such handsome profits encouraged reinvestment and guaranteed rapid expansion.

One of the most talked-about features of the Waltham System was its labor force. Where Slater had employed children, Lowell recruited young women. Women were better able to handle the looms and most of the other machinery than were children, and at $2 a week were cheaper than men. More important, they were available, or rather, could be made so. Only two occupations were seriously open to women, domestic service and teaching. The second paid poorly, and the first imposed limitations on freedom. But New England farmers were not about to let their daughters go off to work in a mill town without any moral and physical protection. Lowell anticipated their objections and met them with the leaf borrowed from Robert Owen's book. He built boarding houses, each under the supervision of a house mother, where the girls were given good meals and decent lodging for a modest charge against their $2 a week pay. Each evening they were all securely locked in. He also built churches, indispensable not only for religious instruction but as part of a normal New England environment, and planted several thousand shade trees.

In the aftermath of the War of 1812, the success of Waltham was conspicuous in its contrast with the rest of New England industry. Britain's 100-plus power looms, turning out a variety of weaves and the new calico prints, easily undersold Rhode Island's now antiquated combination of factory spindles and home hand-weaving. Visiting Pawtucket, Francis Cabot Lowell and Nathan Appleton found David Wilkinson's machine shop silent and motionless, like most of his customers' mill spindles. Lowell prescribed a solution for Rhode Island: buy Moody's power loom, which the Waltham shop stood ready to fabricate for them. But in bad times the mill owners were reluctant to take the plunge. Instead they turned for help to the federal government, from which they besought a protective tariff.

Lowell was probably the sole textile manufacturer in the country who did not need protection. But the outcry among his fellow New England industrialists was such that he could hardly stand aloof, and with his usual astuteness he took advantage of it. Journeying to Washington in 1816, he made the acquaintance of John C. Calhoun and other Southern leaders, arguing the importance to the South of a healthy New England cotton-textile industry. Unlike some New Englanders, he was tactfully reserved about his opinions of the recent war which the Southerners and Westerners had favored, and made a good impression with his command of facts and figures. The agrarian South and West being naturally averse to high tariffs, he proposed only a modest duty on cotton cloth, provided a minimum valuation of twenty-five cents a yard be set on all imports. The India cotton that competed with his Waltham sheeting sold for much less, and the establishment of the arbitrary twenty-five-cent-a-yard figure made the 25 percent duty Congress finally adopted weigh heavily against it, while Rhode Island's fancy hand weaves were virtually unprotected against their British power-weave competition.

Daniel Webster, a congressman from Portsmouth, New Hampshire, who espoused antiprotectionism in the interests of his shipping constituency, listened to Lowell's arguments and perhaps his inducements ("I found [Lowell] full of exact, practical knowledge, on many subjects") and soon after moved from Portsmouth to Boston where Lowell's friends helped him build a lucrative law practice and stay in Congress to protect their interests. Next time the tariff question came up, Webster's was the most eloquent voice for protection.

Lowell, in poor health for years, died in 1817 at only forty-two. By that time he had given American industry an impetus it did not lose. Out of Paul Moody's Waltham machine shop came a steady succession of improvements and original innovations to increase the speed and efficiency of the plant operation. The shop sold looms to other manufacturers at a markup over cost of 28 percent, other machinery for more; Moody's dressing machine for preparing the yarn for the loom, costing $500 to make, sold for $813.50, considered a very good profit in a day of low overhead and insignificant taxes. Licensing of patents was also begun in 1817, with the loom patent going at $10, later raised to $15. A common arrangement was for a mill to buy a license to copy all the Waltham machinery for a fixed rate, typically $6,000 for a 6,000-spindle mill for five years. Not all the improvements came directly from Waltham. Ira Draper of Weston, Massachusetts, patented a self-acting temple for keeping the cloth stretched to proper width in the loom, and many other Yankee mill mechanics contributed improvements.

By 1820 Moody had turned out more machinery than the Charles River could power, and he and Jackson began looking around for a larger site. A friend of Moody's, Ezra Worthen, suggested Pawtucket Falls, located not at Pawtucket but on the Merrimack River at East Chelmsford, Massachusetts, 25 miles north of Boston, where a large volume of water plunged thirty-two feet and where in addition the Middlesex Canal a mile north of the falls gave a direct water route to Boston. The place was a virtual wilderness, but Lowell's experiment at Waltham had showed how the labor problem could be solved. Moody reconnoitered the site and sketched it for Jackson, whose responsive excitement carried the whole company beyond their original intention of a limited expansion. What Jackson now proposed was to build a whole new town, with several complete factories and housing on a large scale. Nathan Appleton joined in with the proposal that the time had come to advance to calico printing. Timothy Wiggin, a Boston businessman in London, was commissioned to hire an English expert, J. D. Prince. Prince coolly demanded a salary of $5,000 a year. "Why, five thousand dollars is more than the governor of the state of Massachusetts earns," the Britisher was told, to which he retorted, "Can the governor of Massachusetts print cloth?" He was hired.

The "Merrimack Manufacturing Company" attracted most of the old Boston Company shareholders and new capital besides. One newcomer, Kirk Boott, formerly of Boott and Sons, Boston, took on major management responsibilities. Boott was almost unique in America in having some professional engineering education. This had come through an ambiguity on the part of his father and himself as to whether the family nationality was American or British. An unreconstructed Boston Tory, Boott, Sr., had sent his son to school at Rugby, brought him back for two years at Harvard, then purchased him a commission in the British army. Young Boott served under Wellington in the Peninsular War, but when his regiment was ordered to North America for what turned out to be the Battle of New Orleans, he balked, though he had no sympathy with "Mr. Madison's War." Resigning his commission, he took the opportunity to study engineering and surveying at the British military school at Woolwich before returning to Boston and the family mercantile firm.

Jackson negotiated the purchase of a company called the "Proprietors of the Locks and Canals on Merrimack River" that owned, but made little use of, the waterpower rights, and also several farms. Kirk Boott took charge of building a dam, corresponding with engineers of the Erie Canal for technical information, and enlarging the Pawtucket Canal around the rapids. Five hundred Irish immigrant laborers were recruited from Boston for the work, which by the late summer of 1823 was far enough advanced for the first machinery in Paul Moody's new machine shop to start operating. Kirk Boott recorded the start of Moody's huge waterwheel:

"Thurs. Sept 4, 1823   After breakfast went to factory, and found the wheel moving around his course, majestically and with comparative silence. Moody declared that was 'the best wheel in the world.' N. Appleton became quite enthusiastic. . . . Both Moody and Borden [Moody's assistant] said 'They never saw machinery start better.' "

The original intention had been to allow the Merrimack Company to operate the entire new development, but in 1824 a change was made in the interest of more convenient corporate management. The old "Locks and Canals Company" was revived and awarded the functions of machinery building, and real estate and waterpower management. The waterpower was divided into fifty "mill powers," each adequate to turn 3,584 spindles and each to be accompanied with a grant of four acres of land for a mill site. The result was the charting of a planned industrial community into which capital rushed like the Merrimack torrent itself. Besides the Merrimack Company, a new "Hamilton Company" was formed, whose shares were snapped up at once. In 1824 a town charter was secured, and the name East Chelmsford abandoned. Kirk Boott wanted to name the new city—half Irish shantytown, half new-laid-out streets—after Derby, his father's birthplace in England. But Nathan Appleton fittingly suggested Lowell. Jackson and Moody strongly seconded him, and the town was so incorporated (March 1, 1826). As the partners fully realized, their new-city concept was no more than an enlargement of Lowell's Waltham pattern: large, integrated mill establishments, boarding houses to attract woman labor, a waterpowered machine shop the heart of the whole enterprise.

Lowell and Waltham presented a different picture from the "Slatersvilles" of southern New England, the villages built around the small "family" mills. On a far larger scale, Lowell also had a more complex plan that included a system of canals to power the mills, sites for future mills, housing, parks, churches, schools, libraries, and public buildings. However, like the mill villages, Lowell planted shade trees.

Yet the city that was named after him could have profited from Francis Cabot Lowell's vision. It was, true enough, an enlargement of Waltham, but the enlarged scale called for something more imaginative than an increase in the size and number of mills and boarding houses. A downtown area surrounding a common or mall, with recreational facilities, would have been farsighted. Kirk Boott may have been inhibited by the speculative interest of his partners, who bought much of the land just to the west and held it off the market for twenty years.

Boott's vision did not at first even encompass enough churches. A Church of England man, he built a single Episcopal church (St. Anne's, named after his wife), even though all his mechanics and mill girls were Calvinists of one sect or another. He even taxed them 37½ cents per quarter for the upkeep of the church, and when he learned of a young mechanic who was trying to start a Universalist (everyone will be saved) Church, and who besides was a member of the radically democratic Workingmen's Party, he ordered him fired. He did, however, lend help to building a Catholic Church, finding it badly needed to tame the wild Irishmen of "Paddy Camp Lands." In spite of Boott's opposition, churches of other denominations soon went up, and in 1834 a visitor reported that there were "churches and meeting houses of every sect," including Baptist, Congregationalist, Methodist, Unitarian, and even Universalist.

In early 1828, while Paul Moody was still striving to meet the voracious demands for machinery of the Merrimack and Hamilton Companies, two new firms, the Appleton Company and the Lowell Company, were incorporated. In 1831 three more firms built mills, the Tremont Mills, the Suffolk Manufacturing Company, and the Lawrence Manufacturing Company, this last the creation of two newcomers to manufacturing, Amos and Abbott Lawrence. The site that had supported five farm families in 1821 numbered 2,500 residents in 1826 and 18,000 in 1836, by which time some of the omissions in planning were beginning to be evident.

Visitors were still impressed by the youthful neatness of the town. "It was new and fresh, like a setting at the opera," reported French economist Michel Chevalier in 1834.

> A pile of huge factories, each five, six or seven stories high, and capped with a little white belfry, which strongly contrasts with the red masonry of the building, and is distinctly projected on the dark hills on the horizon. By the side of these larger structures rise numerous little wooden houses, painted white, with green blinds, very neat, very snug, very nicely carpeted, and with a few small trees around them, or brick houses in the English style, that is to say, simple, but tasteful without and comfortable within; on one side, fancy-goods shops and milliners' rooms without number . . . and vast hotels in the American style, very much like barracks . . . on another, canals, water wheels, water falls, bridges, banks, schools, and libraries. . . .

Lowell seemed a fulfillment of an industrial dream. The young women who flocked to tend its spindles and looms were the marvel of the world for their health, clean good looks, and moral uprightness. When this latter quality was subjected to the suspicion of skeptics, the director of the Lawrence factory reported with a satisfaction not short of smugness,

> There have only occurred three instances in which any apparently improper connection or intimacy had taken place, and in those cases the parties were married on their discovery, and several months prior to the birth of their children; so that in a legal point of view, no illegitimate birth has taken place among the females employed in the mills under my direction. Nor have I known of but one case among all the females employed in Lowell . . . a case where the female had been employed but a few days in any mill, and was forthwith rejected from the corporation, and sent to her friends. In point of female chastity, I believe that Lowell is free from reproach as any place of an equal population in the United States or the world.

Lowell was a stop on every European visitor's itinerary, and the mill girls were its prime exhibit. Dickens made a special excursion to Lowell from Boston in 1842, arriving as the girls were returning to work after the noon meal, and found

Boott Cotton Mills, Lowell, 1852. From *Gleason's Magazine*. (Library of Congress)

them all well dressed and clean, healthy, and well behaved. The mills where they worked had "conveniences for washing," the workrooms "were as well ordered as themselves." In the windows of some were green plants, in all was as much "fresh air, cleanliness and comfort, as the nature of the occupation would possibly admit of." As late as 1861, Anthony Trollope expressed admiration for the mills, the town, and the girls—"They are not only better dressed, cleaner, and better mounted [turned out] in every respect than the girls employed at manufactories in England, but they are so infinitely superior as to make a stranger immediately perceive that some very strong cause must have created the difference." Trollope compared them to the best class of shop girls in a large city, and observed that their wages were fully a third higher than those of British mill women, permitting them to save marriage portions, to help improvident parents or, a surprisingly frequent incentive, put brothers through school.

The best known of the Lowell girls was Lucy Larcom, daughter of a retired ship's captain whose widow opened a boarding house in Lowell in 1835. Lucy's mother "liked to make nice things for the table," and, unable to make ends meet and provide for her boarders on the $1.25 a week contributed from each girl's salary as prescribed by the mill management, sent her children to work in the mills. Lucy found the work "really not hard," changing bobbins on the spinning frame every three-quarters of an hour with half a dozen other little girls, and spending the intervals "frolicking around among the spinning-frames, teasing and talking to the older girls, or entertaining ourselves with games and stories in a corner, or exploring, with the overseer's permission, the mysteries of the carding-room, the dressing-room, and the weaving-room." Lucy became a star contributor to the *Lowell Offering*, a magazine founded by one of the town's "Improvement Circles," or study clubs, and composed a long poem, conventional in form but original in content, in which she described the mill workroom "dim with April's rainy light . . . through greenery of geranium leaves," where three mill girls stood by the window like "three damsels at a casement . . . in some high castle-turret," gazing out on "a river less romantic than the Rhine . . . New England's beautiful blue Merrimack." English travelers, taken on a tour of the mill by the Superintendent,

> . . . paused awhile among the balsam-flowers
> and pinks and marigolds about the gate . . .
> The carding room
> They gave one glance, with its great groaning wheels,
> Its earthquake rumblings, and its mingled smells
> Of oily suffocation; and passed on
> Into another room's cool spaciousness
> Of long clean alleys, where the spinners paced
> Silently up and down, and pieced their threads,
> The spindles buzzing like ten thousand bees . . .
>
> The next great door swung in upon a room
> Where the long threads were wound from beam to beam,
> And glazed, and then fanned dry in breathless heat.
> Here lithe forms reached across wide webs, or stooped
> To disentangle broken threads, or climbed
> To where their countenances glistened pale
> Among swift belts and pulleys, which appeared
> To glow with eyes, like the mysterious wheels
> Seen to Ezekiel once . . .
> And so he led them to the weaving-room.
>
> The door, swung on iron hinges, showed
> A hundred girls who hurried to and fro,
> With hands and eyes following the shuttle's flight,
> Threading it, watching for the scarlet mark
> That came up in the web, to show how fast
> Their work was speeding. Clatter went the looms
> Click-clack the shuttles. Gossamery motes
> Thickened the sunbeams into golden bars,
> Arms, hands, and heads, moved with the moving looms,
> That closed them in as if all were one shape,
> One motion . . .

In a more prosaic vein, a Georgian journalist named William Thompson, who turned out rustic humor under the pen name of "Major Jones," described the "factory galls . . . [who], swarming out of the factories like bees out of a hive, and spreadin in evry direction, filled the streets so that nothin else was to be seen but platoons of sun-bonnets . . . all lookin as happy, and cheerful, and neat, and clean, and butiful, as if they was boardin-school misses jest from ther books." In the evening, the stores were illuminated and the girls strolled in pairs, half-dozens, and dozens, shopping, laughing, and chatting "as if it didn't hurt 'em to spend ther earnins no more'n other people." In the morning the factories were quiet, their yards clean, and the flower-gardens by the doors glittering with dew; the girls were at breakfast in their trim two- and three-story boarding houses near the factories. When the bells rang, they emerged into the street as "merry and happy as if they was gwine to a frollic, insted of to ther work."

After breakfast he visited the mills and saw the girls tending the looms and the spindles, "ther little white hands flying about like they was part of the machinery," while "they found time now and then to steal a sly glance at us." After watching calico printing, visiting the whip factory, the factory that made carding machines, where "a little iron contraption" cut up and bent wire, punched holes in pieces of leather, and inserted and fastened the wire in the holes, and a mechanized carpenter's shop, Thompson met the editor of the *Offering*, who took him to see Lucy Larcom. Lucy was checking off goods in the packing room of one of the mills. "I never met with a more interesting young lady, though I spose she wouldn't thank me for callin her a *lady,* as she gin me her autograf in a very different spirit. It reads—

> Major Jones:
> Sir—I have the honor to be, yours, very respectfully, a *bona-fide* factory girl,
>
> > Lucy L . . ."

When President Andrew Jackson visited Lowell in 1833, (the same journey in which he called on Samuel Slater), the bands, civic leaders, and militia in the welcoming parade were outnumbered and outshone by 2,500 factory girls dressed in white muslin frocks with blue sashes and waving green parasols in salute. The pageant's organizers apologized for their failure to obtain 2,500 green parasols, so that a few of the girls waved blue ones. The gallant old general reassured his hosts with his favorite oath: "Very pretty women, by the Eternal!"

10

"The Eighth Wonder of the World"

ROBERT FULTON'S STEAMBOAT WAS in the first autumn of its Hudson River career when on October 27, 1807, the first of a series of articles appeared in the *Genesee Messenger,* published in Canandaigua, New York, proposing the immediate implementation of the dream of Gouverneur Morris. The anonymous editorialist, later identified as a Geneva flour merchant named Jesse Hawley, who had taken advantage of twenty months' confinement in debtors' prison to write the articles, advocated a canal east to west across New York State from Utica to Buffalo, linking the already planned improvement of the Mohawk River with the Great Lakes.

From the economic point of view, the project seemed promising; from a technical point of view it presented no difficulties that competent engineers could not deal with. The level plain of western New York furnished ideal canal terrain. Yet the logistical magnitude of the scheme—360 miles of wilderness to survey, route, organize, and excavate—was enough to give Europe's most experienced engineers pause, and America had no experienced engineers. The longest canals in Britain and France were barely a third the size. Russia had a 4,500-mile waterway, but it was formed by digging a few canal links to connect large rivers. No European or Asian canal had ever been built of comparable length in a single construction effort.

Hawley may have been influenced by President Jefferson's message to Congress in the fall of 1807 in which the former champion of small government boldly em-

LEFT Gouverneur Morris, who in 1801 envisioned the building of a canal from the Hudson to Lake Erie. (Library of Congress)

RIGHT De Witt Clinton, one of the Canal's most ardent promoters. (Library of Congress)

braced the logic of his Louisiana Purchase by proposing a program of "internal improvements," under which heading the Erie Canal certainly fell. But before the immensity and cost—which Hawley estimated at $5 million—Jefferson grew cautious and refused to commit the federal treasury. When Joshua Forman, member of the New York State assembly from Onondaga County and sponsor of a canal bill, called on the president in Washington, Jefferson declared that the project was a century ahead of its time. "Why, sir, here is a canal for a few miles, projected by George Washington [the Potomac Canal], which, if completed, would render [Washington] a fine commercial city, which has languished for many years because the small sum of 200,000 dollars necessary to complete it, cannot be obtained from the general government, the state government, or from individuals—and you talk of making a canal 350 miles through the wilderness—it is little short of madness to think of it at this day!"

But the project gained a political sponsor who for its purposes was even better than a president—Lieutenant-Governor De Witt Clinton, who won a lasting title to statesmanlike vision by his conviction that the benefits to the state, especially to New York City, outweighed the financial and engineering hazards. Born in a Hudson Valley village and educated at Columbia, Clinton had served as secretary to his uncle, Governor George Clinton of New York, before entering politics himself as state senator in 1795. A United States Senator in 1802, and subsequently mayor of New York City, in 1809 Clinton was leader of the Republicans in the state senate and political boss of New York City. The Platt Bill, outgrowth of an alliance of interested parties, received Clinton's support and was passed in the legislature in March 1810. Three thousand dollars was appropriated for surveying, and a commission was appointed whose six members included elderly Gouverneur Morris as well as Clinton himself.

The question arose of finding a survey engineer. Admitting that there was no one in America qualified in the British or European sense, the Commission had the good luck to have its choice already made in the shape of a middle-aged lawyer, county judge, and salt manufacturer of Lake Onondaga named James Geddes, who had acquired surveying experience in his youth. Geddes had already done preliminary work for the state legislature and had demonstrated ability and vision, identifying a serious problem in crossing the Irondequoit Creek at Rochester, but expressing the conviction that the enterprise was feasible.

In the survey of 1810, Geddes was joined by Benjamin Wright, another county judge and a former state legislator, who in the 1790s had surveyed half a million acres of Oneida and Oswego County farmland, and who had had baptism as an engineer building four flood dams in Wood Creek, west of Rome, in 1802. The dams were part of the canal-building efforts of the Western Inland Lock Navigation Company, which had set out to improve the Mohawk River route to the West by canalizing rivers, a project that had temporarily foundered amid financial and engineering problems. High tolls on the Western Inland Canal, necessitated by the company's fiscal difficulties, had been a factor in Jesse Hawley's bankruptcy and imprisonment for debt in 1807.

European experience had shown the limitations of canalizing rivers, and the advantages of instead drawing water from the meandering river to supply a canal following a shorter line. As an alternative to the Western Inland route, Geddes saw merit in a canal system linking the Hudson with Lake Ontario, paralleling the Mohawk and Oswego Rivers and Wood Creek, with a 12-mile horsepowered railroad to link the Oswego River with westward-flowing Wood Creek. But the Commission perceived a dangerous defect in the Mohawk-Lake Ontario scheme that had nothing to do with canal technology. The St. Lawrence River, broad and deep (though ice-obstructed in winter), offered cheap freight rates—fifty cents a hundred pounds downstream, a dollar a hundred up. If any point east of Niagara Falls were made the terminus of New York's canal, the products of the area around Lake Erie would flow north to Montreal and Quebec. The commission even expressed an apprehension that western New York might be annexed to Canada. Geddes and Wright therefore proposed an interior route heading straight for Lake Erie, with aqueducts to carry the canal over the Genesee River and the heads of Lakes Seneca and Cayuga.

In an attempt to solicit federal support, Robert Fulton and Chancellor Livingston were enlisted on the Commission, and amid rising controversy—the towns on the Western Inland Canal took alarm at being left backwater, while the farmers of the Hudson Valley and Long Island fought the prospect of competition from the West—a new report was made in the spring of 1812. Facing an imminent threat of war with Britain, Congress momentarily looked favorably on the project, but the actual outbreak canceled the prospect of federal aid and postponed any other approach.

As soon as the war was over, the canal's friends in New York and Albany set to work again. A new committee was organized headed by De Witt Clinton, now once more mayor of New York City, and entrusted with the task of drawing up a petition to the legislature. The result was the thoroughgoing and eloquent Clinton Memorial of February 21, 1816. Recalling the prosperity of ancient Egypt and China, achieved through their systems of inland navigation, the Memorial pointed out that more recently England and Holland had built canals and prospered mightily. Now the "great prize" of trade with the American West was at stake among New York, New Orleans, and Montreal, the other port cities all being cut off by mountains. The relative distances from Buffalo to the three ports were cited to New York's advantage, and even, with rather remarkable farsightedness, those from Chicago, at the moment no more than a mark on the map. A ton of farm produce could be hauled 100 miles for $32 by wagon and road; by canal the cost was reckoned as $1, assuming that a loaded canal boat could be towed 30 miles per day by two horses. One horse might even do the job, and the canal provided superior safety and certainty of arrival.

Granting that her rivals would take part of the fabulous Western commerce, New York City, if the canal were built, would "engross more than sufficient to render her the greatest commercial city in the world," a Yankee forecast certain to draw incredulous jeers in London. Clinton visioned the "whole line of the canal [filled with] boats loaded with flour, pork, beef, pot and pearl ashes, flaxseed, wheat, barley, corn, hemp, poultry, ginseng, bees-wax, cheese, butter, lard, staves, lumber, and the other valuable productions of our country; and also, with merchandise from all parts of the world. Great manufacturing establishments will spring up. . . . Villages, towns, and cities, will line the banks of the canal, and the shore of the Hudson from Erie to New York."

On the basis of European experience and the Erie's 360-mile length, the total cost would come in somewhere between $5 million and $11 million. Clinton thought that $6 million would do the job, but that even at double the sum it should be built forthwith. The money would be needed at a rate of $500,000 a year; Clinton boldly advocated selling stock in the enterprise.

Commercial advantages aside, Clinton defended the project on high national grounds. With the Burr conspiracy and the secessionist Hartford Convention fresh in mind, he warned: "However serious the fears which have been entertained of a dismemberment of the Union by collisions between the north and the south, it is to be apprehended that the most imminent danger lies in another direction . . . between the atlantic and the western states." And for his peroration he conjured an image of national and democratic grandeur: "[Following the canal projects of powerful monarchies] It remains for a free state to create a new era in history, and to erect a work, more stupendous, more magnificent, and more beneficial, than has hitherto been achieved by the human race."

The legislature, in which commercial interests had no small influence, bought Clinton's dream, directing the commissioners to go ahead and lay out a canal route. Nevertheless, there was a powerful opposition made up partly of Oswego-

Ontario interests and partly of conservative skepticism. Lieutenant-governor John Tyler fought the project vigorously, and Chancellor James Kent wobbled in his support. Ex-governor Daniel Tompkins, elected vice-president with James Monroe in 1816 (and succeeded as governor by De Witt Clinton), announced his opposition on the grounds that another war with Britain was imminent and New York should concentrate on defense measures instead of the "chimerical" canal project. Kent evidently had little respect for Tompkins's judgment, because he then announced that if another war was indeed on the horizon, "I am in favor of the canal and I vote for the bill."

The profile of the canal route showed a gradual slope from Buffalo east, with one interruption in a net fall of 565 feet to the Hudson. Eighty-three locks would be necessary, with twenty-seven concentrated in the steep slope between Schenectady and Albany. About a third of the way from the Hudson lay the "summit" of the eastern section at Rome, on the Mohawk, at the top of a fifty-foot rise from the Seneca River to the west. Rome was chosen as the starting point for digging, because the ground was easy and rapid progress could be made, "working both ways to oncet," as the upstate Yorkers said.

A fresh reconnaissance of the line of the canal in early spring of 1817 led to a revision of the gross engineering plan. The "summit level" of the canal, the middle portion with least slope, had been designated as from Salina (later Syracuse) northeast to Rome on the Mohawk. It was now decided to carry this summit section southeast to Utica so that if work were suspended after completion of the western and central sections, the canal would reach as far east, and to as navigable a point on the Mohawk, as possible.

The work was divided into three roughly equal sections, each entrusted to a chief engineer. James Geddes, who had done so much of the original survey work, was given the western section, from Buffalo to Seneca Lake; Benjamin Wright the middle section, from Seneca to Rome; and Charles C. Broadhead the eastern section, from Rome to Albany. The eastern section contained the three chief obstacles of the route, the falls of the Mohawk at Cohoes, where the Mohawk joined the Hudson; the "Little Falls" of the Mohawk; and the summit link from the Mohawk to Wood Creek. The eastern section was consequently the most expensive, estimate of its cost running $2,271,690 as compared with $1,801,862 for the western section and only $853,186 for the middle.

During the spring, as Monroe inaugurated the Era of Good Feeling, gangs armed with stakes and sledgehammers, and backed by wagons and teamsters, set to work driving five lines of red stakes entirely across the state of New York. The stakes and their clearings, through forest and swamp, over hill and dale, farmland, populated places, and long stretches of desert wilderness, suddenly made the endlessly talked-about canal project seem real to the public. Up to now, skepticism had been the most sympathetic expression, ridicule the commonest. But as the five lines of stakes, spanning 60 feet, marked off the canal's towpaths, banks (40 feet apart), and center, and as other crews followed up the stake gangs with augurdrills to take soil samples, the last burst of derisive laughter faded off to a surprised and wondering silence.

At sunrise on July 4, 1817, the canal commissioners broke soil at Rome. The three chief engineers, Wright, Geddes, and Broadhead, stood by while Judge Joshua Hathaway of Rome presided. Judge John Richardson, first to take up a contract on the canal, waited with a plow behind a team of oxen while the rest of the company leaned on shovels. As the sun rose, cannon thundered and Richardson opened the first furrow on the canal line. After an address by Canal Commissioner Samuel Young, Judge Richardson took a shovel and dug the first spadeful of earth. Then the cannon sounded once more and everyone fell to digging, "vying with each other," reported the Utica *Gazette,* "in this demonstration of joy, of which all partook on that interesting occasion."

The first task for the "American engineers" who were learning their profession by doing it was to establish the proper level for the middle section. Geddes ran a series of test levels for a distance of more than a hundred miles around Oneida and Onondaga Lakes while Wright laid off the canal line west of Rome. When Geddes's survey returned to the line laid off by Wright, the difference at the junction was less than one and a half inches.

The construction work was organized through small private contractors, mostly well-to-do farmers in the vicinity. The contractors had little or no capital and generally had to be furnished advances of $200 to $2,000 to get started. In December when work was knocked off for the winter they were given fresh advances to buy provisions, since beef, pork, and flour were cheaper in winter than spring and the few roads were slightly better.

That first year Geddes and Wright learned a good bit about their chief-engineering jobs. Merely finding contractors and assigning excavation sections was not enough. In this barren country, the stone, lumber, and lime for construction of the locks had to be systematically programmed for delivery at the proper points along the route, in forest, swamp, or hillside. They also learned that the spade and wheelbarrow, Europe's time-honored canal implements, were too inefficient and expensive for a long project in a labor-short country, and replaced them with horse-drawn plows and scrapers. By the second summer 2,000 men and 1,000 horses were at work, the men earning about fifty cents a day, and the contractors being paid ten to fifteen cents per cubic yard for the excavation of earth, more for shale or rock.

The commissioners pointed out proudly that the contractors were "native farmers, mechanics, merchants, and professional men" who lived near the canal. Most of the canal workers too were recruited locally, but a permanent work force was needed to push the job through the sparsely settled regions, and this was furnished by Irish immigrants, whose fighting, drinking, and wife-beating propensities passed into New York State folklore. Once a gang of Irish did an elaborate put-on for Sunday visitors who came to gawk at their temporary village, the women suddenly emerging screaming from their shacks with the men pursuing them armed with shillelaghs. Sometimes the workers put a keg of beer at intervals along the path of stakes, and when the gang reached it, they paused to drink it up. "Fastest digging and drinking the *canawl* has ever seen," commented an admiring upstate Yorker. One Irish worker became world-famous—Paddy Ryan, who defeated the English boxing champion Joe Goss and became "King of the Erie Canal and Champion of the World." Besides fist fights, there were cockfights and bulldog fights, and less violent sports—caterpillar, cockroach, and bedbug racing.

That winter (1818) the entire remaining middle section was put under contract, with a route change to avoid a large swamp at Marl Meadows near Camillus, 10 miles west of Syracuse. With spring the axes rang through the dense forest, followed by plows, scrapers, and wagons.

New implements appeared, some of European design, some invented on the spot. With a tree feller, using the ancient principles of lever, wheel, and screw, a single man could topple a tree. Stumps were cleared by a stump hauler, capable of grubbing thirty to forty large stumps a day. Another invention was a new kind of plow for cutting the tangled roots that underlay the floor of the dense American wilderness; it could be pulled by two yoke of oxen through any complex of roots not exceeding two inches in diameter. The narrow blade could not turn over the soil, but by cutting up the roots it made them easily disposable by a harrow driven ahead of the shovel-plow and scraper.

For work in wet ground, where heavy equipment could not operate, Jeremiah Brainard of Rome invented a wheelbarrow whose bottom and sides were made of a single bent board, lighter, more durable, and easier to unload than previous barrows.

A final contribution was made by a young "engineer" named Canvass White, an Oneida County farmer who had served as a lieutenant in the New York Volunteers in the War of 1812 and became assistant to Benjamin Wright in the surveys of 1816 and 1817. At De Witt Clinton's suggestion but with his own funds, White went to England to inspect hydraulic works—canals, aqueducts, and tunnels, walking 2,000 miles of towpaths, and paying particular attention to underwater cements. On his return White became an assistant engineer on the Erie's middle section, and in 1818, after experimenting with different varieties of limestone, found a type in Madison County that became increasingly hard under water. Protected by patents in 1820 and 1821, White's cement process was used in all subsequent Erie Canal construction and was one of the canal's valuable contributions to engineering.

During the season of 1818, all but 5 of the 94 miles of the middle section were grubbed and cleared, 48 miles were excavated, and 8 miles completed. In the summer of 1819 the first boats navigated a 20-mile stretch that included masonry aqueducts over Oneida and Onondaga Creeks. The job was staying surprisingly close to the cost estimate despite a grim problem: "fever and ague" struck down over a thousand workmen, mostly in the low-lying valley of the Seneca, where work sometimes had to be suspended for weeks on end.

Exploring parties were meantime laying off the Western Section, parts of which were put under contract, along with the 26-mile portion of the Eastern Section between Utica and Little Falls. As the Erie works reached Wood Creek, they interrupted the operation of the partially completed Western Inland Canal, whose stockholders had been receiving good dividends in the last few years and whose consequent cries of outrage had to be silenced by compensation. The settlement took the form of purchase of their stock by the state for $150,000, a disconcerting cost that might perhaps have been foreseen.

The question arose: was the project too grandiose after all? Did prudence perhaps dictate postponing completion? It was decided that work should be pushed rapidly on the Western Section; if this and the Middle could be completed, the improved Mohawk could be made to answer in the East. Accordingly, more than 40 miles of the Western Section were completed in 1820 between the Genesee River and Montezuma Swamp, while the completed Middle Section became a busy avenue of commerce, with mile markers erected throughout its 96 miles from Genesee Street in Utica to the lock leading into the Seneca River.

By 1821 a glimpse of the canal's true potential was visible on the Middle Section, where barges laden with barrels of flour and salt, with wheat, lime, maple sugar, butter and lard, gypsum, lumber, wagons, and coaches were hauled at a steady pace by horsepower tramping the towpaths. The first tolls amounted to a promising $23,000. The Eastern Section between Utica and Little Falls was also open to barge traffic. Confidence returned, the rest of the Eastern Section was contracted out, and the last doubts about completion were silenced.

Philip Freneau saluted the canal in the *New Brunswick Fredonian:*

> By hearts of oak and hands of toil
> The Spade inverts the rugged soil
> A work, that may remain secure
> While suns exist and moons endure.

Among the public, the epithet "Clinton's Ditch" had quietly altered to a respectful "Big Ditch," while the more effusive section of the press hailed the canal as "the Eighth Wonder of the World."

In 1822 Canvass White executed one of the work's most difficult technical feats by carrying the canal across the Mohawk River by aqueduct. An even larger aqueduct over the Genesee at Rochester was constructed in imitation Roman style, of nine hewn-stone semicircular arches of 50-foot span, and by mid-1823, 220 miles were navigable.

That year the engineers attacked the last major problem, the crossing of Mountain Ridge in the Western Section, a 66-foot rise, by a series of five locks. A thousand men were employed to cut a 7-mile trough, 27 feet wide and from 13 to 30 feet deep, through the ridge, two miles of it through solid rock, with a towpath chiseled from the side of the cutting. Gunpowder was used to blast rock from the bottom of the excavation to be carried off in baskets by tall wooden-armed derricks. Accidents from the flying debris were numerous, and after every rain, water had to be drained from the rocky bottom of the excavation. Progress was slow. At the site, the village of Lockport sprang up, with taverns, shops, and a population of 1,500.

In October 1823 the canal was completed from Brockport, just west of Rochester, to Albany, where the junction with the Hudson River was celebrated on October 8. The next spring, five days after the opening of the canal, 106 canal boats were counted in the Albany basin.

The last phase of construction brought to a crisis a miniature political tempest that had threatened since the commencement. Two tiny harbors, or rather non-harbors, Black Rock, on the Niagara River, and Buffalo, four miles away on Lake Erie, vied for the honor, and especially the profit, of providing the western termi-

Excavation of the Erie Canal's Western Section at Lockport, where a 7 mile trough had to be built, 27 feet wide and from 13 to 30 feet deep, two miles of it through solid rock. Wooden derricks lift baskets of rock, blasted by gunpowder. From Cadwallader Colden's *Memoirs*, 1825. (Library of Congress)

nus. Black Rock was handicapped by a problem of wind and current, Buffalo by a sandbar. The canal commissioners arrived at a politic compromise that built harbors for both villages, terminated the canal at Black Rock, and then reterminated it at Buffalo. Black Rock celebrated victory, but Buffalo won the war, taking over the canal terminus and eventually Black Rock too.

In 1825, after nine years of work (and fifty of dreaming), the "Grand Canal" was completed. That June, the Marquis de Lafayette, as part of his grand tour of the United States, traveled from Buffalo to Albany via the canal, his voyage one long sentimental celebration. Arriving at Black Rock by Lake Erie boat, the elderly hero embarked on a canal boat at Lockport, where work was still in progress and workmen saluted him with blasts that sent splinters of rock into the air. At Rochester he was met by a flotilla of decorated boats, which escorted him to a platform erected at the center of the aqueduct for the welcoming ceremony. After a detour to the Finger Lakes, he returned to the canal at Syracuse, where the reception committee, which had sat up all night waiting, served him for breakfast the supper intended for the night before. At Rome, Utica, and Schenectady, children pelted his boat with flowers from the bridges over the canal.

The canal's original dreamer, Gouverneur Morris, had lived only long enough to see the work started, but Governor De Witt Clinton, the driving force behind the project, was very much alive and star of the lavish ceremony when the canal officially opened. At 9 A.M. on October 26, 1825, a procession formed in front of the courthouse in Buffalo, with band, riflemen, and committees, and marched to the water where lay the *Seneca Chief*, a bulgy, windowed tub, swathed in bunting, loaded with cargo of products from Lake Erie's shores. In the cabin Clinton was

Seneca Chief west of Lockport, 1825. (Canal Society of New York State)

greeted by a huge picture of himself garbed as Hercules resting from his labors, etched by lithographer George Catlin. Jesse Hawley, whose articles had done much to start the dream toward reality, delivered the opening address at the Buffalo basin. At 10 A.M. whips cracked, the horses started down the towpath, and the *Seneca Chief* glided forward, followed by a flotilla of official boats, including a "Noah's Ark" carrying two bears, fish, a pair of eagles, an assortment of other birds, and two Indian boys. A signal cannon was fired, and a line of guns along the canal and the Hudson took up the echo all the way to New York. Every town along the route added its festivities. At Lockport the guns captured by Perry at the Battle of Lake Erie were fired in salute under the direction of an immigrant veteran of Napoleon.

Rome struck a sour note by holding a counterdemonstration, a muffled-drum procession that carried a black barrel of water from the old Western Inland Canal that had built Rome, and dumped it into the new canal. The flotilla stayed in Rome only a chilly hour. Sister Mohawk city Little Falls was equally unenthusiastic, but Schenectady warmed up with the "College Guards" of Union College firing a salute at the passing line of boats, and Albany, which envisioned all the wealth of the West headed its way, delivered a twenty-four cannon salute, speeches, and wining and dining late into the evening. Next morning the flotilla was escorted by eight steamboats down the Hudson, arriving in New York early the following morning (November 4) to receive a resounding welcome from batteries on Manhattan, Governor's Island, Fort Lafayette, and Fort Tompkins. The "Wedding of Waters" took place near Sandy Hook, with De Witt Clinton dumping a Lake Erie barrel into the Atlantic, but saving a pint to send to Lafayette, in a box made by Duncan Phyfe from cedar brought by the *Seneca Chief*. The ceremony moved one New York journalist to speculate that "a display so grand, so beautiful, and we may even add, sublime, will never again be witnessed."

New York threw in a parade. Five thousand marchers in a procession a mile and a half long wound from Greenwich Street through Canal to Broadway, up Broadway to Broome and the Bowery, down to Pearl, and thence to the Battery and City Hall. That night the Lafayette Amphitheater in Laurens Street was turned into the largest ballroom in America by knocking out a partition, and New York danced under a proscenium emblazoned with the giant names of Canvass White, James Geddes, Benjamin Wright, and David Thomas, the self-taught engineers, and of De Witt Clinton and his commissioners.

The Grand Canal had come in at $7,143,789, not quite $20,000 a mile, well within reach of the estimates. Even more important, Clinton's forecast of canal revenues proved amazingly accurate, with the first full year of operation running only $8,000 under his forecast of half a million dollars' revenue and the following year surpassing even Clinton's optimism.

In the canal's early years, passenger barges ("packets") won considerable popularity among foreign visitors, despite an inconvenience that passed into folklore—to placate farmers along the route a great number of ramshackle bridges for livestock crossings were built, but for economy's sake kept low so canalers and travelers on deck had to be alert for the warning cry, "Low bridge!" A Canadian visitor in 1826 complained that one had to lie down flat upon the deck, "often not too clean," and remarked that he had "got once knocked down . . . —rec'd a severe blow, which stunned me a good deal." Edward Westcott's fictional David Harum of the 1890s remarked at a gathering of society of Newport, New York, that if somebody called out, "Low bridge!" most of the gentlemen over fifty would duck, implying that they got their start toward fortune as Erie canallers.

Besides Newport, upper New York State gained Lockport, Brockport, Gasport, Spencerport, Middleport, and Port Byron from the canal, a reflection of the waterway's maritime pretensions despite its modest four-foot depth. Already-established hamlets sometimes changed their names, as the canal suddenly poured its riches into their laps. Rochesterville, profiting from its waterpower source in the Genesee falls, dropped a syllable from its cumbersome name as it hastily built mills to grind the barge loads of flour crowding in from the West. Salina, on the Onondaga salt works, grew overnight into Syracuse. Captain Basil Hall, an English traveler of 1827, was surprised to leave the "dense, black, tangled, native forest" and suddenly come "to such a gay and thriving place as Syracuse, with fine broad streets, large and commodious houses, gay shops, and stagecoaches, waggons, and gigs flying past, all in a bustle. In the centre of the village, we could see from our windows the canal thickly covered with freight boats and packets, glancing silently past, and shooting like arrows through the bridges, some of which were of stone, and some of painted wood. The canal at this place has been made double its ordinary width, and being bent into an agreeable degree of curvature, to suit the turn of the streets, the formality is removed, as well as the ditch-like appearance which generally belongs to the canals. . . . I was amused by seeing, amongst the throng of loaded boats, a gaily painted vessel lying in state, with the words Cleopatra's Barge painted in large characters on her broadside."

Besides the packets there were "lineships," barges taking both passengers and cargo, and running on schedule, with changes of horses at regular stations like

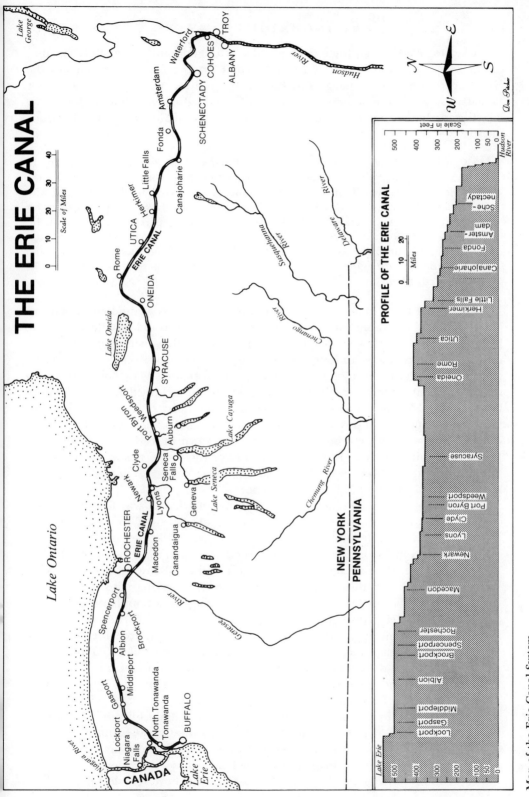

Map of the Erie Canal System.

stagecoaches. Westbound, these were crowded with emigrants who helped balance the heavily eastbound cargoes. In October of 1825, the first emigrant boat, the *Hiram,* deposited fifty passengers in Buffalo "bound for Michigan." A year later as many as 1,200 were arriving in a single day, crowding into Buffalo hotels before they embarked for the lake journey. In 1832 a Buffalo newspaper described the spring influx:

> Canal boats filled with emigrants, and covered with goods and furniture, are almost hourly arriving. The boats are discharged of their motley freight, and for the time being, natives of all climates and countries patrol our streets, either to gratify curiosity, purchase necessaries, or to inquire the most favorable points for their future location. Several steamboats and vessels daily depart for the far west, literally crammed with masses of living beings . . . their decks piled up in huge heaps with furniture and chattels of all descriptions, and even hoisted up and hung on to the rigging . . . a mass of human bodies clustering all over them like a swarming hive.

Larger canal boats sometimes accommodated as many as a hundred passengers. The interior of the cabin was lined with benches, which could be folded out into beds at night, with tiers of sacking-bottomed frames above suspended from the ceiling; in the center were long tables for eating. At night, one end was partitioned off for the ladies by a screen or curtain. Nathaniel Hawthorne, traveling on a canal boat, found himself placed so close to the curtain that he could hear, besides snores, "whispers and stealthy footsteps; the noise of a comb laid on the table or a slipper dropped on the floor; the twang, like a broken harpstring, caused by loosening a tight belt; the rustling of a gown in its descent; and the unlacing of a pair of stays. My ear seemed to have the properties of an eye. . . ." Forgetting that his berth was "hardly so wide as a coffin," America's first great novelist turned over and fell out on the floor.

Perhaps the best of innumerable descriptions of what it was like to ride the Erie Canal was written four years after the canal's opening by an anonymous journalist for the Philadelphia periodical, *The Ariel,* who began the westward journey from New York City to Buffalo by embarking on a night boat to Albany, fare two dollars. After an admiring inspection of the Albany basin, with "extensive storehouses" on a thirty-yard-wide wharf, communicating with the principal streets by a number of bridges, the writer, following the example of many westbound travelers, decided to take the three-hour stage ride to Schenectady, to avoid the tedious day-long canal trip with forty locks in a distance of 28 miles. At Schenectady, the stage was greeted by several packet men, and he contracted for passage to Utica, a distance of 89 miles, for a cent and a quarter a mile, "a York shilling for each meal extra, and . . . no charge for berths. . . . We 'set sail by horsepower,' as the Irishman has it, about 2 o'clock P.M., the horses being attached to a rope about 30 yards long, made fast to the boat amidships, with our ideas pleasingly elevated at the thought of traveling on the Grand Clinton Canal for the first time. . . . A majority of my companions were Western merchants. . . ."

The boat, about 80 feet long, was divided into three apartments, the two at either end for passengers, the stern for eating, the bow for sleeping and sitting. "The roof is in the form of the back of a tortoise, and affords a handsome promenade, excepting when the everlasting bridges and locks open their mouth for your head. The centre apartment is appropriated to merchandise. . . . We really live *well* in our little house . . . with every convenience but short necks, that we could ask or desire. . . . It takes 5 hands to manage a boat of this size . . . we have relays of horses every 20 miles."

At twilight the travelers met their first adventure, at Schoharie Creek, just west of Amsterdam, where the canal traversed the creek, about thirty yards wide, not by an aqueduct but by a dam. "[The creek] is crossed by means of ropes stretched across the stream, which ropes are your only security; should they give way, you must inevitably go down the current and pass over a dam immediately below, of several feet perpendicular descent. In times of a freshet it is very dangerous. Two or three boats have already been forced involuntarily over it." These accidents shook up passengers and crewmen, but produced no serious injury to the boats, though a return circuit via Schenectady was necessary to get back on the canal. "The horses are ferried over in scows, pulled by the same ropes. . . ."

The following morning the writer arose early, after a restless night,

> owing to the continued blowing of trumpets and horns at the approach of every lock, and now and then a tremendous jar received in passing a boat. . . . The boats on the canal have a beautiful appearance at night, being each illuminated by two large reflecting lamps on either side of the bow. . . . I endeavored to count the boats which we passed yesterday, but I soon gave it up for a troublesome job. . . . [He was kept busy watching out for the locks and bridges—one might be knocked down] and rise up without your head on your shoulders. . . .
>
> At 12 A.M. we arrived at the little falls of the Mohawk . . . the wildest place on the canal. . . . The rapids at the Little falls are divided just below the village by an elevated island of everlasting rocks, which arrests its progress and causes an incessant roar and foam. The canal for a mile below this spot is a perfect encroachment upon the bed of the river—the wall which divides it from the river is so powerful and strong, that the labor and expense attending its erection must have been immense. . . .
>
> The passenger can supply himself with provisions and grog at all the lockhouses along the line at a very low rate. . . .

Arriving at Utica at sunset, the travelers found the canal "literally choked up with boats." The writer commented that Utica was "a beautiful place," and that State Street, "truly for two or three squares . . . is in no respect inferior to Broadway of New York City. The Mohawk runs immediately on the north side of the place, and the canal directly through the centre. Nothing can exceed the facility with which boats are loaded and discharged. There is a walk on each side of the canal about 10 feet wide; a boat stops opposite a store, a tackle descends from an upper story, which by means of a rope and windlass within the building, managed by one man, can raise and lower heavy weights with wonderful dispatch."

At 10 P.M. the boat left Utica, "and the ear was saluted from a great distance up and down the canal by the music of bugles, horns and trumpets, some of the boatmen sounding their instruments most sweetly. . . ."

During the night the boat passed Rome and at sunrise reached the stretch of canal known as the Black Snake, from its serpentine course, following a low terrain profile through 20 miles of pine and hemlock swamp. Late in the afternoon the passengers viewed the Onondaga (Syracuse) salt works—"upwards of two hundred acres actually covered with vats filled with salt water in the act of evaporation. . . . The salt water is obtained from two springs or wells, and is pumped by water power obtained from the canal, carried through horizontal logs in every direction for half a mile to a mile and a half, to supply the vats. . . ."

The next morning the journalist, cutting his canal trip short, alighted at Weedsport and took the stage to Auburn, where he boarded a Great Western Mail coach for a quicker trip to Buffalo, "which supports six extensive Hotels, a Theatre and three Churches," where he rejoined the Grand Canal at its termination in "another spacious Basin, filled with boats."

Low bridges, dam floodings, and other mishaps only enlivened the folklore of the Grand Canal without diminishing the universal public approbation. Among many accolades to the canal was a play by William Dunlap, *A Trip to Niagara,* staged at the Bowery Theatre, New York, in 1828. A member of a party of tourists on the canal asks, "When shall we get to the wilderness?" Jonathan Bull, a comic Englishman, answers in words that sound with new irony in a later age: "These curst creatures [the Americans] have spoilt all that. What with their turnpike roads, and canals, they have gone, like tarnal fools as they are, and put down towns and villages, gardens and orchards, churches and schools, and sich common things, where the woods and wild beasts and Indians and rattlesnakes ought to have been."

The Eighth Wonder of the World richly vindicated De Witt Clinton's judgment as its flood of traffic (which forced improvements and enlargements paid for by its swelling tolls) populated the Midwest with farmers and millers who shipped back barrels of flour in a volume that amazed the world. It also paid another dividend, touched on by a journalist describing the New York celebration. Seconding Clinton's faith in American engineers, he wrote: "[The engineers] have built the longest canal, in the least time, with the least experience, for the least money, and to the greatest public benefit."

That year, 1824, one of the canal commissioners, Amos Eaton, founded Rensselaer Polytechnic Institute at Troy. Eaton's thought was mainly to train engineers for New York's future canals, but the school, first in the world to offer its students a scientific laboratory, proved to have a far wider field for its alumni (one of the earliest was George Washington Roebling, who eventually built the Brooklyn Bridge).

More important, the canal itself proved to be a magnificent engineering school. Its own alumni fanned out north, south, and west to direct the country's first great civil-engineering boom. Benjamin Wright became known as the "father of American engineering," by serving as chief engineer on the Chesapeake and Ohio Canal in 1828–31 and the St. Lawrence Canal in 1833, and as consulting engineer on the Welland, the Chesapeake and Delaware, the Delaware and Hudson, and others, and by surveying railroad lines in New York, Illinois, Virginia, and even Cuba.

Canvass White opened a factory at Cohoes where he produced cement by his patented process, diverting Mohawk River water and by a clever system of canals using it six times before returning it, a marvel studied by the Europeans and the Japanese. Meanwhile White superintended construction on several major canals—the Susquehanna and Schuylkill, the New Haven and Farmington, the Lehigh, the Delaware and Raritan—and on the Delaware breakwater.

Nathan Roberts, a Madison County farmer who had become Benjamin Wright's assistant in 1816, and in 1822 had taken charge of the western section, drafting the plan for the elaborate lock system at Lockport, served as consulting engineer for the Chesapeake and Delaware Canal, surveyed a ship canal around Niagara Falls, acted as chief engineer for the western section of the Pennsylvania State Canal and as a member of the board of engineers for the Chesapeake and Ohio Canal Company. For the federal government he surveyed a ship canal around Muscle Shoals, Alabama, and returned to the Erie Canal to direct the enlargement of 1839.

John B. Jervis of Rome, who as a youth quit his father's lumber business to become an axeman in the party that surveyed the Rome swamp in 1817, rose to a supervisory role, and succeeded Benjamin Wright as chief engineer for the Delaware and Hudson Canal and railroad. He invented a braking device for the cable-hauled inclined-plane portages used in the Allegheny canals, and drew up specifications for the "Stourbridge Lion," the locomotive imported from Britain for the pioneer Carbondale & Honesdale Railroad in 1829. In 1831, as chief engineer of the Mohawk & Hudson Railroad, he built an experimental locomotive with a swiveling truck at the forward end, which through a picturesque modification became known as a cow-catcher. In 1836 Jervis planned New York City's Croton Aqueduct, and a decade later built a water-supply system for Boston. He built bridges, dams, and railroads in New York and the Midwest.

The longest, and perhaps the most distinguished career of all the Erie Canal's graduate engineers belonged to William McAlpine, who had become Jervis's apprentice at the age of fifteen, stayed with the canal after its completion, and was appointed chief operating engineer for the eastern division in 1836. He left the canal to design water-supply systems for Chicago, Brooklyn, Buffalo, Montreal, Philadelphia, San Francisco, New York, and Toronto, and to superintend the construction of the Erie Railroad and the Chicago & Galena (later Chicago & Northwestern). Chief engineer for many bridges, he built the New York State capitol at Albany in 1873 and, as engineer of parks of New York City laid out Riverside Drive. This last of the Erie canallers died in 1890, at the age of seventy-eight, busy on his latest project, a New York subway system.

PART III

PART III

11

America 1826: Fifty Years of Independence

A HALF CENTURY AFTER its self-assertive Declaration of Independence the novel republic in the North American wilderness was an object of keen interest to European intellectuals. Many crossed the ocean to take a firsthand look, and returned home to record their impressions. Some, like Frances Trollope, who arrived in 1827, carped; more, like Alexis de Tocqueville, who came in 1832, admired; but all found a wealth of sights and sounds strange to the European eye and ear, and even nostril. William Newnham Blane, an Englishman who journeyed through "the States" in 1822–23, encountered on "the Prairie" a "beautiful little animal, about two feet long, of a dark colour, with longitudinal white stripes down its back, a bushy tail, and very short legs." To the Englishman's mystification, the little American creature stood its ground when he rode up to it. When he poked it with his whip it gave him a surprise he promised to "recollect till my dying day."

Most visitors landed at New York, Philadelphia, or Boston, three colonial provincial capitals whose bursting expansion since the Revolution showed no signs of abating, though when Blane landed in 1822 he found New York's population temporarily diminished. Yellow fever was raging in the city. In Greenwich Village, already overtaken by metropolitan growth, he found the streets in the low-lying parts barricaded and strewn with lime, the houses shuttered and deserted. He estimated that only seven or eight thousand of the city's current 120,000 residents remained in town. "Nothing endued with life was to be seen in any of the streets or neighboring quays, except here and there a cat." He had no difficulty assigning blame for New York's periodic visitations of the scourge—"There is no such thing in the whole place as a sink or common sewer. All the filth and soil is collected in pits, of which there is one in every house, and the very opening of which, when full, is enough to breed the plague itself. Moreover, their contents, instead of being carried to some distance from the town, are conveyed to the nearest slip, or quay, and thrown into the water. . . . The streets in the lower part of the town are notoriously filthy, and the stranger is not a little surprised to meet the hogs walking about in them, for the purpose of devouring the vegetables and offal that are thrown into the gutter."

Applying at a lodging house, Blane was asked if he minded sharing a room, and when he reluctantly agreed, discovered that it meant sharing the bed. He retreated on board ship.

The next year, on his return journey, Blane was more favorably impressed with the city. The yellow fever gone, the New Yorkers had returned to their homes, and "instead of a spectacle of desolation . . . the streets swarmed with an active and numerous population."

Another British visitor, Henry B. Fearon, noted that the laborers on the Manhattan waterfront were "less careworn" than London's navvies, and saw no beggars. He was impressed with the shopkeepers' display of their goods on sidewalk stands, implying a high standard of honesty, and despite the dirty streets, pigs, excessive drinking, violence, and racial prejudice, he saw no evidence of the "irremediable distress" of European cities. Even astringent Mrs. Trollope found much to appreciate in New York—the universal employment of ice to cool water and preserve butter, the gaslight illumination of the shops in the evening, the flagstone pavements, and the handsome new brownstone buildings. "In truth," she wrote on her return visit, "were all America like this fair city . . . I should say, that the land was the fairest in the world."

If metropolitan amenities lacked something from the viewpoint of a later day, they had made large advances over the eighteenth century. New York produced a major innovation in 1828 with the first American mass transit system in the form of a horse-drawn omnibus line. Philadelphia had pioneered an even more striking advance in 1822 with its Fairmount Works that steam-pumped water from the Schuylkill (with Oliver Evans's engine) throughout the city. That year Boston led in adopting gas lighting for its streets, New York following in 1828. None of these improvements, it should be pointed out, was the first in the world of its kind—in the 1820s pumped water distribution, gas streetlights, and omnibus lines were familiar to Londoners, Parisians, and many other European city dwellers.

The best city homes of the 1820s were replacing the medieval kitchen fireplace by the iron range, and heating fireplaces in living rooms and bedrooms by iron heating stoves, generally accompanied by the substitution of coal for wood. Yet the chronic conflagrations were still battled by volunteer companies manning horse-drawn hand pumps, and the night watch still patrolled the streets, lighted the lamps, and sounded alarms. Poorer homes were still unheated, had little furniture, no glass, china, or rugs, and the poor districts, still lacking sanitary facilities, supplied most of the cholera victims.

Great Fire in New York City, 1835. The frequent "Great Fires" were battled ineffectively by volunteer companies manning horse-drawn hand pumps. (Library of Congress)

The new cities of the West were objects of special interest to foreign observers. Mrs. Trollope had heard expansive natives compare Cincinnati with Paris. She found the town in reality "about the size of Salisbury" (actually 12,000) with only one paved street, no sewage system, its square blocks bisected by alleys that on rainy days especially were "abominations." Even well-disposed Tocqueville thought Cincinnati "a town which seems to want to get built too quickly to have things done in order. Large buildings, huts, streets blocked by rubble, houses under construction; no names to the streets, no numbers on the houses," nevertheless, "a picture of industry and work that strikes one at every step."

Yet another Englishman, John Woods, found Cincinnati a "noble-looking town, by far the best I have seen in the western country," compared with Pittsburgh, which "owing to the quantity of ironworks . . . has a black and dismal appearance."

In Erie Canal-created Lockport, Mrs. Trollope found that "as fast as half a dozen trees were cut down, a *factory* was raised up; stumps still contest the ground with pillars, and porticos are seen to struggle with rocks." Buffalo struck her as even queerer: "All the buildings have the appearance of having been run up in a hurry, though every thing has an air of great pretension; there are porticos, columns, domes, and colonnades, but all in wood. Every body tells you . . . and every body believes, that their improvement, and their progression, are more rapid, more wonderful, than the earth has ever before witnessed." American notions of "improvement" struck Mrs. Trollope as questionable. Driving from Utica to Albany, her appreciation of the beauty of the landscape was interrupted by the information from one Yankee fellow traveler that they were passing through property formerly belonging to a wealthy Englishman, a member of Parliament, who "has sold a deal of it, and now, madam, you may see it as it begins to improve"—pointing to a large wooden shed with a gigantic sign, "Cash for Rags."

What repeatedly astonished foreigners about the unfinished, obstreperous West was the abruptness of the transition from civilized milieu to untrammeled wilderness and back again. Tocqueville coasted along the southern shore of Lake Erie in a steamboat, for hours on end seeing nothing but the "dark forest that ends only where the lake begins," then suddenly out of nowhere, "a church tower, elegant houses, an appearance of wealth and industry"—Cleveland. Quitting Detroit, he passed through "one league" of land under cultivation: "After that we enter a thick forest through which a fine road has been cut. From time to time a little cleared space," within which a field covered with stumps surrounded a log cabin "often without windows." Yet there was "no poverty" and the "peasants" were "well-clothed." At the door of one cabin he saw the family drinking tea. Entering another, he found it to consist of a single room, yet "the woman dressed like a lady."

Investigating this mystery further, the French parliamentarian learned the pattern of pioneer life in this broad frontier zone from which the Indians had been driven, but which remained to be cultivated and exploited:

> When a new settler arrives, he goes to live with a neighbor if there is one. If there is not, he puts up a tent. The first operation is to clear the field, which he does with the help of laborers. The expense of this work is estimated at about 3 dollars per acre of land (including the clearing and erection of fences). When the land is thus prepared, the new settler sows an acre of potatoes, and sows wheat or corn in the rest according to the nature of the soil. . . . The new settler has to bring provisions for at least six months. Two barrels of corn for himself and his family, and one barrel of salt pork will be enough: the latter item costs 14 dollars. Tea does for drink. It is generally calculated that to establish a new settlement one must start with 150 to 200 dollars in hand. . . . With that money the new settler also buys animals which do not cost much to feed. They are let loose in the woods with a bell, and graze freely. A laborer costs one dollar when he is not fed, 6 shillings when he is.

Tocqueville noted that his information came from a young Scottish doctor, a new settler, near Pontiac, Michigan.

It was to take advantage of surrounding forest for cattle grazing and hunting that the Midwest settlers often chose the isolated sites that startled foreign visitors, accustomed to the traditional European farm-village cluster. Even where the American settlers built villages, they were closely walled in by the dense forest. Fresh clearings had a particularly desolate look, studded with black stumps or scorched treetrunks that had been girdled—"had their throats cut," in the words of Captain Basil Hall, who thought of them as "the very Banquos of the murdered forest!" In upstate New York, Captain Hall found his coach passing through villages whose white church spires were topped by gilt weathercocks "glittering and crowing, as it seemed, in triumph over the poor forest." His driver told him the name of each village and pointed out "the seminary . . . the polytechnic . . . the wool factory," and "at the next crack of the whip—hocus pocus! . . . again the depths of the wood at the other extremity of civilized society, with the world just beginning to bud, in the shape of a smoky log hut, ten feet by twelve, filled with dirty-faced children, squatted round a hardy-looking female cooking victuals for a tired woodsman seated at his door, reading with suitable glee in the Democratic Journal of New York an account of Mr. Canning's campaign against the Ultra Tories of the old country."

City and country, native and immigrant, Americans were insatiable newspaper readers, supporting some 850 periodicals of all types in 1828. Blane was "both surprised and pleased," when on asking the landlord of an Indiana tavern for something to read, he was presented with a choice of novels of Goldsmith and Scott. In St. Louis he met people who had read all Scott's works, including the latest, *The Fortunes of Nigel,* which had only appeared in England a few months before.

One thing all the visitors admitted: the Americans continued to eat well. Breakfast, especially, overwhelmed travelers with a profusion of ham, roast beef, eggs, steak, fish, broiled chicken, sausages, fried oysters, and preserved fruits. "No people on earth consume as much animal food as the Anglo-Americans—hot meat always eaten at breakfast, dinner and supper," wrote Blane. Even Mrs. Trollope was delighted by Cincinnati's markets selling "excellent" beef at four cents a pound, equally "excellent" fowl at twelve cents apiece, turkeys and geese for fifty cents. Pigs, rounded up in the woods and fattened on corn for a few weeks before slaughter, were so cheap that only the hams, shoulders and sides were saved, the rest being thrown into the Ohio River. Veal was "inferior . . . to the eye, but it ate well," and eggs, butter, nearly all kinds of vegetables were "excellent," and at moderate prices." Only American fruit proved second to European.

In the southwest frontier region of Mississippi in 1835, a Northern novelist named Joseph Ingraham found young men flocking in from the East or Europe filled with dreams of "a broad plantation, waving with the snow white cotton bolls. . . . Cotton and negroes are the constant theme—the ever harped upon, never worn out subject of conversation among all classes." Their eager avarice, he observed, rapidly despoiled the shallow-loam soil of the Mississippi uplands:

> Every plough-furrow becomes the bed of a rivulet after heavy rains—these uniting are increased into torrents, before which the impalpable soil dissolves like ice under a summer's sun. By degrees, acre after acre, of what was a few years previous beautifully undulating ground, waving with dark-green snow-crested cotton, presents a wild scene of frightful precipices and yawning chasms, which are increased in depth and destructively enlarged after every rain. There are many thousand acres within twenty miles of the city of Natchez, being the earliest cultivated portions of the country, which are now lying in this condition, presenting an appearance of wild desolation. . . .

William Faux, a querulous traveler, complained of the physical violence on every hand (even Tocqueville had to admit violence seemed excessive in the South), and the dirt—"soap is nowhere to be seen or found in any of the taverns east or west." Faux thought the Westerners lived "like store pigs in a wood, or fattening pigs in a stye." Tocqueville had a more favorable and more far-seeing comment on the "strange mixture of prosperity and poverty" of the frontier zone: "The Americans in their log houses have the air of rich folk who have temporarily gone to spend a season in a hunting-lodge."

Slovenly and backward in some foreign eyes, upward-mobile and lucky in others, the flood of immigrants from the Eastern states, Britain, and continental Europe, building their log cabins in the clearings amid the massacred trees, advanced irresistibly. The Indians were not so much overcome by armed force as shoved aside by technological superiority. Firearms played an insignificant role in the winning of the Midwest, and in fact probably helped the Indians to resist more than they facilitated the settlers' conquest, the musket invariably being the principal article of exchange for furs at both private and government trading posts. The invaders, cultivating their Eurasian wheat, South American potatoes, and the Indians' own corn with European implements and techniques, could feed a thousand where the Indians fed a dozen.

Add the steamboat, and they could do much more. The very first steamboats cut the keelboat rate from $5 per hundred pounds to $2 and swung open the gate to two-way trade between Midwest and East. Forests fell, farms multiplied, and supporting industry sprang up. Pittsburgh, Cincinnati, Wheeling, and Louisville offended Mrs. Trollope and her fellow travelers with their upstart pretensions and noisome streets, but the rolling mills, foundries, engine shops, boiler works, cotton mills, glass factories, and farm-implement plants wreathed in a perpetual pall of black smoke were transforming the Ohio Valley into one of the world's leading industrial areas. Shipyards abounded, sending a stream of low-decked, heavy-engined, tall-chimneyed steamboats into the many-branched Mississippi system. After the battle of New Orleans in 1815, Captain Henry Shreve took the *Enterprise* a hundred miles up the Red River to the Alexandria rapids, and in 1819 the *Independence* ascended the Missouri, followed next year by several little steamers of the government's Yellowstone expedition.

The first steamers appeared on Lake Ontario in 1816 and on Lake Erie in 1818, and the opening of the Welland Canal, providing a navigable link between the two lakes, gave a tremendous impetus to lake traffic.

Cargo was more important than passengers in the Western boats, but the largest vied with the Hudson steamers in accommodations. All steamboats made a selling point of luxury for cabin passengers. Blane admired their "handsome carpets, ornamented lamps, silk curtains, a profusion of gilding, glass and mahogany; a pianoforte and sofas in the ladies' cabin; baths, &c." Cabin passengers experienced considerable discomfort from noise and vibration, flies and mosquitoes, the aroma of livestock from the lower deck, frequent minor accidents, and the awkwardness of certain necessities, such as doing laundry on board, but for the travelers of 1826, such inconveniences were readily borne in gratitude for escape from the jolting, lurching, jam-packed, breakdown-prone stagecoach.

The steamboat's contribution to air pollution bothered no one, though some objected to its noise pollution. The exhaust from the high-pressure engines sounded like an approaching battle, and their power was indeed excessive for their quivering hulls—"an engine on a raft with $11,000 worth of jig-saw work," was one description. Though the Western boats could not compare with the Eastern for sturdiness, durability, smoothness of operation, and quality of workmanship, nevertheless, in the eyes of a modern scholar, Louis Hunter, they "may well be regarded as the more remarkable achievement." In freight and passenger carrying capacity on a given draft and at a given cost they were unmatched in the world. Gradually, through the efforts of the Stevenses and many other, mostly anonymous, engineers, skippers, designers, and builders, the engines, transmissions, gearing, and boilers improved in reliability and efficiency.

Their evolution was far from complete in 1826, though their future line of development was manifest in the unique solutions their builders were finding for the novel problems of Mississippi-system navigation. The large fluctuations in depth, constantly shifting river courses, and great number of cargo-landing points dictated ever shallower draft, while hulls grew longer and flatter, with straight sides and flat bottoms, returning oddly to much the configuration of Fulton's *Clermont*—for reasons unforeseen by Fulton, right for the Mississippi. The keel gradually shrank to a vestige, reducing draft and increasing cargo capacity, and, to the surprise of the skippers, actually improving steerability by facilitating the sliding movement around the river's sharp bends at which pilots became adept. A distinctive feature of the riverboat's profile dictated by conditions of service was the long rake of the stem, making her an odd sister of the slightly later clipper. The steamboat's prow was so low in the water that the aesthetic effect was slight (though the sheer, or rise of the deck fore and aft, did have an aesthetic intention) but it solved the problem of nosing up to the innumerable "steamboat landings" at plantations, farms and village roads, at all seasons of the changeable river's year.

Along with progress came costs. Steamboats proved efficient vectors of epidemic disease, especially cholera, and disasters were chronic. The thin hulls—the thinner the better for making a single trip's cargo pay and being able to pick it up and land it—were pierced by snags, and high-pressure boilers, overloaded by holding down the safety valves for more speed, exploded just as Oliver Evans's critics said they would. Sparks from the chimneys, careless crewmen, and passengers set fires in inflammable cargoes as well as superstructures and hulls. Often the tiller ropes, by which the skipper in his forward pilothouse controlled the rudder, burned and made it impossible to steer ashore. Apparently few passengers knew how to swim. The blazing *Brandywine* drifted aground fifty yards from shore above Memphis in 1832, and only 75 of the 200 aboard survived. Five years later the loss of the *Ben Sherrod*, with 150 lives, provoked a strong public reaction, including a mass meeting at Natchez that protested the alleged incompetence of the *Sherrod's* captain and the shocking negligence of the captain of another boat that steamed past the stricken craft without stopping to help. A succession of boiler accidents was climaxed in 1838 when the *Moselle* blew up at a landing in the Ohio a mile above Cincinnati in a spectacular explosion that rained fragments of timber and iron along with pieces of humanity from a geyser of steam and smoke that rose hundreds of feet. The gutted hulk drifted into the stream and sank, drowning more, the toll reaching 150 out of 280. The *Moselle's* captain had been much commended by passengers and the press for his success in achieving speed by feeding

Flatboats were not banished from the Mississippi by the steamboat. Flatboatmen could float their cargoes downstream and ride back upstream on a steamboat. Currier & Ives lithograph. (Library of Congress)

his fires with pine resin and holding steam in his boiler during landings by loading down the safety valve. The *Moselle,* everyone said up to the disaster, was "a crack boat."

Professor John Locke of Cincinnati showed that with the engine stopped, all valves closed, and the fires unchecked, steam pressure would climb from 100 to 200 pounds in less than five minutes. Angry public opinion blamed the ships' engineers for the repeated disasters, but the engineers were found to be acting under captains' orders in holding steam during landings. The old controversy of high pressure versus low pressure was muted by a number of boiler explosions on the Eastern low-pressure boats—if a boiler was overloaded, it could explode, whether its designed loading was high or low.

Nevertheless, the Western steamboats were statistically more hazardous, and one of the reasons was popularly recognized as the Western "go-ahead" spirit. Pioneers, prospectors, land speculators, and shoestring businessmen were full of it, and the steamboat skippers and owners (often the same) only had a more spectacular field to exhibit it. A Mississippi fireman boasted to a passenger: "I tell you, stranger, it takes a man to ride one of these half-alligator boats, head on a snag, high pressure, valve soldered down, 600 souls on board & all in danger of going to the devil." A writer in *The North American Review* emphasized the allure of speed: "It is in vain to hold it out as an inducement to passengers . . . that any boat is furnished the patent safety-valve, or supplied with life-preservers; another lying alongside, which has proved the faster in a trial of speed, leaves port crowded, while the empty cabins of the former cause captains and owners mentally to resolve, that the next boat they build, shall at all events be a fast one." The continued boiler explosions finally led to the first federal regulatory law in transportation in 1838, but it had hardly any effect, and not until 1852 were federal standards for construction, equipment, and operation of steamboats seriously applied.

Flatboats were by no means banished from the rivers by the steamboats; on the contrary, the economy and convenience of a steamboat ride back up river gave flatboating cargoes downriver a fresh attraction. Blane saw many, ranging from emigrant-family Huck-Finn-style rafts to the 150-ton-burden "Kentucky Arks" carrying horses, pigs, poultry, flour, corn, apples, peach brandy, cider, whiskey, bar iron, castings, tin and copper ware, glass, furniture, millstones, grindstones, nails, and everything else produced in the Midwest for sale downstream or out in the world.

Brilliantly successful in a commercial if not in a health and safety sense as the American steamboat was in its native river habitat, it was unfit for the deep sea. The *Savannah* had indeed crossed the Atlantic, but had made most of the voyage under sail, its fuel bunkers only capable of holding coal for eighty-nine hours' operation in the twenty-four-day crossing. The advantage the *Savannah*'s engine gave her in calm weather proved insufficient to compensate for the fuel savings of sailing ships, and she ended her career minus engine, sailing up and down the Atlantic coast.

For ocean steamship service, difficult technical problems had to be overcome, such as the strain put on a hull by a heavy engine in a violently rolling sea, the corrosion of boilers by salt water, and the inefficiency of existing coal-burning engines. In the end a British ship, the *Sirius*, was credited with the first all-steam Atlantic crossing. The *Sirius* barely made it to New York in 1838 as her stubborn skipper refused to hoist sails and held off a mutiny while feeding spars and furniture into his furnace, intent on winning a race with a rival British ship built by Isambard Brunel. The *Sirius*'s title is not completely clear, however, a British-built Dutch navy ship, the *Curaçao*, having apparently made an all-steam crossing to the West Indies in 1827.

The American sail merchant marine prospered with the growth of whaling stimulated by the market for illuminating oil. But interior rather than exterior transport was the significant sector. The success of the Erie Canal stirred businessmen and state legislatures up and down the East Coast and into the West. Long-dreamed-of projects like the Potomac-Ohio River and the Lake Erie-Ohio River links suddenly attracted financial support and new proposals met ready acceptance. Besides canals tying the Atlantic states to the Ohio Valley, and those connecting the Great Lakes with the Mississippi-Ohio system, there were the tidewater canals, dug from Maine to Virginia to give the upcountry farms and plantations access to the seagoing rivers.

Canal fever built up until it provoked resistance from competing or otherwise threatened interests—waggoners and turnpike innkeepers, and New England mill owners who objected to the diversion of their precious river waters. Some sensible protests were voiced over the construction of canals in technically difficult or economically barren regions. The first category was represented by the canals of western Pennsylvania which were carried over the Alleghenies by animal-powered haulage up inclined planes at what proved excessive costs, and the second by such New England canals as the New Haven & Northampton, poorly constructed because of a shortage of capital caused by the lack of sufficient traffic, and in turn contributing to economic failure.

Cost of canal construction typically overran engineers' optimistic estimates, and revenues repeatedly fell far below investors' anticipations. Macadamized turnpikes could be built at under $10,000 per mile, whereas canals cost upward of $20,000, and often much more. The Chesapeake and Ohio cost $60,000 per mile; the Boston and Lowell, $71,000; the Susquehanna and Tidewater, $80,000. Maintenance often came as a rude surprise when floods damaged canals or droughts made them useless. Finally, inevitably, canal management was nearly always either incompetent through inexperience or corrupt through absence of oversight, and commonly both.

Most of the money to build canals came from the state governments, which actually meant that it was borrowed in Europe, mainly London. When the canals failed to pay off, a negative reaction set in that snowballed into the disastrous Panic of 1837. Several states had to repudiate their canal debts, in other words declare bankruptcy.

That was a minor matter. Americans were more cheerful about bankruptcy than Europeans, not even socially ostracizing failed businessmen and readily extending them fresh credit, often creating a rags-to-riches-to-rags-to-riches cycle in a business career. But the national canal passion distracted engineers, promoters, state governments, and investors from the true technological solution to inland transportation. The best that can be said for the canal boom is that in several places it solved important local problems, and that it helped train a generation of civil engineers for railroad building.

The 1820 census counted 9,638,453 Americans. That of 1830 counted 12,866,020, the country thus adding during the decade of its fiftieth anniversary more than 3 million people, a considerably greater number than its total population in 1776. Most of the new Americans were the immigrants who crowded the lower decks of the river steamers, sleeping amid the cargo, eating sausage, dried herring, crackers, and cheese they furnished themselves, and supplying most of the victims for the disasters and cholera epidemics. In both casualty lists they shared honors with the crewmen. When the *John Adams* went down, 84 out of 100 cabin passengers were saved, but only 5 out of 87 "deckers"; 11 out of 11 officers, but just 7 out of 32 crew.

Such small losses made little impression on the census figures, universally regarded as reason for national self-congratulation. The domestic market was expanding at a rate neither Hamilton nor Jefferson had foreseen, enriching the New England successors of Slater and Lowell and the New York beneficiaries of the Erie engineers. Panics and depressions hardly interrupted growth, which resumed afterward at an accelerated rate.

America was a technology-hungry giant, feasting in great gulps with occasional digestive pauses. And if America was itself contributing significantly to the banquet, it was taking back far more than it contributed—all the devices and tech-niques invented in old Europe, Asia, and Africa, inherited without effort, and all the innovations of modern Britain and Europe, bought or stolen.

The country was unmistakably getting rich. The principal individual benefi-ciaries were the upper middle class of merchants and professionals. The country's only landed aristocracy, the Southern planters, were doing well too, but not nearly as well as the Yankee industrialists. Industrial capital was now accumu-lating to reinforce commercial capital as a source of new enterprise and encour-agement to invention.

Yet despite headlong growth, Tocqueville found some of the characteristics of smallness and intimacy in the 1830s: "Of all the countries in the world America is that in which the spread of ideas and of human industry is most continual and most rapid. There is not an American but knows the resources of all the parts of the vast land that he inhabits; all the able men in the Union know each other by reputation, many of them personally. I have often been struck by astonishment to find how far that is the case. . . . It has never happened to me to speak to an American about one of his compatriots without finding that he was up-to-date in knowing both how he was now placed and the story of his life."

The center ring in economic America in 1826 still belonged to agriculture, the sector that except for the transportation revolution—about to be completed by the railroad—had up to now been little affected by technological advance. The incompetent but not really stupid farmers of the marvelously abundant Midwest were ready for a technological revolution of their own.

12

The Stevenses, Peter Cooper, and the American Railroad

IN 1812 THE ERIE CANAL COMMISSIONERS received a letter (forwarded to them by De Witt Clinton) from Colonel John Stevens, advising that they drop their canal in favor of a railroad line. Stevens proposed mounting a pair of wooden rails on pillars three to six feet above ground and powering a carriage with cast-iron wheels by a steam engine like that aboard his *Juliana*. The cost per mile, he promised, would not exceed that of a good gravel turnpike.

There was no such thing as a railroad line in the world at the time, and Colonel Stevens's reputation as a steam-power engineer earned only a gingerly reception for his idea on the part of the canal commissioners. Many agreed with Benjamin Latrobe, the Philadelphia architect-engineer who completed the Capitol, that if land steam power was practical, England would have tried it out by now. "We are too apt to look up with reverential awe to what has usually been called the mother-country, for every improvement in the arts," Stevens retorted testily. His old friend and friendly enemy, Chancellor Livingston, argued that his wooden rails would not stand up and should be made of metal, sending the cost way up, and also that a railroad line would be inherently hazardous in comparison with a canal. Stevens composed a lengthy answer, concluding, "Sooner or later, the improvement now proposed will be brought into general use and, if I mistake not, long before the proposed canal will be completed." He mistook, but not by very much.

The pamphlet that Stevens presently published, containing his proposals and various defenses of them, were later called by an American railroad executive "the birth certificate of all railroads in the United States," but at the time, Stevens could get few people to read it. About the only enthusiastic response he got was from Oliver Evans, who expressed himself as "highly delighted [at Stevens's] . . . most comprehensive and ingenious view of this important subject . . . [that] removed all the difficulties that remained." Evans was probably the only man in the United States who did not think Stevens out of his mind in predicting "a steam carriage . . . moving with a velocity of one hundred miles an hour."

Besides the economic significance of the railroad, Stevens appreciated its military and political importance in a vast, underpopulated country. He appealed to Congress on patriotic grounds: "I am anxious and ambitious that my native country should have the honor of being the first to introduce an improvement of such immense importance." But Congress was as wary as the New York commissioners. Oliver Evans sagely concluded that it might be "enough for this generation to try canals, the next to try railways, and the next to adopt steam-carriages."

Stevens also pressed the New Jersey legislature, pointing out the value of a railroad across the state from Trenton to New Brunswick to connect the Delaware and Philadelphia with the Raritan and New York. His own steamboats operating on both rivers gave him an admitted interest in the overland link, which stagecoaches were filling, but not very satisfactorily. Their free-enterprise competition was too competitive and too free—despite all Stevens and his sons could do, the coaches battled each other to the detriment of the passengers, whom they refused to set down except at the inns with which they had financial arrangements. Even Rachel Stevens, wanting to get out at Van Brunt's in New Brunswick, was forced to descend instead at Keyworth's.

The New Jersey legislature in 1815 chartered a company to build a "Rail-Road," but without mention of motive power. Stevens meantime was distracted by his ironclad warship and a new projectile he and his brightest son, Robert Livingston Stevens, had conceived—a shaped charge containing an explosive. The shell was successfully tested under the eyes of Commodore Stephen Decatur and Captain David Porter, and Stevens, in forwarding the results to President Madison, commented, "If I do not grossly deceive myself, these shells are calculated to produce, ultimately, an entire revolution in naval and military tactics." He was right about that too, but the revolution awaited considerable further technical development, notably breech-loading and a better propellant.

As work on the Erie Canal progressed, Stevens shifted geographical tactics and proposed railroads farther south to link the Ohio with east-flowing rivers. To Pennsylvania he suggested a line connecting the Susquehanna with the Ohio, and to the federal government in Washington one linking the Ohio with the Potomac. The Pennsylvania legislature voted an authorization in 1823, but no money, and the length of the line, over 70 miles, was enough to make Philadelphia capital wary.

Stevens turned back to New York. The financial success of the Erie Canal, presaged long before its completion by the tolls on the intermediate sections, suggested the viability of a New York-to-Albany rail line. The terrain was ideal, as

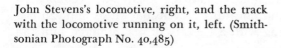

John Stevens's locomotive, right, and the track with the locomotive running on it, left. (Smithsonian Photograph No. 40,485)

he pointed out to De Witt Clinton: "The shores of the Hudson afford a theatre [for steam locomotion] as complete as may be desired." Clinton replied promptly early in 1825, assuring Stevens that he was "fully impressed with the importance of the project," and enclosing a clipping from a London paper. The clipping described a steam railroad experiment to be tried in the north of England coal country, between Stockton and Darlington. Clinton with his usual perspicacity predicted that the success of the pioneer English line would permit capital to be raised in the United States.

Stevens, now seventy-six years old, determined to build a demonstration railroad that would disprove the technical objections to steam locomotion and dramatize its potential. At his old Hoboken workshop he plunged into the project with the enthusiasm of youth. "It is really surprising that Your Papa at his age should be so very active," Rachel Stevens wrote one of her sons. "He enjoys good health and his faculties don't seem in the least impaired."

On the vast tree-shaded lawn below the house Stevens laid out a half-mile circular track on which he assembled a steam engine with a vertical tubular boiler and a round furnace surmounted by a smokestack. A horizontal cylinder transmitted power to a crankshaft connected to a gear wheel that meshed with a rack rail midway between the wheel rails. The whole, mounted on a four-wheeled platform, weighed less than a ton. On February 28, 1825, the colonel wrote a satisfied but modest memorandum of his demonstration:

"In the afternoon of last Saturday week, I made some experiments for propelling a carriage on railways but did not succeed to my satisfaction owing to the great friction of the wheels against the sides. On the following Monday I sent the carriage down to Van Velsen's shop and directed him to insert rollers into each end of two bars; one to be placed in front of the fore-wheels and the other behind the hind wheels, extending beyond their track on each side, so as to roll against the upright pieces placed on the outer side of the ways. This improvement, as far as I know, is original." The friction against which Stevens had to take special measures was caused by the tightness of the curve. The passengers were friends invited from New York. The beaver-hatted gentlemen, wide-skirted and parasoled ladies were whirled around the circular track at a speed of 6 miles per hour. They were the first passengers ever to ride on a steam railroad, not only in America but in the world. George Stephenson's demonstration run on the Stockton & Darlington did not come till September of that same year, 1825.

That, of course, was the year the Erie Canal was completed. The Erie had no immediate meaning to New Jersey, but it had considerable meaning elsewhere. Philadelphia businessmen immediately began talking about canals to the West. Baltimore businessmen began talking about a railroad, not because they were more progressive or farsighted than Philadelphians but because a canal following the route of the Potomac or the Susquehanna was cost-prohibitive. In 1827 the Baltimore interests pushed a bill through the Maryland legislature authorizing a railroad line, to be named the Baltimore & Ohio, to run from Baltimore to Wheeling, Virginia, on the Ohio River. On the Fourth of July, amid a shower of fireworks, Charles Carroll of Carrollton, last surviving signer of the Declaration of Independence, lifted the sod for the first stone of the roadbed.

Real-estate promoters were not slow to seek advantage in Baltimore's railroad enthusiasm. Two New York speculators presently invited a friend to join them in buying up three thousand acres of land at Lazeretto Point, across the bay from Fort McHenry of *Star-Spangled Banner* fame. The friend they invited was not a man either to forego opportunity or to invest lightly, and only came in on the deal after careful on-the-spot study and consultation. He was also not the man to let a business venture fail for want of enterprise and inventiveness, which explains why a New York merchant and philanthropist succeeded Colonel Stevens as American railroad pioneer, building the first American locomotive to run on a regular track.

Peter Cooper is the prototype of the Horatio Alger model success story. On the February night in 1791 when he was born, his father, walking up Broadway, heard a voice advising, "Call his name Peter and he will do a work for the world as important as that done by Peter of old." The elder Cooper was a Revolutionary War veteran who had turned into a peripatetic ne'er-quite-do-well, and Peter grew up with only three terms of schooling, the rest of boyhood helping out with, and thereby learning, one trade after another—hatmaking, brickmaking, brewing. His childhood was by no means unhappy. He remembered his father taking him to see George Washington's funeral parade down Broadway, holding him up to see over the crowd. He also got to see Thomas Jefferson ride up to the building where Congress was meeting, tie his horse to a hitching post, and go in.

Like Eli Whitney and John Fitch, he had a vast curiosity about how things worked, and an irrepressible instinct for making them work better. Helping his mother pound the family wash in a wooden tub, he devised a pump-handle lever with a ratchet mechanism that pounded all around the tub as he worked the handle. Finding an old shoe in the street, he took it apart, studied the pieces, and thereafter made shoes for the family. A go-cart he built brought him $6 with which he made what he later described as the best two investments of his life: a lottery ticket and a cigar, which cured him permanently of gambling and smoking, and by a natural extension, of drinking. He had an adventurous streak that often led to danger from climbing trees, exploring houses under construction, sleighing on Hudson River ice, jumping logs, and swimming. Luckily his mother was a model of calmness; when warned that Peter was climbing the ridgepole of the house, she remarked, "Then he will not be drowned in the Hudson," and hearing that he was swimming in the river, expressed gratitude that he would not fall off the roof.

Peter Cooper, his wife Sarah, and children Edward and Sarah Amelia. (New-York Historical Society, New York City)

At seventeen Peter was apprenticed to a maker of private carriages, John Woodward, for whom he proved an exemplary worker, while spending his few leisure hours visiting New York's museums—Savage's, Scudder's, and Barnum's. He invented a machine for mortising the hubs of carriages, a task previously performed by hand, and sold it to his employers. He never took out a patent on it, and in 1879 noted with satisfaction that his device was still "mortising all the hubs in the country." He remembered himself as a tireless dabbler, "always fussing and contriving . . . never satisfied unless I was doing something difficult—something that had never been done before, if possible." His most ambitious invention was a huge contrivance for harnessing the tidal current of the East River to a waterwheel, using the power to compress air in a chamber on the shore, and transferring the compressed air to cylinders on board ferryboats to be released to drive the paddle wheels. His enthusiasm persuaded Robert Fulton to come and look, but Fulton looked and declined comment.

At the end of Cooper's apprenticeship, Woodward showed his appreciation of the young man's character as well as ability by offering him a loan to go into coach making on his own. Cooper accepted, but before he could open his own shop, Woodward ran into financial disaster as the result of a single wealthy client reneging on an order. The American private coach business, Cooper perceived, was an unreliable luxury trade better left to the British and French imports. As late as 1832 Tocqueville observed, "In all the journeys I have made in the United States I have never seen one single person in his own carriage or with his own horses. The wealthiest people travel in public conveyances without servants."

A brother of Peter's who had settled in Hempstead, Long Island, introduced him to a man who had invented a machine for shearing cloth, and was looking for a partner. Cooper accepted the offer, made improvements in the machine, and profited when the War of 1812 shut off British imports. One of his customers was Matthew Vassar, proprietor of an ale-and-oyster house in the basement of the Poughkeepsie County Court House, who bought a machine at a moment when the firm's fortunes were at a low ebb, and with it the rights to sell it in Poughkeepsie County.

Amid inventions and sales promotion, Peter found an opportunity to socialize in Hempstead, and met Sarah Bedell, his "day star and the inspiration of his life." They were married in 1813, and henceforth, "he never sat near her without holding her hand in his [and] never spoke to her or of her without some tender epithet." Sentiment was fortified by tragedy. The first four of the Coopers' six children died in infancy. The last two, Edward and Sarah Amelia, were the more cherished.

Love and marriage did not deter invention; on the contrary. To meet a new American problem, he invented a lawnmower very like the modern hand mower; he did not patent this, but a little later took out his first patent for a device inspired by his first child. To free his wife from the need to rock the baby's cradle, he ran a wooden rod through a hole in the floor, suspended on "knife-edge bearings." In the cellar the rod was attached to a barrel filled with stones that acted as a pendulum; given a push, the barrel rocked the cradle for hours. Cooper bought a Swiss music box from a Yankee peddler and attached it to the pendulum. He added a flagstaff of cloth strips, also powered by the pendulum, that waved to keep flies off the baby, and patented the whole device. The peddler on his return through Hempstead offered his horse, wagon, and stock for Connecticut rights.

The postwar slump of 1815 put an end to the cloth-shearing business and Peter returned to New York to join his brother-in-law Benjamin Bedell in operating a grocery on the Bowery near Stuyvesant Street. The store was profitable, but storekeeping was tedious, and Cooper soon turned back to invention.

Discussion of the technology of the Erie Canal was at its height. Cooper conceived a device to propel canal boats by exploiting the power wasted in the falling water of the locks. In a mile-long stretch of the East River he built a model consisting of a waterwheel, a reservoir, and an endless chain. The towline of a scow was fastened to a hook on the chain and the scow towed forward as the waterwheel turned. In June 1820 the young inventor took De Witt Clinton aboard and propelled him a mile down the river and a mile back in eleven minutes. Clinton wanted to use the invention on the Erie, but had to give in to the objections of farmers along the right-of-way who had been promised that they could sell horses and feed to the canallers. Cooper ran his waterpowered scow on the East River for ten days, giving free rides to a thousand passengers, but aroused no further interest. In 1870 the president of the Camden & Amboy Canal in New Jersey conceived the same method of propulsion for his waterway, and applying to the Patent Office, discovered Peter Cooper's fifty-year-old, long-expired patent.

Cooper found another use for his endless-chain principle, substituting it for the crank in the rotary steam engine and taking out two patents for a steam-powered chalk grinder.

The depression of 1820–21 brought him a financial opportunity in the form of a chance to buy into a company with good potential, a Manhattan glue manufactory on Kip's Bay. The depression soon turned into the Era of Good Feeling as the steamboats opened up the West, and Cooper set about making his glue factory the best glue factory in the world. The first person in every morning, he lighted the fires himself, and managed the plant, kept the books, sold the product, and did maintenance. His was the first American-made glue to compete in quality with Irish, English, and French, and one of the first American products to achieve what became an American trademark: reliable uniformity. His business reputation was that of a tough but thoroughly honest bargainer, an antiunion but fair boss, and conscientious-toward-consumers sales promoter. He once refused to raise a price as high as the demand seemed to justify, telling a subordinate simply, "The world needs this thing."

Glue started his fortune, New York real estate did the rest. Fed by the Erie Canal and the riches of the West, New York was beginning to make serious use of its fabulous harbor, and the result was spreading the city rapidly northward up Manhattan Island. Starting out merely with the intention of building a nice house for his family, Cooper acquired a section of new, undeveloped Fourth Avenue, several houses and lots on Third Avenue, a tract of land at Third Avenue and Thirty-third Street, a tract fronting the Hudson between 113th and 114th streets (at the moment only lines on a map), and a farm in Mamaroneck, some 25 miles outside of town, in Westchester County. Though he hardly profited to the extent of the Astors, Rhinelanders, and Lorillards, he did well enough to become one of the city's five known millionaires before the Civil War.

His inventive muse was not repressed by business problems or profits. He devised a steam-propelled, wire-guided torpedo and a gas balloon whose explosion cost him part of the sight of one eye. In a more utilitarian vein, and as a byproduct of the glue factory, he created the first widely used packaged table gelatin in America, with Mrs. Cooper writing the recipes printed on the packets.

But the invention destined to put Peter Cooper's name in all the history texts came about as a result of his real-estate speculation in Baltimore. He had already invested much of his capital and borrowing capacity in the purchase and clearing of land (his endless-chain device proved an excellent earth-moving conveyor belt) and in building kilns and forges to exploit the area's bog iron for rails, when the commissioners of the Baltimore & Ohio (B. & O.) suddenly ran into a technical problem. They had hastily pushed their roadbed through hilly country before considering certain problems inherent in steam locomotion, and though George Stephenson's demonstration of his *Rocket* locomotive in England in 1829 confirmed them in their intention to use steam, they found their curve radiuses too tight to be practical for Stephenson's or any other known engine.

The commissioners were in a quandary. Peter Cooper stepped forward to save the day, the future of the railroad, and especially his own investment. "I saw the defeat of my enterprise . . . a terrible defeat to me," he recalled later, and told the commissioners to hold on and "I would put a small locomotive on, which I thought could pull a train around those short curves. . . . So I got up a little locomotive."

Tom Thumb races the horsecar, 1830. From William H. Brown, *History of the First Locomotive in America,* 1871. (Eleutherian Mills Historical Library)

Cooper had a small brass engine shipped from New York to Baltimore on June 15, 1830, found some wheels at the Mount Clare Railroad Shop, had a boiler made, and fashioned pipes out of two musket barrels for tubing to the boiler. To increase draft, he rigged a blowing apparatus driven by a drum attached to a car wheel. The wheelbase was short, and Jonathan Wright, chief engineer of the B. & O., contributed a new wheel design that improved adherence to the rail: each wheel was in section a segment of a large cone. The vertical boiler was about 6 feet high, with a diameter of only 20 inches, the engine one horsepower with a cylinder $3\frac{1}{4}$ inches in diameter and a $14\frac{1}{4}$-inch piston stroke. At first Cooper employed his endless-chain substitute for the crank, but it made a clacking noise during the preliminary trials, and he abandoned it. After various mishaps the little locomotive, christened *Tom Thumb,* finally had a successful run (August 1830) carrying six men on the engine and thirty-six in tow on a car and achieving 15 miles per hour, with a top speed of 18. The safety valves released steam too generously but Cooper "put my hand on them and held them down."

The demonstration and subsequent runs by the little brass engine stimulated the sale of the railroad's bonds, and aroused Baltimore's threatened stagecoach proprietors. The result was an incident that inscribed, or rather engraved, *Tom Thumb* in American folklore. The leading coach company, Stockton & Stokes, organized a race between the locomotive and one of their horses, each drawing a single car, from Relay House to Baltimore, a distance of eight miles. *Tom Thumb* got off to a slow start, as the speed of the wheels had to start Cooper's drumblower going, and the horse had a quarter-mile lead when the safety valve lifted and the steam issued to a whistle. The passengers shouted, the engine gained on the horse and passed him, but just at that moment the blowing device failed, the band slipping from the drum. Cooper managed to get it back on, but the horse had gained an insuperable advantage and won the race, to the widely publicized delight of the coachers and the horse-loving public.

Cooper was chagrined, but not crushed ("It didn't amount to anything," he told reporters) and the success of the B. & O. unaffected. Currier & Ives later made a picture of the race, but with a nice commercial prudence showed the horse and locomotive neck and neck, offending neither conservative horsemen nor progressive railway enthusiasts.

Its demonstration value vindicated, *Tom Thumb* was soon retired from service in favor of the *York,* built by Phineas Davis of York, Pennsylvania, winner of a

John Stevens's son Robert Stevens, inventor of the T-rail and the timber "sleeper," as well as a "pilot" assembly, forerunner of the locomotive cowcatcher. (Smithsonian Photograph No. 644B)

contest sponsored by the railroad. By 1834 the B. & O. had seven locomotives, thirty-four passenger cars, and a thousand freight cars running as far as Harper's Ferry.

But the railroad did not consist only of locomotive and cars. There was also the other component, the rails. These actually antedated George Stephenson's, John Stevens's and Peter Cooper's locomotives by a couple of centuries, wooden rails having supported hand-drawn and animal-drawn cars in Central European metal mines in the 1500s. By the time of *Tom Thumb* several iron-rail profiles had been designed, but the right one not yet hit upon. One night in the foyer of the Park Theatre in New York, Colonel Stevens's two sons, Robert and John Cox Stevens, encountered Commodore Robert F. Stockton, leader of the canal party in New Jersey that was blocking the Stevens rail project. Instead of talking about the play they talked about railroads and canals, and agreed to a compromise by which the Jersey legislature granted charters to both companies. Robert Stevens was made president and chief engineer of the resulting Camden & Amboy Railroad, and went off to England to buy iron rails. On board ship one day he whittled out the cross-section of the standard British "Birkenhead" rail, with an I-shaped cross-section.

Such a section had to be secured to the stone blocks of the roadbed by small angled iron plates called chairs, or pedestals, and it occurred to Stevens that these might present a production problem in America. He then whittled out an inverted T that could be spiked into wooden plugs in the stone blocks, and arriving in England explained his idea to the iron manufacturers. They were dubious, but finally gave in, and in 1831 the sailing ship *Charlemagne* docked in Philadelphia with the first shipment of 550 sixteen-foot iron T-rails.

The T-rail proved a large blessing to American railroads and their passengers. Most of the early American tracks were made by the slapdash technique of capping lengths of wooden rail with iron straps, which had the habit of coming loose and curling upward into "snakeheads" that thrust themselves suddenly through the floors of passing coaches.

In England Robert made friends with the Stephensons—old George and son Robert, another brilliant engineer, from whom the American purchased a locomotive on the model of the Stephensons' new *Planet*. The two Roberts drafted a contract with genially imprecise specifications—"Jones's Wheels, if not found objectionable . . . a vertical cylinder of as great a diameter as convenient. . . . The tubes to be made of iron as thin as possible." The resulting *John Bull* locomotive duly arrived in the United States and made its test run on November 12, 1831. Colonel Stevens, now eighty-two, was the life of the turtle-soup-and-champagne party he threw in Hoboken. When *John Bull* showed a tendency to jump Robert Stevens's rails, Robert invented a "pilot" assembly mounted on guide wheels to run in front of the locomotive, the same solution John Jervis was finding the same year. Matthias Baldwin adopted *John Bull* as the model for his first locomotive in his new Philadelphia works.

Locomotive *John Bull,* ordered in England by Robert Stevens from George and Robert Stephenson in 1831, model for the first locomotive produced by Matthias Baldwin in his Philadelphia works. (Smithsonian Photograph No. 3,661)

Best Friend of Charleston, the first American locomotive in commercial service, 1830. (Smithsonian Photograph No. 14,490)

Building his roadbed toward Amboy that winter of 1831, Robert Stevens found himself frustrated by the delay in delivery of stone blocks (from the Sing Sing prison quarry). Cutting and laying transverse logs and ramming home broken rocks between them, he laid his rails directly on these "sleepers" or cross-ties, and so reached Amboy. To his surprise, he found that the locomotive not only ran well on this simpler bed, but that the ride was more comfortable.

Robert Stevens never patented his rail or roadbed, both of which were freely used by all other American railroads. Stevens was not aware at the time that across the Atlantic another inventor, Charles Vignoles, was simultaneously inventing the same T-rail spiked directly to ties for a French railway. The Industrial Revolution was making strides outside England.

American railroad building slowed down after a flashy start that included several other lines besides the Baltimore & Ohio and the Camden & Amboy. The Charleston & Hamburg's *Best Friend of Charleston* was the first American-built locomotive actually to enter commercial service. The *Stourbridge Lion,* built in Britain to John Jervis's specifications for the Carbondale & Honesdale (later absorbed into the Delaware & Hudson), proved too heavy for the track and trestles. The *De Witt Clinton* made its trial run in 1831 on the Mohawk & Hudson, grandparent of the New York Central. The incipient railroad boom was slowed by the success of the Erie Canal, widely but not very effectively imitated, tying up investment capital through the 1830s and 1840s, and by the Panic of 1837. Most of the early lines radiated from the port cities—Boston, New York, Philadelphia, Charleston, Savannah, Mobile—or formed short links or feeders for rivers or canals.

Robert Stevens and his brother remained in railroading all their lives, Robert contributing a stream of minor inventions. Robert also gained fame in another medium, designing and sailing racing yachts that won international fame and gave the American image, especially in Britain, a touch of polish.

Peter Cooper, on the other hand, his railroading immortality secure as the result of a single impromptu achievement, went on to other fields, pioneering in the iron and steel industry (his Trenton, New Jersey, plant rolled the first I-beams in 1860), aiding the Atlantic Cable project, and presiding over the North American Telegraph Company while inventing a washing machine, a compressed-air engine for ferryboats, and many other devices. He had patents signed by every president

The *De Witt Clinton,* New York's first locomotive, which made its trial run in 1831. (Smithsonian Photograph No. 13,225-C)

from Madison to Fillmore, after whose term presidents ceased personally signing patents. As a New York City alderman he set an example of probity and public spirit, helping to professionalize the city's police and fire departments and improve public sanitation by securing a modern water-supply system. His finest monument was the Cooper Union, which he founded in New York in 1859 to teach science and engineering to young Americans, tuition-free. His civic sense disapproved of encouraging beggars, but his generosity proving ungovernable he compromised by giving a handout to every mendicant who solicited him while warning his grandson never to do so.

He lived to enjoy a rare moment of glory in 1880 as the white-haired, eighty-nine-year-old star of Baltimore's 150th anniversary parade, along with a replica of *Tom Thumb,* cheered by a quarter of a million people, most of whom were not even born when the little engine and its inventor made history.

13

John Hall and Sam Colt: the Birth of the "American System"

ON TOP OF THE STEEPLE of the First Parish Church in Portland, Maine, a slight discoloration is visible on the weathervane, a patch put there to cover up a bullet hole. The bullet hole was made in 1812 when John H. Hall stood at the foot of Temple Street a block away and demonstrated his new breech-loading rifle with an accurate shot. In time, this demonstration became a second shot heard round the world.

Everyone knew rifles were better than smoothbores. The Pennsylvania rifle was an American legend along with Daniel Boone. Because of its small bore and tendency to foul after repeated firing, however, it remained a better hunting than military weapon. Even before the end of the Revolution, Daniel Morgan's sharpshooters had discarded it in favor of the smoothbore Charleville. What was needed to make rifling work militarily, as gunsmiths and ordnance officers knew, was a method of loading the gun at the breech instead of via the muzzle. Breech-loading also promised significant battlefield advantages in rapidity of fire and facility of loading while kneeling, crouching, or lying prone. A clever British officer, Major Patrick Ferguson, had invented a breech-loader with which he armed his regiment in the Revolution, but its battle advantages were evidently limited, since Ferguson was killed and his command wiped out by backwoods militia at King's Mountain. One disadvantage that doubtless troubled Ferguson's men was that the marriage of flintlock ignition and breech-loading was uncomfortable, because it was difficult to make a flint lock that would supply a spark and yet close tightly enough to fully contain the explosion. A basic problem of black powder, not really

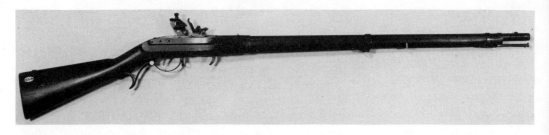

Hall's breech-loader. (National Park Service)

solved until the introduction of smokeless powder in the 1880s, was that the fraction of it that burned did so very quickly, practically all at once. That characteristic put a premium on tight containment of the rapidly expanding gases.

John Hancock Hall—he was born in Portland two years after the Declaration of Independence—was one of a number of inventors still struggling with the flintlock-breech-loading combination when he put his shot through the Portland weathervane. He had patented his rifle the year before, 1811, jointly with Dr. William Thornton, one-time collaborator with John Fitch. Dr. Thornton, intelligent, slippery, a friend of Jefferson but a bit of a rascal, had become chief of the Patent Office. To Hall's application he had returned a refusal on the ground that a breech-loading rifle had already been patented—by himself. Thornton may have thought of inventing a breech-loading gun—many people had—but the deal he presently arranged with Hall to share the patent was evidently a simple shakedown. Hall apparently thought it expedient to go along.

Like Paul Moody, Hall came from an upper-middle-class New England family, his father and grandfather having graduated from Harvard. Hall himself had passed up college in favor of guns, though later sending his son to college (Yale, not Harvard). In 1813, while making guns for the War of 1812 (he also served in the militia, acquiring the title of captain), he married a York, Maine, girl named Statira Preble, relative of the famous Commodore Edward Preble. His gunshop on Richardson's Wharf in Portland was not large, employing only six or eight men, and is not even known to have used waterpower. But in June of 1816 he wrote a letter to the War Department that showed him to be fully abreast of Eli Whitney's mass-production concept:

"Only one point now remains . . . viz.: to make every similar part of every gun so much alike that it will suit every gun, e.g., so that every bayonet will suit every barrel, so that every barrel will suit every stock, every lock or receiver will suit every barrel, and so that if a thousand were taken apart . . . will all come right . . . and although in the first instance it will probably prove expensive, yet ultimately it will prove most economical and be attended with great advantage."

Portland is 175 miles from Springfield and 200 from New Haven, and so John Hall was not exactly a neighbor of either Whitney or Whitney's friend and protégé Roswell Lee at the Springfield Arsenal. Yet he could hardly have been unaware of Whitney's long struggle. At least one other New England gunsmith, Simeon North of Berlin, Connecticut (only 25 miles from New Haven), is known to have striven for interchangeability in his manufacture of pistols on government contract, but North like Whitney evidently used hand methods to finish his parts.

In 1817 the government bought a hundred of Hall's rifles, and the following year gave him a contract to design and construct at Harper's Ferry a factory to manufacture them in quantity. He at once resolved to carry out his plan of fully interchangeable parts. "I had been told that it had been pronounced impossible by the French Commissioners appointed by that Government . . . and I know that all attempts to effect it in Great Britain and this Country had failed; but from an unswerving reliance on my own abilities I expected to accomplish it in a *short* period."

Harper's Ferry occupies a low-lying peninsula between the converging Shenandoah and Potomac rivers. Offshore in the Shenandoah a group of islets are known collectively as the Island of Virginius, or simply the Island. This was the site turned over to Hall for his "Rifle Works," an establishment entirely separate from the "Musket Factory" on the peninsula facing the Potomac.

Hall was fortunate in getting cooperative encouragement from the army in the person of Lieutenant-Colonel George Bomford, assistant chief of ordnance who succeeded Colonel Decius Wadsworth as chief in 1821 and ran Army Ordnance for the next twenty-one years. Despite Bomford's support Hall found his anticipation of a *"short* period" overoptimistic. It was five years before he succeeded in assembling or fabricating machinery capable of producing identical parts, and found it still not satisfactory.

Hall was able to profit from two significant inventions of the Connecticut arms industry. At the Springfield arsenal, a mechanic named Thomas Blanchard conceived and built a machine to carve out wooden gunstocks of identical pattern. Blanchard's machine was a lathe whose rotary cutter was linked by cams to a tracing wheel of the same diameter as the cutter. The tracing wheel followed a master gunstock pattern, and via the cams guided the cutter on its irregular path through a wooden block. Given hard enough steel, such machines as Blanchard's could be adapted to cutting metal parts, but that transition was some distance away. In the meantime the simple "milling machine," mounting a fixed rotary metal cutter with several cutting edges, had appeared in the private arms industry. Once believed an invention of Eli Whitney, the milling machine is now more cautiously ascribed to Simeon North, perhaps in 1818, the same year as Blanchard's lathe. In 1827 John Hall patented a "Machine for Cutting Metal and Other Hard Substances" that improved on the North miller by the addition of an automatic feed.

Like Whitney and North, Hall relied on the forge to produce rough metal parts, and employed his new machine to cut the rough parts to finished precision. In this he was notably more successful than Whitney had been. A commission sent by the War Department conducted a test similar to that by which Eli Whitney had dazzled and perhaps tricked Thomas Jefferson, but on a conclusively large scale. Recalling one hundred Hall rifles that had been shipped to the Springfield Armory two years earlier, the commission mixed them with more recently made parts and found they fitted each other with an "exact nicety." Hall's machinery was not basically different from Whitney's; it was simply better—that is, it permitted closer tolerances. American foundrywork, if it had not caught up with

Harper's Ferry, the confluence of the Potomac, left, and the Shenandoah, right, with the U.S. Armory (musket works) along the river. John Hall's rifle works is hidden behind the hill on the right. (Library of Congress)

British, was not far behind, and in its application to machine tools was opening new horizons.

Hall also made the important move of establishing standard screw threads. Heretofore two screws of the same diameter might vary in pitch, that is, number of threads per inch, or in depth of thread, or even if they were identical in all three of these dimensions might still not be interchangeable if the profile of the threads varied slightly. In still another significant advance in mechanical engineering, Hall introduced the technique of gauging all operations on a given part from the same point, or bearing, to insure uniformity.

Hall's Harper's Ferry machinery attracted European interest. A Prussian and a French diplomatic representative came to inspect and to take away Hall rifles. Ultimately Hall manufactured 9,000 rifles claimed to be fully identical, and of superior accuracy and loading speed to the muskets being made over on the Harper's Ferry mainland.

His triumph was finite. Hall rifles were used in the Black Hawk and Seminole Wars of the 1830s, but the army found fault—Hall's lock had an awkwardly protruding lever that galled the shoulder when carried at shoulder arms, and its sights, offset to the left because of the same lever, made it hard to aim. In the eyes of the generals, the muzzle-loading smoothbore was still the reliable battlefield weapon, and as late as the Mexican War (1846) Winfield Scott opted for Old Reliable.

In the end the Hall breech-loader was allowed to die, and despite all the proven advantages of the breech-loading principle, the Civil War found the army still wedded to muzzle-loading, because of the French invention of the Minié ball, now feasible for rifles.

Of far more importance than the breech-loader was the advance Hall brought in the technique of interchangeability.

The economic character of firearms as government-contracted, mass-produced, identical-form products made them the natural industrial sector for experimental mass production. Hall's breech-loader was no better adapted to interchangeability than Whitney's musket, but its advantages as a firearm, combined with two other inventions, opened a new technical path for the development of firearms that fitted in exceptionally well with the concept of mass production.

The first of these two inventions was percussion ignition. Hall's original rifle used the centuries-old flint-and-iron combination to make a spark to set off the powder in the flashpan to explode the propellant or the cartridge. A Scottish minister named Alexander Forsyth tried exploding a fulminate simply by hitting it with what came to be called the hammer. Inventors on both sides of the Atlantic soon took the next step of packaging Forsyth's fulminate in a little paper envelope or cap, destined for a long life in toy pistols but of immediate value in real weapons. The American version was patented by an English-born Philadelphia artist named Joshua Shaw, and adopted by John Hall for his breech-loader. Simeon North made a number of the new guns for the army under Hall's patent. When the metallic cartridge, securely sealing propellant and bullet to eliminate gas leakage, was developed in France, the stage was set for the modern military firearm, the repeating rifle.

The first inventor to attempt to make a percussion repeating rifle was a Martinsburg, New York, boy named Walter Hunt, who moved to New York City in 1826 to set up a machine shop. Ingenious and eclectic, Hunt invented a flax-spinning machine, a heating stove, an iceboat, a nail-making machine, a fountain pen, and a sewing machine. One day he needed a small, secure fastening for something, and in three hours of tinkering with a piece of wire, invented the safety pin—which he sold for $400, the only money he ever got out of it. Hunt was one of the first mechanics and gunsmiths to perceive that successful breech-loading of a percussion-fired gun opened the way to a repeating weapon. All that was needed was a spring mechanism that would feed a succession of cartridges to the chamber and an ejection device to get rid of the old cartridge case.

Hunt's rifle fired a metal cartridge with a cork stopper over a hollow-based bullet. Despite problems with the breech bolt, the cartridge and gun had unmistakable potential and attracted immediate attention. Lewis Jennings, a gunsmith who had long experimented with the repeating idea, improved Hunt's magazine. Horace Smith, who had been manufacturing the French Flobert target pistol with metal cartridge, sought out Daniel Wesson, an expert employed by Robbins & Lawrence of Windsor, Vermont, one of New England's largest arms firms. Backed by a New York promoter named Courtland Palmer, Smith and Wesson eventually developed a satisfactory breech-bolt mechanism. A New England group that included New Haven shirtmaker Oliver Winchester presently took over manufacture, under the name of the Volcanic Arms Company, and a little later, when financial difficulties brought a reorganization, Winchester assumed managerial

Samuel Colt. (Smithsonian Photograph
No. 42,323)

control and hired an expert mechanic named Tyler Henry as plant manager.
What emerged was the Henry rifle, an adaptation of the Hunt that fired a metallic
cartridge designed by Wesson. Ultimately, the Henry became known as the Winchester, the rifle that allegedly won the West.

That story spanned decades. The primary market for a repeating rifle had to be
the U.S. Army, or some other army, and armies were notoriously reluctant to
adopt new weapons that brought fewer visible advantages than complications
(vulnerability to jamming, maintenance problems, and—a hard-dying myth—ammunition wastage).

A repeating handgun was something else. A promising civilian market existed,
especially in the booming West, and a number of inventors sought to capitalize on
it. Multibarreled, manually rotated pistols were a couple of centuries old, though
not very useful, the weapons being awkward to use and ponderous to carry
around.

Samuel Colt, the man who won the revolver race, was a little like Robert Fulton—not really the inventor of anything, but the possessor of a bold inventive
mind that earned the success it obtained. Son of a Hartford, Connecticut, merchant who pioneered silk manufacture in America, he grew up a lively lad with a
taste for chemistry. From William T. Smith, chief chemist at the silk factory, he
learned about nitrous oxide—laughing gas—and had fun experimenting with it.
He also enjoyed explosives, and was expelled from Amherst Academy in 1830 for
an overboisterous Fourth of July celebration. Sixteen years old, he signed as a
deckhand on a Boston sailing ship bound for India.

In Calcutta he apparently saw a new firearm used by British officers, a pistol with a breech containing several chambers set in a cylinder that could be hand-rotated to fire a succession of shots. The weapon was actually the invention of a countryman of Colt's, Elisha Collier, an American living in London, and dated back to 1818. Collier's gun had been adopted by the British Indian Army, but by no one else, and in fact left much to be desired in the way of simplicity and speed of operation. En route home, which happened to be by way of England, Colt followed the example of Robert Stevens and whittled out the wooden model of a new invention, using a hot wire to bore a six-chambered cylinder that rotated automatically with the action of cocking. The problem of precise alignment of the firing chamber with the barrel he solved by a latching device that, according to his own account, he copied from the ship's capstan, though the Collier weapon had a suspiciously similar principle. He may also have learned something on his return home from a revolving-chamber rifle invented by William Billinghurst of Rochester, New York.

Colt's own first two revolvers, made in the machine shop of his father's factory with the help of Anson Chase, a Hartford gunsmith, were unsatisfactory, and at eighteen he found himself confronted with the problem that had vexed so many inventors before him: how to raise funds for research and development.

His solution was original, and highly successful. Remembering the laughing-gas experiments, he embarked on a lecture tour. His show was a smash hit, the *Albany Microscope* recording one of many admiring notices:

"The museum was crowded to excess every evening. The effect which the gas produces upon the system is truly astonishing. The person who inhales it becomes completely insensible, and remains in that state for about the space of three minutes, when his senses become restored, and he sneaks off with as much shame as if he had been guilty of some mean action. No person will begrudge his two shillings for the gratification of half an hour's laugh. . . ."

In two years Colt earned enough to finance fresh experimentation with the aid of John Pearson, a Baltimore gunsmith who contracted to work for twelve months at $10 a week, ten hours a day, "Sundays excepted." Colt continued his laughing-gas lectures, ranging from Savannah to Montreal, where he memorized his routine in French.

By 1836 with Pearson's help he had produced models worthy of U.S., British, and French patents for a pistol whose rotating breech, securely locked and easily unlocked by the action of cocking, fed five cartridges in succession into the chamber (which held one to start with, making the gun a "six-shooter"). It was one of the last inventions (February 25, 1836) patented under the old permissive patent law of 1793, which in recent years had loaded the Patent Office files with unoriginal and conflicting claims. Congress called a halt in July 1836, with a new law establishing an examination system.

Moving from model-making to manufacturing was expensive, and Pearson, who perhaps deserved to be remembered as a co-inventor, dropped out because of his young employer's slowness in paying: "I suppose you thought you had done fine to send me $100," Pearson wrote sarcastically. "But your account is now over $100 more. . . . By God you use me anything like a man. . . . You are in a Devil of a hurry but not to pay your men."

Patent model of Colt's revolver, 1836. (Smithsonian Photograph No. 45,715)

Meantime several manufacturers came out with a new version of the old multibarreled pistol. The "pepperbox" rotated its barrels automatically with the cocking action, as the Colt rotated its chambers, and kept the barrels so short that the
gun, though not exactly a pocket weapon, could be carried with reasonable convenience. The short barrels made it difficult to hit anything farther away than
across a card table, but that was as far as its eager purchasers—miners, settlers,
merchants, and gamblers of the West—wanted to shoot, and the pepperbox, simpler than the revolver, was cheaper to make. Colt's Patent Arms Manufacturing
Company of Paterson, New Jersey, hardly got into production before it was put
out of business in 1842 by this technological regression.

Frustrated, but far from giving up, the still-young inventor-manufacturer
turned to Fulton's weapon of underwater "torpedoes" for harbor defense, and
succeeded in winning a $20,000 appropriation from Congress to produce the first
electrically detonated underwater explosives. But in 1846 the Mexican War revived the six-shooter. A friend, Samuel Walker, who was raising a regiment of
"Mounted Rifles," helped Colt to a good sale: 1,100 revolvers under the Colt patent to be manufactured by Eli Whitney, Jr., at Whitneyville, Connecticut, using
imported Sheffield-cast steel for barrels and cylinders. The weapon produced, with
a 9-inch-long .44-caliber barrel projecting in front of its revolving chamber,
weighed four pounds nine ounces. It was certainly not a pocket pistol, but could
be carried conveniently in a holster. The newly formed Texas Rangers tried the
gun and liked it, and the Colt revolver was on its way. The next model was the
"Navy Frame," ordered by the U.S. Navy in 1851, followed by the "Army Frame"
and finally the famous "Frontier" or "Peacemaker" model, the immortal six-
shooter of the Old West.

The historical importance of the Colt revolver itself was slight. But the gun
was an ideal product for interchangeable parts manufacture and the factory Colt
built at Hartford in 1848 significantly forwarded mass-production manufacture.
As plant manager and collaborative inventor, Colt brought in a boyhood friend,
Elisha King Root. Root was a product of the machine-tool spin-off of the textile
industry, in which he had started as a bobbin boy at the age of ten in his native
Ware, Massachusetts. Colt, now financially able to avoid the mistake he had committed with John Pearson, made Root the highest-paid man in Connecticut. When
Colt failed to obtain stock-turning machinery from Springfield's Thomas Blanchard, Root not only successfully imitated the Blanchard wood lathe but created
a version with a hardened steel edge capable of shaving and carving iron, following a template (pattern).

Root next introduced in the Colt plant an even more important cutting machine, the "universal" miller invented by Frederick W. Howe for Robbins &
Lawrence in 1848. Howe's was the first milling machine made for commercial

Brown & Sharpe universal miller, 1862 model. (Smithsonian Photograph No. 47,023-C)

production, that is, sale to other manufacturers. But Robbins & Lawrence had suddenly gone bankrupt, so Root designed his own version of the "universal" (i.e., capable of performing many types of metal-cutting operations) miller, and had it made at the Lincoln iron works in Hartford. Known as the "Lincoln Miller," Root's machine became the preeminent American machine tool, with more than 150,000 ultimately made and sold.

Also from the New England arms industry came the "turret lathe," an assembly carrying several different cutting tools so mounted that they could be brought successively into operation against the same workpiece. Another American answer to the persistent shortage of skilled labor, the turret lathe could be set up to perform its operations by an expert mechanic and turned over to a semiskilled operator to run. Stephen Fitch of Middlefield, Connecticut, is known to have built an early, if not the first, version in 1845 to cut a large number of screws required to fulfill a government pistol contract. In Fitch's model, eight cutting tools were mounted on individual cylinders around the horizontal cylinder or turret. Fitch's machine was followed by others, the most important version designed by Frederick W. Howe of milling-machine fame.

In 1851 Great Britain held its mammoth Crystal Palace Exhibition in Hyde Park, London. Fittingly, the exhibition was dominated by the numerous exemplars and products of the British Industrial Revolution. The modest American exhibit at first drew slight attention, except for ridicule over its tardy opening, the Washington government having forgotten to arrange for its transportation from the dock. Even when an American banker named George Peabody came to the rescue and the Yankee exhibit was set up, its display of maple sugar, gold-filled

Turret lathe, manufactured by Jones & Lamson of Windsor, Vermont. (Smithsonian Photograph No. P-64,177)

teeth, magic-lantern slides, stuffed porcupines, cod-liver oil and corn-husk mattresses, spread out amid the brocades and statuary of old Europe, seemed a sort of whimsical junkyard stranded in an art museum. Its own essay in conventional art, an insipid nude sculpture called *Greek Slave,* was coldly received by the critics, though appreciated by Cockney men and boys. But a pair of rival American farm machines, the mechanical reapers of Obed Hussey and Cyrus McCormick, outclassed their British and European competition, and a New York locksmith named Alfred Hobbs, representing the firm of Day & Newell, went about opening British locks deemed impregnable while London's best locksmiths struggled in vain with those invented by Robert Newell. Visitors began to take a closer look at the American exhibit and a ripple of genuine surprise grew.

The Colt revolvers and Sharps rifles (made by Robbins & Lawrence) first drew attention on their merits as weapons, before word spread that the Yankee arms consisted of fully interchangeable parts. Gradually the meaning of this novel information was digested and the technique of mass production, "The American System of Manufacture," became one of the most talked-about features of the exhibition among the knowledgeable.

The Crystal Palace remained primarily a showcase for advanced and varied British technology (the building itself was a landmark in metal-skeleton construction) and the American displays won only five Great Council Awards out of 170 (McCormick reaper, Goodyear rubber, Bond astronomical device, Dick machine tools, and Gail Borden's preserved meat biscuit). Yet two years later, when New York copied London on a modest scale and built its own little Crystal Palace in Bryant Park (back of where the Public Library now stands), Parliament sent Britain's leading machine-tool expert, Joseph Whitworth, to study the American exhibits of special-purpose machine tools. On Whitworth's recommendation, the British government equipped the national armory at Enfield with 157 American machines, including seventy-four of Frederick Howe's universal millers, at a cost of over $100,000. In the next two decades Prussia, Russia, Turkey, Egypt, Spain, Sweden and Denmark equipped arsenals with American machinery.

By the time of Samuel Colt's death in 1862, interchangeable-parts manufacture of all types of military small arms was universally established. Far more important, the native land of the American System of Manufacture was successfully transferring the concept out of the narrow sphere of government-contracted weaponry into the boundless one of production for the civilian market. One early product found suited to it, as we have already seen, was the New England clock. Another was the domestic stove, which enjoyed a tremendous boom. By the time of the Civil War, manufacturers in Philadelphia, New York, Albany, Providence, Cincinnati, and Pittsburgh were turning out 300,000 iron stoves a year with interchangeable panels, tops, lids, fireboxes. Hundreds of thousands of locks, farm implements, axes, springs, bolts, reels of wire, and cooking utensils, as well as machine components for industry, came out of the metal-cutting factories.

The path traced by Eli Whitney and pioneered by John Hall had broadened to an avenue opening into the immensely rich future of the industrial world.

14

Obed Hussey and Cyrus McCormick: Mechanization of Agriculture

THE MCCORMICK REAPER that won a Great Council Medal at the Crystal Palace Exhibition was, on first inspection, derided by the London *Times* as "a cross between a flying machine, a wheelbarrow, and an Astley [circus] chariot." The *Times* soon changed its view, and so did the rest of the British press, as the two American reapers, McCormick's and its rival, the Hussey reaper, demonstrated their supremacy in further contests. "What was curious to see," said one Yorkshire paper, was "two implements of agriculture lying side by side in rivalry, respectively marked, 'McCormick, inventor, Chicago, Illinois,' and 'Hussey, inventor, Baltimore, Maryland'—America competing with America, on English soil."

American agriculture had awakened tardily to the value of technology, but once awake had seized on it with both hands. British inventors had struggled since the eighteenth century with the problem of mechanical reaping, though English and Scottish farms (the best of the British reapers was the product of Scotsman Patrick Bell) were not large enough to invite machinery as importunately as did the huge, fertile new American farms between the Alleghenies and the Rockies. Besides, British farm labor was cheaper, and certain British farming techniques militated against mechanical reaping. Finally, the British may have grown a bit conservative after a century of rapid proliferation of technical devices and processes. As a result, it was not really surprising that two Americans had invented the practical machine to cut cereal crops, mainly the golden wheat that grew so abundantly across the wide Midwest.

Obed Hussey, the one-eyed sailor who co-invented the McCormick reaper but never got rich or famous. From Edward Stabler, *Overlooked Pages of Reaper History,* 1897. (Library of Congress)

Cyrus McCormick. (Library of Congress)

The two inventors presented contrasting personalities to their British hosts—large, athletic, assertive Cyrus McCormick, and gentle Quaker Obed Hussey. Hussey was the older by seventeen years. Born in Maine in 1792, he had moved to Nantucket as a boy and sailed on whaling voyages before settling down as a farmer. An accident cost him the sight of his left eye, over which he wore a black patch that gave him a misleading look of sinister dash. Apt with tools, curious, perceptive, he invented machines for grinding corn and corncobs, for husking, and for crushing sugar cane before beginning work in 1830 on the reaper. He had gravitated to Baltimore, where his workshop was a room of a farm implement factory owned by Richard B. Chenoweth.

Chenoweth's daughter Sarah, about seven at the time, later described the process of invention in 1830–31:

> No grown person was allowed to enter, for in this room he spent most of his time making patterns for the perfecting of his reaper. I, unforbidden, was his constant visitor, and asked him numberless questions. . . . Although very poor at the time, he was a man of education, upright and honorable, and so very gentle in both speech and manner that I never knew fear or awe of him. . . . [The reaper] was talked about morning, noon and night. To this day my brother bears on his finger a scar made by receiving a cut from one of the teeth of the machine. When finally the model was completed, it was brought out into the yard of the factory for trial. This trial was made on a board, drilled with holes, and stuck full of rye straws. I helped put those very straws in place. Mr. Hussey, with repressed excitement, stood watching, and when he saw the perfect success of his invention, he hastened to his room, too moved and agitated to speak. . . . A workman [remarked] that Mr. Hussey did not wish us to see the tears in his eyes.

Sarah's brother Richard also cherished memories of "the best friend of my boy-hood days," who furnished him with pennies, taught him how to put iron runners on a wooden sled, and helped him make his first wagon. "It was not possible to try [the reaper] in Maryland," Richard wrote, "owing to the hilly nature of the ground, and [it] was afterwards taken to Ohio for trials and was rebuilt there, or at least a part of it. . . ."

The machine that Hussey demonstrated near Carthage, Ohio, in July 1833, was horse-drawn rather than pushed, as earlier models had been. Hussey kept the ani-mals from trampling the grain by offsetting to the side the cutting apparatus, a horizontal reciprocating knife consisting of a series of triangular steel plates bolted to a straight, flat iron rod. The triangular cutters moved against stationary upper and lower guards, or fingers. Forerunner of the sickle-bar, the cutter was the machine's chief innovation. As the grain was cut it was thrown onto a following platform, where an operator raked it into sheaves.

Hussey's Carthage demonstration got off to an unpropitious start with a minor mechanical failure. As the inventor worked to repair his machine, a burly farmer picked up a reaping cradle and swung it in the air with the exclamation, "This is [still] the machine to cut the wheat!" The crowd laughed and cheered, but Hus-sey methodically completed his repairs. The horses having been unharnessed, he himself hauled his reaper down a gentle slope through the standing grain, cutting every head clean.

He took out a patent and continued to demonstrate around the country, often traveling on foot like John Fitch, with a horse to pull the machine. The demon-strations drew crowds and won friends, but purchasers were few. Patient Hussey was a little ahead of his time when he established his first manufacturing opera-tion in Cincinnati in 1833.

Meanwhile, on a farm at Walnut Grove in the Shenandoah Valley of Virginia, a well-to-do Scotch-Irish farmer named Robert McCormick had been working on a reaper since 1809. McCormick had his own flour mills, sawmills, distillery, and a blacksmith shop where he had already invented a threshing machine, a hemp-breaking machine, and a blacksmith's bellows.

McCormick's reaper outwardly resembled that of Scotsman Patrick Bell and other early designs in that it was pushed against the standing grain by the horses. In McCormick's machine the wheat was thrust against stationary sickle-shaped knives by rapidly revolving vertical cylinders with projecting teeth, and the cut grain was delivered at the side of the machine by a revolving leather apron studded with nails. Provided the wheat stood up straight, the machine cut it fairly well, but if the grain drooped, the toothed cylinders had trouble forcing it against the blade. At best, the grain was delivered in a matted tangle.

After endless tinkering and repeated trials, Robert McCormick made a last ef-fort in the spring of 1831, and gave up.

His twenty-two-year-old son Cyrus, who had already invented a plow designed for the hilly Virginia fields, picked up his father's discarded machine and set to work. He redesigned along the same line Hussey was trying in Maryland, moving the horses to the side so they could pull instead of push. His first blade was straight, with a smooth edge, a crude divider to separate out the grain to be cut,

Robert McCormick's blacksmith shop and mill at Walnut Grove, where Cyrus built his 1831 reaper. (Authors' photo)

wire or wooden fingers, and a light plank platform. After trying it out in a patch of wheat with promising results, he had the local blacksmith make him a new blade with a serrated edge, while he himself remodeled the divider and added a reel. The finished machine differed from Hussey's mainly in the design of the knife, the fact that the raker walked alongside instead of riding, and the use of a reel to force the grain against the cutter. The reel was not original with McCormick, who had borrowed it from Scotsman Patrick Bell. Hussey had considered it and judged it superfluous.

In July 1831, Cyrus McCormick demonstrated his machine publicly by cutting six acres of late oats on the neighboring farm of John Steele. A boy rode the single horse that drew the machine, and Jo Anderson, a slave who had helped McCormick throughout, walked beside with a rake to sweep the severed grain off the platform.

The machine worked, but not well enough for commercialization. McCormick wrote later, "I found in practice innumerable difficulties. . . . I was often advised by my father and family to abandon [the invention]." Through 1832 he made improvements—iron fingers, a platform that could be adjusted to the height of the knife, better gearing—and held a new public trial at Lexington, Virginia. The owner of the field churlishly complained that the reaper was damaging his grain and ordered it off his land, but William Taylor, owner of the adjoining farm, pulled down a rail fence and invited McCormick to continue. That afternoon the reaper victoriously harvested six acres of wheat, (a good scythe hand might harvest one to two acres a day) and was put on exhibition afterward in the courthouse square. The next year, 1833, McCormick cut all the grain at Walnut Grove and that of several neighbors, gaining considerable local newspaper publicity. Yet he did not patent the machine until April 1834 when he saw a picture in *Mechanics Magazine* of Obed Hussey's reaper, patented the previous fall and already in manufacture in New York City and in Cincinnati. Far from being discouraged, the combative McCormick fired off a challenge to his rival in the form of a letter to the editor:

Rockbridge, Va., May 20, 1834

Dear Sir:

Having seen in the April number of your "Mechanics Magazine" a cut and description of a reaping machine, said to have been invented by Mr. Obed Hussey, of Ohio, last summer, I would ask the favor of you to inform Mr. Hussey, and the public, through your columns, that that principle, viz., cutting grain by means of a toothed instrument, receiving a rotatory motion from a crank, with iron teeth projecting before the edge of the cutter . . . is a part of the principle of my machine, and was invented by me, and operated on wheat and oats in July, 1831. . . . Consequently I would warn all persons against the use of the aforesaid principle . . . as an infringement of my right. . . . I have . . . been laboring to bring it to as much perfection as the principle admitted of, before offering it to the public. I now expect to be able, in a very short time, to give such an account of its simplicity utility and durability as will give general, if not universal satisfaction.

He was not yet ready to back up his words with manufacture and sale. In 1835 Robert McCormick deeded to his son a 500-acre farm, which occupied the young man's attention, and the following year father and son became involved in iron manufacture, buying an ore bank and a tract of timber on the South River and building a furnace. The venture ended in disaster, the result of inexperience, bad management, lack of capital, and the panic of 1837; traditionally Cyrus was said to have emerged with "his honor, one slave, a horse and saddle, and $300." Actually the firm's money loss seems to have been slight—and the yield in experience to Cyrus McCormick was large. He wrote much later, "All this I have ever since felt to be one of the best lessons of my business experience." He had learned about iron, marketing, labor management, business ethics and law, and court procedure. "If I had succeeded in the iron enterprise," he commented, "I would perhaps never have had sufficient determination and perseverance in the pursuit of my reaper enterprise to have brought it to the present stage of success."

Through the middle 1830s, Obed Hussey continued to canvass the Midwest, but unexpectedly began to ring up substantial sales when he turned east into Maryland, which he had quitted a few years earlier as too hilly for mechanical reaping. The *Farmer's Register* told its readers that the Hussey machine's "performance may justly be denominated perfect as it cuts every spear of grain, collects it in bunches of the proper size for sheaves, and lays it straight and even for the binders." In 1838 Hussey moved his manufacturing operation from Cincinnati to Baltimore, almost in McCormick's home territory.

ABOVE AND OPPOSITE Hussey and McCormick reapers in the Crystal Palace catalogue. (Smithsonian Photograph No. 649-L)

As his iron venture turned sour, McCormick reverted to the reaper, and by 1840 was laboriously manufacturing machines. That year he sold his first two. He made improvements in his cutting knife, substituting serrations that were alternately reversed every inch and a half, and causing the knife to vibrate under guards shaped like spearheads. In 1843 he sold twenty-nine machines.

With the two inventors becoming known and operating in close proximity, a match between the rival machines was inevitable. McCormick issued the challenge and Hussey promptly accepted. The first of their long series of competitions took place on a farm north of Richmond, whither Hussey was unable to transport his heavy model because of a flood-damaged bridge. His lighter machine lost the match, in the opinion of the majority of farmer spectators, but a rematch a week later favored Hussey.

Hundreds of later competitions produced no more conclusive results, for the reason that the two machines had equal merit. Modern experts consider McCormick's as slightly superior for reaping (cutting grain, with its hollow stalks) and Hussey's for mowing (cutting the tougher, better-rooted grasses). The competitors, however, met very different fates in the marketplace, a result that was due first to Hussey's bad luck and second to McCormick's genius for merchandising, perhaps even more impressive than his inventive skill.

Hussey's misfortune was to give up on the Midwest too soon. At Baltimore he made reapers for the farmers of the East Coast and sold a few more each year, but Eastern farms were generally too small to use reapers effectively. But in the late 1830s and early 1840s, the Ohio valley had seen its fleet of rickety and explosive steamboats reinforced by an army of clattering, track-jumping railroad trains, while the Erie Canal was supplemented by the Ohio & Erie, dug from Cleveland on Lake Erie to the Scioto, an Ohio tributary (De Witt Clinton came out to turn the first spadeful of earth), to complete the inland water route from New York to

New Orleans. In 1844, six years after Hussey had retreated east, Cyrus McCormick reconnoitered the West, and wrote back to his father that the Ohio valley was now producing more wheat than the available labor could harvest. Thus the transformation of the Midwest reached the point at which mechanical harvesting was needed just when McCormick was ready to produce it. Hussey was equally ready, but Hussey was in Baltimore. McCormick looked for a site in the West, and with the astuteness of Napoleon picking a battlefield chose Chicago.

At the moment, Chicago was not prepossessing. A cluster of timber warehouses along a muddy river and swampy lakefront, backed by rows of shacks sheltering a mixed and none too genteel population of 15,000 going on 30,000, it was the urban version of the frontier. Its Lake Michigan harbor was an open stretch of beach blocked by sandbars, its roads westward planked-over swampland. But two major projects were nearing completion that promised to make the city the hub of the future: the Chicago canal, fulfilling Père Marquette's dream of linking the Great Lakes and the Mississippi system, and the Galena & Chicago Union Railroad, providing farmers to the west with a cheap means of shipping grain and livestock. McCormick moved to Chicago in 1847 and in 1848 both the transportation projects were completed.

The first McCormick factory was a new three-story brick building just east of the north end of the present Michigan Avenue Bridge (today the site of Mies van der Rohe's Equitable Building). Auxiliary buildings housed a steam engine, lathes for turning iron, and six forges. The first year McCormick hired thirty-three factory hands, and within a year he needed 120. His brother Leander supervised the plant operation, brother William sales and purchasing. When in 1851 one of Chicago's frequent fires destroyed most of the main building, Cyrus seized the opportunity to build the most modern steam-powered plant in America and perhaps in the world. McCormick was thoroughly familiar with Oliver Evans's automated flour mill, for which his father had invented an automatic stopping device, and in his new plant he introduced to industrial production a remarkable degree of automation. A reporter from the *Chicago Daily Journal* gave this description:

An angry whirr, a dronish hum, a prolonged whistle, a shrill buzz and a panting breath—such is the music of the place. You enter—little wheels of steel attached to horizontal, upright and oblique shafts, are on every hand. They seem motionless. Rude pieces of wood without form or comeliness are hourly approaching them upon little railways, as if drawn thither by some mysterious attraction. They touch them, and presto, grooved, scalloped, rounded, on they go, with a little help from an attendant, who seems to have an easy time of it, and transferred to another railway, when down comes a guillotine-like contrivance—they are morticed, bored, and whirled away, where the tireless planes without hands, like a boatswain, whistle the rough plank into polish, and it is turned out smoothed, shaped, and fitted for its place in the Reaper or the Harvester. The saw and the cylinder are the genii of the establishment. They work its wonders and accomplish its drudgery. But there is a greater than they. Below, glistening like a knight in armor, the engine of forty-horse power works as silently as the "little wheel" of the matron; but shafts plunge, cylinders revolve, bellows heave, iron is twisted into screws like wax, and saws dash off at the rate of forty rounds a second, at one movement of its mighty muscles. But there is a greater still than this. There by the furnace fire, begrimed with coal and dust, decorated with an apron of leather, instead of a ribbon of satin, stands the one who controls—nay, who can create the whole.

Success bred opposition. In 1847 Hussey's patent had come up for renewal, and thanks to misleading advice from the Patent Commissioner the old sailor had gotten his application in too late and now had to petition Congress. McCormick promptly counterpetitioned against the renewal, claiming that his own reaper had priority even though he had not patented it first. Congress granted Hussey his renewal, and when McCormick's own 1834 patent came up, Hussey retaliated by petitioning in turn, on rather better grounds. Farmers and other reaper manufacturers joined a swelling opposition to McCormick, now pictured as a dangerous monopolist, and after a sharp lobbying fight the renewal was refused.

The loss of his legal advantage enraged McCormick but scarcely affected his business position. His dominance of the reaper industry by now did not really depend on his patent, the loss of which may actually have hurt Hussey more by opening the door to competition from other manufacturers. Far more important were McCormick's efficient production techniques and his innovative business methods, which in sum virtually amounted to the invention of modern business practice. Market research and analysis, customer service, installment credit, and rational pricing policies were all pioneered by McCormick's aggressive firm. He perceived a value in meticulously standardized parts that had not occurred to Eli Whitney, John Hall, or Samuel Colt: mail-order maintenance. A farmer had only to write naming the part and year of purchase to get a replacement from the McCormick foundry room, stocked not with parts but with casting patterns. Mechanics from the factory roamed the countryside in the winter, helping farmers get their often mistreated reapers in shape for the next season. Advertising, by newspaper and handbill, with testimonials, descriptions, and terms of sale, became an important department of the company.

The first sales representative of the firm, cousin J. B. McCormick, who roved the lower Ohio Valley in the 1840s, was soon supplemented by a network of agents grouped under regional managers, all pinpointed by a map on McCormick's office wall in Chicago showing the agents' names and the numbers of reapers each had sold in successive years. McCormick had realized early that farmers could only pay after harvest, or as he put it, "after the machine had paid for itself." Accordingly, he instituted installment buying, with down payments of 10 to 25 percent and the balance collected over a year and a half at 6 percent. Given the risky nature of wheat farming, there were plenty of arrears, but McCormick took care of those by allowing for them in his pricing structure.

A McCormick agent in Waterloo, Iowa, D. R. Burt, described his selling methods in a report in 1850.

> I found in the neighborhood supplied from Cassville quite early in the season one of Manny's [a competitor] agents with a fancyfully painted machine cutting the old prairie grass to the no small delight of the witnesses, making sweeping and bold declarations about what his machine could do and how it could beat yours, etc. etc. Well, he had the start of me, I must head him somehow. I began by breaking down on his fancy machine, pointed out every objection that I could see and all that I had learned last year . . . gave the statements of those that had seen the one work in my grass . . . all of which I could prove. . . . Now gentlemen I am an old settler, have shared all the hardships of this new country with you, have taken it Rough and Smooth . . . have often been imposed on in the way I allmost know you would be by purchasing the machine offered you to-day. I would say to all, try your machine before you [pay] one half or any except the freight. I can offer you one on such terms, warrant it against this machine or any other you can produce, and if after a fair trial . . . any other proves superior and you prefer it to mine, keep [it]. I will take mine back, say not a word, refund the freight, all is right again. No Gentlemen this man dare not do this. The Result you have seen. He sold not one. I sold 20. About the same circumstances occured in Lafayette Cy.

An agent's life was complicated by bad weather and poor crops slowing the demand for reapers, by late delivery, the underselling of competitors, mechanical defects, and, above all, the problem of collecting bills.

A McCormick agent, A. D. Hager, sent to sell reapers in North Carolina in 1854, wrote from Jamestown: "I arrived here yesterday after a tedious stage ride from Raleigh. Upset once on the road with a stage load of 14 passengers, but not severely hurt. . . . Wheat fields here are small, hence the prospect is not the best for selling. . . ." A week later he reported, "I have strove in vain to get a horse to use a week, but now have concluded to take Stage and then foot it. . . . The land is good, but as long as they have a negro to plow it, with one mule and an antediluvian plow with *shafts* to draw by, they will have little use for reapers. I hope I am Yankee enough to sell what we have on hand here, and am inclined to think I shall, when the rubs of harvest come." Faced with the prospect of demonstrating the McCormick machine on the plantation of T. Pollock Burgwyn, vice-president of the United States Agricultural Society, a man who favored the Hussey reaper, Hager wrote, "Wednesday and Thursday are the days for Napoleon to either win or lose the battle of Roanoke Valley," but after the trial: "The day is past. All machs. worked well. Yours cut equal to any of them but the delivery is not as good as the others. . . . I will just remark that I am treated, with the best his house affords (and he lives in tall style), have twice during a time of leisure been invited to take a ride with him, once with his family . . . but Hussey's Agent eats not at Burgwyn's table but with his *overseer* and never to my knowledge has been invited into the house. Today I was furnished with a horse saddled but Hussey's Agt. walked it." A week later in Greensboro he was complaining that he had repaired a machine refused by a customer "to the satisfaction of all—still the d——d villains won't agree to take it. . . . I have forty plans for attack and thirty nine for retreat and when the battle is over I will tell you who is *winner*. . . . Health good . . . weather hot and no rain for one week. Everybody but myself has bowel complaint. If they would take less liquor and keep more *honor* about them, think might enjoy better health."

In the Chicago office, its walls adorned with medals, diplomas, and certificates of merit won by the McCormick reaper, one official supervised the agents, another collections, a third purchasing, a fourth the shipment of machines, a fifth repairs and spare parts, the bookkeeper relating to all these departments. Correspondence was written in longhand, copies kept in great tissue-paper letter books. Cyrus McCormick and the half-dozen other principals dictated their letters to a copyist clerk who took them down in shorthand (Isaac Pitman had expounded his system in England in 1837), made a copy for the files, and signed the originals with a rubber name stamp.

In the 1850s Hussey lost his position as McCormick's chief rival, as several upstart firms made headway: Seymour & Morgan of Brockport, New York; Howard & Company of Buffalo; John S. Wright of Chicago; and John H. Manny of Waddam's Grove, Illinois. While doggedly pressing for a renewal of his 1834 patent, McCormick fought the new competition not only by his own aggressive sales campaigns but by studying their machines to detect infringements of his 1845 and 1847 patents, which included a raker's seat and a reverse-angled sickle. The unremitting struggle in the courts was anticlimaxed by defeat in the Supreme Court in 1858, which, even coupled with a tardy court victory by Hussey in 1859, did not shake McCormick's dominant position. By 1860, court decisions notwithstanding, everyone in America knew who had won the reaper war.

In a letter to a friend, Edward Stabler, Hussey gave voice to a rather touching protest:

> I made no money during the existence of my patent. . . . I would have been better off at the end of the fourteen years if I had filled exactly such station as my foreman holds, and got his pay, and would not have had half the hard work, not a hundredth part of the heart-aching. I never experienced half the fatigue in rowing after a whale in the Pacific Ocean (which I have often done) as I experienced year after year for eighteen years in the harvest field. . . . Why should I not be compensated for toiling to introduce an invention which I thought to be of so much advantage to the World? I know I was the *first* one who successfully accomplished the cutting of grain and grass by machinery. . . . No man knows how much I have suffered in body and mind since 1833, on account of this thing, the first year I operated it in Balto. Three years after I cut the first crop, I could not go to meeting for many weeks for want of a *decent coat,* while for economy I made my own coffee and eat, slept in my shop, until I had sold machines enough to be able to do better. . . . My machines then cost me nearly all I got for them when counting moderate wages for my own labour. . . . Now I do not believe that there

is a reaper in the country (which is good for anything) at so low a price as mine, and not one on which so little profit is made.

In 1858 Hussey sold his declining business. Two years later he was riding a train from Boston to Portland, when a little girl asked for a drink of water. The old Quaker went into the station to get her one, and in trying to reboard the train as it started up, fell beneath the wheels and was killed.

Cyrus McCormick vaulted on to the heights. His reaper won the Grand Medal of Honor at the Paris Exhibition of 1855; Napoleon III awarded him the Legion of Honor; and he was named a member of the Institute of France. His foreign triumphs were promptly exploited in domestic advertising. By 1858 he was a millionaire. That year he finally found time to get married, at the age of forty-eight, choosing pretty young Nancy Fowler, of Clayton, New York. The wedding ceremony in Chicago was ecstatically reported by the *Chicago Daily Press,* which described the groom as "a massive Thor of industry":

> If our townsman, unknown to himself, has delayed the ceremonies for a few more years than is customary, for the express purpose of linking his fate with the one who now bears his name, we risk nothing in pronouncing the prize well worth his waiting, and in *reaping* one of the fairest flowers our city can boast, he has but added the orange blossoms to the laurels of his world famous title of nobility.
>
> Our lady readers will be on tip-toe to learn of the bride, and how she was dressed, and who was there, and how they were dressed. . . . We suppose all who were there have informed those in the immediate vicinity, who were in this respect less favored, that the bride wore a white silk dress with an over-dress of *tulle,* that those who had heard of the rich trosseau [sic] looked to see diamonds and saw nothing of ornament to add to . . . a simple wreath and boquet [sic] of white flowers. . . .

For the honeymoon the groom took his bride to Washington, because his Supreme Court case was just coming up.

The years immediately before the Civil War also saw Virginia-bred McCormick battling abolitionism in the Presbyterian Church and in the Democratic party. He did not permit his Southern sympathies to interfere with business. The thousands of letters in the McCormick office files between 1861 and 1865 scarcely mention the war except to note that the battle of Fredericksburg might affect the premium on gold, and that Gettysburg hurt sales in Maryland and Pennsylvania.

McCormick's position was by now so strong that even important innovations introduced by competitors only supplied grist for his own mill.

The first of these innovations was the machine patented by two Illinois farmers, C. W. and W. W. Marsh in 1858 and marketed in the 1860s. The Marsh "harvester" differed from the Hussey and McCormick "reapers" in that it had an attachment—one of Oliver Evans's endless belt conveyors—that carried the cut grain to a table on the reaper platform where two men could bind the sheaves. In 1870 Charles Withington mechanized the binding operation with a further saving of labor. McCormick declared another patent war, which ended with a patent pool, a device already pioneered in the sewing-machine industry, permitting McCormick to add the mechanical binder to his own machine.

John Deere, inventor of the steel plow.
(Deere & Company)

The Chicago fire (October 8–9, 1871) equally failed to daunt the grizzled tycoon, though it wiped out his plant, much other property, and his handsome residence. Mrs. McCormick hastened home from a vacation to meet her husband, sleepless and with one arm of his coat burned off, on the edge of the smoldering city. He drove her straight to the site, not of their home, but of his factory, and began to outline plans for rebuilding. Instead of simply resurrecting the old factory, he used the location to build a temporary quarters for the business, choosing a larger site, at Canalport, on the Southwest Side, for a huge new plant, which was in operation by the beginning of 1873.

Neither age nor affluence sweetened McCormick's vinegar personality. Despite many philanthropies, his closeness with a dollar became a Chicago legend. Expertly terse in his own telegrams, he underlined superfluous words in those he received from his agents and took the senders to task. Rare was the billing he accepted without argument. Potter Palmer gave him a reduced rate on meals at the Palmer House, but found it necessary to restrict the cut price "to yourself only for the reason that seventy-five cents does not pay me the actual cost of dinners."

Returning to Chicago from Washington on the Penn Central, and notified in Philadelphia of an excess luggage charge of $8.70, McCormick ordered his family off the train and demanded that the trunks be unloaded. The railroad officials refused and took the McCormick luggage on to Chicago, where a fire destroyed part of it. McCormick sued for $5,500, and spent a fortune battling the equally stubborn railroad for eighteen years, all the way up to the Supreme Court, which awarded his heirs $18,000.

Confined to a wheelchair in his last years, McCormick held court in his parlor,

Reconstruction of Deere's 1837 plow.
(Deere & Company)

dispensing aphorisms on rugged individualism. His dying words, in 1884, according to one account, were "Life *is* a battle." The following year his brother Leander, with whom he had quarreled violently over management of the business, published a book seeking to transfer credit for inventing the reaper to their father.

The McCormick reaper, invented by Obed Hussey and Cyrus McCormick, and perfected by the Marsh brothers and Charles Withington, made possible the low-cost harvesting of the huge Midwestern wheat yields, or in a simple phrase of immense meaning to the nineteenth century, brought cheap bread. The reaper does not deserve all the credit, however. Another crucial invention was the John Deere plow.

The plow was more than 2,000 years old when John Deere left Vermont in 1836 to open a blacksmith shop in Grand Detour, Illinois, and had been through a succession of revolutions in design—the iron plowshare, the moldboard for turning the sod, the coulter to cut the soil in front of the plow, all-iron construction. In 1819 Jethro Wood of New York had produced a plow on the Eli Whitney-John Hall principle of standard interchangeable parts, not for speed in production but for ease in mending. But in 1836 a new, literally sticky, problem had emerged in the Midwest. The very richness of the prairie soil made it cling to the iron plowshare so that a farmer needed two teams of oxen to drag his plow and had to stop every two minutes to scrape the share with a wooden scraper.

Visiting a neighbor's sawmill in Grand Detour, John Deere saw a large circular saw blade of imported Sheffield steel laid aside for repairs. The metal was glittering smooth; suddenly the thought flashed into his mind, would soil cling to such shining metal?

He bought the blade from the sawmill, took it home to his blacksmith shop and set to work. Snipping out a paper pattern of share and moldboard, he placed it on the sawblade and cut around it with chisel, striker, and sledge. Heating the piece on the forge, he shaped it with the hand hammer. Then, with a plow beam fashioned from a sapling, he put together, in his own words, "a very rough plow."

The plow was rough but the plowshare smooth, and it did what Deere had intuitively guessed it would. It shed the sticky Midwest soil as easily as iron had the sandy soils of the East and of Europe. Naming his invention the "Self-Polisher," Deere went into business, using sawmill steel for his shares (and polished wrought iron for the moldboard) until the firm grew to a point where he had to import his own steel direct from England. Importing had its drawbacks; Deere thought the salt sea air damaged the metal in transit, and shipping was expensive. By 1846 he was making and selling a thousand plows a year, and journeyed to Pittsburgh to talk to one of the booming industrial city's iron manufacturers. The result was America's first cast plow steel, made by Jones & Quigg, and a subsequent rapid diffusion of the John Deere plow. Up to 1848, one farm journal noted, "Steel plows were as scarce as honest lawyers," but thereafter they spread rapidly on the prairie.

The steel-plow business outgrowing Grand Detour, Deere moved to Moline on the Mississippi, a site that was ideal in some respects, less so in others. When Mississipi navigation was closed by winter ice, it was next to impossible to ship anything out. "To go to St. Louis in winter," Deere recollected, "we had to go by way of Michilimackinac" at the top of Lake Michigan. He continued to work at the anvil himself while a partner, John M. Gould, applied McCormick-like business methods, signing up members of the Iowa state legislature to sell plows.

As railroad and telegraph tamed and transformed the West, Deere & Company grew into a corporation much like Cyrus McCormick's in Chicago (where John's son Charles went to business school). A journalist described the Moline headquarters in 1869: an elegant office with frosted-glass partitions, gas chandelier, walnut desks, carpeted floors, marbleized mantel, central heating, frescoed ceilings, silver-plated doorknobs and locks—"the most convenient and elaborate business office we have ever seen."

When the former blacksmith went to his reward in 1886 in a casket decked with calla lilies crossed by a sheaf of grain, he was an envied shareholder in banks and railroads and a lamented benefactor of churches and Sunday schools.

By that time the American agricultural revolution had made itself felt far beyond the Middle West. Future problems, at the moment masked by consistent weather and fair prices, lurked, but the American farmer with his new technology had opened an era in mass production of food and fiber that at least rivaled in historic impact the American System of Manufacture.

15

Charles Goodyear, Gentle Lunatic

CYRUS MCCORMICK, Peter Cooper, Robert Fulton, Francis Cabot Lowell, Oliver Evans, and other heroes of the American Industrial Revolution have a convincing normality about their personalities. Intelligent, creative, touched with genius, they yet retained a sensible perception of what the world was all about, what they wanted out of it, and how to get it. They were men, in the old expression, with both feet on the ground. Eli Whitney was perhaps a little more of a dreamer, and John Fitch a little more of a crank. But the image of the inventive true believer, the fanatic who sublimates everything else to his single passion, is best represented by the man whose appearance on the street in New York in 1837 led to the observation, wryly recorded by its own subject, "If you meet a man who has on an India rubber cap, stock, coat, vest and shoes, with an India rubber money purse without a cent of money in it, that is he."

Charles Goodyear was born two days before the opening of the nineteenth century, on December 29, 1800, at New Haven, son of a prosperous merchant named Amasa Goodyear who evidently had his share of the Yankee inventive streak—he acquired an interest in a patent for button-making and in 1807 began manufacturing America's first pearl buttons in a waterpowered factory at Naugatuck. Most of the buttons for the uniforms of the recruits of 1812 came from Amasa Goodyear's plant. Branching out into general hardware, he patented a number of farm implements, the most successful of which was Goodyear's Patented Spring Steel Hay and Manure Fork. Initial sales resistance by New England farmers inspired

Amasa with another invention—the promotion giveaway. When users found the new forks actually lighter, stronger and more durable than the old, word-of-mouth rapidly turned the new product into a best seller.

During these years son Charles, the oldest of six children, showed himself to be a studious and hard-working lad, putting in hours at the hardware firm or on the family farm which Amasa maintained, and winning plaudits as one of the youngest and brightest of Reverend Daniel Parker's pupils at Ellsworth, Connecticut. The Reverend Parker may have persuaded him to aim for the ministry; in any case he became an expert on the Bible and remained unshakably pious throughout the vicissitudes of his life. But at this early age, according to his own account, he had an experience like the alcoholic's first taste of wine. "When yet a schoolboy," he wrote in his third-person autobiography, *Gum-Elastic,* "the wonderful and mysterious properties of this substance attracted his attention, and made a strong impression on his mind. A thin scale, peeled from a bottle or a shoe, sometime afterward attracted his attention, and suggested to him that it would be very useful as a fabric, if it could be made uniformly so thin, and could be so prepared as to prevent its adhering together and becoming a solid mass, as it soon did from the warmth and pressure of his hand." That rubber, turned sticky in his hand, he was never able to let go of, though for the next twenty years he was occupied with many other things.

After finishing school at seventeen, he went to Philadelphia to learn the finer points of the hardware business from the firm of Rogers and Brothers, returning to New Haven in 1821 to join his father as part of A. Goodyear & Son, manufacturers and merchants. In 1824 he married Clarissa Beecher, daughter of a Naugatuck innkeeper, who a year later presented him with his first child, a daughter named Ellen. In 1826 Charles moved back to Philadelphia with his family to found the first hardware store supplied entirely with American-made goods, as an outlet for the surplus manufacturing capacity of the Naugatuck firm. For three years all went well, but 1829 suddenly brought disaster for not very clear reasons, evidently rooted in the inexperience or incompetence of both father and son in running a credit business.

An attempt to palliate the calamity by getting extensions from creditors only completed it, and Charles Goodyear landed in Philadelphia debtor's prison. To get out, he closed down the hardware business, promised his creditors shares in his and his father's inventions, and further to stave them off set about producing more inventions: a new model spring fork, a new button-making process, a faucet, a spoon-manufacturing process, an air pump, and several boats built of metal tubes. Meantime Clarissa went on having children, eventually eight more, four of whom died in infancy, leaving three daughters and two sons.

His interest in building metal boats was either stimulated by or in turn stimulated an interest in water safety, a concern that quickly became a second obsession. In 1834 he paid a visit to New York to learn what kind of lifesaving equipment was being manufactured, and in the sales rooms of the Roxbury India Rubber Company found rubber life preservers. Purchasing one to take home and study, he was soon back to show the Roxbury sales representative his life preserver equipped with a new valve. Conversation followed, and the representative told his visitor about

LEFT Charles Goodyear, by C. P. A. Healy. (Goodyear Tire and Rubber Company)

RIGHT Clarissa Goodyear, by C. P. A. Healy. (Goodyear Tire and Rubber Company)

the *real* problem with anything made of rubber. The Roxbury Company had invested heavily in waterproof rubber shoes, had manufactured $20,000 worth and sold them to eager purchasers. Summer had come, and the shoes had stuck together and created so powerful a stench that there was nothing to do but bury them—and with them the aspirations of the company's stockholders.

Goodyear was astonished. He had seen the advertisements for the new rubber industry's products shamelessly promise that they remained "unaffected by the weather." Apart from the lighthearted business ethics of the day, the advertising claims were the result of the absolutely maddening character of rubber, which treacherously promised to mend its ways under the ministrations of an inventor, and then come summer, come winter, reverted to repellent stickiness or rocklike hardness.

Ever since French researchers had found that turpentine or ether could be used as solvents on coagulated rubber brought from its native South America, French, British, and other European experimenters had been trying to get the stuff to take on a reliable elastic form and keep it. Charles Macintosh in Scotland found an even better solvent in naphtha, a by-product of his dye-manufacturing business, and had the bright idea of enclosing rubber between two layers of fabric. His "Waterproof Double Textures," patented in 1823, were soon world renowned, as "mackintoshes." A few years later a London coachmaker named Thomas Hancock accidentally invented a "mastication" process for compounding rubber with other materials and shaping it in molds. Hancock had been cutting garters, suspenders, sides for slip-on shoes, and other clothing accessories from bottles and blocks of natural rubber imported from South America. Seeking to mince up his waste rubber bits, he built a hollow cylinder spiked with teeth in which a spiked roller rotated. To his amazement, the "masticator" turned out not a basketful of minced rubber but a large solid rubber ball. By repeating the process and adding other ingredients Hancock produced the first rubber compounds, whose distinct if not decisive advantages over natural rubber were of immediate commercial value. Hancock did not patent his "pickle," as he called it, but simply swore his employees to secrecy and went about manufacturing rubber rollers, printing blankets, billiard cushions, fire hose, brewery tubes, and other items, which remained largely unaffected by the mild English climate.

In America a different story unfolded. Thomas C. Wales of Boston imported rubber shoes from Brazil that sold so well that he sent American shoe lasts to the Amazon to speed production; soon a half-million pairs of rubber shoes were being imported to the United States annually. The Roxbury India Rubber Company, whose New York showroom Charles Goodyear had visited, was started by Edwin M. Chaffee, a foreman in a Boston leather factory who had invented a machine to coat cloth with a rubber solution. Chaffee also invented a rubber mill and a rubber colander that proved of enduring value, along with many other manufacturing devices. His commercial success brought a swarm of imitators, a huge capital investment in rubber manufacturing in New England and New York, a flooding of the market with glibly advertised shoes and garments, and then the discovery by the public that the North American climate turned rubber into cement in the winter and molasses in the summer. A rubber panic followed, and in scarcely two years the Roxbury company was left alone in the business, and badly worried. This was the moment at which Charles Goodyear discovered the problem.

On his return from New York to Philadelphia, he was rearrested for debt, but merely restricted to living "within jail limits," which meant staying with his family in a small but decent cottage. The cottage had a kitchen, into which Goodyear plunged with the zest of an Escoffier. He had obtained some raw rubber, which he cut into small pieces with one of Clarissa's kitchen knives, kneaded with turpentine into a dough, compounded with other ingredients, and rolled with her rolling pin. A mixture with magnesia he found produced a hard white rubber which for a moment appeared very promising, but a book bound with it presently sagged into the usual rubbery collapse.

A New Haven friend named Ralph Steele advanced a little capital, and Goodyear tried another mixture. His enthusiasm enlisted that of Clarissa and the children, and the family worked together to produce several pairs of shoes. He had another idea. The turpentine instead of helping might be hurting, so he stored the shoes while checking out pure latex (natural rubber) on an Irish helper. The Irishman's rubber trousers stuck together and he had to be assisted out of them to the merriment of onlookers. Meantime the stored shoes turned into a mass of melted gum. Goodyear sold most of the family's few belongings, paid the cottage rent by pawning linen Clarissa had woven, boarded his family in the country near Naugatuck, and went off to New York by himself, apparently forgiven or forgotten by his Philadelphia creditors. In New York he boiled rubber, turpentine, and magnesia in quicklime and water and exhibited his "tanned" rubber at the fairs of the New York American Institute and the New York Mechanics' Institute. Both fairs awarded him medals, but he soon found that his "tanning" was barely skin deep—a little vinegar made the rubber as sticky as ever.

Like so many nonviolent monomaniacs, Goodyear aroused sympathy, and friends repeatedly came to his rescue. Two New Yorkers did so now. John W. Sexton invited the threadbare fanatic into his house in Gold Street, a few blocks from City Hall, and Simon Carle opened his drugstore to him. In addition, he won permission to use Pike's Mill in Greenwich Village, whither he daily trudged three miles with a gallon jug of slaked lime prepared in his room, to mix with the gum elastic in the hope of making it flexible. A former tutor from Connecticut, William DeForest, ran into him in Gold Street on his way home and was invited to the room in Sexton's house where they sat knee to knee amid kettles and chemicals as Goodyear assured dubious DeForest, "William, here is something that will pay all my debts and make us comfortable."

It was during this period that he took to wearing the all-rubber costume that drew New York's attention. But by 1837 he had quit the city for a cottage in New Haven where he could rejoin his family and where, in one of the experiments which never ceased, he came near to asphyxiating himself working in a closed room, and after rescue was under a doctor's care for six weeks.

Once more, he thought he had found the magic answer in his "acid-gas process," and his conviction was so sincere that he persuaded another friend, one made during the exhibiting at the Mechanics' Institute in New York. The friend, William Ballard, helped him establish a factory with steam power in Bank Street, on what was then New York's upper west side. Momentarily business boomed and the new firm took over an abandoned rubber factory on Staten Island, but the Depression of 1837 ruined Ballard even before Goodyear's product, as falsely promising as all its forebears, could.

The Goodyear family huddled in a cottage on the grounds of the Staten Island factory, paying no rent, pawning and borrowing, and not infrequently begging, for food. Charles's younger brother Robert Goodyear joined them with his wife, and contributed to the food supply by fishing in New York Harbor. On one of his ferryboat trips to the pawnbroker in New York, unfailingly sociable Charles ran into John Haskins, a veteran of the old Roxbury company, who listened to his latest theories and was persuaded to offer financial support, the first fruit of which was the recovery of Goodyear's umbrella, which he had had to leave with the ferry master as security for his fare. Haskins was a Millerite (forerunner of Seventh-Day Adventists) and believed the Second Coming was at hand, so perhaps felt he had little to lose. With his help, and the permission of Chaffee and other partners, Goodyear moved his family to New Haven while he himself journeyed to Roxbury, where the rubber machinery now lay idle. For a year he made and sold shoes, piano covers, tablecloths, and other items in a desultory novelty-goods way, but in 1838 he moved again, to Woburn, Massachusetts, a northwest suburb of Boston. This town had already suffered two industrial disasters, the failure of a promising silk-farm venture, followed by that of the Eagle India Rubber Company. The superintendent of the defunct Eagle firm was a capable though illiterate ex-livery stable keeper named Nathaniel Hayward, who had his own secret process for treating rubber. Hayward filtered his turpentine through sulfur and used a little sulfur in his compounds, afterward exposing them to the sun. The process was originally intended to whiten the product, but had the more important result of seeming to retard melting. Seeming to—Hayward was not sure enough to have applied for a patent. Goodyear supplied all the missing enthusiasm, hiring Hayward, getting him to apply for a patent, and offering him $1,000—never mind where the money was coming from—for the rights.

This time he was sure he had the answer. He put everything he could borrow into manufacturing life preservers, beds, cushions, coats, capes, carriage blankets, and was rewarded with a totally unexpected bonanza—an order from the United States Government for 140 waterproof mailbags. The Goodyears tossed their rubber caps in the air, and for several months it seemed as if salvation, not to mention vindication, was achieved. The mailbags were manufactured and shipped. But hung by their handles, the bags began to sag and were soon unfit for duty. The government shipped them back to Woburn, whither the new Goodyear life preservers also began returning. Not only was the family once more penniless, but the inventor's reputation was destroyed.

His friends did not desert him—he was simply too sympathetic a figure to desert. They gave him good advice—forget rubber and get into some other business—any other business, and they would help. Gently, fanatically, he turned them all down and set his family once more to work handcrafting small rubber items for sale while he reverted to the pawnbroker. The family remained in New Haven, while the inventor commuted between there and Woburn, where he kept a small residence near the factory. The kitchen of the Woburn house was, naturally, another rubber laboratory. One day while his brother Nelson, daughter Ellen, and some friends were visiting him, he was busy testing the effect of heat on the compound he had used for the disastrous mailbags. A piece of it dropped on the hot wood stove, and on recovering it he gave an exclamation: instead of melting, the piece had charred "like leather." Nelson and Ellen later corroborated Goodyear's account, including the fact that the visitors adopted a distinctly remote demeanor. They had experienced too many of Goodyear's "discoveries" already. Their coolness made no impression on the inventor, once more positive he had the secret of rubber. He nailed the piece to the door outside and in the morning, to his exultant gratification, found it flexible. The compound he was using included sulfur, and experiments soon showed him that rubber could not be melted in boiling sulfur at any temperature, but always charred, or in his own optimistic leather-derived expression, acquired a "perfectly cured" exterior.

Now the trick was to control the process. That proved not at all easy. To multiply and enlarge his experiments he haunted the smithies and workshops of Woburn and the surrounding neighborhood, borrowing furnaces and boilers in nonworking hours, heating mixtures in kettles full of hot sand and hot soap, in melted lead and boiling water. He moved with his family to Lynn, so that he could try steam in his experiments at a factory there (Baldwin & Haskins). A few weeks later he moved everyone to Woburn. Each morning he gathered his own fuel on the Woburn Common, and in the cottage he used the residual heat of the oven after Clarissa had baked bread. He hung rubber over her teakettle spout, and toasted it over the open fire. He kept altering his mixture, and tried every heating period from an hour to a day. Every now and then he produced another well-cured sample, just often enough to drive a sane man crazy.

He got permission and found the means to build a brick oven in the Eagle India Rubber factory yard, paying a carpenter and laborers in rubber products. Professor Benjamin Silliman, the chemist and geologist who had expanded Yale's scientific program from its promising beginnings in Eli Whitney's day, visited the kiln and pronounced his benediction, but that winter (1839–40), Goodyear, having pawned all his own books, pawned his children's school texts for $5. A neighbor, Elizabeth Emerson, recalled later, "I found they had not fuel to burn, nor food to eat, and did not know where to get a morsel . . . except it was sent in to them [as charity] . . . I heard many remonstrate with him. I have talked with him considerably myself. . . ." Another neighbor remembered seeing the Goodyear children digging up potatoes before they were half ripe, and that "We used to furnish them with milk, and they wished us to take furniture and bedclothes in payment rather than not pay for it."

In the nick of time, a guardian angel appeared. Oliver B. Coolidge was ex-president of the defunct Woburn Silk Farm and Eagle Rubber Company. One day a heavy snowfall left the Goodyears bereft of food or fuel. Goodyear decided to apply to Coolidge for help, and set out in the storm for Coolidge's house some miles away. Ill and weak, he had to stop and rest frequently in the drifts. He made it to Coolidge's place—and proudly displayed his best rubber samples. Even at this low ebb of fortune, he was no beggar asking for a handout, but an inventor seeking backing. Coolidge soberly examined the samples and was impressed. For the rest of the winter he supported the Goodyears, advancing a total of $600 without security, and paying one dunning storekeeper after another. Goodyear insisted on giving mortgages on his rubber, turpentine, and machinery, but Coolidge dryly observed later, "I did not consider them a great deal of security." Goodyear's own view of that winter, as recorded in *Gum-Elastic,* was, "[I felt] in duty bound to beg in earnest, if need be, sooner than that the discovery should be lost to the world."

Despite Coolidge's help, Goodyear was housed once more in debtor's prison for various brief intervals in the winter and spring of 1840, and the lowest psychological point for the family was only plumbed in May when after a fruitless trip to Boston for a promised loan, Goodyear journeyed to East Cambridge, spent the night with a friend, and then walked the ten miles home to be greeted at the door with the news that two-year-old William Henry was dying. There was no money for a coffin, and the small body was borne to the graveyard in an open wagon, the father trudging behind. Not long before, Goodyear had fantastically but all too believably turned down a good offer from France for the old acid-gas process, writing back that the process had been superseded by a better one on which he was still working.

It was three more years before the interminable experiments finally produced reliably flexible and durable rubber. Several other backers contributed along the way, notably wool manufacturer William DeForest who later married Goodyear's sister, and the Rider brothers, New York businessmen. Hayward came back to Woburn to help in the research. Elizabeth Emerson, in whose house Goodyear lived for a period, recalled that "after we got through our work in the kitchen, he used to take possession of our stove in experimenting . . . when he took [the bits of rubber] out, he used to nail them up in the house . . . often till twelve o'clock at night."

His progress, if slow, was genuine. He found that white lead was a good additive, and he found that the white lead and sulfur had to be bone dry and free of acid. He found that rubber-coated goods had to be produced without turpentine, and that nothing was more important than precise temperature regulation (and few things were harder to achieve with the heating technology of the 1840s). Under pressure from his backers he applied for a "caveat," or warning of an impending patent, in 1841, but that year the Riders went broke. DeForest, now his brother-in-law, stayed with him to the eventual tune of $46,000. By 1843 Goodyear was turning out a product he felt reliable enough for a full patent, which he obtained the following year. Haskins, his old Millerite backer, still waiting for the Second Coming, helped him acquire some of Edwin Chaffee's patents from the Roxbury Company's production days, and soon the new "Naugatuck India-Rubber Company" was licensed to manufacture the new rubber. Even then Goodyear was picked up by the law one more time and went through bankruptcy, a process he had been at great pains to avoid up to now.

But his invention was a resounding success. A licensee following directions properly could turn out any amount of rubber that would remain flexible under all weather conditions. The vast market demand, despite the residue of skepticism from the earlier rubber fiasco, manifested itself quickly, and dozens of companies sprang up. Many were careless with the process and turned out inferior rubber. Many others pirated, some, like Horace H. Day of New Brunswick, making a fortune.

Goodyear, naturally, did not make a fortune. Most of what money he made from the license royalties he poured into further experimentation and an unbelievably fertile invention of new rubber applications, many far in advance of their time—squeegee mops, tents, power and conveyor belts, printers' rolls, pump valves, rubber bands, engine hose, pump parts, even tires (for wheelbarrows). With Peter Cooper he designed a doughnut-shaped pneumatic cushion, copies of which sold for many years under the name of "Peter Coopers." Though remaining thrifty in regard to his own needs, he treated his family to some luxury to make up for the years of penury, often coming home so loaded with gifts that they thought he must have bought out a whole store. Yet he never actually got out of debt. Thomas Hancock, the English manufacturer, cleverly pirated his process by acquiring some samples, analyzing them, and beating Goodyear to a British patent. Out of the British experience Goodyear at least got a great name for his invention—one of Hancock's associates, William Brockedon, dubbed it "vulcanization." Goodyear at first resisted the name, but its popularity induced him to give in. Meantime France gave him a patent but then took it away because he had exported vulcanized rubber shoes to France before getting the patent.

At home Horace Day's larceny ultimately led to the greatest patent-law case in

Goodyear's Vulcanite Court at the Crystal Palace Exhibition, 1851. (Goodyear Tire and Rubber Company)

United States history up to then, with Rufus Choate, "the wizard of the law," arguing on Day's side against Daniel Webster for the Shoe Associates, a powerful New Jersey-New England combine. Webster was taking time off from his job as Secretary of State, for a fee of $10,000 plus a $5,000 bonus if he won. Goodyear met the old legal champion on his arrival in Trenton from Washington and put a fine black horse and carriage at his disposal. When Webster expressed his admiration later, Goodyear gave him the horse along with the victory fee. Webster's summation reached one of his characteristic perorations: "We want to know the name, and the habitation, and the location of the man upon the face of this globe, who invented vulcanized rubber, if it be not he who now sits before us. . . ." And pointing to the bent and white-haired figure of Charles Goodyear, he drew the applause of the packed courtroom: "I say that there is not in the world a human being that can stand up, and say that it is his invention, except the man who is sitting at that table." It was Webster's last speech ever to a jury, and it took care of Horace Day with a permanent injunction.

In London Goodyear was less fortunate, a jury concluding (erroneously) that Thomas Hancock had understood vulcanization without Goodyear's help. But Goodyear enjoyed the suit, keeping a handsome brougham throughout his London stay and as often as not putting the coachman inside while he drove. He had the time of his life with the Crystal Palace Exhibition, at which he exhibited "Goodyear's Vulcanite Court," a suite of three rooms in which walls, roof, furniture, carpets, and draperies were all made of rubber, while rubber combs, buttons, musical instruments, carvings, and balloons were displayed. Thomas Hancock's rival exhibit was totally eclipsed. Faithful Clarissa died in London in 1853, and after a whirlwind courtship he married Fanny Wardell, of London, by whom he presently had another three children, only one of whom survived.

When he went to Paris for the Great Exhibition of 1855, he had more mixed luck. Business failures in the United States affecting European firms licensed by him, and the adverse court decision on his French patent, combined to bring an abrupt ruin—he had signed notes and suddenly could not meet them. For the last time he was carted off to debtor's prison—at Clichy, on the Paris outskirts, where he stayed several days till a payment from a solvent licensee allowed him to purchase release. But Napoleon III meantime visited his display at the Exhibition, awarded him the Grand Medal of Honor and the Cross of the Legion of Honor, the latter decoration brought to him in his prison cell by his son Charles. Napoleon III, a sovereign who appreciated the practical arts, then called on him in his hotel and took him riding in the Bois de Boulogne, Napoleon and Goodyear in the first carriage, the Emperor's brother and chief statesman, the Count de Morny, in the second. In the pond in the Bois, Goodyear demonstrated his rubber pontoons, a farsighted military application that finally matured in World War II.

Meantime at home he won a victory of value to future inventors. Commissioner Joseph Holt of the Patent Office ruled in favor of an extension of his patent despite the active opposition of Horace Day and Thomas Hancock, describing inventors as "the true jewels of the nation to which they belong," and Goodyear in particular as a "public-spirited inventor, whose life has been worn away in advancing the best interests of mankind."

The saintly old gentleman passed his last years in a home he bought for himself in Washington, large enough to assemble the whole Goodyear family, including the sons from his first marriage, and still provide laboratory space and a tank for testing rubber life-saving apparatus. He died on a trip to New York in 1860, and the refusal of the Patent Office to grant another extension to Charles Goodyear, Jr. (this time *Scientific American* and much of the press supported the still truculent Horace Day), shut off the flow of royalties to his heirs, who were left with heavy debts. The heirs did not do badly, however; Charles Jr. invented a number of shoe-manufacturing machines and seized on a French invention to make a fortune of his own from the Goodyear Welt Shoe Machinery Company, while second son Nelson Goodyear took family revenge on British pirate Thomas Hancock by patenting Hancock's own hard-rubber process in the United States. Transatlantic piracy had definitely become a two-way affair.

16

Joseph Henry, Samuel Morse (and Several Others) Invent the Telegraph

THE TANTALIZING MYSTERY of electricity that had fascinated Benjamin Franklin and other eighteenth-century savants was solved in the first three decades of the nineteenth by the discoveries, in sequence, of four Europeans: Alessandro Volta of Italy, who built the first battery; Hans Christian Oersted of Denmark and André Ampère of France, who explored electromagnetism, the intriguing mutual relationship between electricity and magnetism; and Michael Faraday of England, who demonstrated electromagnetic induction, that is, the fact that not only did an electric current produce a magnetic effect, but, reversing the process, a magnet could be made to produce an electric current. By rotating a copper disk between the poles of a large permanent magnet, Faraday produced a current in the disk. In effect he had built the first dynamo. He published his findings in a scientific paper in 1831, and his European colleagues were impressed, though not surprised, England being in the vanguard of scientific as well as technological development.

They would have been surprised if a diffident young American named Joseph Henry had published his own demonstration of the principle the year before, when he had made his experiment in the laboratory of the Albany Academy. That was more or less the story of Henry's life, to be a little too modest, or a little too late, or both. His own self-evaluation was that he was indecisive; he frequently told the story of a childhood dilemma over whether to order square-toed or round-toed shoes from the shoemaker, who solved the problem by making him a pair of shoes with one round and one square toe.

America's second great scientist, Henry came like Franklin from what the nineteenth century liked to call a humble background, and in fact from an even humbler one—Franklin's father was a Boston soap and candle maker, Henry's an Albany drayman. Henry was born in 1797. In 1812, at fourteen, he was apprenticed to a watchmaker and silversmith. At the end of two years his master pronounced him "too dull to be a silversmith." The truth was rather the opposite; silversmithing was too dull for Joseph Henry, who plunged briefly into the theater, and then entered academic life with the aid of a scholarship awarded by the discerning principal of the Albany Academy, a school of near-college level.

He fell in love with science upon exposure, and tutored Henry James, father of the future novelist and the future philosopher, en route to becoming a professor. Tall, handsome, and dignified—the external effect of shyness—he was popular with his students, who profited from his own pleasure in scientific demonstrations. He was only nineteen when on a visit to New York he saw one of the new electromagnets built by William Sturgeon of England. Sturgeon had exploited Ampère's discovery that an electric current produced magnetism by winding copper wire around an insulated soft iron core and sending an electric current through it. The advantage of an electromagnet over an ordinary permanent magnet was that it could be turned on and off by making or breaking the current. Back in Albany, Henry built an improved electromagnet of his own, insulating the wire instead of the iron core, and winding many more turns, producing a much stronger magnetism. He then plunged into the experimentation that by 1830 led him to the discovery of induction. Possibly he was distracted from publication by falling in love with and marrying his young cousin Harriet Alexander. On his honeymoon he combined scientific business with pleasure by visiting New Haven where he called on Benjamin Silliman, Yale's scientific luminary. Two years later, in 1832, after Faraday had bagged all the glory, Silliman published Henry's paper on his induction experiments in his *American Journal of Science and Arts* (widely known as *Silliman's Journal*).

What Henry did was to set up an electromagnet (Sturgeon's creation based on Ampère's discovery, with his own improvements), powered by a battery (Volta's invention), and wind a coil of copper wire around a piece of soft iron fastened to the poles of the magnet, the ends of the wire connected to a galvanometer (made possible by Oersted) to detect current in the wire. When he connected the battery and thereby activated the electromagnet, the galvanometer needle was momentarily deflected in one direction; when he disconnected the battery and deactivated the electromagnet, the needle was momentarily deflected in the opposite direction: "It appears that a current of electricity is produced, for an instant, in a helix of copper wire surrounding a piece of soft iron whenever magnetism is induced in the iron; and a current in the opposite direction when the magnetic action ceases. . . . We have thus, as it were, electricity converted into magnetism [in the electromagnet] and this magnetism again into electricity [in the coil]."

That year (1830) Henry did gain a measure of fame, however, by publishing the results of earlier experiments in which he had succeeded in lifting a weight of 750

Joseph Henry. (Library of Congress)

Electromagnet built by Joseph Henry for Benjamin Silliman of Yale in 1831. (Smithsonian Photograph No. 13,346)

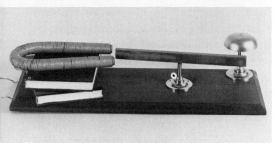

Joseph Henry's telegraph device of 1832. The closing of a circuit activated an electromagnet that repelled a permanent magnet, causing it to swing against a bell. (Smithsonian Photograph No. 47,797-A)

pounds with a huge electromagnet—made of 500 feet of copper wire wound in nine separate coils—the most powerful magnet ever built. Silliman commissioned him to build one for Yale that proved capable of lifting 2,300 pounds, and practical application was quickly found by an iron works in Crown Point, New York, in extracting iron from pulverized ore. In 1831 Henry took the next logical step by building an electric motor. A bar electromagnet tilted to make an electrical connection that caused a permanent magnet to repel and tilt the bar in the opposite direction, breaking the circuit and continuing the rocking motion. Henry recognized the limitations of his device, though he noted that "it is not impossible that the same principle, or some modification of it . . . may hereafter be applied to some useful purpose."

A young blacksmith from Brandon, Vermont, Thomas Davenport, studied the Crown Point magnets, bought one himself, and in July 1834 succeeded in making an electric motor consisting of a seven-inch-diameter wheel, two spokes of which were electromagnets. Two other electromagnets were placed near the periphery of the wheel. In Davenport's description, "The north poles of the revolving magnets attracted the south poles of the stationary ones with sufficient force to move the wheel . . . until the poles of both stationary and revolving magnets became parallel with each other. At this point the conducting wires from the battery changed their position by the motion of the shaft; the polarity of the stationary magnets was reversed, and, being now north poles, repelled the poles of the revolving magnets that they had before attracted, thus producing a constant revolution of the wheel."

Like Eli Whitney and other inventors, Davenport ran into a maddening last-minute difficulty, an inability to break the current quickly enough to prevent the wheel stopping. Like Whitney, he got help from a woman. "It's no use," he told his wife Emily, according to an account by his brother Oliver, "there is no power short of the Almighty quick enough to do that." Emily suggested trying to find a better conductor, and asked if quicksilver (mercury) wasn't a conductor. Tom tried it, and working through the night until three o'clock in the morning they made the wheel spin. With only a Voltaic battery available to supply current to the electromagnets, the device's application was limited, but Davenport used his motor to power shop machinery and even a small experimental car on a circular track, the world's first electric railway (1836). In England Robert Davidson carried on a similar experiment, while in Russia M. H. Jacobi operated an electric boat on the Neva River.

All these experiments were premature in the absence of a large source of current. Henry and Faraday had pointed the way to the generator, but development took several decades, during which the dry cell and lead-acid batteries also appeared. Meanwhile, the water turbine (1837), like the batteries invented in France, and seized on immediately by the New England textile industry, had a tremendous potential application in hydroelectric power generation that occurred to no one for forty years.

For the time being the future of electricity lay in communication, a field in which it had been the subject of experimentation for a century past. The word "telegraph" was already in existence, as well as the principle of the alphabetic code, both having been invented by Claude Chappe for his visual semaphore system that during the French Revolutionary wars permitted news from the front to reach Paris in a few hours. Noting the phenomenon of electrolysis, the decomposition of certain liquids by electric current, German researchers sent impulses over wire to cause bubbles in a trough at the other end. A young American named Harrison Gray Dyar did the same thing on Long Island, producing signals in the form of discolorations on paper, and was apparently the first to put telegraph wires on poles (1826). The electrolytic telegraph was a blind alley, however, too slow-acting to be practical. Dyar went off to Paris and made a fortune out of inventions in textile dyeing.

Ampère meantime envisioned the use of a current-deflected magnetized needle to spell out signals, and in 1832, the year when so much happened in the electrical world, such a needle telegraph was actually installed in Russia to connect the Czar's winter and summer palaces.

The magnetized needle telegraph was one way. Another was demonstrated in

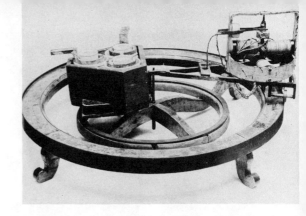

Thomas Davenport's electric motor, built to operate a small electric car on a track, 1836. (Smithsonian Photograph No. 44,988)

1831 by Joseph Henry to his science class in Albany, to show that current could be sent through a long wire by means of a special high voltage "intensity" battery. Stringing almost a mile of wire around the classroom walls, he connected one end to a battery and the other to an electromagnet. Close to one pole of the electromagnet he placed a permanent magnet on a pivot, so that it was free to swing. When the circuit closed and the current flowed, the electromagnet repelled the permanent magnet and caused one end to swing sharply against a bell. Typically, Henry did not patent what was in reality a simple practical telegraph, and which he in fact recognized as such. He did not, he said later, consider it "compatible with the dignity of science to confine benefits which might be derived from it to the exclusive use of any individual. . . . In this, I was perhaps too fastidious."

The drayman's son was indeed too fastidious. Samuel F. B. Morse, scion of a patrician family from Charlestown, Massachusetts, was not. A few years older than Henry, Morse was born in 1791 and in due course followed his father's footsteps to Yale (his grandfather had been president of Princeton), where he studied under Henry's friend Benjamin Silliman. Under Silliman's instruction and that of Jeremiah Day he learned about Voltaic batteries and constructed some of his own. Science, newly introduced into the American college curriculum, was one of the few things that interested Morse at Yale. Outside class, like Robert Fulton, whose career his was to parallel in other ways, he spent his time sketching, drawing caricatures, and painting portraits—five dollars for a miniature, one dollar for a profile. Graduating in 1810, Morse studied painting in England, remaining there during the War of 1812, and returning to America in 1815 to earn his living as a portraitist. In 1816 he married Lucretia Walker of Concord, Massachusetts. More talented than Fulton, he became one of America's best-known portrait artists, executing commissions for many wealthy and influential people. Nevertheless, he found it difficult to support his wife and three children, who had to live with his parents in Charlestown while he did portraits in Albany and New York City. When Lafayette visited America in 1824, Morse undertook a commission to paint his portrait, hoping to earn enough from it to build his own home. But while he was in Washington completing the painting, Lucretia died in Charlestown.

The bereaved artist moved to New York City, where he quickly became the

Samuel F. B. Morse, with a model of his telegraph, in a Mathew Brady photograph. (Library of Congress)

leader of a group of young painters rebelling against John Trumbull, the autocratic president of the American Academy of Fine Arts. In 1825 Morse led his group into a secession that founded the National Academy of Design.

Morse was studying art in Paris during the period when Henry was carrying out his experiments with electromagnets and induction, returning to the United States in the historic year of 1832 aboard the packet *Sully*, where a conversation over the midday meal changed his life. Talk turned to the electromagnetic experiments of Ampère, and a young Philadelphian, Dr. Charles T. Jackson, asserted that Franklin had passed electric current through many miles of wire almost instantaneously. Jackson was in error, but Morse (according to his later recollection) remarked that if this were so, "I see no reason why intelligence might not be instantaneously transmitted by electricity to any distance." Nothing further of moment was said, but in his cabin Morse played with the idea in his sketchbook, drawing rows of dots and dashes to be made on moving tape in response to electrical signals generated from a battery. The marks indicated the ten digits, which could be turned into words, phrases, and sentences by means of a code book.

Morse envisioned a long stick of sawtoothed type which he called a "portrule," to be drawn rapidly under contacts, opening and closing a battery-powered circuit. The receiver would either print the dots and dashes at the receiving end chemically by means of a spark, or mechanically by a pencil controlled by an electromagnet. When he got home he cast some type in brass molds. He soon began to run into the typical development problems that plagued all inventors, including how to support himself and his motherless children.

As a result, the Europeans jumped off to an early lead in the telegraph sweepstakes. Two Germans, Karl Gauss and Wilhelm Weber, built a two-wire copper telegraph line in 1833 that they carried over housetops in Göttingen for more than a mile. Their receiver was a bar galvanoscope whose deflections right and left spelled out a code. Another German enterprise used the pivoted magnetic needle to send signals between Munich and a small town 6 miles away. In 1837 the first large, serious application of the same principle was made by William Fothergill Cooke and Charles Wheatstone, who patented an apparatus with five pivoted needles to send coded signals for British railways.

Morse had taken a job teaching art at the new New York University. In a suite of rooms overlooking Washington Square, he painted, taught painting and sculpture, wrote, cooked his meals, and slept, and in every spare moment experimented with the telegraph. He had devised a sending instrument and a receiver. Each key in the sending device was a lever, the end of which, a conductor, stroked against a disk on which were raised metal conductors with varying spaces and lengths. The contacts produced long and short electrical impulses on a wire leading from the disk. An electromagnetic receiver at the end of the wire penciled a wavy line whose narrow and wide bumps could be readily interpreted as dots, dashes, and spaces. Morse demonstrated the device for friends and callers who were delighted to hear the words they had dictated at one end of the room read from a strip of paper at the other end.

After a time Morse discarded the key sender and went back to the portrule. But the instruments were still too crude for public demonstration or patenting, and Morse could not afford equipment or skilled help.

In the midst of his struggles with the telegraph, Morse's ambitions as a painter—in his own eyes, his real career—suffered a crushing disappointment: in the summer of 1836, Congress failed to include him among painters chosen to decorate the Capitol rotunda. Morse regarded telegraphy as a means of getting rich in order to devote his life to art, but now art seemed to be turning its back on him. Years later he wrote of painting as of a beloved mistress: "I did not abandon her, she abandoned me."

News of a fresh telegraph venture in France stirred panicky fears that his invention had been pirated. Even apart from his inventive career, Morse seems to have had a mild streak of paranoia; during these years of frustration, he took time off from both science and art to run twice for mayor of New York on an anti-Catholic nativist (American Republican) ticket. He got few votes, and soon dropped politics (though anti-Catholicism continued to flourish in New York, Philadelphia, and Boston, New York even electing a nativist mayor in 1844).

Until 1836 Morse remained totally unaware of the fact that Joseph Henry had invented an electromagnetic telegraph in 1831, a year before the idea occurred to him aboard the *Sully*. A fellow professor named Leonard Gale called his attention to Henry's 1832 article in Silliman's journal, and particularly to a decisive scientific truth that had escaped Morse: the one-cell battery he was using generated a quantity of current, but of inadequate intensity (voltage). Intensity rather than quantity was needed for transmitting over a long distance. The necessary voltage could be produced, as Henry had demonstrated, by using a many-celled

Morse's apparatus of 1837, using his original portrule sender (foreground), with sawtooth type at top center; the receiver, rear, produced a penciled wavy line on a roll of tape. (Smithsonian Photograph No. 14,593-B)

battery and increasing the number of turns of wire around the electromagnet. Enlightened, Morse rebuilt his apparatus and soon sent signals (November 1837) through 10 miles of wire wound on reels in Gale's lecture room.

That fall Henry returned from a year's leave of absence to Princeton, where he now occupied the chair of natural philosophy (science), and where he had continued his experiments, stringing his wires all around Nassau Hall. Among other things he demonstrated the ground-return, making use of the earth's conductive property to complete an electrical circuit—an effect which he did not realize had been discovered in Italy a generation before. In England he had visited Faraday and Wheatstone in Wheatstone's laboratory, hitting it off splendidly with the British scientists. When the two Englishmen failed to produce a certain result and Henry succeeded, Faraday exclaimed, "Hurrah for the Yankee experiment!" Wheatstone demonstrated his needle telegraph and the supplementary local circuit he used to lengthen the distance the signal could be carried. Henry promptly explained a recent invention of his own, a remote-control relay using an intensity battery to operate a small-intensity magnet at a distance, which in turn powered a large-quantity magnet and battery.

On his arrival home, Henry's friends urged him to act at once to claim his rights in the telegraph. Morse, now confident that he had overcome all the technical difficulties, and nervous over reports of Wheatstone's and other European telegraphs, was moving to obtain patents at home and abroad, and even more important, financial backing from Congress. Leonard Gale had already become a partner; now Alfred Vail, whose family owned the Speedwell Iron Works at Morristown, New Jersey, supplied Morse with money to build a demonstration model, and Morse was able to file a caveat, or preliminary patent claim, for a device to transmit numbers in the form of dots and lines, to be translated into words and phrases by a code book. The pencil he abandoned in favor of a stylus, still assuming that the receiver had to print or record rather than simply make sounds.

In the face of Morse's flurry of activity, and despite his friends' warnings, Henry was still procrastinating when he accidentally ran into Morse in a chemical-supply store on Broadway. According to Henry's later account, Morse's scientific knowledgeability did not impress him, but apparently his personality did, because Henry decided not to oppose the petition Morse had presented to Congress for an appropriation.

Henry went further, writing Morse encouragingly from Princeton to offer the relay he had already told Wheatstone about (and which Wheatstone had promptly incorporated, although he never gave Henry credit). At Morse's entreaty Henry joined in the campaign for a government subsidy, writing a warm letter of support: "Science is now fully ripe for this application, and I have not the least doubt, if proper means be afforded, of the perfect success of the invention." Pointing out that the telegraph had been suggested by many people, from Franklin's time forward, but that until the recent discoveries in electromagnetism it had been impracticable, he dismissed the controversy over authorship of the invention: "The mere suggestion, however, of a scheme of this kind is a matter for which little credit can be claimed, since it is one that would naturally arise in the mind of almost any person familiar with the phenomena of electricity; but the bringing it forward at the proper moment, when the developments of science are able to furnish the means of certain success, and the devising a plan for carrying it into practical operation, are the grounds of a just claim to scientific reputation as well as to public patronage." As for the telegraphs of Wheatstone and German physicist Karl von Steinheil, "I should prefer the one invented by yourself." Henry was nothing if not obliging; Morse could not have put the thing better himself.

Morse was lucky in his enemies. The man who actually chose to challenge him was bereft not only of serious claim but even of competence as an advocate. Dr. Jackson, the fellow passenger who had started the discussion in the dining salon of the *Sully*, wrote him a pugnacious letter saying that he had seen notices of "our" telegraph in the newspapers, "but observe that my name is not connected with the discovery." The Philadelphian had the nerve to demand that he be included forthwith in all rights and honors. Morse, who had never acknowledged his large debt to Henry and had baselessly suspected English, French, and Ger-

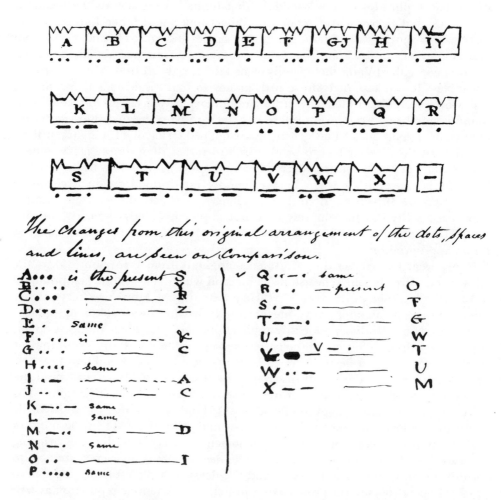

A page from a Morse notebook, showing his original code of 1837, represented by saw-tooth type, and later changes, below. (Smithsonian Photograph No. 18,456-A)

man inventors of stealing his ideas, was outraged by the effrontery of Jackson, who actually stated his case in court in the course of later litigation, but got nowhere. Jackson subsequently claimed credit for the invention of guncotton (a European innovation) and for the use of ether as an anesthetic (a discovery of Dr. Crawford Long of Georgia).

Despite this distraction, the powerful support of Alfred Vail and the Speedwell Iron Works permitted Morse to push ahead in developing his invention, and he had his one original, or nearly original, inspiration (Claude Chappe and Karl von Steinheil had thought of it), throwing out the clumsy bookful of numbered words and phrases in favor of a simple alphabetic code of dots and dashes, forever to be remembered as the Morse Code. Its early form was random; not till six years later did Morse sensibly modify it to assign the shortest signals to the commonest letters.

But technical perfection, Vail's backing and the Morse code still did not bring fruition to an invention which required either a very large private capital investment, or, what Morse deemed more obtainable, the subsidy of the federal government. He succeeded in enlisting Congressman Francis O. J. ("Fog") Smith, chairman of the House Committee on Commerce, as a full partner—conflict of interest was scarcely a concept yet—but even Smith could not appreciably speed action.

Sailing to Europe in 1838, Morse obtained a patent in France but was refused one in Britain on a technicality, despite the difference between his telegraph and Wheatstone's. In Paris he picked up a welcome bonus in a meeting with Louis Daguerre, who had just perfected his photographic process and who taught it to his Yankee visitor for nothing. Morse brought it home and made good money with it in New York, casually dealing a fatal blow to his own former profession of miniature portrait painting.

On his return to America, he heard from Wheatstone and Cooke. The two Englishmen, who had 200 miles of wire strung along British railroad right-of-ways, proposed to Morse that they divide up the American market. Morse refused, and the Englishmen applied for an American patent, obtaining it eight days before Morse obtained his own on June 20, 1840. The almost simultaneous patents were clearly based on differing technology, so that there was no question of a legal battle. The problem was rather the acquisition of enough support to provide a dramatic demonstration either for the government or for private investors. Doggedly Morse lobbied for a government subsidy, hiring a professional lobbyist to help. Fog Smith's Commerce Committee finally proposed a $30,000 appropriation for a demonstration line 40 miles from Washington to Baltimore, with Morse included as superintendent at $2,000 a year (not a great salary, but no insult—unskilled labor earned about a tenth that). The House was divided along now familiar sectional-economic lines, the agrarian South opposing, the commercial North favoring, but the arresting aspect of the opposition had nothing to do with regional interests. Congressmen in general shared with the press and public a deep-seated incredulity about the technology of the telegraph. All Morse's and Henry's experiments and all the reports from Europe to the contrary, everyone found the thing too uncanny. Steamboats and locomotives they could grasp, a wire that talked was something else.

With the helpful support of the chairman of the Ways and Means Committee, future president Millard Fillmore, the bill was finally passed, 89 to 73, with no fewer than 70 members taking refuge in the cloakroom (February 1843).

Between the atmosphere of skepticism and the short time remaining for the Senate to act, Morse had abandoned hope, going to bed on the last night of the session believing his bill lost. Commissioner of Patents Henry L. Ellsworth stayed till midnight adjournment, saw President John Tyler sign the bill, and next morning sent his daughter Annie to Morse's hotel with the news. Morse promised Annie that she could write the first telegraph message.

The obvious route for the telegraph line was along the right-of-way of the Baltimore & Ohio Railroad, which had made large technical progress since Peter Cooper's *Tom Thumb* of thirteen years earlier, but whose management, despite the experience of Wheatstone and Cooke with British railways, had not an inkling of the tremendous significance of the telegraph to the railroad. Grudgingly the B. & O. gave permission for the line, provided it did not interfere with railroad operations!

A reasonable but wrong assumption was that the wire should be buried in the ground. Fog Smith, pocketing the construction contract, undertook to fulfill it with the aid of a young stranger named Ezra Cornell, who designed a trenching plow in the Portland, Maine, editorial office of Smith's *Maine Farmer*.

In August 1843, with a new improved battery, Morse sent an experimental message through reels carrying 160 miles of high-voltage wire without relays. The result stimulated him to the vision of telegraphic communication across the Atlantic, an idea less premature than it seemed at first glance. But production of pipe-encased wire for the Washington-Baltimore demonstration line lagged, and Morse communicated to Cornell his suspicion that it was inadequately insulated anyway. Cornell arranged an accident to his plow to delay the laying of the pipe so Morse could test the wire. His fears were confirmed. Leonard Gale resigned, and Morse took to his bed.

Alfred Vail came to the rescue by reading in an English journal how Wheatstone and Cooke had abandoned underground wire in favor of overhead. Vail proposed to insulate each wire individually, but Ezra Cornell, who was proving a bright young man indeed, suggested a simpler expedient—glass insulators on the poles. Morse at first vetoed the radical notion, but after an enlightening visit to Joseph Henry in Princeton, reversed himself and adopted it. Neither Henry, Morse, Cornell, nor Vail were aware that Weber, Gauss, and Steinheil had already done the same thing in Germany. Nor did they realize that their telegraph poles were not even the first in America, never having heard of Harrison Gray Dyar's Long Island chemical-decomposition telegraph of 1827.

On April 9, 1844, when the overhead line extended along the B. & O. tracks for 6 miles, a signal telegraphed from the end of the line was answered from Washington in seconds.

By a splendid coincidence both the Whigs and the Democrats scheduled their conventions for Baltimore, the very publicity godsend the telegraph needed. On May 1, when the Whig convention opened, the wires extended only to Annapolis Junction, 22 miles from Washington, but Vail was stationed there to get the nominations from the B. & O. train and wire them to Morse at the Capitol. At 3:30 the train steamed in with the news that favorite Henry Clay had been nominated for president and obscure Theodore Frelinghuysen for vice-president. The delegates on board the train, en route to Washington to deliver the news, voiced derision as Vail began clicking away. A few moments later similar skepticism was expressed at the other end of the line. In his room at the Capitol, Morse read off the message, "The ticket is Clay and Frelinghuysen." The assembled congressmen and officials were surprised and puzzled—"Who the devil is Frelinghuysen?" was the general query—but unconvinced. Even when the train arrivals confirmed the message, the skeptics refused to admit that the telegraph worked, preferring to believe that Morse had made a lucky guess.

By May 24 the line was completed to Baltimore. Morse fulfilled his promise to Annie Ellsworth, who had studied her Bible and come up with an unforgettable quotation, from the prophecy of Balaam (Numbers 23:23). This time the company was assembled in the Supreme Court chamber, where Annie gave Morse her text. A minute later back it came from Baltimore: "What hath God wrought?" A great piece of American folklore was born, but neither blasé Washington nor the country paid much attention. Something more dramatic was needed. One week later the Democratic convention opened in Baltimore.

Cornell and Vail had their instrument set up in a warehouse at the Baltimore B. & O. depot, while Morse had now moved to a room below the Senate Chamber. The Democrats were angrily divided, with Ex-President Martin Van Buren the leading candidate but the opposition strong enough to put over the politically memorable two-thirds rule on the second day. Morse announced the news as it broke, orally through a window of the Senate chamber and visually on a bulletin board in the Capitol rotunda, but captured only slight attention. The balloting began; Morse reported Van Buren slipping, Lewis Cass of Michigan gaining. As the race grew hotter, the crowds grew thicker in front of Morse's window and at the bulletin board. On the seventh ballot, Morse announced that Cass had passed Van Buren. On the eighth ballot a new candidate appeared, James K. Polk of Tennessee, the original dark horse. Excitement was at its height when on the ninth ballot Morse read the message, "Polk is unanimously nom." By this time Washington Democrats were crowded in front of his window, fully impressed, and showing it. Minutes later a delegate rose in the convention hall in Baltimore to read a "telegraphic dispatch" from Washington: "Three cheers for James K. Polk, and three cheers for the telegraph!"

Better yet was coming. The convention nominated Senator Silas Wright of New York for vice-president; Vail forwarded the news to Morse, who informed Wright. Wright requested Morse to telegraph that he refused the nomination, and minutes later the Baltimore convention was startled when the presiding officer read the message. By telegraph Wright was asked to reconsider; by telegraph he again refused. Nobody at this point really doubted the mysterious wire's capability, yet even now, just to make sure, a committee boarded the B. & O. to check personally with Wright. He confirmed the accuracy of the telegraphic message, and the convention turned to George M. Dallas of Pennsylvania as vice-presidential nominee.

On the last day of its session, March 3, 1845, Congress voted to maintain the Baltimore-Washington line under authority of the Post Office, but there was little sentiment for a nationally owned telegraph. Fog Smith and a crony named Amos Kendall seized the real handle on the future by organizing the "Magnetic Telegraph Company," which along with numerous other private enterprises was soon building telegraph lines under patent from Morse, generally paid for in stock. The idea's time had come: the lines paid, the stock rose in value, Morse grew rich.

Another European effort netted him no sales but a valuable technical improvement. From France's Paris-to-Rouen telegraph line in 1845 he pilfered the Breguet magnet, all the while strenuously complaining that Louis Breguet had stolen his telegraph—despite the fact that Breguet used the Wheatstone rather than the Morse principle.

Wherever the technology came from, the telegraph was a great American success. By 1846 a New York newspaper could exult: "While England by her government has got with great labor 175 miles [actually 200] of telegraph into operation . . . the United States with her individual enterprise has now in successful operation 1,269 miles. This is American enterprise."

More truthfully, it was American need and opportunity. The large, fertile, mineral-rich country with its scattered centers along the shores of splendid waterways, needed the telegraph as it needed the steamboat and railway, and could pay for it. The press, which had been as slow to recognize the telegraph as it had the steamboat, awoke to discover that what it now called "the greatest invention of the age" was, for the press itself, exactly that. The Mexican War brought this truth home. A British traveler of 1846–47 described the Yankee competition among news correspondents for telegraph priority:

The strife was between several Baltimore papers for the first use of the telegraph between Washington and Baltimore. The telegraph office was close to the post office, both being more than a mile from the wharf, at which the mail steamer, after having ascended the Potomac from the Acquia Creek, stopped, and from which the mail bags had to be carried in a wagon to the post office. The plan adopted by the papers to anticipate each other was this. Each had an agent on board the steamer, whose duty it was, as she was ascending the river, to obtain all the information that was new, and put it in a succinct form for transmission by telegraph the moment it reached Washington. Having done so, he tied the manuscript to a short heavy stick, which he threw ashore as the boat was making the wharf. On shore each paper had two other agents, one a boy mounted on horseback, and the other a man on foot, ready to catch the stick to which the manuscript was attached the moment it reached the ground. As soon as he got hold of it he handed it to the boy on horseback, who immediately set off with it at full gallop for the telegraph office. . . .

On an important occasion, one of the agents . . . beat his competitors by an expert manoeuvre. He managed, unperceived, to take a bow on board with him, with which, on the arrival of the boat, he shot his manuscript ashore, attached to an arrow, long before his rivals could throw the sticks ashore. . . .

Next evening, however, when still more important news was expected, and arrived, he was in turn outwitted. On her way up the boat touches at Alexandria, on the south side of the river, to leave the bags directed to that town, and take others from it. On this occasion one of the newspapers had a relay of horses between Washington and Alexandria, the rider receiving the news from the agent on board the latter place, and galloping off with it to the capital. The bow was then of no use, for by the time the news-laden arrow was shot ashore, the intelligence designed for the rival paper was being telegraphed ahead to Baltimore. It will thus be seen that the American press partakes of that "go-aheadism" which characterizes the pursuit of business in so many of its other departments in America.

By that time Morse was involved in the explosion of legal actions that now burst over every important patent. At his son Charles's wedding he had met a charming deaf girl named Sarah Griswold, whom he married in 1848. Before settling down with her at Locust Grove, the Italian villa his new wealth had built on the Hudson, he took her on an inventor's honeymoon to Frankfort, Kentucky, where he was suing a Kentuckian named Henry O'Rielly for building a telegraph line from Pittsburgh to Nashville in competition with the Morse-Kendall-Smith line. The press supported the defendant, reasoning that the destruction of the Morse patent would give it cheaper rates. O'Rielly's claim was that Morse's patents were invalidated by the earlier Steinheil telegraph in Europe, but the judge ruled against him. As other cases arose in Boston, New York, Washington, and in the Midwest, O'Rielly took his appeal to the Supreme Court. When it arrived there in 1854 after the usual delays, irrepressible Dr. Jackson of the *Sully* luncheon party turned up, but the court had no trouble dismissing his fantasy. Another witness was more compelling.

Joseph Henry had left Princeton in 1846 to accept the post of secretary, or chief executive officer, of the newly created Smithsonian Institution. Congress had wrangled for a decade over accepting an astonishing gift of half a million dollars from an Englishman for "the increase and diffusion of knowledge among men," but Henry quickly proved a brilliant choice to handle the dazzling bequest. In 1854, far from being an obscure professor at Princeton, Henry was one of the most distinguished men in Washington. Furthermore, he had a legitimate grudge against Morse. Alfred Vail had written a book about the telegraph completely omitting Henry, and though Morse had promised to do something about it, he had allowed a second edition to appear with no changes made. Subpoenaed to testify for the defense in the O'Rielly case, Henry accorded Morse credit for his success in the practical application of electricity to communication, but stated, "I am not aware that Mr. Morse ever made a single original discovery in electricity, magnetism, or electro-magnetism, applicable to the invention of the telegraph." In rebuttal, Morse produced Henry's letter of 1842, which did not contradict his testimony, but put a different face on it.

The defense showed that many others had preceded Morse, among them Harrison Gray Dyar, who refused to appear against Morse. Chief Justice Roger Taney, speaking for the majority of the court, awarded Morse the credit for having the invention in complete form and publicly exhibiting it in the spring of 1837, ahead of Steinheil, Wheatstone, and Davy. Even if his patent had been later than the others, Taney ruled, it would not be invalidated unless one of the others had previously patented a similar instrument in the United States (Wheatstone's 1840 patent was not a "similar instrument").

The victory left Morse with a sense of frustration. He was assured of royalties beyond his own hopes, but the money had never really been very important to him. He sincerely believed himself to be the inventor of the telegraph, and Chief

Justice Taney to the contrary, the evidence was now fairly clear that he was so, if at all, only in a qualified degree. He was especially nettled by the fact that Henry had preceded him in every feature of the telegraph and guided him in some aspects. After getting his patent extended that same year (1854), he wrote an aggrieved "Defense Against the Injurious Deductions Drawn from the Deposition of Professor Henry," in which he ungraciously (and untruthfully) asserted, "I am not indebted to him for any discovery in science bearing on the telegraph." Henry, more easily hurt than angered, appealed to the Board of Regents of the Smithsonian Institution. A committee of distinguished personalities (Stephen A. Douglas was among them) was appointed to judge the case. After reading Henry's written statement, one from Gale telling about his suggestion to Morse that he read Henry's paper, and hearing other testimony, the committee condemned Morse's "Defense." Modest Henry was satisfied with the blue-ribbon vindication, and never sought a more material reward.

The committee's finding evidently chastened Morse. In a speech in London shortly after, he voiced a more realistic appraisal of his own role in the invention of the telegraph than theretofore:

> When the historian has made his search, and brought together the facts, if anyone connected with a great invention or discovery has attracted to himself the more concentrated regard or honour of mankind, or of a particular nation, how significant is it that time, and more research, bring out other minds, and other names, to divide and share with him the hitherto exclusive honours. And who shall say that it is not eminently just? Did Columbus first discover America, or does Cabot, or some more ancient adventurous Northman dispute the honour with him? . . . It is surely sufficient honour to any man that he be a co-laborer in any secondary capacity to which he may be appointed . . . in a great benefaction to the world.

Modesty in an inventor is always becoming, even when a little belated, and well compensated by royalties.

17

The Sewing Machine Completes the Textile Revolution

AMONG THE CROP of apprentice mechanics joining the cotton-mill labor force at Lowell in 1835 was a frail sixteen-year-old named Elias Howe who had grown up working on his father's farm, grist mill, saw mill, and cotton hand-card factory, where with his brothers and sisters he stuck wire teeth into strips of leather. In Lowell he worked for two years in a machine shop, helping to make and repair cotton-spinning machinery, before the Panic of 1837 shut down the Lowell mills and sent Howe and many of his fellow workers to Boston to hunt scarce jobs. After a stint as a machinist in a hemp-carding shop in Cambridge, he obtained a place as an assistant to a man named Ari Davis, who made and repaired precision instruments—mariners' compasses and scientific apparatus. Davis was known for his short temper and loud voice, and one day Howe heard him berating a friend who was talking about inventing a knitting machine: "Why are you wasting your time on a knitting machine? Take my advice, try something that will pay—make a sewing machine!" The friend said it couldn't be done, but Davis contradicted him: "Can't be done? Don't tell me that—why, I can make one myself!"

It was the first Elias Howe had ever heard of a sewing machine, but it was by no means the first time the idea had been voiced. For fifty years, inventors, in England, on the Continent, and in America, had been struggling with the logical last link in the chain of machines needed to mass-produce cloth garments. Six basic elements proved to be indispensable to a successful sewing machine: a surface to support the cloth, a needle to carry the thread through the cloth, a combining device to form the stitch, a feed mechanism to move the cloth steadily along so that one stitch could follow another, tension controls to provide an even delivery of the thread, and finally a control mechanism to insure that each part of the machine performed its operation in the proper sequence.

In 1790 Thomas Saint, an English cabinetmaker, patented a machine to sew leather and heavy canvas that included several of these features: a vertical awl to punch a hole, a spindle to push the thread across the hole, and a forked needle to force it through the fabric to the underside where a looper caught hold of it. A crude feeding device, activated from the lower mechanism, moved the fabric along and a second loop was formed inside the first, producing a chain stitch. A shaft activated by a ratchet wheel moved the needle bar up and down, and the machine contained two tension assemblies and a device for holding the thread supply. The cloth was supported on a flat table. Apparently Saint's machine could not be made to operate successfully; it never progressed beyond the patent model stage.

In the early 1800s inventors, most of them British, produced machines that imitated hand-sewing, one actually armed with pincers to act as fingers in alternately seizing and releasing the needle on either side of the cloth. One machine patented in England in 1807 by Edward and William Chapman, designed to stitch ropes for belting, introduced an important innovation: the "eye-pointed" needle, with an eye on the point rather than the base so that the needle did not have to be passed completely through the fabric as in hand stitching. The Chapmans intended their machine for short seams only; for most sewing it was impractical.

The first technically successful sewing machine was finally built in 1829, after many years' experimentation, by a French tailor named Barthélemy Thimonnier, who obtained a patent the following year. Thimonnier's machine employed a hook-tipped needle something like a crochet hook. Moved downward by a foot treadle, and returned by a spring, the needle pierced the fabric and caught a loop of thread, returning it through a previously made loop, thus producing a chain stitch on the upper side. The cloth, held in place on a horizontal table by a retractable presser foot, had to be advanced by hand; there was no feed mechanism.

Thimonnier's original purpose for the machine was embroidery, but he soon realized its potential for tailoring. With two financial backers, he began manufacture and by 1841 had a plant with eighty machines turning out uniforms for the French army. But the tailors of Paris reacted as had the British Luddite weavers threatened by machinery. Storming the factory one night, they destroyed all the sewing machines. Thimonnier survived to found the first sewing-machine company and the first civilian garment factory to use sewing machines, but ultimately fled to England where he died bankrupt.

In 1834, only four years after Thimonnier produced his first model, Walter Hunt, the New York mechanic who created the original prototype of the Winchester rifle (as well as the safety pin), built America's first sewing machine of record. Hunt's model featured an eye-pointed needle, set in a horizontal vibrating arm, that pierced cloth held vertically by a feeding device. An oscillating shuttle held a second thread that combined with the needle thread to form a lock stitch. The machine represented an advance of prime importance in conceptualization

LEFT Thimonnier and his sewing machine patented in 1830. (Smithsonian Photograph No. 10,569-C)

RIGHT Walter Hunt, inventor of the lockstitch and the eye-pointed needle—as well as the safety pin and a prototype of the Winchester rifle. Hunt never patented his sewing machine, and abandoned it when he had trouble with the feed mechanism. (Smithsonian Photograph No. 10,569-O)

in that it did not try to imitate hand stitching, while the lock stitch seam promised superior operating efficiency to the Thimonnier chain stitch.

The Hunt machine's chief drawback lay in its feed mechanism, which had to be constantly reset, and which limited the machine to straight seams. But Hunt, an impatient tinkerer, had other inventions in mind, and did not consider the sewing machine important. After demonstrating that it would sew, he sold his interest without ever bothering to take out a patent.

Five years later an Austrian tailor, Joseph Madersperger, who had patented a sewing machine for embroidery twenty-five years before, produced a multiple-needle quilting machine with some of the features of Hunt's device—the eye-pointed needle, and the use of threads from two different sources to produce a kind of lock stitch. But Madersperger's feed mechanism functioned poorly, and after spending a lifetime neglecting his tailoring business in attempts to perfect the invention, the Austrian died in the poorhouse.

The early 1840s produced several more machines, including the first American patents, without achieving any substantial advance. (One inventor, George Corliss, abandoned sewing machines for steam engines, eventually producing the giant engine that powered Machinery Hall at the Philadelphia Exposition.) In 1844

English inventors John Fisher and James Gibbons obtained a British patent for an embroidery machine that produced a decorative stitch (not a lockstitch, as in Hunt's machine), with an eye-pointed needle and a shuttle—the first patent for that combination (since Hunt had not patented his machine ten years earlier).

Thus when Elias Howe's interest was aroused, apart from several embroidery machines, there existed one practical sewing machine (Thimonnier's) that had actually been used in clothing manufacture, but which utilized the inferior chain stitch, while a superior lock-stitch machine (Walter Hunt's) had been invented but abandoned.

Just before his twenty-first birthday Howe married a Boston girl, Elizabeth Ames, and presently found himself with a wife and three small children to support on his $9 a week mechanic's pay. One of his frequent bouts of illness put an end to his earning even that, and Elizabeth had to take in sewing to keep the household going. The sight of his wife hand-stitching late into the evening recalled to Howe's mind the sewing machine Ari Davis had shouted about, and he began trying to visualize the device. At first he followed some of his predecessors into the blind alley of trying to duplicate the motions of hand sewing—pushing a needle all the way through the fabric and returning it. After many frustrating experiments, he suddenly glimpsed the insight that had come to Walter Hunt (just possibly he had heard of Hunt's invention) to use threads from two different sources, an eye-pointed needle and an oscillating shuttle. Howe built a little prototype, about the size of a portable typewriter, mainly of wood, with some wire and a little metal.

Totally lacking funds for development, he appealed to his father and older brother Amasa, who had invented a machine for splitting palm leaves and opened a straw-hat factory in Cambridge. They lent Elias their loft, where he set up a lathe and started to produce a second-generation machine, but the hat factory caught fire and burned down. A run-of-the-mill disaster for an inventor, it might have been fatal, but Howe had the luck to encounter a friend named George Fisher who had recently come into a modest inheritance. Fisher listened to Howe's description of his sewing machine, and in exchange for a half interest in the future patent, boarded Howe's family, lent him tools, and put up $500 cash for wood, iron, and incidentals.

Working through the winter in his quarters on the top floor of Fisher's house, Howe completed a model, and in April 1845, sewed a complete seam on it. He spent a month more in modifications, and in May stitched all the principal seams on the machine for new suits for himself and Fisher.

Howe's model, similar to Hunt's in many ways, employed a curved eye-pointed needle mounted in a lever that vibrated horizontally, working in conjunction with a shuttle that moved back and forth. The needle pierced the fabric, throwing a slack loop on the other side. The shuttle carrying the second thread passed through this loop, linking the two threads. Needle and shuttle then returned to respective starting positions, tightening the thread and forming a lock stitch. The shuttle had a pointed nose and a square end, like a boat, with an opening on the side for inserting and removing the bobbin on which the second thread was wound. The machine was powered by a hand crank. The feed system consisted

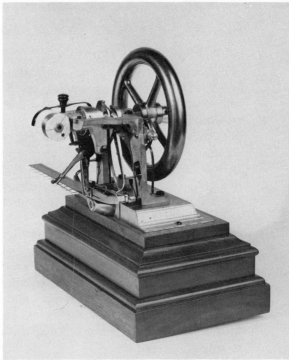

LEFT Elias Howe. (Smithsonian Photograph No. 649-K)

RIGHT Patent model of the Howe sewing machine. (Smithsonian Photograph No. 45,525-B)

of a thin narrow strip of metal several inches long, with pins projecting from one side. The material to be sewed was secured in a vertical position to this "baster plate" by the pins (which also held together the two pieces of cloth to be sewed, making basting unnecessary—hence the term "baster plate"). The baster plate moved forward with each stroke of the needle. When it had passed entirely, it had to be moved back to its starting position, and the cloth unpinned and moved forward. Thus the chief weakness of Howe's machine lay in its feed system, which was defective on two counts: it had to be reset by hand every few inches, and the straight-line path of its needle could not be modified to sew curved or angular seams.

Despite these defects, the modern sewing machine was now practically invented, but its customers, unlike those of the McCormick-Hussey reaper, were not easy to identify. The hand labor that went into the fabrication of its precisely fitted parts pushed the retail price up to $300, putting it entirely beyond the range of the household appliance. It could only be used for commercial production.

The manufacture of ready-made clothing in America, born in the 1820s, had grown rapidly in the following decade, in spite of the setback of the Panic of 1837. New York had a wholesale garment industry by the mid-1830s, made up mainly of small businesses, many of which cut the garments and farmed them out to seamstresses to stitch at home; other cities, principal among them Boston and Cincinnati, followed, creating a large potential market for machine sewing.

But Howe first approached the hand tailors, the very people whose skills would be rendered obsolete by the sewing machine. An intelligent, enterprising tailor might indeed figure that a sewing machine would give him an advantage in speed over his professional brothers, but the first to take the plunge would have to be courageous as well as intelligent and enterprising, because his professional brothers would not applaud him. To Howe's invitation to come and inspect his invention, only one New England tailor responded, and he was talked out of actually going.

Howe finally called on the large clothing factories in Boston, whose owners thought woman labor cheaper than $300 sewing machines. To disprove that fallacy, Howe performed a cleverly dramatized demonstration. Setting up his machine in the Quincy Hall Clothing Manufactory, he challenged five of the fastest seamstresses in the plant to a seam-sewing contest. Ten seams of equal length were cut, one given to each of the women, and five to Howe. Bets were made, the race was begun, and Howe finished all five of his seams seconds before the first girl finished her single seam. Not only that, but his sewing, examined by the tailor-judge, was pronounced the strongest and neatest.

The demonstration was interesting, and even convincing . . . yet the businessmen still held back. Francis Cabot Lowell's Boston successors had grown conservative.

Defeated, Howe took a job as a locomotive engineer to support his family while continuing to tinker with his machine. But he was soon ill again, and had to quit. Somehow by the fall of 1846 he finished an improved model and, accompanied by Fisher, traveled to Washington and obtained a patent (September 10, 1846). The patent changed nothing in Boston. Trying New York, Howe experienced an equally negative reception, and made not a single sale.

At his father's farm in Massachusetts, the Howes held a family council. The American garment industry, they decided, was still too primitive to mechanize, but perhaps the more mature British industry would respond. Amasa Howe was commissioned to cross the Atlantic and make the effort.

Amasa did not turn out to be the world's shrewdest businessman. In England, he met with much the same difficulties that Elias had had in America, at last found a prospect, and then let himself and his brother be swindled. William Thomas, a large manufacturer of umbrellas, corsets, and leather goods, whose Cheapside plant employed more than 5,000 workers, offered £250 for the British rights with the verbal understanding that he would patent it in his own name and pay Elias Howe a royalty for each unit he sold. The Englishman did indeed patent a sewing machine, though the British court threw out part of his claim on the grounds that it conflicted with the 1844 Fisher-Gibbons eye-pointed needle and shuttle combination. Nevertheless, Thomas (at least according to Howe) exacted from three to ten pounds' royalty for every sewing machine manufactured by others or imported into England without ever paying Howe a penny.

Meantime Thomas decided he wanted the machine modified for his own corset-manufacturing use, and sent Amasa back to America with an offer of a salary of £3 a week for Elias to come to England to do the job. Elias was reluctant, but no better prospect being in view, he embarked with Amasa in February 1847, taking along the original model of the sewing machine and his United States patent papers. They traveled steerage, cooking their own food below decks.

For eight months Howe worked at modifying the machine to sew corset stays in place, and when he was finished Thomas first mistreated and then fired him. By this time his wife and three children had joined him in London, but he now had to send them home again for economy's sake, pawning clothes to pay for cab fare to the boat. Borrowing a spare room and some tools, he built a new sewing machine in four months and was able to sell it—for £5, paid in a promissory note that he had to discount to £4. At last he gave up on England, pawned his original model and his patent papers for his passage, and in April 1849 landed in New York with empty pockets.

Renting a room in a boardinghouse for immigrants, he got a job as a machinist. A few weeks later he learned that his wife was dying in Cambridge. His father had to send him ten dollars so that he could visit her deathbed. The inventor of the Howe sewing machine attended his wife's funeral in a borrowed suit.

So far Howe's life had paralleled that of John Fitch and other inventive Jobs whose patience was tested by the commercial failure of a technically successful device. But in Boston he suddenly discovered that the sewing machine's hour had struck. During his absence in England, Boston had gone sewing-machine mad. Tailors and garment manufacturers alike had adopted the machine, which was being produced in half a dozen different models, advertised in handbills, and demonstrated at exhibitions.

What had happened was that a number of inventors had seized on the Howe formula of eye-pointed-needle-and-shuttle-produced lock stitch and added their own improvements, many of genuine value. One inventor, John A. Bradshaw of Boston, frankly based his patent on improvements on Howe's machine. Two other Bostonians, Charles Morey and Joseph B. Johnson, had in turn adapted Bradshaw's machine to the chain stitch, producing a machine that *Scientific American* asserted to be in use "in most of the Print Works and Bleach Works in New England, and especially by the East Boston Flour Company. It sews one yard per minute."

Another inventor, John Bachelder, had patented the first continuous, intermittent feed mechanism, an endless belt with projecting pointed wires to hold the cloth, and a device to control the length of the stitch. His machine had several improvements of enduring value: a straight (instead of curved) eye-pointed needle that operated up and down from above, a horizontal surface to support the cloth, and a yielding presser foot to hold the cloth in place.

Perhaps most ingenious of the sudden crop of inventors was Allen B. Wilson, a cabinetmaker, who had apparently arrived independently at the lock stitch, with an improvement in the form of a shuttle pointed on both ends that passed on both its forward and backward journeys through loops left by the needle. Litigation forced Wilson to sell his rights, but later, in partnership with Nathaniel Wheeler, he patented several other devices, the most valuable of which was a simple and effective solution to the problem of the feed mechanism, still used today in almost every sewing machine: the four-motion feed, a flat-toothed surface that moved forward to carry the cloth ahead, dropped away from the cloth, moved backward, and finally rose against the cloth again.

Examining the galaxy of new machines, Howe found that every one of them infringed on some part of his 1846 patent. Exasperatingly, his patent model and papers were reposing in the London pawnshop, and might even be irrecoverable. By good luck a friend named Anson Burlingame was about to depart for London on business, and agreed to try to find Howe's property. Burlingame proved a friend indeed; he located the model and papers, redeemed them, and by autumn had them in Howe's hands.

To prosecute the infringers, Howe needed one more thing, money. He turned again to George Fisher, but Fisher had sold his rights in the machine to three friends and was no longer interested. The three friends could not or would not help either, and in the end Howe had to borrow against a mortgage on his father's farm.

The first suit to come to a hearing was against the manufacturer of a machine patented in 1849 by Boston tailor Sherburne C. Blodgett and his partner John A. Lerow. The Blodgett and Lerow model had many of the Howe features—including the curved eye-pointed needle and the awkward feed mechanism that had to be constantly reset—plus a novelty that proved to be something less than an improvement: a shuttle that revolved in a circle instead of moving back and forth. The defense resurrected Walter Hunt's sewing machine of the 1830s, maintaining that it contained all the essentials of Howe's 1846 patent, but Howe showed that the Blodgett and Lerow model had features of his own patent that were not present in Hunt's machine, and the case was decided in Howe's favor (1854). Even before it was settled, Howe was selling royalty licences—to Wheeler, Wilson & Company, to the Grover & Baker Company of Boston, to his own brother Amasa, and to others—giving the licensees the right to use any part of the Howe patent.

Howe followed up his victory with suits against other infringers. Among them was an ex-actor turned inventor named Isaac Merritt Singer, who proved to be Howe's most formidable opponent. Eight years older than Howe, Singer had been born in upstate New York (Pittstown) in 1811, the youngest of eight children of German-Jewish immigrant parents who separated in a divorce action, rare at the time, when he was a child. Isaac joined a carnival at twelve and for the next sixteen years worked as pitchman, roustabout, manager, and repertory actor (taking the stage name of Isaac Merritt), and finally founded his own company, the Merritt Players. The young actor proved unexpectedly mechanical, and in 1839 invented an excavator, a practical version of a Robert Fulton idea, which he sold for $2,000. In the 1840s, when the Merritt Players were stranded in Fredericksburg, Ohio, Singer got a job in a plant that manufactured wooden type. Recognizing the need for a better type-carving machine, he invented and patented one, and went to New York in search of backing. Ensuing tribulations took him to Boston, where he presently (1850) encountered the Blodgett and Lerow sewing machine, which immediately fascinated him.

The steam-powered workshop of Orson C. Phelps, where Singer rented display space for his type-carving device, was one of the shops manufacturing the Blodgett

Isaac Singer. (Singer Company)

and Lerow. Phelps complained that his customers were constantly returning their machines for repairs, claiming that the threads chronically broke. The machine's main departure from the original Howe, the rotary shuttle, had a serious flaw: it either twisted the thread too much or completely removed its twist. Examining the shuttle with the eyes of a machinist, Singer, knowing nothing of the Howe design, suggested that it move to and fro; a straight needle used vertically he also thought would be more practicable. As both Bachelder and Wilson had done, he included in his improvements a table to hold the cloth horizontally rather than vertically; and like Bachelder, a yielding presser foot to hold the cloth down as the needle was drawn up.

Singer had still another idea. A feed wheel projecting from below through a slot could move the fabric continuously, a definite improvement over the Howe. When he learned that John Bachelder had included such a device in his continuous feed patent, Singer purchased the rights.

With two partners, George Zieber and Orson Phelps, of the machine shop, Singer set to work to produce his own model. Later, in the course of a patent suit, he reported:

> I had no money. Zieber offered forty dollars to build a model machine, Phelps offered his best endeavors to carry out my plan and make the model in his shop; if successful, we were to share equally. I worked at it day and night, sleeping but three or four hours a day out of the twenty-four, and eating generally but once a day, as I knew I must make it for the forty dollars or not get it at all.
>
> The machine was completed in eleven days. About nine o'clock in the evening we got the parts together and tried it; it did not sew; the workmen, exhausted with almost unremitting work, pronounced it a failure and left me one by one.

Zieber held the lamp, and I continued to try the machine, but anxiety and incessant work had made me nervous and I could not get tight stitches. Sick at heart,
about midnight, we started for our hotel. On the way we sat down on a pile of
boards, and Zieber mentioned that the loose loops of thread were on the upper
side of the cloth. It flashed upon me that we had forgot to adjust the tension on
the needle thread. We went back, adjusted the tension, tried the machine, sewed
five stitches perfectly and the thread snapped, but that was enough. At three o'clock
the next day the machine was finished [September 30, 1850]. I took it to New York
and employed Mr. Charles M. Keller to patent it. It was used as a model in the
application for the patent [filed April 16, 1851].

Under the name of I. M. Singer Company, the little firm launched manufacturing operations, Singer stumping the Boston and New York garment districts,
demonstrating before church and social groups, at carnivals and circuses. He invented two new features, both completely original and of significance: a packing
case that could be turned into a stand for the machine, and, probably Singer's
best contribution to the sewing machine, the heel-and-toe-action foot treadle by
which generations of home sewers were to power it, leaving both hands free to
guide the cloth. Later he added a flywheel to smoothe the treadle action and improved the treadle by giving it an iron stand and making it wide enough to be used
by both feet. By a bizarre irony Singer, who had invented several features that
turned out to be already patented, failed to patent the treadle until it was into
public use and too late.

But the firm prospered. Entering the market just after the beginning of the
sewing-machine boom, Singer proved as able a businessman as Cyrus McCormick.
His advertising soon brought his operation to the attention of Howe, who through
his lawyers demanded $25,000 for the Singer machines already manufactured and
sold, plus royalties via licensing. At this point Singer and Zieber bought out the
evidently more faint-hearted Phelps, and Singer looked around for the best lawyers in sight. He chose Jordan and Clark of New York, and talked junior partner
Edward Clark into taking the case in return for a third interest in the company.
When Zieber became ill, Clark and Singer bought his share for $6,000, forming
what proved to be a highly effective if somewhat oddly assorted partnership. Self-
made actor-mechanic Singer took charge of research and production, New York
patrician Clark of marketing, financing, and litigation.

In the sewing-machine business, they were equally shrewd and equally tough.
To try to prove that Elias Howe had invented nothing original, Clark instituted
a diligent patent search in Europe, and even tried to show that the sewing machine was a Chinese invention. Unable to find an earlier patent that described
the lock stitch, he turned, as the Blodgett and Lerow manufacturer had before
him, to Walter Hunt. Hunt unearthed one of his thirty-year-old models, Singer
had it renovated to make it sew, but when Hunt admitted in court that he had
never applied for a patent, the Boston judge ruled unequivocally that "there is
no evidence in this case that leaves a shadow of a doubt that, for all the benefit
conferred upon the public by the introduction of a sewing machine, the public
is indebted to Mr. Howe." The Patent Commissioner sensibly commented: "When
the first inventor allows his discovery to slumber for eighteen years, with no proba-

Model operating Singer Model 1. (Singer Company)

bility of its ever being brought into useful activity, and when it is only resurrected to supplant and strangle an invention which has been given to the public, and which has been made practically useful, all reasonable presumption should be in favor of the inventor who has been the means of conferring the real benefit upon the world." On July 1, 1854, Singer bought a Howe license and paid $15,000 for the machines he had already manufactured.

The Singer sewing-machine case had a larger result. Because it conclusively demonstrated that all the necessary and desirable features of the sewing machine could not be assembled under the patent claims of Howe or any other single inventor, it led to the first United States patent pool. After a succession of suits and countersuits among the embattled inventors (in which Howe was the defendant more than once), a sensible businessman named Orlando B. Potter, president of the Grover & Baker Company, suggested a "combination" of manufacturers. Howe's company, Singer's, Grover & Baker, and Wheeler, Wilson & Company each owned valuable patents. Howe owned the eye-pointed needle and the shuttle that combined to make the indispensable lock stitch. Singer had the Bachelder feed device, Bachelder's yielding presser foot, and his own patented heart-shaped cam to move the needle bar. Wheeler, Wilson owned the rights to the four-motion feed. Grover & Baker less important patents, which may explain why the combination idea originated with its president (in 1856, however, Grover & Baker patented a sewing case that turned theirs into the first portable sewing machine).

The other companies agreed to an even split, but Howe held out for and got a royalty of $5 for each machine sold in the United States by any of the manufacturers in the Combination, and $1 for each sold abroad. Between 1856, when the pool was formed, and 1867, when his patent expired, he collected $2 million. The license deal freed him from the cares of manufacturing, which he left mainly to his brother Amasa, who was often mistaken for the inventor while accepting exposition prizes abroad.

The patent pool cleared the way for the rapid development of manufacturing technique. Given the large commercial market, and the tremendous potential of the home sewing market, the product, with its basic technical character of an assemblage of precisely machined metal components, lent itself brilliantly to application of the "American System" of interchangeable parts manufacture. The outbreak of the Civil War multiplied the demand for commercial machines (and heightened that for domestic) as the government placed orders in the hundreds of thousands for uniforms, overcoats, shoes, tents, knapsacks, cartridge belts, blankets, and sails.

All New York and New England jumped at the opportunity, except for Elias Howe, whose reaction to the war was astonishing. While his brother Amasa, Isaac Singer, Wheeler, and their clients in the garment-making, blanket-making, tent-making businesses plunged happily into their war orders, forty-two-year-old, chronically sick Elias Howe organized and equipped the 17th Connecticut Volunteers and enlisted in their ranks as a private. His modest heroism did not prevent his being slandered as a profiteer. One day in Baltimore he overheard two Copperheads reviling "the damned Abolitionists" for their war profiteering and asserting that "old man Howe" had been given a contract to carry mail to the whole Union army. The tale had apparently grown out of Howe's volunteering to act as mailman for his regiment, which he also occasionally served as unofficial paymaster when the government was slow with the soldiers' pay.

He survived the war but died in 1867 at the age of forty-eight. He had started a sewing-machine company of his own a few months before his death which, combined with Amasa's company and managed by Elias's son-in-law, continued for another twenty years as the Howe Sewing Machine Company.

Allen Wilson, inventor of the four-motion feed, reaped few profits. He had retired from Wheeler, Wilson & Company in 1853 because of ill health, receiving only a salary and a percentage from the patent renewals, while the firm went on to become the Singer Company's chief rival, especially in the home sewing-machine market. In 1874 Wilson's petition to have his patents extended on the grounds of hardship met with violent protest from antimonopoly ideologues. The *New York Daily Graphic* wrote: "So valuable has been this latter four-motion feed that few or no cloth-sewing machines are now made without it. The joint ownership of this feature of the Wilson patents has served to bind the combination of sewing-machine builders together, and enabled them to defy competition by force of the monopoly. The inventor has probably realized millions for his invention. . . . A monopoly of this feed motion for seven years more would be worth from ten to thirty millions to the owner—and would cost the people four times as much." Wilson had made no millions, but his petition was denied, and he died in mediocre circumstances in 1888.

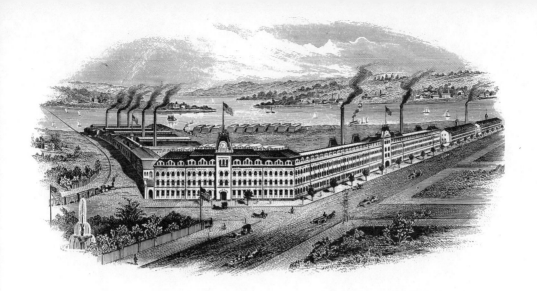

Singer sewing-machine factory in Elizabeth, New Jersey, founded 1873, then the largest single product manufacturing facility in the world. (Singer Company)

Isaac Singer prospered better. Besides his war orders, he profited from the growing home sewing-machine market, which his partner Clark cleverly exploited by hiring girls to demonstrate the machine, and by emulating Cyrus McCormick with the "hire-purchase" or installment plan. The Singer home model sold for $50 cash (a dramatic illustration of the economics of mass production) or $5 down and $3 a month until the company had collected $100, an arrangement appliance manufacturers, encyclopedia publishers, and others were not slow to copy. Singer and Clark also introduced two other modern business devices, the trade-in (especially with his competitors' models) and special sales at reduced prices. Within a few years the company was selling a thousand machines a week and making a thousand dollars a day. The home sewing machine's success was enhanced by the invention of the garment pattern by a Massachusetts tailor named Ebenezer Butterick, who published a man's shirt pattern in 1859 and sold so many he followed it up with children's and women's fashions.

Ex-carnival pitchman Isaac Singer rose on the wings of his inventive and business skill from pushy parvenu to flashy man-about-town, readily recognized by New Yorkers in a five-horse diligence in Central Park, his furred and jeweled mistress of the moment beside him. In 1875 he chose England as his retirement home, but died of a heart attack while building a suitable mansion. Besides a $13 million fortune for his heirs, he left behind one of America's first and most euphonious consumer trade names, almost a lyric, though like so many lyrics misleading, the "Singer Sewing machine."

PART IV

18

America 1851

P RINCE A LBERT DID NOT PLAN the Crystal Palace Exhibition of 1851 to celebrate the seventy-fifth anniversary of American independence, but the crowning there of the "American System of Manufacturing" was a fitting coincidence. On its seventy-fifth birthday America signaled to the world a critical change of relationship. After several decades as an eager devourer of other people's technology, it had acquired a capacity to create technology for others. From a technological importer, the country had grown into an importer-exporter.

The McCormick-Hussey reaper, so much appreciated in England, was only the foremost of a number of mechanizations taking place in American agriculture as farm families from rocky New England, soil-exhausted New York and Pennsylvania, and from Scandinavia, Germany, and Britain flocked into the bountiful Midwest prairie. For the first time, or with significantly improved effectiveness, horsepower was being applied to nearly every important task in growing crops— plowing, cultivating, seeding, raking, threshing, reaping, mowing, baling, corn shelling, and straw and root cutting. Calvin Delano's patented sulky rake of 1849, soon improved by wire teeth, was ten to twenty times as productive as hand-raking. George Brown's two-row horse corn-planter of 1853 could plant in hills at a rate of fifteen to twenty acres per day. Corn was primarily a western crop, and Brown's implement remained virtually unknown in the East, but Moses and Samuel Pennock's seed drill for wheat moved from East to West, pioneered by a progressive farmer named John Jones who used it in Delaware and Pennsylvania despite the jeers of conservative neighbors: "Some would advise me to take the implement home, break it up and cook my dinner on it. I . . . persevered. And now . . . all my neighbors have adopted the drill for sowing their wheat and most other small grain."

John and Hiram Pitts of Winthrop, Maine, first successfully combined mechanical threshing (a Scottish invention), separating, and fanning in one machine in 1837, moving their manufacturing operation westward by stages to reach Chicago in 1851, by which time several other manufacturers were turning out similar machines. The device made custom threshing possible, the entrepreneur, often a nonfarmer, using the farmer's horses to thresh his grain for three to ten cents a bushel. Some farmers argued that the old-fashioned hand flail, though far slower, had an advantage—it kept hired help, an increasing element as farming grew in scale, over the winter.

Steam power in the form of stationary engines for threshing, pumping water, and operating churns, made its first appearance on the farm in the 1850s, and spread rapidly in the 1860s. Mechanization in general diffused swiftly in the decade of the 1860s as the war sent prices up.

Nonmechanical improvements in agricultural technology also made significant appearance. In 1847 the Mormons, driven west by persecution, introduced large-scale irrigation to the United States by diverting water from City Creek, near what became Salt Lake City, eventually spreading the technique through Utah and other Western states (some of which had experienced it much earlier under the rational agriculture of Indians). Commercial fertilizers were introduced in 1843 in the form of a shipload of Peruvian guano, a source which, however, declined in quantity and nitrogen content after midcentury, to be replaced by chemical fertilizers, pioneered in Europe.

Oneida, New York, dairy farmer Jesse Williams was an expert cheese maker, so his son brought his milk over to the older man's milkhouse, and out of the father-son collaboration grew the "American System of Dairying," or cooperative dairy-farming, that spread through the Midwest.

Western farm products were at first regarded as inferior to those of the East, whose place names became marks of quality—Genesee flour, Orange County or Goshen butter, Herkimer cheese. The Western middlemen cheerily adopted the Eastern labels, but by midcentury genuine improvement made Western products fully competitive. The half-wild razorback hogs disappeared in favor of scientifically bred Poland Chinas and Chester Whites, kept in pens and fed cereals. By the 1860s British travelers thought the Western hogs superior to England's.

The stockyard operation at Cincinnati afforded diversion to many travelers. William Chambers (1854) described it:

> The greater number of the hog slaughterhouses are behind the town, on the road towards the higher grounds, and are generally wooden structures of a very plain description. Each is provided with a series of pens, whence the animals walk in single file along an enclosed gallery towards the apartment where they meet their doom.
>
> When a pig is killed in England, the sufferer usually takes care to let the whole neighborhood hear of the transaction. On such occasions, it is the prescriptive right

of the pig to squeak, and he is allowed to squeak accordingly. In Cincinnati, there is no time for this. Impelled along the passage from the exterior pen, each hog on entering the chamber of death receives a blow with a mallet on the forehead, which deprives him of consciousness and motion. The next instant he is bled to death and by means of an extensive system of caldrons and other requisites, the carcass is speedily cleaned, dressed, and hung up to undergo the proper cooling, previous to being cut in pieces and pickled.

Across the river in Covington, Chambers noted, the largest slaughterhouse rose four stories, with the pigs driven up an inclined plane to the top floor to be slaughtered, dismembered and pickled on the way down, on the flour-mill principle. Though the Englishman was unaware of it, Cincinnati's hogs also had an important contribution to make to mass production.

In 1851 the United States Agricultural Society was established to push for expansion of the Agricultural Division of the Patent Office, whose enterprising Commissioner, Morse's friend Henry L. Ellsworth, distributed seed packages and published farm statistics. By 1854 the division employed three researchers (a chemist, a botanist, and an entomologist) and by 1856 was conducting experiments in a five-acre garden. In 1860 the Republican Party, new political instrument of the Midwest farmers, pledged establishment of a Department of Agriculture, a pledge fulfilled by a bill President Abraham Lincoln signed in 1862 (though cabinet status was withheld another quarter century). That year an even more significant piece of legislation, the Morrill Act, originally passed in 1857 but vetoed by reactionary James Buchanan, gave vast tracts of public land to state colleges whose primary mission was designated as teaching and experimenting in "agriculture and the mechanic arts." Pennsylvania, Michigan, Maryland, and Iowa had already established state agricultural colleges, and were swiftly joined by institutions in every state until some seventy land-grant colleges and universities flourished. Their contribution to the development of American (and world) scientific agriculture was critical, and in addition they provided a tremendous accretion to engineering and science education (as well as liberal arts and all other areas of higher learning). Ezra Cornell combined a generous part of his telegraph fortune with a New York land grant to found his namesake university in his home town of Ithaca.

The agricultural expansion stimulated the long-stalled boom in railroad building. At midcentury only one long line reached into the Midwest, and on it freight and passengers were carried by sixteen different companies. Vast inefficiency had been created by the failure to adopt a standard gauge, a blunder made by other countries but compounded in the United States by the multiplicity of states as well as railroad companies.

Most of the major technical problems had been solved, though not completely, or even very well. Brakes were manually operated and too weak to handle increasing inertial forces. Both locomotives and cars frequently jumped the track, among other reasons because many were built as "compromise cars," loosely adaptable to slightly varying gauges. Link-and-pin couplings sometimes failed, and provided a fearful hazard for yardmen doing the coupling. Burning cinders from the smokestack set coaches, boxcars, wheat fields, and pastures ablaze, and

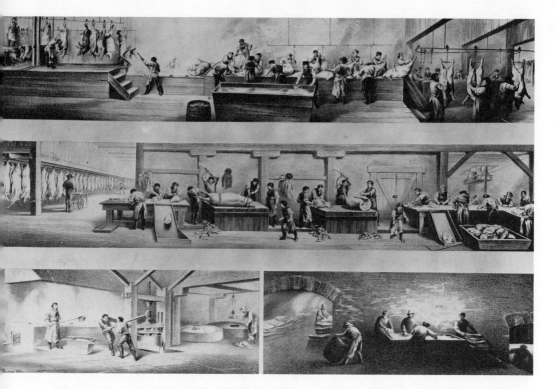

Pork-packing in Cincinnati: a dis-assembly line, predecessor of the modern assembly line. (Library of Congress)

collisions or track-jumpings overturned pot-bellied stoves used to heat cars. Road-beds were rough, springs inadequate, and breakdowns commonplace. Despite these and other shortcomings, the railroad was universally extolled as a vast improvement in speed (15 to 20 miles per hour) over stagecoach and steamboat, and even admired for its comfort—springs or no springs, sleeping cars and dining cars were early and popular innovations.

Defects notwithstanding, railroads were needed, and breakneck construction was launched in the Old Northwest, between western Pennsylvania and Missouri. Overnight Chicago jumped onto the map as the nation's railroad capital. The great consolidation known as the New York Central came in 1853, and the same year New York-to-Chicago rail service was inaugurated.

Grain as well as flour now became a standard commodity, since grain could be more easily handled in loose bulk. Chicago exported much more grain than flour, as did Detroit, Toledo, Milwaukee, and Cleveland. Novelist Anthony Trollope, repeating in 1861 his mother's venture of the 1820s, waxed lyrical about the "rivers of wheat" that flowed through the Midwestern grain elevators and were carried on trains and lake and canal boats to the East. In Chicago and Buffalo,

> I began to know what it was for a country to overflow with milk and honey, to burst with its own fruits, and be smothered by its own riches. . . . Chicago may be called the metropolis of American corn [wheat]—the favourite city haunt of the American Ceres. The goddess seats herself there amidst the dust of her full barns, and proclaims herself a goddess ruling over things political and philosophical as

well as agricultural. . . . I went over one great grain store in Chicago. . . . It was a world in itself—and the dustiest of all worlds. It contained, when I was there, half a million bushels of wheat. . . . But it was not as a storehouse that this great building was so remarkable, but as a channel or a river course for the flooding freshets of corn. . . . There were not bottoms enough to take the corn away from Chicago, nor indeed on the railway was there a sufficiency of rolling stock or locomotive power to bring it into Chicago. . . . The country was bursting with its own produce and smothered in its own fruits.

American bulk handling startled the Englishman:

Nothing is known of sacks or bags. . . . We in England are not accustomed to see wheat travelling in this open, unguarded, and plebeian manner. Wheat with us is aristocratic, and travels always in its private carriage.

Trollope marveled at the towns in the Midwest created and dominated by the railroad.

The line of the rails runs through the main street of the town, and forms not unfrequently the only road. . . . The panting and groaning, and whistling of engines is continual. . . . This is the life of the town; and indeed as the whole place is dependent on the railway, so is the railway held in favor and beloved. The noise of the engine is not disliked, nor are its puffings and groanings held to be unmusical. With us a locomotive steam-engine is still, as it were, a beast of prey. . . . But there, in the western States, it had been taken to the bosoms of them all as a domestic animal; no one fears it, and the little children run about almost among its wheels. . . . With us in England, it is difficult to realize the importance which is attached to a railway in the States. . . . In America, especially in the North, the railways have been the precursors of cultivation. They have been carried hither and thither, through primeval forests and over prairies. . . . The face of the country between one settlement and another is still in many cases utterly unknown; but there is the connecting [rail]road by which produce is carried away, and new comers are brought in. The town that is distant a hundred miles by the rail is so near that its inhabitants are neighbors; but a settlement twenty miles distant across the uncleared country is unknown, unvisited. . . .

A French visitor, G. T. Poussin, also found something peculiarly American in the swiftly spreading continental rail network, writing in 1851: "Steam, with the Americans, is an eminently national element. . . . With them it is applied as much to extend their liberty as to augment their physical welfare. . . . The American seems to consider the words democracy, liberalism, and railroads as synonymous terms." The ideological association did not interfere with business, the Philadelphia firm of Harrison and Estwick building Russia's first railroad line from Moscow to St. Petersburg and selling the Czar 160 locomotives plus rolling stock.

In the Eastern cities, the iron rail acquired another significance as New York, Philadelphia, and Boston laid rails in their streets for horse-drawn commuter cars. The volume of traffic, reaching into the tens of millions annually, presaged a future for the electric motor with which Thomas Davenport, the Brandon, Vermont, blacksmith, had moved a car in 1836. In 1847 Moses Farmer drove a two-passenger electric car in Dover, New Hampshire, and in 1851 Charles G. Page of the Patent Office, supported by a grant from Congress, ran a car fitfully between Washington and Bladensburg, Maryland. The technology was there, except for the large power source.

In water transportation, progress was uneven. Ocean shipping, America's original industry, had expanded steadily, and in midcentury was in a glowing state of prosperity, with American ships in every sea, carrying every kind of cargo to all the ports of the world. Two new types of sailing ship were especially American, the whaler and the clipper. The virtual extinction of the Atlantic whale only stimulated exploitation of the Pacific species, hunted from New Bedford and Nantucket after a harrowing trip around Cape Horn that discouraged nobody. The knell of the American whaler was sounded by the world's first oil well, drilled at Titusville, Pennsylvania in 1859 through pipe driven to bedrock by an ex-train conductor named Edwin L. Drake. The new "mineral oil" immediately began replacing whale oil in the world's lamps and animal fat in axles and machinery.

The whaler's technology, the ancient harpoon and lance, and the blubber-boiling try-works amidships, had little to do with navigation. The clipper, on the contrary, was the ultimate triumph of sailing-ship design, her maximum length-to-breadth ratio, enormous sail area, long concave bows making possible an absolutely astonishing speed. One ship, built by Donald McKay of Boston for the Australian Black Ball Line, set the all-time Atlantic sail-crossing record of 12¼ days (Samuel Slater's 66-day crossing was about par for the old-style ships).

The clipper was the ultimate in wooden sailing-ship design, but wooden sailing ships were out of date, and the clipper's American origin actually implied an environment of conservatism rather than innovation. The future of shipping lay in the less aesthetic, and at first not even speedier, iron ship propelled by steam power. Iron ships of over 2,000 tons, about the limit in wood, could be built without breaking in two, and steam provided reliability of propulsion and therefore of scheduling.

Reluctantly turning to iron and steam, American shipbuilders, dominated by the conservative New York industry, stuck to the paddle wheel long after British builders had proven the superiority of the screw propeller—originated by David Bushnell, Robert Fulton, and Colonel Stevens, perfected and patented by Swedish-born American John Ericsson. The American Collins Line gave Britain's Cunard a battle in the Atlantic for several years with its swifter-than-clipper crossings of nine to ten days, but the Collins ships had chronic mechanical problems despite a larger government subsidy than Cunard's, and in the mid-1850s one of the four Collins ships sank after a collision and another vanished without a trace. Congress suspended the subsidy and Collins gave up.

Cunard's ships were paddle-wheelers like Collins's (though iron instead of wood). The first iron screw ships were those of another British shipper, William Inman, who managed to weather a pair of disasters uncannily identical to those of Collins, whose sailing dates he had taken over. Gradually the screw demonstrated advantages of economy and power in ocean cruising, though Inman probably owed his success more to a competitive innovation, the provision of livable quarters for steerage passengers, whom Collins and Cunard had both snubbed, and for whom the sailing ships provided sanitary facilities alternatively described as appalling and nonexistent.

At least one American steam line made money in ocean navigation. Cornelius Vanderbilt, a rowdy veteran of the Hudson River, conceived the idea of carrying Forty-Niners to California via Nicaragua. When an adventurer named William Walker seized control of the Nicaraguan government and allied himself with Vanderbilt's New York enemies, blocking passage across the isthmus, Vanderbilt organized a coalition of Nicaragua's Central American neighbors and overthrew Walker. By 1853 the "Commodore," as he liked to be called, had made so much money that he built himself a steam yacht and made a triumphal tour of Europe, taking along his entire family and a clergyman to write a fulsome history of the voyage.

John Ericsson, who had designed a screw propeller and competed with George Stephenson in early locomotive building, had emigrated to the United States from Sweden in 1840. After inventing a number of valuable maritime instruments he was seduced by the fantasy that heat, or "caloric" in the terminology of the day, could be used over and over to produce power. In 1852 he built a ship named for himself that mounted by far the largest steam engine ever put aboard a vessel, featuring a "regenerator" whose thousands of wire interstices were supposed to trap the "caloric" as it escaped to the atmosphere. The *New York Tribune* was fully convinced by a demonstration cruise: "The age of Steam is closed; the age of Caloric opens. Fulton and Watt belong to the Past; Ericsson is the great mechanical genius of the Present and the Future." The *Times* thought the demonstration an event "which will be held memorable in the ages to come."

A skeptical exception to the press chorus was the voice of *Scientific American*, a new and already distinguished magazine with a twenty-seven-year-old publisher, Alfred Ely Beach, and a twenty-eight-year-old editor, Orson Munn. Munn shocked everyone as the vessel docked by calling out, "Vive la humbug!" In its editorial columns, *Scientific American* expressed the view that "the good opinion of one eminent practical engineer . . . would be worth more than all the rest of the daily paper fraternity." Britain's celebrated engineer and shipbuilder Isambard Kingdom Brunel pronounced the caloric theory a version of perpetual motion, and the *Ericsson* was gradually recognized by its designer as a ponderous will-o'-the-wisp, whose significance today lies in the light it casts on mid-nineteenth-century technology's spirit and substance; John Ericsson knew a thousand times as much about steam power as had John Fitch, but still could be trapped into a gross scientific blunder.

Isambard Brunel's own chef d'oeuvre, the mighty iron ship *Great Eastern*, assisted in the frustrating but ultimately dazzling Anglo-American engineering enterprise of laying the Atlantic cable. The company organized by young retired industrialist Cyrus Field (he had made a swift fortune in wholesale paper in New York) twice tried to carry the huge weight of cable across the ocean on two ships, and in 1858 got the thing in place long enough for Queen Victoria to send a message to President Buchanan, but it broke. Even the *Great Eastern* had problems in stowing 5,000 tons of iron, but Samuel Morse's dream was finally consummated in 1866.

LEFT Squire Whipple, designer of the all-iron "bowstring" truss bridge, who wrote the first American theoretical study of bridge engineering. (Library of Congress)

RIGHT John Ericsson, designer of the *Monitor* and pioneer of the locomotive and the screw-propeller, pursued the chimera of "caloric" in his 1852 ship, the *Ericsson*. (Library of Congress)

Brunel and other British engineers and shipbuilders gave England a lead in oceangoing iron steamship technology that America did not challenge. In wooden paddle-wheelers for inland waters, however, America reigned supreme. By 1845 Western builders were able to float 500 tons of cargo in eight feet of water, and, by 1867, 2,000 tons. Two smaller boats launched in 1856 could navigate (unloaded) on fourteen and eleven inches respectively, not far from the legendary "heavy dew" of skippers' boasts. In the 1850s, the decade of Mark Twain's boyhood, the Mississippi steamboat reached glorious maturity, rising from the water like a layer cake, with a main deck, a boiler deck, a hurricane deck, and a "texas," the officers' deckhouse, so-named because all the cabins were named after states (hence, "staterooms"), and the officers' quarters were the largest. Three-fourths to four-fifths of a fully laden steamboat stood above the water. Yet lateral stability was critical because a list could cause a boiler explosion. It was achieved by concentrating weight on or below the main deck—engines, boilers (down from the boiler deck), cargo, fuel, heavy structural members. Then a fresh instability factor developed with the addition of "guards," extensions of the main deck over the paddle wheels to protect the wheels and facilitate loading and unloading. To compensate, cargo was arranged for easy shifting. Chain wagons and coal cars were especially useful. At that, the officers often had to order passengers to quit one side of the deck when they congregated to watch something ashore.

To resist hogging and sagging, the tendency of the ship to break in two longitudinally because of its shallow draft in proportion to its length, Hudson River and other Eastern builders borrowed the arch-truss from the covered bridge, allowing it to rise above the superstructure on either side. Western builders used "hog chains" made up of iron rods carried over a series of struts and masts. Cross chains were also run through the hold from wheelhouse to wheelhouse to help support the heavy paddle-wheel assemblies. Despite such bracing, a collision with a sandbar or shore often broke a vessel's back. Such accidents, added to fire and explosion, kept the average life of a Western steamboat below five years, compared with twenty years for an ocean sailing ship and forty for a whaler. Some improvement in combating hazards was brought by the Act of 1852 (supplanting the ineffective Act of 1838), which prescribed inspection and testing of vessels and machinery, examination and licensing of officers, and specification of types and uses of equipment. The wire rope recently introduced to the United States by John Roebling proved the answer to the problem of the tiller ropes burning and stranding a blazing vessel in midstream.

The much-advertised elegance of the saloons was not universally admired. One traveler from the East dismissed the splendor—Turkish carpets, lamps, silk curtains, gilt, mirrors, paneling—as "sham . . . half-disgusting and wholly comical." Also on the negative side was the notorious carelessness of the Western public, which required posted rules against whittling the furniture and sleeping with boots on. Meals on board were sumptuous, with emphasis on meat and fowl, at breakfast as at supper. The bill of fare assigned French names to the dishes, but according to two European visitors, "The passengers obviously do not care how the dishes taste, provided that they sound well on the bill of fare, satisfied to find on it everything they could command at the Cafe de Paris. . . . They are fond of the idea that America is the first country in the world, also as respects the culinary art."

Some boats were less generous with the helpings. John James Audubon, complaining that the steamer that took him from Louisville to St. Louis in 1843 offered fare "so scanty . . . that our worthy commander could not have given us another meal had we been detained a night longer," found the bed linen correspondingly scanty, the pillows stuffed with corn husks, the washing facilities inadequate and his cabin roof leaky.

Gambling was the universal diversion, and professional gamblers numerous. But fiction evidently exaggerated the stakes. A riverboat gambler reminiscing in 1873 wrote: "As for the tales regarding the fabulous sums bet at poker tables on our western rivers, they are all pure humbug. I have grave doubts whether a brag of two thousand dollars has ever been lost and won at a card table on the Mississippi River. . . ."

Crime was dealt with summarily, either by the captain or by a court convened by the passengers, with the culprit usually sentenced to a whipping or being set on shore, sometimes on a sandbar. Aside from gambling, the moral atmosphere was strict. Prostitution was rare, and one young couple who offended by sharing

Salon of the river steamer *J. M. White,* about 1880, showing the opulence of steamboat interiors. (Library of Congress)

a stateroom were taken ashore, licensed, and wedded while the boat waited at the dock.

As transportation technology, the storied riverboat was already obsolete in the very decade of its greatest glory. The impact on steamboating of the railroad-building boom of the 1850s was postponed by the Civil War, which set the river shipyards humming as never before. But by 1870, despite the Currier & Ives-memorialized race between the *Natchez* and the *Robert E. Lee,* the beautiful riverboats were on their way to join the clippers in folklore.

In another area of transportation technology, tunnel building, America in 1851 jumped far out in front—even a little too far. The place was the Berkshires, the motivation an attempt by Boston to challenge New York's commercial supremacy.

Boston in the 1850s was at the height of its literary glory, with Emerson, Haw-thorne, Longfellow, Whittier, and Lowell established luminaries (Melville, whose *Moby Dick* was published in 1851, was less appreciated), but already far outdis-tanced as a business center by less literate New York, which continued to profit from its facile access to the Midwest. By midcentury New York had become the chief distributing center for the whole nation in respect to both foreign and do-mestic products. To the congeries of warehouses of jobbers and wholesalers clus-tered around Pearl Street came retail merchants from as far off as the deep South and the far Midwest who seized the opportunity of a visit to the big city to enjoy the theater and restaurants. In the next decade regional jobbing centers sprang up—Augusta, Memphis, Louisville, Cincinnati, St. Louis, Chicago—but New York

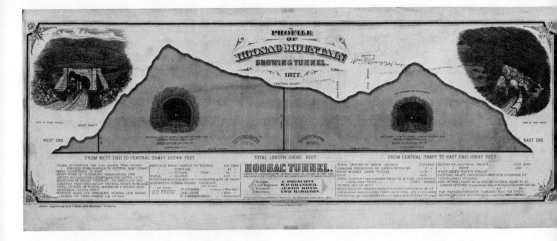

The Hoosac Tunnel, profile of the mountain, with sectional views of tunnel superimposed, east and west portals on either side. (Library of Congress)

lost none of its commercial vitality, and continued rapidly to increase its tonnage and dollars traded.

Philadelphia had tried to counter the Erie Canal by making canals climb the Allegheny Mountains. Boston in 1851 tried to match the New York Central Railroad's Hudson-Mohawk water-level route by pushing a railroad line through the Berkshires at North Adams.

To appreciate the hardihood of the Hoosac Tunnel project, it is necessary to realize that not a single Alpine tunnel yet existed, and in fact not a single rock (mountain) tunnel of any length anywhere in the world. The 4¾-mile Hoosac took twenty-four years to complete, starting with a technological fiasco in the form of a seventy-ton steam-powered drilling machine that was supposed to drill holes for gunpowder blasting, but didn't, and at last triumphantly holing through with the help of Alfred Nobel's just-invented nitroglycerin. Nobel's invention was simultaneously used on the first Alpine tunnel, the French-Italian Mont-Cenis, longer than the Hoosac, but efficiently driven in fourteen years. The Hoosac cost the state of Massachusetts millions, earned a derisive nickname as "The Great Bore," and failed dismally in its intended effect of catching Boston up commercially with New York. But technology's interrelationships are unpredictable, and the Hoosac made a major contribution to the exploitation of the metal-rich Far West by giving birth to the compressed-air-drill industry. It also gave American engineers experience in rock tunneling, needed for the West's railroad development.

If railroad tunneling proved costly, railroad bridging in America was a wonder of thrift, thanks mainly to the Howe truss whose wood and iron components could be mass-produced and shipped to the construction site. Increasing railroad loadings were met by doubling or tripling the vertical iron rods used as tension members. A turnbuckle made it possible to tighten joints loosened by passage of trains.

Howe introduced a more advanced mechanics into bridge building. He did not, any more than had Timothy Palmer, Theodore Burr, or Ithiel Town, introduce

Laying the Atlantic Cable, 1857; the moment when the cable broke. From *Frank Leslie's Magazine*. (Library of Congress)

science. With their hewn or sawn timbers, their trunnels and bolts, iron rods and turnbuckles, the covered-bridge engineers built thousands of bridges that stood up under railroad loadings. But technology in America as in Britain and Europe was now reaching a point at which its marriage with science needed to be consummated. In 1847 Squire Whipple (Squire was his name, not a title) of Utica, New York, published *A Work on Bridge-Building*, the first American theoretical study of bridge engineering. In a truss design, the vertical and diagonal members are always either respectively in tension and compression or vice versa. William Howe's wrought-iron verticals were in tension. Wrought iron was more expensive than cast iron, but cast iron was not strong in tension. Squire Whipple, borrowing a "bowstring" form from France, designed an all-iron truss in which the tension members were wrought iron and the compression members cast iron; the large curved upper chord, in compression, could also be made of the cheaper cast iron. The Howe truss, too, was increasingly made in all iron to carry railroad loadings (for the first time over the Erie Canal at Frankfort, New York).

The same principle, iron framing, had already been applied to buildings in Britain and Europe, typically to the vast one-story open-air markets of London and Paris. The first multistory metal frames were an American accomplishment, the substitution of iron for wood gradually expanding until Daniel Badger of New York made a business of iron-framing in the 1840s. The best-known fully iron-framed building was that of another New Yorker, machinist-inventor James Bogardus, whose four-story foundry of 1848–49 at the corner of Centre and Duane streets made architectural history.

An even more significant American contribution to the future of the new city structure, the office building, was a hit exhibit at the New York Crystal Palace in 1853. Its inventor stood on a square platform, whose means of lifting he explained to the crowd, while the platform rose above their heads. When it reached its highest point, he produced a large knife and cut the suspending rope cable. The crowd gasped, and nothing happened; the platform rested uncannily in space. Elisha Graves Otis had invented the safety elevator.

Vertical lifting devices dated from classical antiquity, the counterweight from the Middle Ages, and steam power applied via a hydraulic fluid from early in the nineteenth century. But because hemp ropes often failed from wear, the elevator was restricted to freight handling until Otis came along. A Vermont Yankee born on a farm in 1811, he had showed the mechanical bent of Fitch, Whitney, and McCormick, quit the farm to run a flour mill like Oliver Evans, to build carriages like Peter Cooper, and to become master mechanic like Paul Moody, in a bedstead factory in Albany. There he began inventing and presently, to meet a need for a plant in Yonkers, New York, he designed and installed the world's first elevator equipped with an automatic device for preventing a fall in case of cable failure. When tension was released by the breaking or loosening of the main cable, clamps snapped outward to grip the guide rails within which the platform descended.

Yet another American innovation in building construction brought a revolution in the centuries-old pattern of domestic architecture. Once more, a shortage of skilled labor, this time in swiftly growing Chicago, was the catalyst. The "balloon frame" principle is believed to have originated with Augustine Taylor, first of a line of great Chicago architect-engineers. Arriving in 1833, Hartford-born Taylor was commissioned to build the prairie hamlet's first Catholic church. Confronted with a shortage of skilled labor and building materials, Taylor designed a structure consisting "of scantling and siding" (studs and boards) easily nailed together. Since wood was plentiful, the studs and joists could be closely ranked, with diagonal bracing providing a rigid cage to be covered with clapboard. As Chicago transitioned overnight from village to town to city, the Taylor "balloon frame"—an epithet of carpenters who feared its lightness—by doing away with the massive timber framing laboriously assembled in Europe and America since the Middle Ages, conjured up hundreds of rows of houses stretching west from Lake Michigan. Like the Town Lattice covered bridge, the balloon frame supplied an appropriate technical solution for a timber-rich, skilled-labor-short country, and spread swiftly through the West to become the universal American dwelling unit for generations.

Taylor's invention incidentally depended on an earlier one, the rotary power saw, which economically cut timber into small pieces. The rotary saw had long been known to watchmakers and the principle had apparently been used in some European sawmills. But its American form originated with the Shakers, a communal sect related to the Quakers and noted for their efficient farming, skillful handicrafts, and practical inventions, including the clothespin. The rotary saw is usually attributed to Sister Tabitha Babbitt of the Harvard, Massachusetts, Shaker community—the Shakers did not believe in patenting—who was watching her spinning wheel whirl its spindle one day in 1812, when she conceived a circular saw blade spun by a waterwheel. Sister Tabitha's invention, freely given to the world, was universally adopted by sawmills, heretofore armed with the medieval vertical pit saw powered via a crank. It also led to the introduction of other sophisticated rotary cutters such as the planing mill and turning mill.

To many Europeans Chicago seemed the most American of cities. W. F. Rae, an Englishman who crossed the continent by rail in 1860, observed the city's breakneck expansion with approval: "None but the idle starve; none but the stupid die poor. . . . [Chicago] is the paradise of the modern man of business. Compared with the bustle of Chicago, the bustle of New York seems stagnation."

But Rae, like most Europeans, also admired New York, whose skyline he had observed as his Cunard liner steamed into the harbor: "The water is studded with steamers and sailing vessels. In the distance are islands covered with verdure, and in the background are the masses of red-brick buildings which constitute the chief city of the Empire State. Conspicuous among the various structures is a towering edifice, imposing in outline and white in colour. I was told that this was the office of the *New York Herald*."

That the most imposing building in New York belonged to a newspaper signaled another aspect of the new age, by no means unrelated to technology. Richard Hoe, son of an English-born mechanic who had built several presses in New York, conceived the idea of mounting type on a revolving cylinder. The Hoe "lightning" press, patented in 1846, first used by the Philadelphia *Public Ledger* in 1847, sent into discard the centuries-old flatbed and opened the way to mass-circulation dailies. William Bullock of Philadelphia, who completed the transition to modern letterpress printing by adding the web (continuous roll of paper), was victim of a not-at-all-unheard-of type of industrial accident when he got caught in a power-transmission belt, yanked into his press, and fatally mangled.

Tourists in that day as in this invariably commented on hotels, and midcentury visitors to America were particularly impressed with the facilities. American hotels were by European standards immense and ultramodern. Their barber shops with reclining chairs were "only to be matched in the dressing-rooms of nobles and princes," thought William Chambers in 1853. Chambers also admired the hotel laundries, where he saw clothes dried by "rapidly whirling machines, which wring out the wet, and cause the articles to pass through currents of hot air, so as to turn them out ready for the ironer in the space of a few minutes. Anywhere, in an hour or two, [the traveler] can get everything washed and pressed, as if he had just started from home." The expansive American hotel already included a range of shops—"an American hotel is not a house: it is a town." Such establishments were by no means limited to New York; Anthony Trollope in 1861 found that "the first sign of an incipient settlement is an hotel five stories high, with an office, a bar, a cloak-room, three gentlemen's parlours, two ladies' parlours, a ladies' entrance, and two hundred bedrooms. . . . Price nearly always $2½ dollars a day, for which a bedroom and as many meals as the guest can contrive to eat. . . ." The spanking new Sherman House in Chicago boasted the latest in hotel technology—not, however, perfected: "There were pipes without end for cold water which ran hot, and for hot water which would not run at all."

The hotels, like so much of what midcentury well-to-do travelers saw, furnished a superficial image of American cities, whose growth in the previous decade had broken all world's records. While the national population increased by 35 percent in the decade before 1850, the cities grew by 92 percent, a rate never again matched even in America. The growth abated only slightly in the decade of the 1850s. By 1860 New York had 800,000 people, not counting Brooklyn, still linked only by the ferry sung by Walt Whitman. Seven other cities exceeded 100,000. Their geographical distribution showed the country's shifting demographic pattern. New York was still followed by her three East Coast sisters, but only Philadelphia was near her in size at 565,000. Baltimore (212,000) and Boston (177,000) were not much larger than New Orleans (168,000), the only metropolis of the Deep South. "Old" Midwest cities Cincinnati and St. Louis were close behind at 161,000, and in eighth place was toddling Chicago (109,000), in 1860 hosting its first political convention, to nominate Abraham Lincoln.

Such rapid urban growth implied gross social disjointedness. Behind the Fifth Avenue hotels, rutted alleys were ankle deep in garbage, ashes, and sewage. Dogs, hogs, and geese acted as scavengers, abetted by hordes of rats. In Southern cities the rats got help from vultures. Sewage systems were still designed only to carry off storm water, and in any case only the rich had flush toilets that could be connected to them. Chicago's neat rows of balloon-frame houses fronted on plank sidewalks covering open sewers that a visitor noted gave off "a frightful odour in summer."

The situation of the American city working class may for the first time have deteriorated. The hungry American labor market had enticed a flood of immigrants whose numbers had pushed wages down or held them level while living costs rose. Horace Greeley estimated a minimum weekly budget for a New York family of five at $10.37, while most of the city's workers were earning $4, $5, and $6 a week.

In Lowell, the "Lowell girls" with their poetry and parades vanished from the scene, their places at the machines taken by Irish men and boys who formed the largest contingent of the new wave of destitute immigrants of the 1840s, a cutting from Europe's new proletariat grafted directly onto the American working class. The ragged newcomers did not need to be enticed with high pay and agreeable working conditions. Their advent coincided with the expansion in scale of the textile and other industries that replaced the old intimacy between resident mill owners and their operatives with an impersonal, competition-conscious, profit-oriented management that had the capability, thanks to the new technology, unilaterally to impose higher machine speeds and lower wages. The union movement that had begun among craft labor as early as the 1820s spread rapidly in the cities of the East Coast and Middle West in the 1840s and 1850s, won and lost a number of strikes, and succeeded in getting several state legislatures to enact ten-hour-day laws. In 1850 the Typographical Union became the first to found a nationwide organization, and was soon followed by the Stone Cutters, Hat Finishers, and Machinists and Blacksmiths.

Another emerging trouble with the increasingly complex American economy was its now evident pattern of eccentric cycles—the Panic of 1857, like that of 1837, was followed by a severe depression. Once more the disaster reached all classes, but not equally. A number of rich and middling businessmen went bankrupt, but most weathered the storm without personal deprivation, while workers, like their medieval ancestors of Britain and Western Europe, had to fall back on charity, begging, or crime. As in centuries past, protest meetings and riots followed.

The capitalist survivors of the panics, and sometimes the recovered victims, lived to make good and occasionally splendid profits. Philadelphia banker Stephen Girard's $8 million estate was thought in 1831 to be the largest private fortune in the country, but seventeen years later New York fur merchant John Jacob Astor left $20 million. The "millionaire" was becoming a character on the American scene.

Even if they had lost a bit of ground recently, city workers of 1851 were substantially better off than in 1826 or 1801. Despite boom and bust, and notwithstanding the immigrant competition, the long-range direction of the living standard was still up, though gains were unevenly distributed. Weavers and other hand workers forced to compete with machines were losing out, while skilled metalworkers and members of the building trades gained status and income.

On the upper political level, the wealth created by an adept technology's exploitation of an abundant continent also had evident impact. At the very moment the Washington government seemed helpless to mend the dangerous rift among its constituent states, it took to rivaling London, Paris, and St. Petersburg as a bully on the world stage. The two-sided Monroe Doctrine—America will stay out of Europe, Europe should stay out of America—was turning visibly one-sided: America owns the Western Hemisphere. National power was crudely flaunted by the aggressive war against harmless Mexico in 1846–47.

General Winfield Scott's large and efficient amphibious operation to Vera Cruz and Mexico City was a convincing demonstration of the growth of American military capacity since the Battle of New Orleans thirty-three years earlier, even though a closer look made it somewhat less impressive. The Mexicans, for various reasons, put up a feebler resistance than they might have, and Scott's expeditionary force showed little in the way of technological innovation: wooden ships, smoothbore cannon, muzzle-loading muskets—nothing Andrew Jackson would not have been familiar with.

There was some kind of irony in the Gold Rush that two years later turned facilely conquered California into El Dorado. No technological innovations were employed either in the animal-traction-and-sailing-ship (hardly even any steamboats) stampede to the gold fields or in the prospecting and recovery processes. But the sudden growth of California, especially San Francisco, stimulated expansion and development of the national communication and transportation networks, in the midst of which the Pony Express (April 1860–October 1861) briefly resurrected a piece of Persian Empire communications technology—the mounted relay.

California in turn heightened American interest in the Pacific, leading to another crude, though this time harmless and even constructive, assertion of power. Japan would have been opened up anyway, under the pressure of its own merchant class, and the kick at the door might as easily have come from Russia, Britain, Holland, or France. In his threat of force against a technologically weaker nation, Commodore Perry sounded exactly like a British, Russian, or

French admiral, though it was probably just as well that the Japanese government decided not to oppose him. An attempted follow-through by Perry's small flotilla might have been embarrassing. The Japanese were not so backward as to lack fire-arms and other seventeenth-century technology, and Japan was not, like Mexico, a small country.

What the Japanese lacked, and wanted, was the West's new nineteenth-century technology. Perry showed them samples from the workshops of the United States, including original American contributions: Morse telegraph instruments and John Hall breech-loading rifles.

For good, ill, or mixed, Andrew Jackson's winged prophecy that America was "manifestly called by the Almighty to a destiny which Greece and Rome, in the days of their pride, might have envied" was coming true. Whatever the future of manifest destiny, at the moment an impending disaster loomed even larger. Two other technologically fueled forces—the cotton-gin empire of the South and the American System–McCormick reaper empire of the North—were on converging courses. It was a matter of time before they would collide.

19

John Roebling Bridges the Niagara Gorge

ONE OF THE MOST FORMIDABLE OBSTACLES in the path of the expanding American rail network was the Niagara River, forming the United States-Canadian border between Lakes Erie and Ontario, and blocking the direct route from western New York to southern Michigan and the upper Midwest. Though short in length, the swift Niagara carries a large volume of water, and over the millennia had created the celebrated falls with extensive upper and lower rapids and a deeply carved 240-foot gorge. With the optimism bred by the era's combination of engineering breakthroughs and entrepreneurial profits, two bridge companies, an American and a Canadian, were formed in 1847, with the goal of building a rail-highway bridge.

The depth of the gorge ruled out intermediate supports; the bridge had to be a single span of over 800 feet. Theodore Burr's arch-truss at McCall's Ferry had measured less than half that, and clearly approached the maximum feasible for the type. An iron arch of the necessary length was even less conceivable. In England, Robert Stephenson, whose father George had built the first successful locomotive, had designed a huge square-section tube of iron to bridge the Menai Strait in Wales with a pair of 430-foot spans meeting on Britannia Isle in the middle of the sea crossing. Lengthened to 800 feet, such a solid iron tube was dubious in terms of strain, not to mention in terms of cost. The cantilever form had not yet been invented (or reinvented, as it soon was in Germany, following the ancient Chinese). There was only one kind of bridge that could possibly be erected in mid-nineteenth century over the Niagara Gorge—a suspension bridge.

The suspension bridge, like the arch, had a very ancient pedigree. Boston historian William Prescott had just revealed in his book, *The Conquest of Peru*, that the Peruvians had long fashioned footways out of the tough fibers of their native maguey tree. The Peruvians were far from alone. West Africans, Indians, Chinese, and others had slung footbridges across rivers and gorges for centuries, progressing from vines to walkways suspended by iron chains. The dizzily swaying spans were tricky even for pedestrians to negotiate, and until the eighteenth century no one had thought of the suspension principle for wagon traffic. Early attempts had not fared well. An eyebar-chain suspension bridge built over the Schuylkill by Judge James Finley of Philadelphia in 1801 failed under weight of snow and ice. Others blew down in storms or gave way under traffic. Yet some stood up, and remarkable span lengths had been achieved. Jean Chaley's Grand Pont over the Sarine at Fribourg, Switzerland, had set a world's record at 870 feet, even longer than what the Niagara bridge companies needed, and the Grand Pont had been standing for twenty-five years, supported not by chains but by four wire cables, each made up of over a thousand 1/8-inch-thick wires. French engineer Louis Vicat had invented a way to install such large numbers of wires by a "traveling wheel" sent back and forth between the two towers at either end of a suspension bridge.

Thus by 1847 the suspension bridge had developed a sophisticated construction technique without achieving stability. No one could say for sure if a given suspension bridge would stay put or, like one recently at Broughton, England, or another at Angers, France, would suddenly give way under the tread of marching soldiers. Or, as in several built in America by Judge Finley and others, under that of cattle or pigs.

When the Niagara bridge companies commissioned Charles Ellet to bridge the Niagara chasm in 1849, a few engineers in the world were beginning to solve the problem of the bridge's weakness—in engineering terms, its tendency to deflect vertically under load and laterally under wind force. This second was an extraordinarily complex phenomenon, though nobody yet realized it.

Charles Ellet was the best-known builder of suspension bridges in America. When Lewis Wernwag's elegant white "Colossus" over the Schuylkill in Philadelphia had fallen victim to fire, Ellet had replaced it with the first suspension bridge in America supported by wire cables, in the new European fashion. The Philadelphia bridge was a trifle, however, compared to a project on which Ellet was engaged at this very moment, over the Ohio River at Wheeling—a bridge with a center span, tower to tower, of 1,010 feet, 240 feet longer than Chaley's Grand Pont, the longest in the world.

Ellet was a brilliant Pennsylvania intellectual who to his own self-teaching had added a year's study in Europe, chiefly at the Ecole Polytechnique in Paris. He had worked on canals and railroads in Pennsylvania and elsewhere, but was still only thirty-seven when he received the Niagara commission. Though the Niagara bridge was shorter in span length than the Wheeling, its mission as a railroad (as well as highway) span demanded much greater strength. Ellet declared the project to be entirely feasible, a bold opinion in which he was joined by only three others

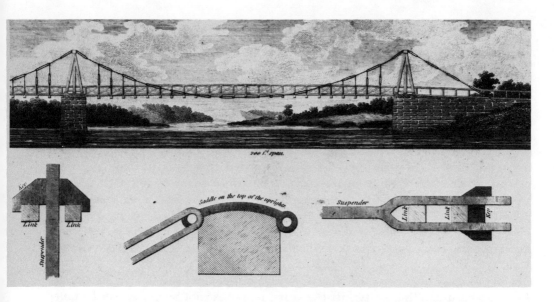

Judge James Finley's suspension bridge over the Schuylkill in 1801 failed under ice and snow, but its truss rail was a glimmer of the future. (U.S. Bureau of Public Roads)

of the numerous bridge builders in North America. He sketched a broad roadway that would accommodate two carriageways, two footways, and a single railroad track, and in the spring of 1848 set to work to hang a light service span across the gorge.

There were easier ways to get the first strand for the service bridge across, but Ellet, who had more than a dash of showmanship, chose one that passed into American folklore. He offered a five-dollar prize to the local boy who could fly a kite across. A farm lad named Homan Walsh, who won the prize, remembered it proudly nearly eighty years later when David Steinman, distinguished twentieth-century bridge engineer and bridge historian, interviewed him. As soon as an iron-wire cable was in place, Ellet had a basket carrier made and pulled himself across, the first man ever to cross the Niagara gorge. He then put the basket carrier on a paying basis, charging a dollar apiece for a death-defying ride over the swirling waters below. As soon as the narrow service bridge was finished, and before it had acquired railings, Ellet mounted his horse and rode across. A breathless crowd witnessed the passage of the horseman in the sky, and women are said to have fainted. Adding railings, Ellet opened his service bridge to the public and collected nearly $5,000 in a year. But audacious, enterprising Ellet was also a bit irresponsible, and quarreling with the promoting companies over money, he took his leave.

A few years earlier Ellet had received a letter congratulating him on his Schuylkill project: "The study of suspension bridges formed for the last few years of my residence in Europe my favorite occupation," wrote his correspondent. "Let but a single bridge of the kind be put up in Philadelphia, exhibiting all the beautiful forms of the system to full advantage, and it needs no prophecy to foretell the effect which the novel and useful features will produce upon the intelligent minds of the Americans." The writer was John Augustus Roebling, an immigrant to the

John Roebling. (Smithsonian Photograph No. 57,253)

United States of the Samuel Slater type—middle class (son of a shopkeeper in Muhlhausen, Saxony); well educated (Royal Polytechnic Institute of Berlin); unoppressed politically, religiously, or militarily; and financially well off (he landed in Philadelphia at the age of twenty-five with $400 in his pockets). Intellectually he was as gifted as Ellet and had more staying power. In Berlin besides mathematics and engineering he had studied philosophy under Hegel, whose favorite pupil he was reputed to be. More significantly for American technology, he wrote as his thesis an analysis of a small suspension bridge he had seen and sketched in Bavaria.

Roebling had ventured west with a party of Saxon farmers, in whose company he had sailed from Europe, and who founded the town of Saxonburg, Pennsylvania. For a while he did some farm work himself while continuing his engineering studies and looking out for a vocational opportunity. In 1837 he got a job with the Sandy and Beaver Canal and two years later was helping survey the route for the new railroad from Harrisburg to Pittsburgh. The famous canal inclines of western Pennsylvania were operated by winch-driven hemp cables that frequently broke. One day in 1841 Roebling saw a cable part and kill two men. He had just read in a German technical magazine about a new European invention: wire rope. No one else in America had ever heard of wire rope, much less made any, and his idea elicited little enthusiasm from the canal men. Roebling was too robust an intellect to be discouraged by a pallid majority negative. He turned his Saxonburg neighbors into a winter labor force to fabricate machinery of his own design, and began manufacturing wire rope whose advantages, once the product was visible and tangible, the canal owners could not miss. The Kentucky hemp makers fought the innovation with the contemporary business methods of violence and chicanery—they cut Roebling's wire-rope cables—but Roebling won the battle by the sheer superiority of his product.

When an ice storm wrecked an aqueduct carrying a canal over the Allegheny River at Pittsburgh, $100 was offered for the best, i.e. cheapest, plan for replacing it. Roebling proposed a suspension bridge, with wrought-iron cables to be spun on the site, got the $100 and the commission, and built his aqueduct for the low price of $62,000, of which a modest $3,500 represented his profit. He hung seven wooden spans of 162 feet each from two cables made up of 1,900 wires apiece, laid parallel and wrapped by outer wire to protect against the weather. The public was impressed. A Pittsburgh newspaper reported that at one moment the new aqueduct carried "six line boats, heavily laden" simultaneously, not realizing that the structure always carried the same 2,000 tons' weight, since, as Archimedes had discovered, boats merely displace a volume of water equal to their own weight.

Over the next few years Roebling built several more suspension spans, one as a carriageway over the Monongahela, the others as canal aqueducts. From his experiences came two important products, first, a wire mill that on the advice of Peter Cooper he located in Trenton, New Jersey, and which formed the original basis of one of America's largest industrial complexes, and second, some well deliberated conclusions about the nature and characteristics of suspension bridges. When the Niagara Bridge Companies first sought engineering advice on their project Roebling was among the experts they consulted. His letter to them of January 1847 contains a remarkably advanced theoretical discussion of the suspension bridge (David Steinman calls it "startling."):

> Although the question of applying the principle of suspension to railroad bridges has been disposed of in the negative by Mr. Robert Stephenson [builder of the tubular Britannia Bridge] . . . I am bold enough to say that this Celebrated Engineer has not at all succeeded in the Solution of this problem. . . . It cannot be questioned that wire cables, when well made, offer the safest and most economical means for the support of heavy weights. *Any span within fifteen hundred feet* [italics added], with the usual deflection, can be made perfectly safe for the support of railroad trains as well as common travel.
>
> The greater the weight to be supported, the stronger the cables must be, and as this is a matter of unerring calculation, there need be no difficulty on the score of strength. The only question which presents itself is: Can a suspension bridge be made stiff enough, as not to yield and bend under the weight of a railroad train when unequally distributed over it; and can the great vibrations which result from the rapid motion of such trains and which prove so destructive to common bridges, be avoided and counteracted?
>
> I answer this question in the affirmative, and maintain that wire-cable bridges, properly constructed, will be found hereafter the most durable and cheapest railroad bridges for spans over one hundred feet.
>
> There is not one good suspension bridge in Great Britain, nor will they ever succeed as long as they remain attached to their chains and present mode of superstructure.
>
> The larger the span, the stiffer it can be made, on account of its great weight, which is necessary to insure stability. To obtain the greatest degree of stiffness, all the timber applied, should, as much as possible, be disposed in the direction of the

floors; truss frames . . . are useful. . . . To counteract the pliability of a cable, stays must be applied by which a number of points, which must necessarily correspond with the knots of vibration, are rendered stationary, and so that the stays and cables act in concert in supporting the bridge.

In 1851 Roebling took over the Niagara project from Ellet. He was meantime occupied with several other enterprises, including a railroad suspension bridge over the Kentucky River at Danville. He scarcely had time to visit his wife in Trenton or even keep up with the result of his visits, writing from Niagara Falls to a Trenton plant official: "You say in your last, that Mrs. Roebling and the child are pretty well. This takes me by surprise not having been informed at all of the delivery of Mrs. R. . . . Please answer by return of mail."

The bridge that gradually rose over the swirling gorge differed from Ellet's design. Instead of a single very broad deck, Roebling constructed a double deck, the upper for the railroad line, the lower for the carriageway. Only a few feet shorter than Chaley's celebrated Grand Pont (821 feet against 870 feet), it was much heavier than the Swiss bridge, whose single span carried highway traffic only.

It was also much heavier than the daring bridge that Charles Ellet had just completed (1849) over the Ohio at Wheeling, and which now held the world's record for span length at 1,010 feet. In mid-1854, as his Niagara work was nearing completion, an electrifying piece of news suddenly arrived by telegraph: Ellet's Wheeling bridge had collapsed. Details were slow in arriving, but even before they did Roebling took alarm. He had himself warned that the Wheeling bridge was too long in proportion to its weight to be safe in a storm, and had recommended that it be strengthened by diagonal stays running from the shore to points underneath its deck. He now made haste to complete such stays on his own bridge, a precaution not at all minimized by additional news from Wheeling. Ellet's bridge had failed, not in any 80-mile-an-hour gale, but in a moderate wind. The editor of the *Wheeling Intelligencer* reported in a story reprinted by the *New York Times* that just before the disaster he had

walked toward the Suspension Bridge and went upon it, as we have frequently done, enjoying the cool breeze and the undulating motion of the bridge. . . . We had been off the flooring only two minutes, and were on Main Street when we saw persons running toward the river bank; we followed just in time to see the whole structure heaving and dashing with tremendous force.

For a few moments we watched it with breathless anxiety, lunging like a ship in a storm; at one time it rose to nearly the height of the tower, then fell, and twisted and writhed, and was dashed almost bottom upward. At last there seemed to be a determined twist along the entire span, about one half of the flooring being nearly reversed, and down went the immense structure from its dizzy height to the stream below, with an appalling crash and roar.

. . . The great body of the flooring and the suspenders, forming something like a basket swung between the towers, was swayed to and fro like the motion of a pendulum. Each vibration giving it increased momentum, the cables, which sustained the whole structure, were unable to resist a force operating on them in so many different directions, and were literally twisted and wrenched from their fastenings. . . . It is a source of gratulation that no lives were lost.

Roebling's Niagara suspension bridge, Currier & Ives lithograph. (Library of Congress)

To the mid-nineteenth century the failure of the Wheeling bridge under ordinary traffic loading and a moderate wind was a mystery whose disturbing character was masked by its externally commonplace nature. Bridges fell down all the time. So did other structures. Amazingly, its real meaning was not even investigated for almost a hundred years, until the day in 1940 when a 2,800-foot bridge over the Tacoma Narrows failed under identical conditions, sending a shock wave through the whole world's engineering profession. In 1854, with scarcely such a thing existing as an engineering profession, John Roebling was one of the few to give the problem serious thought. In a report to the Niagara directors, who had doubtless expressed concern, he gave an analysis that Steinman calls "proof of his genius":

> A competent eyewitness [of the Wheeling collapse] stated that the waves of the floor, caused by the wind, rose to a height of over twenty feet. . . . No ordinary strength of cables can resist the momentum produced by such a weight falling even fifteen feet. . . .
>
> The bridge was destroyed by the momentum acquired by its own dead weight, when swayed up and down by the force of the wind. . . . A high wind, acting upon a suspended floor devoid of inherent stiffness, will produce a series of undulations. . . . These undulations *will increase by their own effect* [italics added] until, by a steady wind, a momentum may be produced that may prove stronger than the cables. . . . Weight should be simply an attending element in a still more important condition, viz.: *stiffness*.
>
> The destruction of the Wheeling bridge was clearly owing to a want of stability, and not to a want of strength. This want of stiffness could have been supplied by over-floor stays, truss railings, under-floor stays, or cable stays.

Roebling's Niagara Bridge was protected by a combination of all these things. Viewed from up or down stream, its huge symmetry of lines ran horizontally, vertically, and diagonally, with an intricate network of stays both above and below a double-deck roadway passing between a pair of heavy masonry towers rising from either bluff. Each roadway was stiffened with a strong railing, that of the upper, railroad deck, made up of especially heavy truss panels. This was the first genuine stiffening truss ever used on a suspension bridge, and it proved the most significant contribution of John Roebling to bridge engineering. The extent to which the idea was original with Roebling is unclear; a Philadelphia engineer named John C. Trautwine had planned a bridge for the Delaware whose wire-cable-suspended roadway was to be stiffened with deep trusses, and Roebling may have seen the model of it that Trautwine exhibited at the Franklin Institute and the Merchants' Exchange. Some British and European engineers were also groping toward the truss, and even James Finley had a vestigial truss in the railing of the Schuylkill Bridge. But John Roebling was the first to grasp, articulate, and act on the basic principle that a suspension bridge roadway had to be rendered rigid against ordinary loading, eccentric loading, storm wind pressure, and—rare but destructive—the mysterious oscillations, started by moderate wind forces and gathering momentum on their own, that had wrecked Ellet's Wheeling bridge.

Roebling's rationalism was unequal to another problem that afflicted his Niagara project, an outbreak of cholera that felled workers by the score. He tried "hydrotherapy," a current nostrum consisting of application of water internally and externally, but his men died anyway. When he felt himself stricken, he walked his room all night, pitting his will power against the devilish malady. "Keep off fear—this is the great secret," he wrote with a sort of heroic pathos as he himself recovered and the epidemic waned.

On March 6, 1855, in defiance of cholera, storm, and the inscrutable treachery of suspension bridges, the Niagara Bridge carried the first train in history to cross a span sustained by wire cables. It consisted of a locomotive hauling a string of double-loaded cars weighing a total of 368 tons.

In his final report to the bridge companies, Roebling reiterated the indispensability of "Weight, Girders, Trusses and Stays" in suspension bridges, "to resist either the action of trains, or the violence of storms . . . no Suspension Bridge is safe without some of these appliances. The catalogue of disastrous failures is now large enough to warn against light fabrics, suspended to be blown down. . . . A number of such fairy creations are still hovering about the country, only waiting for a rough blow to be demolished."

Robert Stephenson had written him from England: "If your bridge succeeds, then mine have been magnificent blunders." Roebling wrote a paper that constituted a courteous but affirmative reply to the effect that the suspension form could be made rigid enough for railroad loadings. As Peter Barlow, another distinguished British engineer, pointed out, the Niagara bridge used only a fourth as much iron as Stephenson's Britannia and carried even heavier loading, while its single span of 821 feet was not far short of the Britannia's two spans of 460 feet each.

Other engineers were quick to copy Roebling's suspension successes, but a little slower at grasping the stiffening principle. Besides Ellet and Roebling, two other engineers had offered plans for the Niagara railroad bridge, and both won commissions elsewhere in the neighborhood. In 1851, while Roebling was still assembling his materials and work force, Edward Serrell built a carriage and pedestrian crossing at Lewiston, a few miles below the falls, of 1,043 feet, longer even than Ellet's ill-starred Wheeling span. But like Ellet's, Serrell's bridge was inadequately stiffened, and when a storm shook it in 1855 it was saved only by a hasty addition of bracing guys by Roebling. These were loosened by an ice jam a few years later, and when somebody forgot to tighten them, the bridge blew down.

Samuel Keefer, the fourth of the quartet of engineers who had believed in the Niagara project, built another record breaker in 1867–69; it was 1,268 feet long and only 10 feet wide, close enough for a view of the Falls. Keefer's tourist-view span, titled the Honeymoon Bridge—Niagara Falls had already acquired a vocation—was designed with some of Roebling's insights, but not enough, and blew down in 1889. Meantime the double-decker, railroad-loaded bridge north of it remained in continuous service until 1897, by which time it was carrying three times its original design loadings, and when it was retired undefeated to make way for a double-track bridge.

It had not pleased all visitors to the Falls. Mark Twain noted sourly: "You drive over to Suspension Bridge and divide your misery between the chances of smashing down two hundred feet into the river below, and the chances of having a railway-train overhead smashing down onto you. Either possibility is discomforting taken by itself, but, mixed together, they amount in the aggregate to positive unhappiness."

Mark Twain to the contrary, Roebling's Niagara bridge was a stunning vision of the future, an engineering marvel that showed the way. Ahead of it lay the Brooklyn Bridge (which Roebling's Rensselaer-educated son, George Washington Roebling, would complete despite a permanently crippling attack of caisson disease), the Golden Gate, the Verrazano Narrows, and a hundred long-span crossings all over the world of the twentieth century. John Augustus Roebling did not invent the ancient, even prehistoric suspension bridge. He did something better: he made it work.

20

William Kelly
and Mass-Produced Steel

SOME INVENTORS ARE EASY TO REMEMBER because their names are popularly attached to their inventions—the Franklin stove, the Colt revolver, the Howe truss. One such invention is mass-production steel, an innovation that opened the way to world-shaking revolutions in building construction, factory machinery, and production of durable goods.

The name of the technique is familiar to everyone: the Bessemer process. Besides his knighthood from Queen Victoria, Sir Henry Bessemer had namesakes in an American steel company and a town in Pennsylvania to attest to his authorship. Yet Bessemer was only one of the two inventors of the process, and not the first. The first man to produce modern steel was William Kelly of Kentucky, and the process should be known as the Kelly-Bessemer process. A third name should probably be added, that of Scotsman Robert Mushet, who was perhaps even more cheated of fame than Kelly.

Kelly was the son of a middle-class Irish rebel who had fled the British repression following the 1798 uprising, and had settled in Pittsburgh in 1801. Marrying another Irish immigrant, Elizabeth Fitzsimons, John Kelly built the first brick house in Pittsburgh (88 Front Street), made money in the burgeoning iron town's real-estate boom, and enrolled his son William (born 1811) in the newly founded Western University of Pennsylvania (later renamed the University of Pittsburgh) to study metallurgical engineering. William Kelly was thus one of America's first academically trained metallurgists, but he did not immediately put his education

LEFT William Kelly. (American Iron and Steel Institute)

RIGHT Kelly converter used in his demonstration at the Cambria Iron Works in 1862. (American Iron and Steel Institute)

to use, going to work on graduation as a traveling salesman for the flourishing wholesale textile ("dry goods") business of his brother and brother-in-law.

In 1846, a tall, slender thirty-five-year-old with a drooping black mustache, Kelly met and courted Mildred Gracy, the pretty sixteen-year-old daughter of a tobacco merchant of Eddyville, Kentucky. Eddyville had a furnace and forge, and the neighboring country abounded with red hematite ore, which could be made into high-grade iron. Kelly proposed to his brother John that the two sell out their mercantile interest and get into iron production. Dry goods had evidently done well for them, for they were able to buy the Eddyville furnace plus 14,000 acres of land rich in both ore and timber, extending several miles along the Cumberland River.

By 1847 the new company was in production, making pig iron and refining it into wrought iron. Kelly soon brought his metallurgical knowledge to bear on the production process, in which he quickly identified the main problem of cost as the enormous amounts of timber that had to be burned to make charcoal for the long refining process. "I conceived the idea," he wrote later, "that, after the metal was melted, the use of fire would be unnecessary—that the heat generated by the union of the oxygen of the air with the carbon of the metal would be sufficient to accomplish the refining and decarbonizing of the iron."

As so often happened, an idea original to an inventor was actually not new. Japanese ironmasters of three hundred years earlier had succeeded in removing some carbon from iron by blowing cold air over the surface of the molten metal, and British ironmakers of the eighteenth and nineteenth centuries had experimented with a similar process, though only glimpsing its possibilities. But Kelly was the first to perceive the potential in blowing air *through* the molten iron. What he was trying to produce was conventional refined "wrought" iron; harder, and equally malleable steel was not yet in his thoughts. He ran into immediate opposition from his experienced forge men, who were unanimous in the opinion that his blast of cold air would have the effect of cooling rather than superheating the molten metal. But Kelly went to work designing a small blast furnace with two *tuyeres,* or nozzles for the air blast, one above the other. The upper tuyere was to melt the ore, the lower to force air blasts into the molten metal after it was separated from the ore.

The new furnace was begun in the autumn of 1847, but Kelly suspended work to build a new blast furnace to take advantage of rich surface ore outcroppings discovered seven miles away. By the end of a year the surface ore was exhausted, and the underground ore at the site proved to be deeply impregnated with a black flint called shadrac, after Daniel's companion, because it refused to melt in a fiery furnace. Better veins of ore were available, but too far from timber supplies to be economical, so Kelly returned to his experiments with the cold air blast, in an effort to develop a cheaper way to produce refined iron. In 1851 he built a furnace consisting, in his words, of "a square brick abutment, having a circular chamber inside, the bottom of which was concave like a molder's ladle. In the bottom was fixed a circular tile of fire clay, perforated for tuyeres. Under this tile was an air chamber, connected by pipes with the blowing engine. . . .

"The first trial of this furnace was very satisfactory. The iron was well refined and decarbonized—at least as well as by the finery fire. . . . The blowing was usually contained from five to ten minutes, whereas the finery fire required over an hour. Here was a great saving of time and fuel. . . ." But Kelly now had his eye on a larger goal than mere economy in the production of wrought iron. "I was not satisfied with making refined . . . metal; my object was to make malleable iron," by which he meant the mild steel of ancient and medieval metallurgists. Heretofore mild steel had been produced solely by such laborious and unreliable remeltings of iron to get exactly the right amount of carbon (less than 1 percent) that it had remained an exotic metal, its production half-accidental and tinged with magic.

In the next year and a half Kelly continued experimenting, temporarily returning to a hot-blast furnace, but abandoning it again in favor of the cold blast, and finding that a longer blast sometimes produced the metal he sought. From one batch that proved highly workable, Kelly forged a four-foot bar that he used for exhibition purposes, giving away bits of it until he had only a few inches left, which he saved—"the first piece of malleable iron or steel ever made by the pneumatic process."

Yet the new mass-production technique remained as uncertain in its results as the old small-scale production method. By now Kelly had married Mildred Gracy, the tobacco merchant's daughter, and had enlisted financial backing for his iron works from his father-in-law and other local magnates, but none of them had any sympathy with the inventor's "air boiling process." Accusing him of neglecting his old-fashioned iron furnaces for a delusion, they demanded that he abandon his "air boiling" experiments and concentrate on production by conventional means.

Kelly placated them but continued to experiment in secret, building a new converter away from the main works and slipping off thither in his spare time. Father-in-law Gracy had his physician, Dr. Edward H. Champion, examine Kelly to ascertain whether he was crazy. Dr. Champion proved patient and sensible enough to listen to Kelly's explanation of his process, and to report to Gracy that his son-in-law's mind was sound, as, so far as the doctor could judge, was his metallurgical theory.

Kelly turned out enough kettles for making sugar and boiler plate for steamboats to keep the business flourishing, but conservative customers, hearing about his experiments, were suspicious. A Cincinnati firm ordering boiler plate specified that they did not want their iron made by the "new fangled process. We want our iron made in the regular way or not at all."

Nevertheless, he made progress. He demonstrated his technique to visiting ironmasters, who invariably arrived skeptical but usually departed convinced, after watching the cold air blown into the molten pig metal in the converter, and seeing the blacksmith take liquid metal out, cool it, and hammer out horseshoes and nails in minutes.

The new process saved time and fuel, but unfortunately it often removed not nearly all, but all, of the carbon, producing not steel but pure iron, malleable but softer than steel. Through the early 1850s Kelly postponed application for a patent in the moment-to-moment expectation of nailing the elusive secret of reliability. Then in November 1856, he learned that Henry Bessemer of England had applied for and obtained an American patent for making steel by the application of a cold air blast.

Kelly at once put in his patent application. The Patent Office held hearings, calling many witnesses, including Dr. Champion, and concluded that "Kelly made the invention and showed it by drawings and experiments as early as 1847, and this testimony appears to be reliable in every respect. . . . Priority of invention in this case is awarded to said Kelly, and it is ordered that a patent be issued accordingly. . . ."

Bessemer had arrived at his discovery of the air blast by an even more circuitous route than had Kelly. The son of a type founder, he had worked out several improvements in typesetting machinery when the Crimean War in 1854 drew his interest to the problem of gunnery. He devised a shell that could be made to rotate when fired from a smoothbore cannon, thus avoiding the necessity of breechloading. Britain's War Office experts derided his idea, so he took it across the Channel and showed it to Napoleon III in a demonstration at Vincennes one brisk December day (1854). Afterward, over the mulled wine in the fortress, Major Claude-Etienne Minié, who had just invented the Minié ball that made possible the muzzle-loading of a rifle, sounded a sagacious warning: The size of Bessemer's propellant charge made it hazardous to fire from existing cast-iron cannon. Reflecting on the major's comment in the carriage back to Paris, Bessemer was led to the study of improving the strength of gun metal.

After a little research, he identified steel as the right metal for high-powered cannon. In Britain steel made in fifty-pound batches by the "crucible process"— two weeks of melting and remelting wrought iron in clay crucibles with the ex-

Sir Henry Bessemer. (American Iron and Steel Institute)

penditure of much fuel—cost £50 to £60 ($250 to $300) a ton. The same idea soon occurred to Bessemer as had occurred to Kelly seven years earlier, that since the main problem was reducing the amount of carbon from 4 percent to 1 percent, a blast of oxygen (meaning air), with which carbon readily unites, might do the trick.

The inspiration was less original with Bessemer than it had been with Kelly, for a British patent was taken out in 1855 for a technique involving blowing air through molten iron. This was the invention of Joseph G. Martien, an American engineer from New Jersey whose idea was tried out at Ebbw Vale Works in South Wales with mediocre success. Martien, and for that matter Bessemer, had slight grasp of the chemistry involved, and were not sure whether they preferred a blast of air or of steam, as had been advocated even earlier by James Nasmyth, Scottish inventor of the steam hammer.

Bessemer constructed a "converter" with a blowing engine and a hydraulic mechanism for tipping the kettle to pour out the contents. With this ingenious furnace he was able to make steel in twenty to thirty minutes from pig iron costing £7 a ton.

By the time Bessemer was ready to announce his invention in a paper before the British Association for the Advancement of Science (August 12, 1856) the Crimean War was over. But the demand for steel did not abate; in fact Bessemer was flabbergasted at the "wild pack of hungry wolves," the highly competitive British ironmasters, that his paper brought down upon him, "fighting with me and with each other, for a share of what was to be made of this new discovery." In a month he had sold royalties worth £27,000. The wolves were drawn less by the character

Bessemer converter. (American Iron and Steel Institute)

of Bessemer's metal than by its amazing cheapness, and when after buying their licenses they tried the process out, the results were uniformly catastrophic. All the carbon was removed from the iron, without leaving enough to make steel, and on top of that a strong strain of phosphorus remained, making the product not only weak but brittle. Bessemer found himself reviled not only as a failure but as a fraud.

Without really taking note of it, Bessemer had experimented entirely with imported Swedish iron ore, which happened to be free of phosphorus in which most British ore was rich, and which was also rich in manganese, a desirable addition. The phosphorus problem proved stubborn (and was only solved by the work of two other British inventors, the Gilchrists, in 1876), but some native British ore was phosphorus-free, and besides, Bessemer protested, imported Swedish ore was cheap. But that was only one part of the problem. The other was the baffling unreliability of the air blast, the factor with which Kelly in America had struggled for the past decade.

The solution was found neither by Kelly nor by Bessemer, but by a Scottish ironmaster's son, Robert Mushet, a scientifically trained metallurgist and scholar who had been carrying on experiments in steelmaking since 1848, and who in his lifetime patented fifty-four steelmaking improvements. After hearing about Bessemer's difficulties with the air blast, Mushet came to the conclusion that the solution to the problem was not mechanical but chemical and metallurgical. Bessemer was not only eliminating all the carbon, without any means of putting back the 1 percent necessary to change the iron into steel, he was producing "burnt iron," overexposed to heat and air, and therefore containing undesirable oxygen. Mushet stumbled on a German compound called *Spiegeleisen*—"mirror iron"—containing manganese and carbon. When added to pure iron the Spiegeleisen united its manganese with the oxygen, passing out in slag, while its carbon stayed with the iron, making steel.

Mushet patented his process in Britain, France, and America. But through a slip on the part of trustees who held his patent as collateral against a loan, his British patent lapsed in 1859, and Bessemer, who had been trying to pry Mushet's secret from him, pounced on it. Bessemer's converters began pouring out reliable steel, and Bessemer's fortune began piling up, while he used Mushet's process without the payment of a cent of royalties.

Meantime, across the Atlantic, Kelly was in trouble. The panic of 1857 suddenly reduced him to bankruptcy, and he transferred his patent to his father's name to prevent its being seized by his creditors. When John Kelly died suddenly in 1860, Kelly's sisters inherited the bulk of his estate, including the patent. The sisters had always thought their brother's experiments foolish, if not crazy, and it took him two years to persuade them to turn the patent back over to him.

Consequently it was not until 1862 that Kelly was able to take advantage of Mushet's Spiegeleisen. Finally he was able to demonstrate his process at the Cambria Iron Works, in Johnstown, Pennsylvania (where the converter he built is today on display) before the usual crowd of skeptical ironworkers. On his first trial, the skeptics had their doubts confirmed when a too-strong blast sent most of the contents of the converter flying into the air in a tornado of sparks. But in a second demonstration Kelly produced conclusive results and the scoffers left the yard in amazed silence.

With his steelmaking process proven, Kelly obtained backing to build a steel works in Wyandotte, Michigan. A Detroit businessman named Z. S. Durfee, one of the Wyandotte partners, arranged for rights to Mushet's American patent by making Mushet a partner. One of Durfee's trips to England to study British methods added a curious episode to the history of inventors' paranoia.

Durfee brought back a picture of Bessemer, in which Kelly thought he recognized an Englishman who had worked for him in Kentucky and who had departed precipitately after learning the Kelly process. Though Kelly and all his family went to their graves under the delusion that Bessemer had stolen the invention, the idea was fantastic. Yet there is some historical interest in the fact that half a century after Samuel Slater, touchy American inventors like Morse and Kelly could suspect the British of stealing their secrets.

Kelly's suspicion may have justified in his own mind his borrowing without license Bessemer's hydraulically tilted kettle for the Wyandotte plant. Another American group, at Troy, New York, reversed the action by purchasing a Bessemer license but pirating Mushet's Spiegeleisen. After a bout of litigation the two companies decided to merge, with the more heavily capitalized Troy company awarded 70 percent of the stock. Kelly objected to the split, but his partners accepted the deal, sweetened, it was charged, by payments under the table.

The merger was not fatal to Kelly's financial interest. A clause in the contract, however, dealt a lethal blow to his fame. By this time British and European "Bessemer" steel was being bought by American railroads (though the first steel rails in Britain had been made from steel produced by Mushet, not Bessemer); therefore, the Troy people specified that, though the product was to be made primarily under the Kelly patent, it should be marketed under the better-known Bessemer name. The term "Kelly steel" soon disappeared from the American language.

In 1870 both Kelly's and Bessemer's United States patents came up for renewal, and only Kelly's petition was granted, the Patent Office ruling that Bessemer had not been entitled to a patent in the first place. It was a golden opportunity for Kelly to squeeze a better deal out of his new and old partners, but characteristically he passed it up, turning the patent license back to his company on the previous terms. The seven-year renewal period saw the company prosper and Kelly pocket a tidy, if not gaudy, $450,000.

Now sixty years old, Kelly moved to Louisville, invested in real estate and banking, and expanded his fortune, though he passed up opportunities that would never have escaped Bessemer. Genial and altruistic, he sold land and houses along the river at Louisville at cost to the Chesapeake & Ohio Railroad, and even refused the offer of a free pass from the Pennsylvania Railroad.

By the time of Kelly's death in 1888 at the age of seventy-six, steel had established itself as the metal of the industrial age. Chicago, making its instant recovery from the fire of 1871, had just built the world's first steel-skeleton buildings, carrying James Bogardus's beginning of 1849 to a logical conclusion and opening up the future of steel as the basic structural material in a dazzling new American city architecture. The second great steelmaking process, the Siemens-Martin or open-hearth, a French-German invention of 1867, was introduced in the United States by Peter Cooper's son-in-law Abram S. Hewitt, who had been the first to try Bessemer's method. The two processes dominated the world steel industry for nearly a century, until the 1950s, when the basic oxygen process, more economical of coal, was invented in Austria, though Kelly-Bessemer and open-hearth furnaces continued to operate.

Robert Mushet, who had trouble wringing a modest £300 a year pension out of Bessemer, had more to complain about than Kelly, and he did complain:

"I have sometimes thought that the [British] Iron and Steel Institute might have made me an honorary member and the Royal Society an F.R.S. [Fellow of the Royal Society], or that Her Gracious Majesty might have revived my ancestors' title of knights banneret, which was forfeited during the [thirteenth century] rebellion of Montrose. At all events, the vast industry of steel makers, including his Grace, the Duke of Devonshire, who gets 12,000 pounds per annum out of my little process, might at least accord me a vote of thanks for the wealth my invention has brought to them. . ." Mushet concluded perceptively if not philosophically, "The world shuns the man who does not get the money."

21

The Technology
of Civil War

WHEN THE SOUTH CREATED by Whitney's cotton gin and the North created
by the technology of Slater, Lowell, Hall, and McCormick came to grips on the
battlefield in 1861, the advantages on the side of the North seemed preponderant.
Yet the South, heavily outnumbered in military manpower and totally outclassed
in industrial facilities, offered a stubborn and prolonged resistance. Historians
have generally credited geography, the South's defensive posture, and superior
Southern military leadership with neutralizing the North's advantages. Apart
from these factors, the technological-industrial component of the North's superiority has probably been overrated. Military and military-support technology was
only at that moment approaching the point at which an advanced industrial apparatus guaranteed substantial military dividends.

In the 1860s, military materiel of all kinds was either readily available, easy to
produce, or needed in only small quantities. Traction power meant horses and
mules, of which the South had plenty. Gun carriages, caissons, supply wagons
were easy to fabricate by hand methods. The North's sewing-machine-equipped
garment factories, fed cloth from New England mills, could turn out uniforms
and overcoats at a highly efficient rate, but the women of the South sewing by
hand—and even spinning and weaving—could make enough shirts and pants to
keep their men from going naked. By concentrating what textile machinery it
had, the South was even able to do a fair amount of factory production. Confed-

erate soldiers were sometimes barefoot—Gettysburg was brought on by a Confederate detachment looking for a shoe factory—but barefoot soldiers can march if they must, and can fight, provided they have weapons and ammunition.

That the Confederate armies had these indispensables in sufficient quantity was partly the result of Southern foresight and Northern lassitude. Before the conflict broke out, Southern governors, abetted by Southerners in the Washington government such as Secretary of War John B. Floyd, were able to buy arms from the United States and get others transferred to Southern arsenals where they could easily be seized. At the war's outset, the Harper's Ferry arsenal and the Norfolk naval base were foolishly allowed to fall into the hands of Virginia state troops. Though the lieutenant commanding the small garrison at Harper's Ferry destroyed most of its stock of rifles and set the arsenal ablaze, the Virginians were able to salvage John Hall's rifle-manufacturing machinery. Priceless to the Confederacy, this technological trove was loaded on wagons and hauled away to the Virginia Manufactory Armory, adjacent to the South's only important ironworks, the Tredegar Works in Richmond.

Shortly after, the tamely abandoned and ineffectually destroyed Norfolk base yielded to the South no fewer than 1,198 cannon, including 52 heavy Dahlgren guns, an armament that was deployed to guard the Southern coast from Roanoke to Mobile and even helped supply Vicksburg.

In addition to these windfalls, the South was able to bring in arms and ammunition from abroad before the blockade became effective, and afterward by blockade running. It also profited from battlefield salvage, a natural advantage to the technologically weaker side in war since the stronger side has no need of it. The North captured its share of enemy weapons but rarely made any use of them, whereas the Confederates diligently scavenged the battlefield and appropriated Union cannon, rifles, canteens, and knapsacks.

Cannon and rifles are useless without ammunition, but gunpowder—black powder—was no insuperable problem. Urine collection for lixiviation (leaching) of saltpeter (potassium nitrate) became an important part of the Confederacy's intensive effort. The low rate of fire of single-shot weapons and the modest numbers of artillery (twenty-four guns to a division) permitted the South to get through the entire war on 6,000 tons of powder.

The limitations of horsepower provided the South another dividend. Though the North's foundries could far outproduce the Tredegar Works in heavy artillery, and though many large-caliber guns were made for the Navy and the Washington fortifications, the Union armies in the field rarely had more than modest advantages in artillery firepower because the heavy guns were too difficult to move.

In respect to food, the South's very lack of industry was an advantage. Since practically the whole country was agricultural, and since slaves were not conscripted (though late in the war Robert E. Lee and Jefferson Davis seriously discussed "arming the blacks"), labor was available. It was rather the North that faced a food-supply problem in feeding an army of several hundred thousand while depleting the Midwest farms of most of their mature manpower. How the North solved its problem, with the aid of farm women and boys, was explained by

Secretary of War Edwin M. Stanton: "The reaper is to the North what slavery is to the South. . . . Without McCormick's invention I fear the North could not win and the Union would be dismembered."

The new military technology that the Civil War introduced, if not very decisive, was at least spectacular, and promised immense importance in future wars.

A few wholly new weapons appeared: the land mine, the booby trap, land and naval mine fields, and the minesweeper. More significantly, several existing weapons were tried in combat for the first time, or experienced important development: the ironclad warship, the submarine, the repeating rifle, and the machine gun.

The ironclad warship burst on the world's consciousness with an éclat a dramatist might envy in the *Monitor-Merrimac* duel. Ironclads were nothing new, having been pioneered by Fulton and Stevens forty years earlier. By 1862 several European navies had Fulton-type harbor-defense ironclads, the French and British had both used "floating batteries" in the Crimean War, the French Navy had launched the full-scale seagoing iron ship *Gloire* (1859), and the British were building more advanced versions. When the Civil War began, the United States Navy was one of the few with no iron ships built or planned. The Confederacy, of course, had no navy at all, and the shortages on both sides opened the way to fertile innovation.

When the Navy Department hastily called for proposals for armored ships to be built overnight, John Ericsson, whose "caloric engine" had proved a nine-days' wonder in 1852, won the contract with his novel, low-freeboard, two-gun revolving turret "cheesebox on a raft" design. The modesty of its armament permitted the *Monitor* the luxury of 8-inch-thick armor. In contrast to the wholly new *Monitor,* the South's *Merrimac* (or *Virginia,* her Confederate name, ignored by Northern newspapers and historians) was simply a stripped-down wooden ship the Southerners had captured at Norfolk and armored by bolting to her sides iron plates from the Tredegar Works. Yet the jerry-built *Merrimac,* overweighted and underpowered, threw a terrific scare into the Union's wooden-hull fleet and proved a doughty adversary even for the *Monitor.*

The *Monitor* and *Merrimac* were the first ironclads to fight each other. Yet they were not the first to engage in combat with other ships, or the first to fight in American waters. Those honors, and some others, go to a flotilla of vessels created months earlier by a self-taught engineer and Mississippi River boatman named James Buchanan Eads. A later feat of Eads demands full treatment in the next chapter; here let it suffice that in 1861 he was a leading citizen of St. Louis with a unique knowledge of the Western river system and a patriotic Union sentiment that contrasted with the soft-on-slavery attitude of his distant cousin President Buchanan. Eads saw control of the Mississippi and its lower tributaries as the key to the rebellion in the West, and urged the War and Navy Departments to build the right kind of warships to win the control. After a fierce battle with the bureaucracy, he was able to set to work and in barely three months of round-the-clock labor that "neither the sanctity of the Sabbath nor the darkness of night were permitted to interrupt" (in the words of a contemporary), eight of the strangest warships any Navy man would care to see were afloat. Their iron-plated

Captain James Eads's ironclad *St. Louis*. (U.S. War Department General Staff)

sides sloped outward from top deck to waterline, while twin black smokestacks rose above their well-protected engines to drive a partly enclosed stern wheel.

One of the eight, the *Benton,* was larger than the other seven, and built on a twin hull completely enclosing the wheel. All mounted a dozen or more heavy guns, yet could navigate in six feet of water. Commodore Andrew Foote led them up the Tennessee River in February of 1862 and poured a storm of shot and shell into Fort Henry that forced the Confederate garrison to decamp without waiting for Ulysses S. Grant's approaching army. The Eads boats then joined in the attack on Fort Donelson that brought the first major Union victory of the war, and hammered a third Confederate stronghold, Columbus, Kentucky, into submission on Washington's Birthday, still three weeks before the *Monitor-Merrimac* clash.

Captain Eads's creations next became the first ironclads in the world to engage enemy warships—the Confederates' rinky-dink but heavily armed wooden Mississippi squadron. Powerfully seconded by a flotilla of ironclad rams that were the brainstorm of Charles Ellet, the daring engineer who had commenced Roebling's Niagara bridge, and who died a hero's death leading his own rams, they went on to capture the important Mississippi fortress of Island No. 10, defeated Confederate ironclads in two battles, and joined hands with Farragut's ocean warships at Vicksburg, cutting the Confederacy in two. "Only give me the ironclads built by Mr. Eads, and I will find out how far Providence is with us," Farragut messaged Washington, and at Mobile Bay two new Eads ironclads, the low-profile, twin-turreted *Chickasaw* and *Winnebago,* led the assault column. Eads's turrets were an advance over Ericsson's. Where the *Monitor* had fired only one shot in seven minutes, the *Chickasaw* could get off two in a minute.

Despite its shortage of foundries, the embattled South answered ironclad with ironclad, building altogether the astonishing total of thirty-seven. The *Merrimac* was not even the first; she had been preceded by the *Manassas,* a curious little cigar-shaped gunboat built in New Orleans on the hull of a tug. Pursuing the

A Confederate "David" torpedo boat aground at Charleston, S.C., in 1865. National Archives. (U.S. War Department General Staff)

same design sense further, the Southern Yankees created a class of formidable little craft called "Davids," double-ended, with crews of only four men, and equipped with ballast tanks that on going into action were filled to lower the deck to the water's edge. Off Charleston in 1863, the first "David" attacked Admiral Du-Pont's flagship *New Ironsides,* the pride of the Union navy, with a spar torpedo, putting the 3,500-ton giant out of action for several months.

Going beyond the nearly submerged "Davids," the Confederates followed up the lead of David Bushnell and Robert Fulton by designing a true submersible. She was built at Mobile under the financial and other encouragement of Horace L. Hunley, and named for her backer.

One of Hunley's concepts was remarkably ahead of its time—propulsion by electric motor. Not at all surprisingly, none could be provided by the Confederacy and the submarine went into action propelled exactly as David Bushnell's *Turtle* had been, by a hand crank, only this one a shaft turned by eight men. Moved by railroad to Charleston, the *Hunley* had a career of disaster before ever getting into action, sinking three times and drowning three crews, among one of them Horace Hunley. The Confederate Navy did not give up easily. The *Hunley* was salvaged, manned a fourth time, and on the night of February 17, 1864, made history by detonating her spar torpedo against the hull of the blockading cruiser *Housatonic.* The explosion blew the *Housatonic*'s magazine, and the cruiser went to the bottom, the first ship ever sunk by a submarine. The blast also sank the *Hunley*—

for the last time. After the war, divers clearing Charleston harbor found the little *Hunley* on the bottom, her torpedo spar still pointed straight at the *Housatonic's* hulk thirty yards away.

Thus a navy that at the beginning of its only war had possessed no ships and no sailors was responsible for a historic innovation in warfare. The Confederates also improved the undersea weapons David Bushnell and Robert Fulton had pioneered. The famous "torpedoes" (naval mines) damned by Admiral Farragut sank twenty-seven Union ships during the war, including the twin-turreted monitor *Tecumseh,* just in front of Farragut's flagship at Mobile Bay.

The Confederate mines were the creation of Matthew F. Maury, formerly head of the United States Naval Observatory and Hydrographic Office. General G. J. Raines's Richmond Torpedo Bureau produced a number of ingenious types for water. One that sank the ironclad *De Kalb* in the Yazoo River in 1863 had a conical hat that when knocked off by an enemy vessel pulled a lanyard that released a spring-loaded plunger that exploded the primer. The Union Navy, adopting torpedoes in its turn, sank four Confederate ships, memorably the hulking ironclad *Albemarle* that late in 1864 was threatening the wooden Union flotilla in the Roanoke River. Lieutenant William B. Cushing got permission to invent perhaps the world's first P-T boat, a steam launch fitted up with a fourteen-foot boom carrying a new kind of torpedo invented by John L. Lay. Cushing picked a dark night, somehow bumped his little boat over the log boom protecting the *Albemarle,* planted his torpedo under the enemy hull, moved out again and pulled the line that set off the explosion, blowing an irreparable hole in the ironclad's unprotected timber bottom.

The success of the naval mines led to two further naval innovations: the minesweeper, whose first examples were crudely rigged small craft sent ahead of large Union vessels, and the secondary mine, a surprise the irrepressible Confederates prepared for the Union sailors in the form of an explosive charge that went off when somebody jiggled the main mine. Later the Union armed some of its monitors with a huge sweep attached to the bow that proved effective in clearing Charleston harbor.

The torpedo-mine was also converted into a booby trap, most notoriously in the form of the "coal torpedo" invented by Captain Thomas E. Courtenay of the Confederate Secret Service. Explosive containers made to resemble lumps of coal or billets of wood were introduced into fuel supplies destined for Union gunboats in Southern waters.

The land side of the Civil War was less innovative than the naval. The North sought to exploit its industrial advantage by introducing breech-loading rifled artillery, but the effect was largely canceled out by the deficiencies of the old-fashioned black gunpowder still in use. The pall of smoke that overhung all artillery in action handicapped aiming the more accurate rifled guns, and their shaped projectiles tended to bury themselves harmlessly in uneven terrain ("the ground looked as though a drove of hogs had been rooting there for potatoes," observed Confederate general Imboden of the hot but ineffective fire of a Union rifle battery at Bull Run). The improvement in range was also limited by the inefficiency of the black powder, whose combustible 40 percent burned almost instantly, giving the projectile one quick push down the barrel. The powder was also too weak to make a good explosive charge except where it could be used in large quantities, as in demolition.

Certain innovations in ammunition brought controversy, such as the incendiary shells fired into Charleston in 1863 from a heavy Parrott gun known as the "Swamp Angel." That they represented no real novelty in warfare was underscored by the fact that they were sold to the government under the name of "Short's Solidified Greek Fire," and purported to be an adaptation of the incendiary weapon of the Byzantine Greeks. General Beauregard protested the barbarity of using such a weapon against "a city . . . filled with sleeping women and children," but Federal General Gillmore kept the bombardment up until the Swamp Angel's breech blew out. The Confederates used incendiary mixtures themselves in guerrilla warfare, setting fires in New York that among other things destroyed P. T. Barnum's famous museum.

Another controversial novelty was the improvisation of Confederate general Raines, who in 1862 commanded the rearguard in the retreat from Williamsburg. Finding a wrecked ammunition wagon loaded with artillery shells containing explosive charges, Raines had a number buried at a road obstruction, with primers · set to detonate under pressure. Federal cavalry set them off, killing men and horses. Northern newspapers protested, and Raines's own superiors, General Longstreet and Secretary of War Randolph, agreed. Later as chief of the Torpedo Bureau, Raines caused his weapon to be reintroduced against Sherman's army in 1864. Sherman dealt with it characteristically by making a captured Confederate officer lead his men in digging up what later terminology called a minefield.

A quite different kind of controversy was generated by the Union army's infantry weapons. Colonel James W. Ripley, the chief of ordnance in Washington, became the target of criticism by contemporaries and historians that appears to be at least in part justified. Faced with the problem of not merely arming very large numbers of troops, but of keeping them supplied with ammunition, Ripley opted understandably for mass manufacture of the current army model, the .58-caliber Springfield muzzle-loading rifle firing the Minié ball. The Springfield was a good rifle, if clumsy to load (in the heat of battle even veterans got mixed up: out of the 37,000 rifles salvaged after Gettysburg, 18,000 had more than one load, making them unfirable, and one had its barrel stuffed with twenty-three loads). It could kill at 600 yards, three to four times the range of the old smoothbore. But the universal use and retention late in the war of the Springfield was a great boon to the Confederates, who added to their prewar seizures much battlefield salvage and 400,000 British Enfields brought in ahead of the blockade or on blockade runners. The South's small-arms ammunition problem was immensely simplified by the fact that the Enfields, made on the American machines purchased on Joseph Whitworth's recommendation in 1853, were virtually identical to the Springfields and fired the same .58-caliber ammunition.

But the North had in its hands the capacity to produce the Henry (future Winchester) and Spencer breech-loading repeating rifles. The Spencer, which held six rounds in its magazine plus one in the chamber, and was easily reloaded by a tubular magazine that fitted into the butt, was highly reliable in operation and had a much greater range than the Springfield. The Henry rifle, with its Smith & Wesson breech-loading mechanism, was said to be even better, firing fifteen shots from a single magazine. The 7th and 66th Illinois, the 97th Indiana, and some other regiments bought Henrys out of their own pay.

Had Colonel Ripley boldly opted for Spencers and Henrys his Richmond opposite number would have been put to a severe test, because not only did the South have no machinery for making repeaters but even captured weapons would be useless without metallic cartridges, much more difficult to manufacture than paper. The combat performance of the repeaters, where used, was convincing. At Olustee, Florida, in early 1864, the Spencer-armed Seventh Connecticut Regiment easily broke up an attack by a superior enemy force, and at the decisive battle of Nashville in December 1864, according to Confederate general E. P. Alexander, "Casement's [Union] brigade with these arms [Spencers] decided that battle with terrific slaughter."

Ripley has also been criticized for his shortsightedness in rejecting machine guns, but here the evidence is not conclusive. Breech-loading and metal cartridges had opened the way to a rapid-fire weapon whose conceptual history went back to a gun invented by James Puckle of England in 1718. Before the Civil War several American inventors were at work on the idea. The Confederates were again surprisingly first in the field with a battery of multibarreled volley-firing weapons at the battle of Fair Oaks (May 31, 1862), the Union following shortly with the Ager or coffee-mill gun, so-called from its top-feeding hopper. Both these weapons and others tried out had problems with overheating; some had mechanical defects besides. The machine gun that finally worked satisfactorily, in fact beautifully, was invented by a transplanted Southerner.

Like Cyrus McCormick, Richard Jordan Gatling was the son of an inventive mechanic, in Gatling's case in Hertford County, North Carolina. The younger Gatling invented a screw propeller simultaneously with Ericsson, though losing the patent race. Moving to St. Louis in 1844, he successfully adapted a cotton-sowing machine invented by his father to planting rice, wheat, and other grains, contributing significantly to the mechanical revolution on the American farm. He later added a hemp-breaking machine and a steam-powered plow, one of the first applications of steam to agriculture.

By the time the war broke out, Gatling was rich and famous. Despite his Southern origin, he had no sympathy with the Confederacy, and set to work at once producing a victory weapon for the Union. Studying all the existing machine-gun designs, he adopted the best features—hopper loading, crank operation, rotating multiple barrels, and by 1862 had a smooth-running weapon that could fire 350 shots a minute. "It bears the same relation to other firearms that McCormick's Reaper does to the sickle, or the sewing machine to the common needle," wrote Gatling, with a neat if chilly appreciation of his invention's place in the new mass-production technology. The Gatling gun met Ripley's objection to variant ammunition by using the .58 Springfield cartridge. Ripley had another complaint: machine guns used up ammunition so fast they might create a supply problem.

He was already using this argument against the repeating rifles, and despite its speciousness, it retained validity in most professional soldiers' eyes until late in the war.

Oddly, the argument against the Gatling gun that Ripley used most feebly—the general uncertainty of the effects of a novel weapon—seemed to be borne out by the Gatling gun's later history. The opposition of Ripley and other officers kept it from more than token use in the Civil War, and it had a long career in minor colonial wars in the remainder of the century, but neither it nor any similar type ever proved of substantial value in a war against a well-armed enemy. The trouble was that the multiple-barreled machine gun was too heavy to be hand-carried, and the requirement of carriage mounting and horse traction meant that it could not easily be used in the front line where it belonged. At even intermediate ranges its mediocre aim (because of the multiple barrels) was a handicap. The true future machine gun (the Maxim, also American-invented) derived from the introduction of nitrocellulose-based (smokeless) powder, whose progressive-burning character made it possible to divert gas to operate a belt-fed action, thus eliminating the multiple barrels.

Among its lesser innovations, the Civil War brought one of numerous modern-era attempts to revive the body armor of the Middle Ages. Neither government sponsored the move, but a number of iron breastplates were made by blacksmiths and sold to recruits. A few were actually worn in combat, and may even have saved lives, but were simply too heavy to carry.

Tents were millennia-old military equipment, but the Civil War brought two new models of lasting value. One was the "shelter half" still issued in World War II and beyond. In the Civil War version, two soldiers pitched their canvas half-tents over a rope stretched between the trigger guards of their rifles, stuck into the ground by their bayonets. The large Sibley tent was actually an Indian invention. Conical, open at the top to permit smoke to escape, it was patented by West Pointer Henry H. Sibley in 1858 after seeing Indian teepees on Fremont's exploring expedition. Sibley also designed a conical stove for inside the tent. The War Department was enthusiastic and adopted the Sibley tent on the basis of a $5 royalty to the inventor for every tent purchased. Southerner Sibley, however, joined the Confederacy, and the War Department suspended payment just when it began to order the tents in quantity. Sibley's heirs sued after the war, but failed to collect.

To traditional military hardtack (waterless, saltless biscuit), bacon, salt beef, and pork, and canned and dehydrated vegetables (French inventions of the Revolutionary and Napoleonic wars) the Union commissary was able to add Gail Borden's condensed milk, patented in 1856. Fresh meat still meant preservation on the hoof, and was hardly ever available through official channels.

Some of the most significant innovations of the war came in the areas of non-military technology. The telegraph had been used in the Crimean and Italian wars, but in the Civil War it became for the first time a decisive element in military communications. At the war's outset wires were strung from the War Department in Washington to the Navy Yard, Capitol, Chain Bridge, and other important points, and soon after to the army in Virginia. The Confederates were equally quick to utilize the invention. Throughout the war both the Richmond and Washington governments kept in hour-by-hour contact with the armies in Virginia, Tennessee, Mississippi, and elsewhere. General Beauregard, informed by his Washington spy Rose O'Neal Greenhow that McDowell was coming, not only notified Richmond and General Joseph E. Johnston in the Shenandoah Valley, but had time for back-and-forth discussion of the strategy for the first battle of Bull Run (1861).

Besides governments and field commanders, the press used the wires to give the public for the first time a ceaseless flow of prompt reportage from the front. So accustomed did the public get to the luxury that when Sherman moved out of Atlanta in 1864, cutting himself off from the telegraph, the effect in the North was a state of breathless suspense until a blockading gunboat brought word of the capture of Savannah.

In the Peninsular campaign in Virginia, civilian balloonist Thaddeus Lowe carried a telegraph wire aloft to scan Confederate defenses through binoculars and send information down to guide artillery fire, the first use of aerial spotting. Lee's secret march west commencing the Gettysburg campaign was first detected by balloon observation by Captain George Washington Roebling, son of the famous bridge engineer.

If the telegraph revolutionized military communications, the railroad revolutionized logistics. The railroad-building decade of the 1850s had turned a scattered 8,000 miles of track into a 30,000-mile national system. The South lagged behind the North in railroad building, and faced major problems in locomotive production and repair, rolling stock, and track maintenance. Nevertheless it got invaluable service from its lines, especially in keeping Lee's army supplied. Stonewall Jackson cleverly seized a number of trains at the war's outset. Occupying Harper's Ferry, he permitted the B. & O. to run freely in both directions for two weeks, then just before pulling out stopped all trains from leaving the area while continuing to let them enter. His haul of 42 locomotives and 386 cars was too large to carry off, so taking what he could, he burned the rest, putting the B. & O. out of commission from Baltimore to Wheeling.

French troops had been railroad-moved to the theater of combat in the Italian war of 1859, but in the American Civil War for the first time large-scale strategic movements by rail took place. In the first Bull Run campaign, Johnston, alerted by telegraph early on July 18, 1861, had his vanguard, under Stonewall Jackson, arriving at Manassas next day, after 20 miles of forced marching and 35 miles of rail transportation. Shuttling back and forth, the locomotives hauled all of Johnston's 12,000 men to Manassas by the 20th, in time to provide the decisive element in the battle next day.

Of many more railroad maneuvers, the most spectacular were those that resulted in the battles of Chickamauga and Chattanooga in 1863. Lee sent Longstreet's corps by rail to reinforce General Bragg, defending Tennessee; because a Union force under Burnside held Knoxville, Longstreet had to take a circuitous route via Augusta and Atlanta. Scraping together locomotives and every kind of rolling stock there was—freight, passenger, baggage, mail, coal, flatcar—the Confederate railroad department got Longstreet's 18,000 men with their guns and horses to Tennessee in time to play a decisive role at Chickamauga.

That maneuver placed the large, defeated Union army under Rosecrans in a critical situation and set the stage for an even more remarkable move. At 9:45 A.M. on September 23, 1863, Secretary Stanton received the telegram detailing the danger at Chattanooga. Stanton called a council of war and asked General Halleck, the chief of staff, how long it would take to move 20,000 men from Virginia to Chattanooga. Halleck thought they could make it in three months. The government's chief of telegraph, a railroad man by background, at first estimated forty to sixty days, but then restudied his timetables with growing optimism. If food depots could be prepared in advance, and pontoon bridges built to replace those destroyed at Louisville, he thought the maneuver could be completed in fifteen days.

Two days later the first troops from Virginia were detraining in Washington. By October 8 the last of two army corps were arriving on the Tennessee, having covered 1,200 miles in thirteen days. All artillery and equipment followed within a week, and barely a month after the first telegraph alert to Washington, Hooker delivered the attack that relieved Chattanooga.

The following year Sherman carried the Northern counteroffensive into the heart of the Confederacy, an extraordinary logistical feat whose basis Sherman fully appreciated. "That single stem of railroad," he wrote, referring to the 472-mile line winding through the mountains from Louisville to Atlanta, "supplied an army of 100,000 men and 35,000 horses for the period of 196 days. . . . To have delivered that amount of forage and food by ordinary wagons would have required 36,800 wagons, of 6 mules each, allowing each wagon to have hauled two tons 20 miles a day, a simple impossibility in such roads as existed in that region."

The value of the railroads made the Civil War also the first in which destruction of rail lines became a part of the technology of war. By the time Sherman cut loose for his March to the Sea the art was highly developed. Parties of soldiers were assigned in three sections. The first lifted ties, prying up and overturning track; the second followed up, collecting the ties, setting fire and piling on the rails; the third twisted the hot rails into doughnuts (often around trees—"Sherman's neckties"). General Slocum noted that it was hard work, "the only thing looking toward the destruction of property which I ever knew a man in Sherman's army to decline doing."

That winter (1864–65) another large-scale troop transfer excelled Hooker's record. Moving from Tennessee to the Potomac to effect a junction with Sherman in North Carolina, Schofield's 23rd Corps covered 1,400 miles in eleven days. Though the move was improvised on notice of only five days, the boxcars were equipped with seats for thirty men, with hay or straw to sleep on, and with stoves. Longstreet's, Hooker's, and Schofield's maneuvers, demanding cooperation among a number of different lines, gave powerful impetus to the postwar movement toward railroad consolidation.

The very havoc the lines were subjected to contributed to improving railroad technology. Track-laying became more scientific as a result of the constant de-

General Haupt, standing on bank at right, inspects a military railroad in 1863 near Bull Run. Mathew Brady photo. (U.S. Signal Corps)

struction and repair. Trestle-supported bridges became an art and a science. The Union's Construction Corps learned to build a 150-foot span with a 30-foot elevation across a creek in fifteen hours. The timber superstructure of the Chattahoochie Bridge, an 800-foot covered truss span in Georgia, was rebuilt from unfelled timber in four and a half days.

The most endlessly harassed and tirelessly rebuilt railroad line in the whole vast war theater was the Louisville & Nashville, whose bridges and rolling stock were targets of Morgan's Confederate raiders and the armies of Kirby Smith and Bragg, as well as the bands of guerrillas that infested Kentucky and Tennessee. The L. & N.'s chief engineer was Albert Fink, a German immigrant and inventor of a widely used bridge truss, whose ability to keep his line operating made it the only railroad in the war zone not seized by the government. All other railroad maintenance became the responsibility of Colonel Herman Haupt, who had been called to Washington from the Hoosac Tunnel, and General Daniel McCallum, another truss inventor, appointed by Grant to head all the western railroads. Haupt and McCallum repaired the incredible total of twenty-six miles of bridges during the war. How they did it was described to his Cabinet by Lincoln:

"Gentlemen, I have witnessed the most remarkable structure that human eyes have ever rested upon. That man Haupt has built a bridge across Potomac Creek, about four hundred feet long and eighty feet high, in nine days, with common soldiers, over which loaded trains are running every hour, and upon my word there is nothing in it but bean poles and corn stacks."

The railroads also contributed to an alleviation of the ghastly, time-honored neglect of wounded soldiers. By melancholy irony, the very years 1861 to 1865 were those in which Joseph Lister in Glasgow was carrying out the experiments

Railroad bridge over Potomac Creek built in nine days by General Haupt's construction corps, in Lincoln's words, "with common soldiers . . . and upon my word there is nothing in it but bean poles and corn stacks." (Library of Congress)

that led to antisepsis. Union and Confederate surgeons innocently slew tens of thousands of men who would have recovered if the doctors had washed their hands and instruments. But moving the wounded to base hospitals by railroad instead of slower wagon or boat sharply reduced the incidence of gangrene, and after a hideous first experience with ordinary boxcars—"they arrive a festering mass of dead and living together," wrote nurse Katherine P. Wormley—converted passenger coaches brought so visible an improvement that by 1863 the first specially designed thirty-stretcher hospital cars made their appearance.

Another railroad modification destined for a military future was the armored car, or, multiplied, armored train—a Union defense against regular and irregular Confederates, all of whom liked to take a shot at a target hard to miss.

In the end, if technology conferred few battlefield advantages on the North, it probably at least made victory inevitable by making it possible to supply and transport large armies while keeping both soldiers and civilians fed. By expanding industrial production and extending the railroad lines—they grew almost as rapidly in war as in peace—it also set the stage for a fresh international surprise. Many Europeans thought that the largest and costliest war in history, as Bismarck called it, would end in exhaustion and depression. Instead the country burst into a perverse springtime of economic and technological energy, a wave that with temporary setbacks was to carry the United States triumphantly into the twentieth century.

22

Captain Eads Builds the St. Louis Bridge

W A R T I M E D E S T R U C T I O N entirely aside, mid-nineteenth-century railroad bridges had a terrific propensity to fall down. The Howe truss in timber and iron and even in all iron was not really strong enough for the ever-increasing loadings, safety margins were irresponsibly stingy, and calculations often inexact. Bridges built to carry one ton per lineal foot failed under a ton and a half. Cast iron was susceptible to failure by flexure, the buckling caused when a side truss was pulled inward or pushed outward by an undesigned strain, e.g., a car jumping the track. Hundreds of bridges had their rails spiked directly to the stringers without any ties, a method inviting derailment, but even with ties, derailments were frequent, the car wheels striking and piling up the ties, lifting the following cars and dumping them right or left, throwing successive fatal strains on stringers, cross-bracing, and trusses. Weak pin connections and angle-block joints, still in use in America long after British and European engineers had adopted riveted joints, contributed to disaster.

Before American railroad bridges could be made safe, many reforms were needed in the realms of construction, maintenance, and inspection, nearly all of which the railroad companies used their large profits not to implement but to resist. But one great basic improvement required an innovative, in fact daring, technological change. The man whose imagination, engineering ability, and nerve brought it about remains a neglected American hero. James Buchanan Eads's achievements in war and peace entitle him to a place beside his friends and contemporaries, Grant, Sherman, and Farragut.

Captain James Eads. (Library of Congress)

Born in Indiana during the typical westward migration of an Eastern (Maryland) family, young Eads was thirteen when he arrived in St. Louis in 1833 on a steamboat that burst into flame as it neared the dock, and barely succeeded in discharging its passengers. His father was an impoverished patrician too genteelly incompetent to make a living. To help out his mother, who opened a boarding-house, James sold apples on the street, then got a job in a dry-goods store whose owner gave him free access to a collection of books in the loft.

In 1839, eighteen years old, the books all read, he quit the shop and headed for the river. "When I was a boy," Mark Twain wrote, "there was but one permanent ambition among my comrades in our village; that was to be a steam-boatman." Mark Twain was taken on as a cub pilot by the immortal Mr. Bixby; James Eads landed a berth as "mud clerk"—so named because the chief duty was legwork along the muddy waterfronts collecting freight bills and bargaining for fuel.

Late in the first winter, his vessel, an elderly steamboat named the *Knickerbocker,* ripped open her hull on a snag in the dawn hours as she turned into the Ohio. A passing flatboat flotilla rescued passengers and crew, but the mishap set Eads to thinking. In the next three years he was exposed to plenty of wrecks, many of which had salvageable cargoes. One morning in 1842 he walked into the office of Calvin Case and William Nelson, St. Louis boat builders, with a scheme. Though their caller was only twenty-two, the two businessmen listened to his proposal with increasing respect. He had designed a twin-hulled boat equipped with derricks and pumps, which he called the *Submarine,* a word designating its function rather than its character as a vessel; if Case and Nelson would build it, he offered them a partnership in a salvage enterprise.

For the next three years Captain Eads—anybody on the Mississippi who had his own boat was a captain—took his *Submarine* to the site of wrecks, climbed over the side in a diving bell fashioned out of a whiskey barrel, and felt his way to the wreck's hold, where he fastened a line to a pig of lead or iron, a tub of butter, or a barrel of whiskey, and signaled by a tug on the line to his crew above. Up and down the Mississippi, the Missouri, the Ohio, the Tennessee, and the Cumberland he worked his way, recovering cargoes that within a five-year limit insurance companies paid him for, and older cargoes that he and his partners owned outright.

By 1845 he had acquired enough capital to start a business on shore, an ambition he nourished for an unbusinesslike reason; he had fallen in love. Martha Dillon was the beautiful daughter of a well-to-do distant relation of the Eads family named Colonel Dillon, who was shortsighted enough to regard the young salvager as a poor catch for his girl. Martha took a different view. She sent Eads a pen, with the admonition, "Do not use this pen until you have occasion to write to her whom you have selected for your companion as you journey through this vale of life." They were married in the Cathedral Church of St. Louis de France, and shortly after, Captain Eads founded a glass factory. The idea was good but the timing bad—the Mexican War made many businesses boom, but not glass. By 1848 Eads was broke and back on the bottom of the Mississippi. But salvaging was better than ever, with steamboats launched daily up and down the river system and sinking nearly as fast. Eads and his partners built several new *Submarines,* one of which was capable of pumping out a wreck and raising it to the surface.

Despite his profits from wrecks, Eads was shocked by the abandonment of the federal government's snag-clearing program in 1856, and journeyed to Washington to lobby against the decision. He got a new snag-clearing bill passed by the House, but it was defeated in the Senate by the opposition of Jefferson Davis, who thought it a mistake to take up the proposal of a person "whose previous pursuits gave no assurance of ability to solve a problem in civil engineering."

That same year a steamboat wreck occurred that had tremendous bearing on Eads's future, and indeed that of the Mississippi. The first bridge over the mighty river had been built west of Chicago at Rock Island, Illinois, a timber truss in five spans mounted on stone piers, to carry the Rock Island Railroad into Iowa. Two weeks after its completion, the *Effie Afton,* steaming north against the current, careened into a pier and a pot-bellied stove on board overturned, setting ship and bridge ablaze. The steamboat companies brought suit to have the bridge taken down as a hazard to navigation. The railroad directors, justifiably alarmed, decided they needed a good lawyer, and hired Abraham Lincoln. Lincoln got a no-verdict from the jury, a victory for the railroad and the bridge. The steamboat companies appealed but eventually the Supreme Court handed down an enlightened decision in favor of the defendants, finding that if the steamboat suit were granted, the bridging of the Mississippi could be permanently prevented. By then Lincoln was in the White House, the Civil War was on, and Captain Eads was busy with his ironclads. Simultaneously a prolonged North-South argument over the route of a transcontinental railroad had been automatically settled by secession, and the Union Pacific began building westward from Nebraska to meet the Central Pacific. Eastward from Nebraska, a line was built to connect with the track coming west from Chicago that crossed at the Rock Island bridge, helping to make Chicago, western terminus of several eastern railroads, the transportation capital of the nation.

The St. Louis business community watched the development with much of the jealousy and apprehension with which Baltimore had viewed the Erie Canal and Boston the New York Central. Across the river, the Illinois Railroad had long ago reached East St. Louis, and the westward connection with the Union Pacific was easily feasible, but freight had to be clumsily ferried across the Mississippi and during severe winters often piled up on the shores.

Talk of a bridge at St. Louis was as old as the town, but the technical difficulties had seemed insurmountable. Yet a "St. Louis and Illinois Bridge Company" was formed in 1866, and charters obtained from the two legislatures, on the condition that either a main span of 500 feet, or two center spans of 350 feet each, be provided to safeguard navigation. For a bridge strong enough to carry post-Civil War railroad loading, the requirement was a challenge even to the country's corps of trained and experienced bridge engineers. Many of them thought it impossible. But James Eads, who had no formal engineering education, was certain it could be done, and if he had no formal training, he had experience that no engineering school taught. He knew a good bit about iron and ironworks, a great deal about construction in the form of shipbuilding, and how to organize labor and materials in widely separated places into an effective pattern. Finally, he knew more about the Mississippi River than any man alive.

At St. Louis, the Mississippi consisted of 225,000 cubic feet of water moving 12½ feet each second in high-water time, in a stream 1,500 feet wide and varying unpredictably in depth. Its bed, as Eads knew well, swirled and flowed to a depth of a foot or more, creating terrific scour against any structure built in it. The depth of mud presented a profile shelving away steeply from west to east so that on the Illinois side an abutment could only reach secure bedrock at a depth of well over a hundred feet. In winter huge irregular chunks of ice drifted down from the north, freezing together in intense cold to form massive ice fields. In narrow passes, where islands occupied part of the stream, the ice jammed, with more ice wedging underneath to form miniature glaciers, sometimes closing the river from December to late February. Then came the flood.

By 1867 several engineers had sketched designs for a St. Louis bridge. Charles Ellet and John Roebling proposed suspension spans, theoretically possible, but of doubtful strength for the ever-increasing loadings promised by railroads. Another proposal was for a solid iron tube of square section, in imitation of Robert Stephenson's famous Britannia Bridge over the Menai Straits in Wales. The most popular design among 1867 engineers was a multiple-span iron truss.

Eads decided against all these. To make the St. Louis Bridge as strong and secure as he deemed necessary, he decided on the ancient, indestructible arch form, but not in stone, wood, or iron. The St. Louis Bridge, he told his backers, should be built of steel.

No structure had ever before been made of steel. Kelly's Cambria demonstration was only five years in the past. Whether steel could be produced in quantity sufficient for three giant arches made up of tubular ribs, with reliable uniformity, was not known. Eads thought it could, provided there was enough care and determination. Very few engineers agreed with him. The Keystone Bridge Company of Pittsburgh was the leading bridge construction firm of the day, and its president, J. H. Linville, the foremost bridge engineer. The company decided to invite Linville's participation as consulting engineer, and sent him Eads's design specifications. Linville sent them straight back. "I cannot consent to imperil my reputation by appearing to encourage or approve [the design's] adoption," he announced. "I deem it entirely unsafe and impracticable."

Eads was unimpressed, and so, remarkably, were his backers. A Chicago-based rival bridge company headed by one Lucius Boomer (Mark Twain later had fun with that name) made considerable trouble via the Illinois legislature, but in the end had to give in to Eads—"one who," in the words of Professor C. M. Woodward, author of the compendious *History of the St. Louis Bridge,* "possessed to an uncommon degree the confidence of his fellow citizens."

To sell the necessary bonds, Eads wanted to get his project off to a convincing start, and chose to begin with his West Abutment, one of the four foundations of the triple arch. Lucius Boomer's engineers claimed that deep bedrock foundations were not necessary. Eads knew they were, because of the violent abrasive action of the deep Mississippi scour. He chose the site of his West Abutment strictly on the basis of the bridge's usefulness, now and in the long future. Consequently it was located in the heart of the busy waterfront, at a point where an 1849 fire and innumerable lesser mishaps had littered the riverbed with debris. "The old sheet-iron enveloping their furnaces, worn-out grates, old firebricks, parts of smokestacks, stone-coal cinders and clinker, and every manner of things entering into the construction of a Mississippi steamer seemed to have found a resting place," recorded Professor Woodward. Two steamboats reposed one on top of the other, the bottom hull immersed in mud and only two or three feet above bedrock. The wharf had been built out since the fire, and rubble dumped to support it pinned the wrecks. Eads devised a sort of monster axe, with a steel blade and oak handle, to cut through the mass, and into the cleft he wedged the sheet piling of a cofferdam, the enclosure within which his foundation presently began to rise.

Eads's design called for a center arch of 515 feet, resting on two piers sunk to bedrock, with side arch spans of 497 feet spanning from the piers to the two shore abutments. The arches would carry a double-deck roadway, highway above and rail line below. On the strength of the completion of the West Abutment and an able summarizing report by Eads, the necessary enabling legislation was passed by both state legislatures and by Congress, and the support of the financial community in New York—and London—gained.

But because of the shelving of the Mississippi profile, the West Abutment, aside from the debris, was the shallowest of the four foundations—only 40 feet below mean high water. Both the piers in the stream had to go deeper, and to touch bedrock the East Abutment had to reach over 100 feet—exactly how far down no one knew.

American engineers realized that the deeper a foundation went, the more intense the pressure became from the accumulating weight of water and mud above. But they had little experience in coping with the problem—taking a work gang down to the river bottom and permitting them to dig down through 40, 60, or 80 feet of mud under tremendous pressure. Deep foundations had not yet become a problem in American civil engineering.

In the spring of 1869 Eads went to France to convalesce from a bronchial infection and to show some of his plans to a French engineering firm that was considering a bid on the St. Louis superstructure. The firm's chief engineer invited him down to Vichy to inspect a deep-foundation bridge under construction with the aid of the pneumatic caisson. This device was not entirely unknown in the United States. West Pointer Sooy Smith had used it in two bridges in the Carolinas in the 1850s, but the Peedee River was not exactly the Mississippi, and Smith's work crews had not had to go very deep. Eads had probably never even heard of Smith's experience. But in Europe he learned that French and British engineers had taken foundations as deep as 70 feet. The caisson they had developed consisted of a working chamber connected to the surface by a masonry column containing two shafts, one for men and one for materials, with an air lock at the top of each. The air lock, invented by British Admiral Thomas Cochrane, was a small, tightly sealed room with two closely fitted doors opposite to each other. The work crew entered, closed the door, opened a valve, and increased the air pressure until it equaled that of the working chamber down below. Then they opened the door to the shaft and descended. Coming out, they reversed the process.

French and British engineers had encountered a puzzling medical problem in connection with the caisson, but no one mentioned it to the American visitor.

Studying the caisson at Vichy, Eads thought it could solve his problem at St. Louis. En route home he stopped off in New York to explain the caisson to a meeting of bondholders, and at home in St. Louis he soon had William Nelson, his old *Submarine* builder, busy on a pair of the strangest structures the riverfront had ever seen: huge, rectangular iron-sheathed boxes mounted on boat bottoms. In October 1869, the first of them slid into the water at Carondelet and was towed to the bridge site where a cluster of boats and barges bristling with hoisting and pumping machinery waited. The ungainly gray box was freed from its false boat bottom and moored in place. A week later, on a cold, raw day darkened further by the smoke of the construction fleet, the cornerstone of the St. Louis Bridge was laid at the East Pier, second deepest of the four foundations.

The ceremony was brief; the hammers hardly paused. Barges loaded with limestone were nudged into place and the huge blocks swung into the masonry column that was growing atop the caisson roof. The column's weight pressed the caisson down through the water till within a few days it rested on the bottom. Down a spiral stairway in the middle of the column went the working crew, for whom the word "sandhog" had not yet been invented. They numbered immigrant Germans along with the inevitable Irish, and were the usual tough lot. On the job Eads always carried a sheath knife and a revolver, but never had any trouble. Despite his slight build, he was a man of exceptional physical prowess, thanks to his years of cargo-mauling on the bottom of the river. He sometimes staged weight-lifting contests on the blacksmith boat, and could outlift everybody except the chief blacksmith.

The work was pushed all fall and into the winter—the crews in the compressed-air chamber digging away, sending the sand up through the sandpump, the construction men aloft building the pier. A bitter cold spell filled the river with ice cakes, and for several days the men were stranded on the barge *Hewitt,* armed with blankets and rations for such an emergency. Eads got his most powerful tug, the *Little Giant,* out to the "Hotel de Hewitt" on Christmas Eve and found the men in good spirits. The ice subsided for a few days, then came back stronger than ever and threatened to smash the pier. Eads had built a breakwater against this danger, and for a few days it was touch and go; then the weather warmed a little, and the work tempo picked up.

As the working chamber sank, the air pressure was slowly raised, to 20 pounds per square inch, to 25, to 30. Some of the men emerging from the caisson complained of stomach pains; one or two reported moments of fleeting paralysis. To relieve the cramps the men doubled over slightly, and sardonically named their affliction the "Grecian bends," after a current fashion in feminine posture. At a depth of 76 feet, with air pressure at 32 pounds, one man suffered such severe abdominal pains that he had to be hospitalized.

European engineers had long been familiar with caisson disease, and an English doctor had even prescribed the remedy—slow decompression. But scientific and medical news traveled slowly unless it had a direct bearing on making money, and the compressed-air tragedy was acted out over and over on the bridges and tunnels of Europe and America.

Eads did his ignorant best. He forbade any but the most physically fit to work in the caisson, cut the day shift to three watches of two hours each, with rest between, and abolished the night shift. The measures were partially effective, and the East Pier was driven to bedrock at 93½ feet without further serious cases, the deepest structural foundation ever sunk. The event was signaled up and down the riverfront on February 28, 1870, with booming cannon and steamboat whistles.

The working chamber, resting solidly on scraped rock, was now filled with masonry "till it was the size of an Irishman," and when the last Irishman crawled out, the last space was filled. The danger from the Grecian bends seemed to be past. But it was spring, the Mississippi began its rapid rise, faster than the masonry column atop the caisson could be completed. Ten days after the freshet began, the air pressure had to be raised to 44 pounds to prevent collapse of the column. A new man named James Riley came out after a two-hour watch, remarked that he felt fine, and ten minutes later toppled over and died, America's first caisson-disease fatality.

Horrified, Eads summoned his personal physician, Dr. Jaminet, to the pier, and a floating hospital was added to the barge flotilla. But in the next few days five more men were fatally stricken. Eads cut the day shift to two two-hour watches, with a long rest between, then to three one-hour watches. He enforced Dr. Jaminet's strict rules on sleep and diet, despite the men's protests. A new freshet sent the water level up, the bends came back, and the watches were cut to 45 minutes. On April 13 the deluge broke through, flooding the pier. However, the men escaped, the damage was repaired, and two weeks later the East Pier stood complete.

Eads had already started on the shallower West Pier, which hit bedrock in a submersion of 78 feet. Dr. Jaminet, keeping a close check on the workmen, himself was stricken with the bends on his return to his office. Recovering from the painful experience, he analyzed it and hit on the solution already arrived at in Europe— slow decompression. The rate he prescribed—6 pounds per minute—was dangerously rapid by modern standards, which call for 1 pound per minute, but it worked, and saved lives. Unfortunately, Dr. Jaminet's discovery was not diffused any more widely than those of the British and French, and in the following years Washington Roebling at the Brooklyn Bridge and De Witt Haskin tunneling under the Hudson reenacted the tragedies.

On the deep East Abutment slow decompression produced dramatic results. The caisson did not find bedrock until 103 feet below the river surface, 136 feet below high water, with a pressure in the working chamber of 49 pounds, yet few cases of the bends occurred, and only a single fatality.

The East Abutment was replete with other hazards, however. A tremendous ice gorge nearly collapsed Eads's breakwater, which he desperately fortified with more rock. A tornado raged in from the southwest with no warning, leveling buildings, uprooting trees, hurling trains from embankments, and crumpling the superstructure of the East Abutment in seconds. By a miracle, only one man was killed and eight injured. The damage repaired, the East Abutment was soon completed, and confounding forecasts of orthodox engineers, the four foundations of the St. Louis Bridge stood solidly planted on bedrock, ready to receive their triple-arch superstructure.

Iron and steel companies all over Europe and America had sought the contract, but Eads's specifications of quality were so rigorous they sobered all and discouraged most. The three huge pairs of arches Eads had designed consisted of ribs made up of sections of steel tube. The tube is a highly efficient structural form; that is, it has a high strength-to-weight ratio. But no one had ever made an arch out of metal tubing, let alone steel tubing.

The superstructure contract was offered to the Keystone Bridge Company, the nation's largest bridge contractor, almost as a matter of course. But Keystone's president was J. H. Linville, the engineer who had deemed Eads's design "entirely unsafe and impractical," and Linville had not changed his mind. He was nevertheless talked into the contract by his vice-president, a thirty-five-year-old Scottish-born American go-getter named Andrew Carnegie, who had acquired an affection for the St. Louis Bridge by profitably selling its bonds on the London financial market. From Junius Morgan in London, father of J. Pierpont Morgan, Carnegie had won acceptance contingent on specified changes in terms, and had astounded Morgan by reappearing two days later with the changes in hand, having used the new Atlantic cable to contact the bridge company.

Accepting the superstructure contract for Keystone, Carnegie subcontracted the steel to the Butcher Steel Works of Philadelphia, while reserving the easier wrought-iron skewbacks—the plates and sockets into which the arch tips fitted at the piers—for his own newly formed Carnegie and Kloman Company.

But the contracting companies were all soon embattled with their exacting customer over his demands for quality and uniformity. "Nothing that would and does please engineers is good enough for this work," Carnegie complained. When

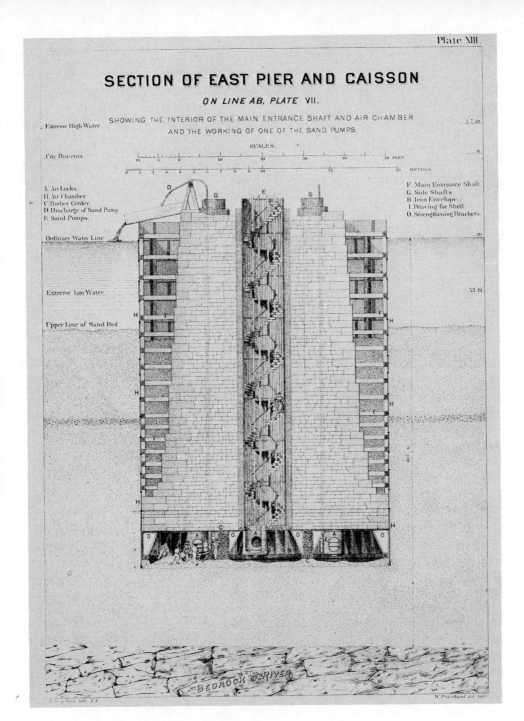

Plate XIII

SECTION OF EAST PIER AND CAISSON

ON LINE AB, PLATE VII.

SHOWING THE INTERIOR OF THE MAIN ENTRANCE SHAFT AND AIR CHAMBER
AND THE WORKING OF ONE OF THE SAND PUMPS.

SCALES.

Extreme High Water

City Directrix

A. Air Locks.
B. Air Chamber.
C Timber Girder.
D. Discharge of Sand Pump.
E. Sand Pumps.

F. Main Entrance Shaft.
G. Side Shafts.
H. Iron Envelope.
I. Bracing for Shell.
O. Strengthening Brackets.

Ordinary Water Line

Extreme Low Water

Upper Line of Sand Bed

BEDROCK OF RIVER

Section of caisson, St. Louis Bridge. (Smithsonian Photograph)

Butcher gave up, Eads found a New York firm, the Chrome Steel Works, that could meet his requirements, but at a higher cost. Carnegie called for appointment of "an experienced engineer," meaning Linville, to "alter, amend or curtail" the bridge plans. Unruffled, Eads accepted the proposal, but got a well-known neutral engineer named James Laurie appointed, who went over all Eads's drawings, specifications, bills, and contracts and turned in a report recommending only insignificant changes.

On every arch bridge ever built, the arch had been supported during construction by centering—timber falsework in the river. Eads had pledged that he would not obstruct the Mississippi channel. To keep his promise, he cantilevered the arches out from the piers, that is, held them suspended by cables and timber falsework built on top of the piers. As the arches thrust farther and farther out over the water in the spring and summer of 1873, a final problem set the shoreline observers guessing: how would Captain Eads join the arch halves when they met? He had his solution ready. The final two steel tubes of each arch rib would be truncated five inches, and screw threads cut inside them. A short wrought-iron plug, fitted with two sets of threads, could then be screwed in, and at the arch closing, drawn out just enough to fit across, bolting the two together. A steel band would give the joint superior strength.

Colonel Henry Flad, Eads's chief assistant, had conceived an alternate plan for the arch closure. Flad's idea was simply to hump the arches slightly by means of the cantilever cables, bring the joining ribs together and let the arch assume its proper form as the cables were removed. Eads gave his approval for Flad to try his idea, and went off to London to negotiate a new loan bond issue with Junius Morgan. Morgan agreed, contingent upon closing one of the arches as a sign to the investing public that the bridge was nearing completion. Eads promised to have an arch closed by September 19, and so cabled Flad. On the 14th, Flad set the men to jacking up the cables of the west arch ribs. Unluckily an unseasonable hot spell hit St. Louis and the ribs expanded instead of contracting slightly as Flad had anticipated. To chill the tubing Flad hastily built a trough and filled it with 30,000 pounds of ice, but the ice melted faster than the ribs cooled, and in the end the colonel gave up and used Eads's screw connection. He cabled Eads, care of Morgan, that the arch was complete—Morgan himself opening the dispatch, as Eads, with cheeky confidence, had taken the boat train to Paris.

A last threat to the bridge was posed by the powerful Keokuk Steamboat Company, which induced President Grant's corruptible Secretary of War William W. Belknap to demand that the bridge company build a canal around the East Abutment so that steamboats would not have to lower their smokestacks. Eads and his general manager, Dr. William Taussig, journeyed to Washington to see Grant. The interview had potential for embarrassment, because Eads had supported the Democrats in the last election and Taussig had years earlier helped bar ne'er-do-well Captain U. S. Grant from the post of county surveyor. But on this occasion as on others Grant proved himself a bigger man than his small physical stature, and after listening to his callers summoned Belknap and ordered him to "drop the case." Shortly afterward, he visited St. Louis and accompanied Eads and Colonel Flad on a stroll across the precarious plankway laid from arch to arch, and joined them in brandy and cigars in Eads's office.

Early in 1874 Eads returned to New York to reassure the American bondholders and bankers that the job was nearly done. He had just gone to bed in his hotel

Cantilevering the arch of the St. Louis Bridge. (Smithsonian Photograph)

when the bellboy woke him with a telegram. It was from Theodore Cooper, the young assistant inspector; the arch ribs had begun to break. Two tubes in the first span had ruptured.

It was a stunning piece of news, even apart from coming on the eve of an important meeting with the financial backers. Eads refused to panic. Lighting the gaslight, he sat down and thought. Finally he figured the thing out. Although the arch was finished, the steel cantilever cables had not been removed. These were contracting in the cold and pulling the ribs up and back, a direction in which these compression members were not meant to take strain. He shot off a telegram to Cooper: loosen the cables. Next morning he addressed the investors with his usual confidence.

Arriving home, he found the shores lined with people waiting for the bridge to break up as the cables were removed. Instead the huge arches settled firmly into place, and on May 24, 1874, the highway deck was opened for pedestrians to walk across. On June 3 it was opened for vehicles, and a few days later the first locomotive crossed on the lower deck, carrying Eads, company officials, and General Sherman, the Army chief of staff, who drove the last spike on the Illinois side. On July 2 Eads treated the public to a demonstration of the bridge's strength by running fourteen locomotives and tenders back and forth in a variety of formations. On the Fourth of July a hundred artillery rounds signaled a parade with floats and

costumed marchers—the stove-makers, brewers, bakers, buggy manufacturers, har-
ness-makers, shoe manufacturers, temperance clubs, German singing societies, and
fire departments of St. Louis, and the U.S. Cavalry from Jefferson Barracks, winding 15 miles under flags and bunting to a triumphal arch near the bridge portal,
topped by a medallion portrait of Eads, with the inscription:

The Mississippi discovered by Marquette, 1673;
Spanned by Captain Eads, 1874

Steamboats, abandoning their hostility, formed a rainbow arch and blew their
whistles in response to rockets arching from the top of the bridge.

The cost ran to $6,500,000, an excess over Eads's estimate of $5 million that
brought criticism in an age when cost overruns had not yet become a familiar engineering phenomenon. A larger economic loss was incurred by the stubbornness
of the railroads in refusing to use the bridge for a considerable period while arguing over the tolls (which were only half the ferry charge, but the railroads, instead
of middlemen cargo handlers, had to pay them).

These were small matters. The St. Louis Bridge was built to serve and built to
endure, and it did both. The first bridge over the wide lower Mississippi, involving
the first significant use of compressed air in America, it was the largest, strongest
bridge built up to then in the world. Its caissons, the largest up to that time, were
sunk to record depths rarely exceeded in the twentieth century. Its arches were
the first ever constructed of steel and the first to be erected by cantilevering.

Not only was it the first steel bridge, but the first steel structure, and Eads's
confident faith and inflexible standards helped make William Kelly's mass-produced steel the construction material of the modern world.

Beyond all this, the St. Louis Bridge—the Eads Bridge, as St. Louis eventually
named it—was the first of the series of American civil engineering feats that did
much to give the world its image of emerging America.

The bridge was not the last of Eads's achievements. A few years later, again in
the teeth of skepticism and reactionary opposition, he built the South Pass jetties
that made New Orleans a true ocean port, eliminating the tow over the sandbar
in the delta that handicapped shipping. His triple claim to fame—ironclads,
bridge, and jetties—is scarcely matched among civil engineers, American or European. Fittingly enough, he was the first engineer to be enshrined in the American
Hall of Fame at New York University. Yet he remains as little known as Oliver
Evans, Colonel John Stevens, Samuel Slater, and John Fitch.

At least, the Eads Bridge still spans the Mississippi in the shadow of the St.
Louis Arch, and a bridge makes a rather magnificent monument.

23

Christopher Sholes and the Typewriter

KATE (*She presses her hand on the typewriter as lovingly as many a woman has pressed a rose*): I learned this. I hired it and taught myself. I got some work through a friend, and with my first twelve pounds I paid for my machine. Then I considered that I was free to go, and I went. . . . If I was a husband—it is my advice to all of them—I would often watch my wife quietly to see whether the twelve-pound look was not coming into her eyes. . . .

LADY SIMS: May I come in? . . . (*Kate is escorted off the premises.*) . . . She has a very contented face. . . .

SIR HARRY (*snapping*): One would think you envied her.

LADY SIMS: Envied? Oh no—but I thought she looked so alive. It was while she was working the machine.

SIR HARRY: Alive! That's no life. It is you that are alive. . . .

LADY SIMS: Are they very expensive?

SIR HARRY: What?

LADY SIMS: Those machines?

—*The Twelve-Pound Look*
by James M. Barrie, 1910

The machine that James M. Barrie dramatized as an instrument for the emancipation of women was still something of a novelty in 1910, but it had antecedents going back to 1714, when an Englishman named Henry Mill patented "an Artificial machine . . . for the Impressing or Transcribing of Letters." Mill must have encountered some of the considerable technical problems in the way, because he apparently never built his machine. Later in the eighteenth century, French and German inventors produced devices for embossing printed characters for the blind that bore an obvious relationship to the writing machine. In 1829 William A. Burt of Detroit patented a sort of toy printer dubbed "Burt's Family Letter Press," with type arranged in a semicircle on a wheel that was revolved manually until the desired letter reached the point of printing, when it was hand-pressed against the paper. Despite its description by the *New York Commercial Advertiser* as "a simple, cheap, and pretty machine," Burt's device never got beyond the model stage, and was certainly unknown to French inventor Xavier Projean who in 1833 produced the first significant proto-typewriter, with typebars converging at the center. A decade later Charles Thurber, of Worcester, Massachusetts, reverting to the problem of printing for the blind, contributed another valuable principle for a writing machine by effecting letter-spacing with a horizontally moving cylindrical platen. Four years later Dr. Samuel William Francis produced a writing machine embodying several of the already established principles, arranging his keyboard in four rows, and adding an ingenious inked ribbon.

All the necessary major components were now present, yet the typewriter stubbornly refused to be born. Two basic requirements of the device itself were difficult to meet: rapid, legible printing and durability under daily use. Beyond these problems arose a third, still quite novel and not fully appreciated by inventors: a design compatible with the technique of mass production.

One of the impractical models that continued to emerge from workshops in Europe and America inadvertently played a catalytic role. Invented by an Alabaman named John Pratt and exhibited in London in 1867, the "Pterotype," another typewheel device, represented no great advance over earlier machines, and in one way was a retrogression since it discarded the inked ribbon in favor of printing through newly invented carbon paper. But Alfred Ely Beach, publisher of *Scientific American,* and himself the inventor of a "Printing Instrument for the Blind," described it in his magazine and informed his readers, "The subject of typewriting is one of the interesting aspects of the near future. Its manifest feasibility and advantage indicate that the laborious and unsatisfactory performance of the pen must, sooner or later, become obsolete for general purposes."

Among *Scientific American*'s subscribers was a Milwaukee lawyer named Carlos Glidden. A blacksmith's son, Glidden hobby-tinkered with farm implements in his office over Kleinsteuber's machine shop between the Milwaukee River and the Milwaukee and Rock River Canal. Next door a couple of ex-printers, Christopher Sholes and Samuel Soulé, were working on an invention, a device to sequentially number pages, tickets, coupons, and checks. Soulé was a capable mechanic, Sholes something more out of the ordinary. Born in a Pennsylvania log cabin in 1819, the son of a cabinetmaker, he had become a master printer by the age of eighteen and editor of the *Wisconsin Enquirer* at twenty. He had served two terms in the Wisconsin state senate, one in the assembly, and had held other public offices as a member of the radical Barnburners' wing of the Democratic party. In the 1860s, as editor of the *Milwaukee Sentinel,* he had been provoked by a compositors' strike to attempt the invention of a typesetting machine. He

LEFT Christopher Sholes. (Sperry Remington)

RIGHT Kleinsteuber's machine shop in Milwaukee, where Sholes built his first typewriters. (Sperry Remington)

had also conceived the novel method of addressing newspapers by printing the subscriber's name in the margin, and the device for serial numbering of pages that he was at work on with Soulé.

There was one other element in Christopher Sholes's background that he himself always thought played a role in his career. As a boy in a one-room school in Mooresburg, Pennsylvania (where, true to a fine old American tradition, he met the girl he eventually married), he developed a powerful aversion to the second of schooling's three R's. His own full name, Christopher Latham Sholes, was a challenge to "the laborious and unsatisfactory performance of the pen," and later, when he learned typesetting, he amused himself by setting it in type and printing it, a "recreation" that he thought "implanted in my mind the embryo of the mechanical typewriter."

But it was loft neighbor Carlos Glidden who, inspecting the number-printing mechanism, exclaimed, "Sholes, why cannot you build a machine to print letters and words as perfectly as these figures?" Glidden showed him Alfred Beach's article in *Scientific American*. Infected by Beach's enthusiasm, Sholes began turning over the problem in his head, and one morning a week later arrived at Kleinsteuber's with a theoretical solution. A cough had kept him awake the night before and he had worked out a preliminary model in his head which he now described to Soulé and another mechanic neighbor, H. W. Roby. The three set to work with bits of wood, glass, and metal. They soon assembled Sholes's conception in the form of a little device consisting mainly of a Morse telegraph key af-

fixed to a small brass typebar carrying the single letter *W*, and a horizontally positioned glass disk under which was affixed a piece of thin paper covered by a sheet
of carbon paper (borrowed from the Western Union office). Advancing the paper
with his free hand, Sholes gave the Morse key a series of smart blows, and to the
admiration of the group of onlookers a neat series of capital *W*s appeared on the
paper.

"Well, Mr. Sholes," said Glidden, "I guess you have coughed up something
pretty good and I'd like to have a hand in it." Sholes promised everyone a share
in the development of the invention, and a partnership was formed among himself, Glidden, and Soulé to develop a full-scale model.

As they worked, the question arose of what to call the invention. Sholes's partners suggested "printing machine" and "writing machine," but imaginative Sholes
came up with "type-writer," which, dropping the hyphen, stuck.

Despite newspapers and magazines, technological news still traveled slowly,
and except for the *Scientific American*'s description of Pratt's "Pterotype," Sholes
apparently had little information about his predecessors. He seized on a suggestion from Soulé that the typebars be positioned on the rim of a circle to strike toward a central printing point. That wheel had already been invented by Projean
and others. At first Sholes followed Pratt in printing by carbon paper, but during
the course of building the first full-scale model—perhaps after learning about
Samuel Francis's machine—he bought several yards of silk ribbon, soaked it in ink,
and hung it to dry in the loft.

For his boxlike frame, he cut up an old kitchen table. The typebars, suspended
in a circle underneath, were operated by wires connected to key bars cut out of
black walnut and modeled after piano keys, arranged in two rows with letters
painted in white, in alphabetical order. Shorter keys resembling the black keys on
a piano were inserted between the letters, for numbers and punctuation marks—
semicolon, dollar sign, hyphen, comma, question mark, and a diagonal stroke for
parenthesis.

All the letters were capitals, since accommodating lower-case letters on a piano
keyboard would necessitate a machine the size of a piano. The paper, at first a
tape, then a sheet, placed on top of the typewriter, was moved to the left as each
key was struck, by a weight-driven clockwork mechanism (escapement). At the end
of each line a bell rang, and the paper frame was moved by means of a foot
treadle. The horizontal position of the paper and the fact that the keys struck
it from below resulted in a curious relationship between keys, paper, and inked
ribbon: the ribbon was placed on top so that the keys struck the paper and forced
it against the ribbon, producing printing on the upper surface of the paper. In
order to produce a legible impression, the paper had to be very thin. Two years
later Sholes transposed ribbon and paper, producing the modern relationship.

As soon as the model was finished, Sholes sat down before it and with his colleagues and friends watching in suspense, neatly pecked out, "C. LATHAM
SHOLES, SEPTEMBER, 1867." For the remainder of his life, Sholes never used
a pen, even to sign letters. One man's rebellion against school was triumphant.

The "type-writer," however, had a long way to go. The Milwaukee kitchen-
table model, successfully assembling all the essential components in a simple

machine, represented the decisive step forward, but it was still clumsy and subject to jamming, and formed letters that frequently strayed out of line. During the course of the experimentation someone, inspired by the ongoing Grant-Seymour presidential campaign, typed out the practice sentence: "Now is the time for all good men to come to the aid of the party."

As so often happened in the development stage of a new invention, money ran short and Glidden and Soulé had to drop out of the enterprise. Sholes was then inspired to compose the world's first typewritten sales letter. The appeal, couched in the very language of the product, proved irresistible to its recipient, a Pennsylvania publisher named James Densmore. A large, florid, unkempt man with a shaggy red beard, Densmore had already demonstrated his acumen by making a fortune out of the burgeoning Pennsylvania oil industry. In return for an interest in the patent, Densmore agreed to pay Sholes's outstanding debts and finance continued development.

The following year (1868) Sholes took out his patent. The patented machine had radial typebars cut out of brass, with the letters on the ends, guided to strike the center point by an annular (ringlike) disk with radial grooves and slots; the clockwork ratchet to move the paper carriage ahead; a hinged clamp to hold the paper; and inked ribbon on spools, also advanced by clockwork.

Later, taking his cue from the compartments of a hand-typesetter's case, Sholes rearranged his keyboard to position the characters most often used nearest the working center. Then, to prevent the keys' fouling, he placed the letters that occurred most frequently in sequence as far apart as possible in the type basket. The result was the "standard" typewriter keyboard memorized by generations of typists since.

"The machine is done, and I want some more worlds to conquer," Sholes exultantly typed out (in capital letters) to Charles Weller, the Western Union operator who had supplied him with the carbon paper for his first model. His conclusion was premature. Densmore hired a court reporter named James O. Clephane to test Sholes's successive models as they strove for increased speed, reduced friction, and more durability. When Clephane sat down at the keyboard, he pulled no punches, wrecking one model after another to the accompaniment of a string of caustic comments. Sholes grew understandably enraged, telling Densmore, "I am through with Clephane!" Densmore alternately bullied and cajoled him to continue. "Sholes, this thing isn't worth a damn and it never will be!" he roared, and then reminded the inventor that it was better to get all the criticism possible in the development stage. "Where Clephane points out a weak lever or rod, let us make it strong. Where a spacer or an inker works stiffly, let us make it work smoothly. Then depend upon Clephane for all the praise we deserve."

One after another, Sholes constructed or reconstructed fifty models before all three men were satisfied. The Sholes machine of 1870 had an iron frame enclosed at the sides with thin polished wood boards. The platen was a rubber roller twice as thick as modern versions but otherwise similar, except that instead of moving laterally with each stroke of the key, it turned as it now does in changing lines. For a new line, the Sholes roller moved a space to the right. The roller-length paper was inserted sidewise, curving around the roller, the edges overlapping to provide a margin. A spring motor powered the movement of the paper frame and ribbon, in contrast to the clumsy weight-driven clockwork mechanism of the earlier model. For the crude wooden keys were now substituted metal rods each with a brass button on the end, on which was painted the letter or figure. The typebars were set in steel bearings. Because the typekeys still struck upward from below, the typist could not see the line as it was printed unless he raised the carriage out of the way. In the succeeding three years, Sholes reduced the platen to its present size, with the paper inserted as it is today, and adopted the modern system of advancing the paper and changing lines.

Searching for a manufacturer, Densmore found the ideal firm in the Remington Arms Company of Ilion, New York. Remington was a microcosm of the history of the American System of Manufacturing. Having commenced with mass production of rifles and pistols and progressed to the sewing machine, it was now ready for the typewriter. Philo Remington tried out Sholes's machine and told the superintendent of his sewing-machine division (according to one story), "We must on no account let it get away! It isn't necessary to tell these people that we are crazy over the invention, but I'm afraid I am pretty nearly so."

Sholes and Densmore undertook to sell the first thousand typewriters, and got their first large order from the R. G. Dun cigar company, a hundred machines for $5,500. Despite this and a succession of other orders, Sholes sold his entire rights to Remington for $12,000. The giveaway reflected a surprising lack of confidence in the typewriter's commercial future. "You know my apprehension," he type-wrote, "that for a while there may be an active demand for them, but that like any other novelty it will have its brief day and be thrown aside. . . . Densmore laughs at the idea when I suggest it." Densmore evidently kept laughing as he made his own royalty arrangement with Remington and eventually pocketed a million and a half dollars.

The first machine Remington brought out under its own name, the "Remington No. 1," was a Sholes typewriter with all the established Sholes features, including the arrangement and actuation of typebars, the printing through an inked ribbon, the standard keyboard. It was still limited to capital letters, and the typist could still not see the line being typed.

Nevertheless, it was an immediate success in the market, adding to the sophistication of mass-production technology, still a virtual American monopoly. At the Philadelphia Exposition it was noted that American machine tools, if a little coarser than British, cost only half as much, the arms, clock, lock, stove, farm-implement, sewing-machine, and typewriter industries having caused machine tools themselves to become mass-produced by interchangeable parts.

Thanks to McCormick, Singer, and other entrepreneurs, marketing techniques for mass-produced machines were now well advanced. Mark Twain, who bought one of the early Remingtons, described how a Boston salesman explained its operation,

> showed us samples of its work, and said it could do fifty-seven words a minute—a statement which we frankly confessed that we did not believe. So he put his type-girl to work, and we timed her by the watch. She actually did the fifty-seven in sixty seconds. We were partly convinced, but said it probably couldn't happen

TOP LEFT Sholes's first single-key typewriter, 1867, now in the Milwaukee Public Museum. The type, a letter W, swung upward to strike a piece of paper held against the underside of the circular glass platen. (Sperry Remington)

TOP RIGHT Sholes and Glidden typewriter, patent model June 23, 1868. Still in the experimental stage, this typewriter had eleven keys, could write only a few letters. (Smithsonian Photograph No. 30,532)

ABOVE LEFT Sholes and Glidden typewriter, patent model July 14, 1868. (Smithsonian Photograph No. 30,530)

ABOVE RIGHT Early model of Sholes's typewriter. (Sperry Remington)

LEFT Sholes and Glidden typewriter, patent model Sept. 19, 1876. The typewriter has now acquired a cylindrical platen, brass button keys, a spring-powered movement. (Smithsonian Photograph No. 18,657G)

LEFT Remington Model One. (Sperry Remington)

RIGHT Lillian Sholes operating an early model of her father's typewriter. (Sperry Remington)

again. But it did. We timed the girl over and over again—with the same result always: she won out. She did her work on narrow slips of paper, and we pocketed them as fast as she turned them out, to show as curiosities. The price of the machine was $125. I bought one, and we went away very much excited.

At the hotel we got out our slips and were a little disappointed to find that they all contained the same words. The girl had economized time and labor by using a formula which she knew by heart. However, we argued—safely enough—that the *first* type-girl must naturally take rank with the first billiard-player: neither of them could be expected to get out of the game any more than a third or a half of what was in it. If the machine survived—*if* it survived—experts would come to the front, by-and-by, who would double this girl's output without a doubt. They would do one hundred words a minute—my talking speed on the platform. That score has long ago been beaten.

At home I played with the toy, repeating and repeating "The Boy stood on the Burning Deck," until I could turn that boy's adventure out at the rate of twelve words a minute; then I resumed the pen, for business, and only worked the machine to astonish inquiring visitors. They carried off many reams of the boy and his burning deck.

By-and-by I hired a young woman, and did my first dictating. . . . I remember the first letter I dictated. It was to Edward Bok, who was a boy then. . . . He was accumulating autographs, and . . . wanted a whole autograph *letter*. I furnished it—in type-machine capitals, *signature and all.* . . . I said writing was my *trade,* my bread-and-butter; I said it was not fair to ask a man to give away samples of his trade; would he ask the blacksmith for a horseshoe? would he ask the doctor for a corpse?

Now I come to an important matter—as I regard it. In the year '74 the young woman copied a considerable part of a book of mine *on the machine*. In a previous chapter of this Autobiography I have claimed that I was the first person in the world that ever had a telephone in his house for practical purposes; I will now claim—until dispossessed—that I was the first person in the world to *apply the typemachine to literature*. That book must have been *The Adventures of Tom Sawyer*. . . .

Mark Twain's memory slipped—that first typewritten book was *Life on the Mississippi*.

Businessmen began by resisting the new machine. It was noisy, and typed letters seemed offensively impersonal. Many testy replies were dictated asserting that the writer was quite capable of reading longhand, and did not enjoy correspondence all in capital letters. In the big central offices of companies like McCormick, Deere, and Singer, secretaries (usually still male) continued to copy letters laboriously by hand. But in the end business office conservatism was overwhelmed by the pressure for efficiency created by the business office's own growth.

What was needed was a more efficient typing technique. Strangely, or naturally, it was supplied by Christopher Sholes. Bereft of material interest in the typewriter but aware of its problems, Sholes saw a blind Civil War veteran tapping his way along a Milwaukee street and it occurred to him that a blind person could learn to type by memorizing the keys through touch. The idea proved sound for sighted typists as well, and touch typing was born, bringing improved accuracy and the superior speeds Mark Twain had foreseen. To teach the new skill, business schools were founded.

Simultaneously Remington introduced an elegant solution to the problem of lower-case letters in its 1878 Model 2 through two inventions, the cylinder-shifting device of Lucien Stephen Crandall, and double type mounted on a single typebar, invented by Byron A. Brooks. A rival machine unimaginatively equipped with two complete banks of keys was destroyed by the competitive advantage of the Remington for touch typing.

The next development was the "visible typewriter," achieved by arranging the typebars to strike from the front rather than from below. The first widely distributed model was produced by Underwood in 1894, though Christopher Sholes is said to have made his last technical contribution to a similar model developed by his son.

Suffering from tuberculosis, and widowed in 1888, Sholes lived the last two years of his life with his daughter Lillian, who had often demonstrated the typewriter for her father. A gaunt old gentleman with white hair and swallowtail coat, he was long remembered by small boys to whom he liked to give candy.

To Lillian he remarked, "I do feel that I have done something for the women who have always had to work so hard. This will enable them more easily to earn a living." In one of his last typed letters he called the typewriter "a blessing to mankind, and especially to womankind," adding rather plaintively, "I builded wiser than I knew, and the world has the benefit of it."

24

Alexander Graham Bell Invents the Telephone

NO INVENTOR EVER APPEARED in a more propitious environment at a more timely moment than did Alexander Graham Bell when he arrived in Boston from Canada in the spring of 1871. At the same time that Boston was falling behind New York in industry, commerce, and population, the New England metropolis was finding a more distinctive role as America's chief center of intellectual activity—scientific-technological as well as literary-artistic. To ancient Harvard had been added new Boston University and, thanks in good part to the Morrill Act, Massachusetts Institute of Technology, all providing facilities in the physical sciences—laboratories, libraries, lectures. In addition, Boston's traditional navigational instrument industry had contributed to making the city a center for the manufacture of electrical instruments. Probably the leading shop in the country for making Morse telegraph sending and receiving instruments, fire alarms, batteries, bells, and school laboratory apparatus was that opened by Charles Williams, Jr., at 109 Court Street in the 1850s; by the 1870s it employed twenty-five workers and had two steam-powered lathes and a forge.

At the moment of his arrival, Bell was not particularly concerned with electricity, though he was no stranger to its possibilities. An immigrant of the highly educated John Roebling type, he was son and grandson of a pair of distinguished Edinburgh researchers into the mysteries of human speech. Grandfather Alexander Bell had taught corrective speech and written a classic text, *The Practical Elocutionist*. Father Alexander Melville Bell had invented a universal phonetic

LEFT Alexander Graham Bell in 1876, the year he patented the telephone. (American Telephone and Telegraph)

RIGHT Thomas A. Watson in 1874, the year he met Bell. (American Telephone and Telegraph)

alphabet which he called Visible Speech, a venture into acoustical science that he later as an afterthought realized might be used to help the deaf. Deafness was a common affliction; Alexander Melville Bell's own wife was deaf. Young Alexander Graham (the Graham was his own addition at the age of eleven, after a Canadian friend) crowned a formal education at the Royal High School in Edinburgh with a year's stay with his grandfather in London, where he read all the older man's books on acoustics. His father, taking him home in 1863, stopped off to visit Sir Charles Wheatstone, inventor of the magnetic-needle telegraph, who showed them a model of a curious device constructed by the eighteenth-century savant Baron de Kempelen for mechanical imitation of the human voice. Home in Edinburgh, Aleck enlisted his brother to help build a speaking machine of their own, and succeeded in making it cry "Mama!" so realistically that a neighbor came running to see "what can be the matter with the baby."

At sixteen, Aleck got a job as a student teacher in music and elocution at Weston House in Elgin, on the Scottish north coast, and presently enrolled for a year at Edinburgh University. During the holidays he joined his brothers in helping their father demonstrate Visible Speech. Linguists dictated to the elder Bell in any language or dialect they chose; he wrote the speech down in his phonetic alphabet, then summoned one of the boys from another room to read it off. Aleck once astonished and amused the audience by accurately reproducing the sound of a yawn.

More and more interested in his father's acoustical analysis, Aleck began experimenting with tuning forks to determine the pitch of vowels—an unwitting first step toward the telephone. A friend of his father's told him that German scientist Hermann von Helmholtz had conducted similar experiments and had also succeeded in synthetically producing vowel sounds. Helmholtz used a tuning-fork device reinforced by an electromagnet to make and break a current at regular intervals, causing the intermittent current thus produced to activate eight other electromagnets with magnetized tuning forks between their poles. Knowing that each vowel was made up not only of a composite of frequencies (pitches) but of a complex pattern of amplitudes (loudnesses), Helmholtz also devised a means of adjusting the loudness of each fork independently. The result was a composite sound that had an uncanny resemblance to a vowel.

Bell's father's friend offered to lend him Helmholtz's *Sensations of Tone,* but Bell was disappointed to find that the book was in German, which he could not read. As a result he was temporarily left with the stimulating misconception that Helmholtz had not only generated but had transmitted his vowel sounds. If one could find a way to transmit consonants, apparently one could transmit speech.

He conceived the idea of transmitting music by rigging up a piano with electromagnets under each wire on a circuit with tuning forks arranged as in Helmholtz's apparatus. Vibratory current from one of the tuning forks would produce magnetic impulses of that frequency in all the electromagnets, but only the string tuned to a particular fork would sound, by a phenomenon known as sympathetic vibration. Sympathetic vibration, or resonance, is vibration produced by an outside force vibrating at the same pitch, e.g., a guitar string that sounds when a note of the same pitch is sung, or a thin goblet that vibrates to a singer's voice.

From the idea of thus making a piano play at a distance, he moved to a concept with valuable practical possibilities, a "harmonic telegraph," or what came to be known as a frequency multiple telegraph. Several messages could be sent simultaneously over a single wire by transmitting them in different pitches, to each of which a single receiver would respond.

Before he could try out his idea and explore the mechanical problems involved in the multiple telegraph (which were considerably more complex than he imagined), the Bell family suffered a typical nineteenth-century tragedy. Both of Alexander's brothers died of tuberculosis, and there was some apprehension that he had also been infected. In the medical helplessness of the age, the family made the rather pathetic decision to move to Canada in the summer of 1870, settling near Brantford, Ontario.

By that time Alexander had embarked on a career as a teacher of the deaf. For several years his father had considered the possibility of using Visible Speech to aid the deaf, and in the spring of 1868 Alexander had experimented with it at a private school for deaf children in London, with almost magical success, accounted for in no small part by his own contagious enthusiasm. One eight-year-old girl went home for the summer holidays rehearsing the words, "I love you, Mama. I love you, Mama." Opening the lines of communication with the world for these isolated children became a lifelong vocation for Bell.

As a result of his father's description of Alexander's methods on a lecture tour, the young man was invited to Boston in April 1871, to initiate the Visible Speech system at the Boston School for Deaf Mutes, and the following March visited the Clarke School for the Deaf at Northampton. The president of Clarke was a prominent Bostonian named Gardiner Hubbard who had made a fortune out of the Boston-Cambridge street railway, the Cambridge water supply system, and the Cambridge Gas Light Company. Hubbard's concern for the education of the deaf derived from the fact that his daughter Mabel had suffered a permanent loss of hearing from scarlet fever at the age of five. Hubbard had become a fanatic of the "oral method"—speech and lip-reading, as opposed to sign language in teaching the deaf—and had won state support for the Clarke School by bringing Mabel before a legislative committee to show how well she spoke and lip-read.

Coincidentally, Hubbard also had an interest in telegraphy. By profession a patent lawyer, he had lobbied in Congress for years for the authorization of a private corporation (with himself as one of the incorporators), the United States Postal Telegraph Company, to break Western Union's monopoly. To provide service at lower rates, costs would be cut by improved technology. But in the first meeting of Hubbard and Bell, and through many subsequent meetings, the subject of the telegraph somehow failed to come up.

In the fall of 1872, Bell took a two-room apartment at 35 West Newton Street and opened his own private school for the deaf. At the same time he began experimenting with the idea that had occurred to him four years before, the multiple telegraph, probably spurred by reading in the Boston papers that Western Union had bought the "duplex telegraph" invented by Joseph B. Stearns of Boston. The Stearns duplex, on an entirely different principle from Bell's concept, sent two messages in opposite directions simultaneously over the main telegraph line. Bell began to tinker with wires, electromagnets, batteries, and tuning forks, spending the better part of his spare time in the next year in an effort to duplicate Helmholtz's synthetic vowel device.

The following year (1873) he became professor of "Vocal Physiology and Oratory" at Boston University, moving to Salem, where he received free room and board in return for instructing six-year-old George Sanders, deaf since birth, who had become his pupil the year before. Among Bell's new private pupils was Gardiner Hubbard's daughter Mabel, now fifteen, back from two years' schooling in Germany. Mabel's first impression of the tall, thin young man with the black side-whiskers, big nose, and crest of black hair was unfavorable. "I did not like him," she recalled later. His dress was old-fashioned and careless, and on the whole, "to one accustomed to the dainty neatness of Harvard students, he seemed hardly a gentleman." But as a teacher he was irresistible—"so quick, so enthusiastic, so compelling, I had whether I would or no to follow all he said and tax my brains to respond as he desired."

Bell's determination to build a multiple telegraph was strengthened by the electrical science he absorbed from the Boston atmosphere. One afternoon in the fall of 1873 in the public library he came across an English translation (1872) of a recent book by a French scientist named Jean-Baptiste Alexandre Baile, *The Wonders of Electricity,* in which he read an arresting sentence: "Some years hence, for all we know, we may be able to transmit the vocal message itself with the very inflection, tone and accent of the speaker." It was the first Bell knew, except for his misconception about Helmholtz's vowels, that anyone was thinking seriously about transmitting speech. In actuality, at least three men, one in Europe and two in America, had conducted experiments. One of the Americans was a professor at M.I.T., Edward Pickering, who in 1870 had constructed a "tin-box receiver," with a vibrating tuning fork, as in the Helmholtz device, making and breaking a battery-powered circuit that passed through an electromagnet fixed near the tin-plate bottom of an open box, causing the tin plate to vibrate to the same pitch as the tuning fork.

The European, a German scientist named Philipp Reis, had coined the word "telephone" for an earlier (1861) apparatus which went a step further than Pickering's, picking up pitches from outside and transmitting them via a membrane diaphragm, rather than simply transmitting its own tuning-fork sounds. Reis's "telephone" could not transmit speech because, like Pickering's, it operated by making and breaking a circuit, producing an intermittent current that reproduced variations in pitch, not in amplitude, or loudness; but his device had drawn considerable interest in the European scientific community. Neither Reis nor Pickering was an inventor, however, and neither of them patented his apparatus.

The other American was an obscure Ohio-born electrician who turned out to be Bell's chief rival for the honor of inventing the telephone. Eleven years older than Bell, Elisha Gray was an ambitious son of the American working class who had put himself through high school and, by age thirty-one, Oberlin College, in preparation for a career as an inventor. Conceiving the idea of transmitting music over telegraph wires, Gray had in the winter of 1866–67 built an intermittent-current device that could generate and transmit sounds, but again pitch only, not amplitude (and like Pickering's and unlike Reis's, it could not pick up outside sounds). But other electrical inventions distracted him from his prototelephone experimentation, and he organized a predecessor of the Western Electric Company, a firm destined to have a fabulous future.

In addition to the suggestion that speech could be transmitted, the Baile book provided Bell with a suggestion for a new device, an "acoustic telegraph," in which a sound vibrated a metal plate, making and breaking an electric current, activating an electromagnet that caused another metal plate to vibrate with the same pitch—a kind of combination of Reis's telephone and Pickering's "tin-box receiver." Baile also gave Bell an idea for a variation on Helmholtz: for the hard-to-adjust tuning fork, substituting steel strips or "reeds" that could easily be altered in length and so changed in pitch.

Bell tinkered with Baile's idea and presently was surprised to notice that when he pressed an ear against a tuned receiver reed while transmitter reeds of different pitches were sounding, he heard not merely the pitch of the receiver but a faint compound sound. The pressure of his ear, damping the reed's natural vibration, caused it to respond to whatever frequencies touched it, like the metal plate in Pickering's "tin-box" and the membrane in Reis's telephone. Bell made note of the phenomenon, although at the moment it was exactly the effect he did *not* want—he wanted his receiver to respond only to its own frequency. The significance of what was in reality the first faint cry of the telephone eluded him. In trying to work out the problems of the telegraph, however, he hit on another

LEFT Alexander Graham Bell with Helen Keller. (American Telephone and Telegraph)

RIGHT Elisha Gray, described by his partner as "of all the men who didn't invent the telephone . . . the nearest." (Smithsonian Photograph No. 42,469)

telephone concept, that of using the steel-reed and electromagnet combination as transmitter as well as receiver.

The new arrangement led him to a crucial insight, one that set his telephone ideas apart from those of his predecessors, whose devices were no more than elaborations of the telegraph. In basic terms, the telegraph, by closing and opening a Morse key, or by drawing type past a contact, or by whatever other means, activated and deactivated an electromagnet at a distance, ringing a bell (as in Joseph Henry's apparatus), making a clacking noise, or operating a recording device. It was but a step from the telegraph to an arrangement in which the Morse sender and receiver were replaced by reeds, tuning forks, or diaphragms, the vibrations of the sending device producing an intermittent current which made the receiver vibrate with the same frequency.

In contrast, Bell's new idea was a revolutionary concept: If he plucked the magnetized reed of the transmitter or blew on it to make it vibrate, it would induce a current in the coil of its electromagnet—not an intermittent current, such as those of Reis, Pickering, and Gray, and such as those with which he himself had been experimenting—but a current that was continuous and fluctuating. Such an "undulatory" current would, he speculated, reproduce in electricity the shape of the sound waves that caused it. Sent through the coil of a receiver reed, it would make the reed vibrate not simply in the same pitch, but in exactly the .

317

same way, reproducing variations in loudness as well as pitch. He was a thought away from the telephone, but without trying his idea out he decided that a magnetized reed's vibration could not generate a current strong enough to travel over a wire and make another reed vibrate audibly.

That spring (1874) he was intrigued by some new acoustic toys M.I.T. researchers were playing with—the "phonautograph" and the "manometric flame." The first produced tracings on a sheet of smoked glass when someone spoke or sang into a cone with a membrane diaphragm—providing Bell with another precious insight: the resultant of all the vibrations of the voice could be projected through a single point, such as the stylus of the phonautograph. The second used a similar diaphragm's vibrations to vary pressure in a gas pipe, causing the flame to produce a picture of the sound waves. Bell thought of both devices as possible aids in teaching the deaf—still his profession and chief interest.

Meantime Elisha Gray made a discovery of his own. A young nephew used one of his transmitters to extract a sound from the zinc lining of a bathtub, i.e., using the tub as a receiver, and Gray seized on the idea to build a metal-diaphragm receiver like Pickering's tin box—the "wash-basin receiver," he called it. In May he built a transmitter with eight keys of different pitches to sound a tune on the metal diaphragm. Gray was close to the telephone receiver, closer than Bell, each of whose receivers reacted to a single frequency, because that was what was wanted in a multiple telegraph. But Gray's transmitter, like Pickering's, did not capture sounds, it merely generated them, and while his apparatus could transmit and receive musical sounds, even chords and simple tunes, it was powerless to transmit speech because it reproduced only pitch, not the complex variations in loudness that make up speech.

That spring Gray demonstrated his invention to Western Union officials in New York and to Joseph Henry at the Smithsonian. In July (1874) the *New York Times* devoted an article to his "music by telegraph," reporting that with this device, which Gray called a "telephone," "anyone at the receiving end can distinctly hear . . . the tune or air which is being played 500 or 1000 miles away." The article quoted a Western Union spokesman as predicting that "in time the operators will transmit the sound of their own voice over the wires," and reported that Gray had applied for patents in the United States and Europe. Bell did not see the *Times* or hear of the article, or of another in the *Hartford Courant* reporting the convention of the American Association for the Advancement of Science, which described Gray's musical telegraph "called a 'telephone'; Mr. Gray hopes one day to be able to transmit the sound of the human voice also by telegraph."

Home for a visit in Brantford, Ontario, and weighing his idea of a multiple telegraph transmitter with air-vibrated magnetized reeds that would induce an undulating rather than an intermittent current, Bell wondered if mere sound waves might not after all be strong enough to generate an appreciable current. He thought of another passage in the Baile book that had caught his attention, a description of a device that worked by resonance: "A series of vibrating plates . . . each of which vibrates when struck by a particular sound, and sends off electricity to create at the end of the line the same vibrations in a corresponding plate, or in other words, to produce the same sound."

Suddenly the elements fell into place, and he envisioned the fundamental principle of the telephone. If one spoke or sang into Baile's "series of [tuned] vibrating plates" as Bell himself had done into the strings of a piano, the plates or reeds would, if there were enough gradation of pitches among them, echo the speech. If instead of Baile's battery-powered intermittent currents, each vibrating polarized reed induced a continuous undulating current, then amplitude (loudness) as well as pitch would be properly proportioned for each. The resultant of all the currents could be transmitted through a single point, like the phonautograph stylus; at the other end of the line, an electromagnet would transform the resultant current into undulations of magnetic force, which, acting on another array of tuned reeds, would reproduce the original sound.

Bell sketched such a device, but did not try to build it. Still committed to the multiple telegraph, he turned back to his work on battery-powered intermittent currents. But in a letter of November 23, 1874, he consulted Moses Farmer, one of Boston's leading experts in electrical engineering, about his "harp apparatus." Farmer assured him of its theoretical soundness.

By now Bell had become a frequent caller at the Hubbards' house in Cambridge. One afternoon he asked Gardiner Hubbard if he knew that a piano string would repeat a note sung into it. Demonstrating the trick, he remarked that a tuned instrument would also respond to a telegraphic impulse having the same frequency, and therefore, on principle at least, several messages could be sent together over a single wire. To Bell's astonishment, Hubbard could hardly contain his excitement.

Embroiled for almost a decade in his struggle against the Western Union monopoly, Hubbard was well aware that the multiple telegraph was the most eagerly sought technical innovation on the horizon. Western Union had already acquired the Stearns duplex telegraph in 1872, and this year (1874) acquired rights to Edison's new quadruplex. Now Bell asserted the possibility of a telegraph capable of carrying five or six more messages than Edison's. If Bell could make the idea work, Hubbard was sure there were several fortunes in it.

Bell returned home to Salem and told his pupil's father, Thomas Sanders, about his conversation with Hubbard. Sanders, who already knew about Bell's multiple telegraph, intimated suspicions of Hubbard's integrity, and urged Bell to patent the invention. Sanders offered to provide money to build a model and pay legal costs in return for a half-share. The upshot was a three-way partnership, the two promoters and Bell.

At the very moment of the agreement, Bell heard for the first time the name of Elisha Gray. Dr. Clarence Blake, a Boston ear specialist with whom Bell had done acoustical work, told him that Gray was experimenting with "telegraphing vocal sounds." Blake's information was incorrect, or rather premature, but it spurred Bell to heightened activity.

Bell's father had advised him to sell his plans outright to Sanders and Hubbard and go back to teaching—"Take what you can get at once." The young man decided against that, but also resisted Hubbard's importunate demands that he concentrate all his energies on the telegraph, abandoning not only his lectures and teaching but the telephone, in which Hubbard took slight interest.

On November 14, 1874, after working "day and night," Bell sent off caveat papers on his multiple telegraph. That same day he read in a Boston paper a reprint of the *New York Times* article of the previous July about Gray's "musical telegraph." He would have been even more concerned if he had realized that Gray's reasoning had followed the same path as his own, and that some months earlier Gray had progressed from the idea of transmitting music to harmonic multiple telegraphy. Hubbard now wrote from Washington that Gray had applied in August for a patent on his telegraph improvements. The partners' patent lawyer advised Bell to withdraw his multiple telegraph caveat, the filing of which might alert Gray to his progress. Bell complied.

Under the building pressure, Bell consented to get expert help on the mechanical work, at which he had only fair aptitude. First he hired one of Moses Farmer's assistants; then, in January 1875, a twenty-year-old electrical worker from Charles Williams's shop named Thomas A. Watson. Son of a Salem livery stable foreman, Watson was much impressed by Bell's crisp diction, his "punctilious courtesy to every one," and his table manners—the fact that he used a fork instead of a knife to convey food to his mouth. The immigrant intellectual and working-class native congenially began a laborious struggle, the effort to achieve transmitter pitches that would not interfere with each other.

In February 1875, feeling that the multiple telegraph was at last patentable, Bell went to Washington. In spite of his longstanding feud with Western Union, Hubbard had arranged for William Orton, president of the company, to call at Hubbard's Washington house (long maintained for his lobbying purposes) for a demonstration of the multiple telegraph. Orton reacted favorably, and a few days later, on February 27, 1875, Bell, Sanders, and Hubbard wrote down their agreement to share equally in Bell's telegraphic inventions, including "any further improvements he may make in perfecting said inventions." They had no inkling that they were founding the largest single business enterprise in history.

In Washington (March 1 and 2) Bell seized the opportunity of visiting the venerable Joseph Henry at the Smithsonian to discuss both the multiple telegraph and the telephone. Henry thought Bell's "harp apparatus" for transmitting speech "the germ of a great idea," but expressed some doubt about a newer inspiration, a membrane diaphragm transmitter. The old scientist showed his visitor a Reis membrane transmitter, the first Bell had seen.

In the light of the frustrating problems involved, Bell finally asked whether he would not be best advised simply to publish his ideas and let others work them out. Henry, doubtless remembering his experience with Morse, told him to perfect the invention himself. Bell protested that he lacked the necessary knowledge. Henry answered firmly, "Get it!"

Later that month, Bell received an unexpected setback in New York, whither he had gone to conduct a trial of his multiple telegraph on Western Union lines. Though the trial "went like clockwork," William Orton bluntly told him that his apparatus was crude compared to Elisha Gray's. Objectively considered, the two devices were very similar, except that Bell's made no demand on the operator to distinguish pitches and separate out messages. Orton finally added with robber-baron candor, "Western Union will never take up a scheme which will benefit Mr. Hubbard." Bell threatened to take his instruments to the rival Atlantic and Pacific Telegraph Company, and Orton backed down a little, declaring that if Bell perfected the device, Western Union would buy it.

When Bell returned to Boston, Hubbard naturally pressed him to stick to the multiple telegraph, but Bell could not put his heart into it. Neither Bell nor Hubbard had any idea that the multiple telegraph, in the form of the modern frequency multiplex telegraph (based on Bell's principle), was still many years and much technological development (e.g., vacuum tube circuitry) away from realization. Bell had simply lost his zest for the multiple telegraph, or rather had transferred it undiminished to the intriguing, elusive telephone.

Nevertheless Bell returned that summer to the stifling loft of the Williams shop where he and Tom Watson set up a three-station telegraph and tuned their reeds, seeking frequencies that would not interfere with each other. Bell supervised the transmitters and one receiver station, while Watson, in the next room, manned a second set of receivers. One of Watson's receiver reeds stuck to its electromagnet, and work halted while Watson disconnected the battery-powered transmitters and plucked the reed free. Bell's eye wandered to one of the receivers in his own station, and he was startled to see it vibrate strongly "at the very time I supposed Mr. Watson to be plucking the reed of his instrument. . . ." He called to Watson to repeat the action, and again the receiver reed vibrated. Just what he had speculated on the previous year and had dismissed as impossible was happening before his eyes. With only the strength of residual magnetism, the plucked reed induced a current strong enough to travel over the wire and excite the receiver's electromagnet, making it vibrate. While commanding Watson to keep plucking the reed, Bell held the variously tuned receiver reeds against his ear, one after the other. As two years before when he first experimented with Baile's ideas, the pressure of his ear damped the reeds, causing them to respond to frequencies other than their own natural vibrations. When Watson plucked, Bell heard a musical tone of the pitch of Watson's reed, regardless of the pitch of the reed he held to his ear. More exciting yet, the sound was equivalent not only in pitch but in loudness. The current generated was the undulatory one he had postulated the year before, but had failed to pursue experimentally. Traveling to the electromagnets in the next room, it had made their reeds vibrate exactly as had the reed that created it. Scarcely ready to believe what he heard, Bell repeated the experiment over and over, until no possible doubt remained that the instrumentation in his hands "could be practically utilized" not only for multiple telegraphy, the object of the experiments, but "speech transmission."

Forgetting all about multiple telegraphy, Bell sketched a diaphragm transmitter for Watson to make. The first model had too light a membrane ("gold-beater's skin," made of ox-intestine lining) and too heavy a steel reed; the reed tore loose from the membrane and ruptured it. An unimportant setback; a month later, with a heavier membrane and lighter reed, Bell sang into the transmitter, and Watson heard the tune on the receiver. So far, so good, but they had still

Bell's vibrating reed receiver. (Smithsonian Photograph No. 59,565)

done no more than Reis had with his intermittent-current, make-and-break action. The intricacy of speech, with its two components of pitch and loudness, was another story entirely. Sung into such a device as Reis's, a tune might be heard clearly but the words remain unintelligible. But when Watson built a diaphragm receiver much like the transmitter, Bell both sang and declaimed into the transmitter, and Watson ran up the stairs to the Williams's attic. "I could hear your voice plainly, I could almost make out what you said." The Williams shop was noisy; four years later Bell tried the same equipment out in a quieter place, and was able to carry on a conversation.

Bell at once informed Gardiner Hubbard, but Hubbard, though impressed, was distracted by a new telegraph idea Bell had hit upon shortly before, an "autograph telegraph" with styluses that would trace closely spaced parallel lines on a sheet of paper, producing a fine grid that could transmit a drawing or a message in its original handwriting.

As for the telephone, even if it worked, Hubbard doubted its commercial value. His attitude was a factor in what followed, but far more important was his daughter Mabel. Inconceivably, Bell at this point abandoned his experiments.

The story was a perfect movie script (though the movie made about it in the 1940s somehow avoided the real, wonderfully romantic story in favor of a colorless fiction): The brilliant, sensitive, impulsive young man had fallen so desperately in love with deaf, pretty, self-possessed Mabel Hubbard that he could think of nothing else. He confided his feelings to the senior Hubbards, who pointed out that Mabel was only seventeen. He followed her to Nantucket, where she was vacationing, but was not allowed to see her. From the hotel he wrote an impassioned letter: "Tell me frankly all that there is in me that you dislike and that I can alter. . . . I wish to amend my life for you." She wrote back primly: ". . . You have both my respect and esteem. I shall be glad to see you in Cambridge and become better acquainted. . . . Gratefully your friend, Mabel G. Hubbard." When she came home she told him she did not love him but on the other hand did not actively dislike him.

With this encouragement Bell went off to Brantford to recuperate from the emotional crisis and write up his patent specifications on the telephone for the United States Patent Office. While there he casually commissioned a neighbor and friend of the senior Bells, George Brown, owner of the *Toronto Globe*, to see about a British patent for the telephone. Back in Boston in October (1875), Bell distractedly resumed his teaching at Boston University, the patent specifications for the telephone still incomplete, rival Elisha Gray working away.

Hubbard grew vehement. Bell should abandon his Visible Speech and his teaching and get back, not to the telephone, but to "telegraph matters." He was in danger, Hubbard told him, of accomplishing "nothing of value to anyone." In November Hubbard presented Bell with an ultimatum; he must choose between teaching and Visible Speech on the one hand and telegraphy and Mabel on the other. Bell grew impassioned; Visible Speech was his life work, he was needed, and he refused to give up helping deaf children to communicate, at least until he had trained others to take his place. If Mabel loved him, she would marry him anyway.

With the two grown men furiously stalemated, teen-age Mabel intervened. On Thanksgiving Day 1875, her eighteenth birthday, she told Bell that she loved him better than anyone except her mother, and if that satisfied him, they could become engaged.

Hubbard groaned, but overjoyed Bell was at last able to return to the telephone patent specifications. To his description of the reed-electromagnet telephone, he added, almost as an afterthought, a completely new idea, that of producing his undulatory current by varying the resistance in an electric circuit. This proved to be the principle on which the telephone was eventually based, and his inclusion of it in the patent was of critical importance. Although Bell had tinkered with variable resistance in building a device to prevent sparking, he had not actually used it as a means of transmission, sticking to his magnetized reeds and electromagnets to produce the undulatory current.

The specifications were completed in mid-January 1876. Bell sent them off to Hubbard in Washington, who agreed to help with the patent. Bell instructed him not to file until he heard from his Brantford friend George Brown, who had exacted a promise to be allowed to make his application first lest a prior United States patent prejudice British rights. Hubbard replied that Elisha Gray had arrived in Washington and was filing new patent applications; they must lose no time.

As usual only one step behind Bell, Gray had worked along a similar path to similar conclusions. During the winter of 1874–75, experimenting with his washbasin receiver, which reproduced electrically generated sounds, Gray had speculated that if he could find a way to pick up speech and transmit it electrically, such a diaphragm receiver could also reproduce it. A tin-can toy telephone that transmitted sound gave him another insight. At first glance it may seem surprising that the tin-can telephone antedates the real telephone, but it had long been known that the vibrations of a taut string, or a length of metal, as in a ship's speaking tube, can carry sound. Gray's discovery from the toy telephone was that the resultant of vibrations caused by sounds at a single point on a diaphragm could be reproduced at a single point on another diaphragm, recreating the original sounds. Instead of using Bell's reeds and electromagnets, he hit upon Bell's important secondary idea, variable resistance. He proposed to build (but had not yet built) a transmitter with a diaphragm that had one lead in the form of a metal rod extending from its center into a vessel of water. Just below the rod was a sec-

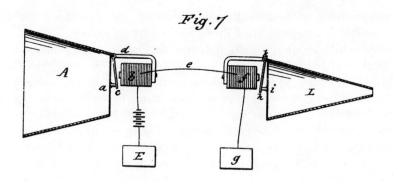

Fig. 7

Diagram of telephone from Bell's March 1876 patent, the basic telephone patent (No. 174,465). Sounds uttered into cone *A* are converged by the cone upon membrane *a,* causing it to vibrate. Armature (reed) *c,* loosely attached by one leg to the membrane, also vibrates, creating electrical undulations in the circuit *E* (battery) *b* (electromagnet) *e* (wire) *f* (electromagnet) *g* (battery). The undulatory current passing through electromagnet *f* causes its armature *h* to copy the motion of armature *c,* and membrane *i* to copy that of membrane *a,* and a sound similar to that uttered into *A* is heard from cone *L.* (Smithsonian Photograph No. 20,944)

ond lead. The vibrations of the diaphragm made the rod approach and recede from the second lead, varying the resistance and therefore the current in proportion to the vibrations of the voice. Like Bell's reed-electromagnet telephone, Gray's apparatus would produce an "undulatory current," although Gray did not so postulate in his caveat.

The first two weeks of February passed in mounting tension with no word from George Brown about the English patents. On February 14 Hubbard wisely went ahead and filed anyway—only hours before Gray filed his caveat. The closeness of the race, due mainly to Bell's six months' abandonment of the telephone for Mabel, helped no little to lay the foundation for one of the most extensive patent litigations in the history of technology, which left behind a long-smoldering controversy over the priorities and relative contributions of the two inventors.

Five days later Patent Examiner Zenas Wilber handed Bell's Washington lawyers a "notice of interference" with Gray's claim. The lawyers had no difficulty showing that they had won the race on February 14, but Wilber came back with a charge that Bell was interfering with an earlier caveat filed by Gray on January 27 for the use of a continuous current that underwent abrupt changes. The question was technical, and on February 26 Bell came to Washington to resolve it by explaining the difference between Gray's "pulsatory" current and his own "undulating" or gradually changing current, amending his application to clarify the terms. With natural curiosity, Bell then asked what had been at issue in Gray's February 14 caveat. A caveat, unlike a patent, is secret, in order to protect an inventor from plagiarism while he is perfecting his invention. In this case, since the interference charged against Bell had been dissolved, he presumed his query innocuous. Wilber obligingly, but indiscreetly, told him: liquid variable resistance—thereby warning Bell that Gray was on the track of this fundamental telephone principle.

On Bell's twenty-ninth birthday, March 3, 1876, the Patent Office examiners formally approved Bell's Patent No. 174,465, the basic telephone patent.

His invention legally secure (he thought), Bell returned to Boston to construct a model. After some random experiments, he decided to try the liquid variable-resistance transmitter. Gray had not built one, and Bell was determined to be first. In his new lodgings on Exeter Street, he and Watson set to work with an apparatus that consisted of a dish of water, one lead from a battery draped over the edge into the water, the other connected to the handle of a tuning fork. When he vibrated the arms of the fork and partially immersed them at an angle, he heard a "faint sound" from the reed receiver. Adding acid to the water, he increased its conductivity, and the sound became "much louder." The two young men then set up a horizontal membrane diaphragm from the center of which a needle dipped its tip into a dish of water, a stationary lead hanging at the side of the dish, variations in area of contact of the needle with the water causing variations in resistance. That afternoon Bell sang into a hole at the top of a box with the diaphragm at its bottom. The tune came through on the reed receiver, and when Watson talked into the box, Bell could hear "a confused muttering sound like speech, but could not make out the sense."

On the morning of Friday, March 10, 1876, Bell had Watson make a similar device, substituting for the box a chamber with a speaking-tube mouthpiece. That afternoon in Bell's Exeter Place rooms, Watson waited in the bedroom with the reed receiver pressed against his ear; in the laboratory at the end of the entry hall, with two intervening doors closed, Bell bent over the transmitter. In his laboratory notebook two days later, he wrote:

"I then shouted into M [the mouthpiece] the following sentence: 'Mr. Watson—Come here—I want to see you.' To my delight he came and declared that he had heard and understood what I said. I asked him to repeat the words. He answered, 'You said— "Mr. Watson—come here—I want to see you." ' We then changed places and I listened at S [the receiver] while Mr. Watson read a few passages from a book. . . . The effect was loud but indistinct and muffled. . . . I made out 'to' and 'out' and 'further'; and finally the sentence 'Mr. Bell, do you understand what I say? Do—you—un—der—stand—what—I—say' came quite clearly and intelligibly. No sound was audible when the armature [reed] S was removed [in other words, the sound was transmitted electrically, not mechanically, as in the tin-can telephone]."

In his autobiography published fifty years later, Watson described Bell as using the famous "Mr. Watson, come here" to call for help after spilling acid on his clothes, but Watson evidently confused the occasion with another, creating a long-lived myth.

Excited and confident, the two young men now narrowed and intensified their efforts, seeking an optimum receiver and transmitter arrangement. Bell devised a mouthpiece that flared like a funnel, and at the beginning of April tried a mixture of graphite from a lead pencil in a cup of mercury in place of the acidulated water, a step in the direction of the final form of the telephone, as it emerged two years later in Edison's carbon-button transmitter: a pressure-sensitive solid conductor. Lack of time and money, and Hubbard's resumption of nagging about the autograph telegraph, kept him from exploring further, and he returned to the tested, and easier to control, electromagnetic transmitter, which remained the telephone form for the next two years. Bell now devised a small flat-coiled clock spring as the transmitter reed. One evening at Hubbard's house, with this new transmitter, they succeeded in sending several sentences "perfectly."

In the course of the spring Bell went on to invent another form of receiver, which came to be known as the "Centennial iron-box receiver," a hollow iron cylinder closed at one end, with an iron rod inside wrapped in a coil of insulated wire. A current through the wire turned the device into an electromagnet, the rim of the open end of the cylinder constituting one pole, the free end of the rod the other. When a sheet-iron lid was fastened to the open end, and the rod adjusted so that it was close but not touching, the lid acted as a diaphragm, responding to the electromagnetic fluctuations induced by the undulatory current.

On May 10, Bell gave a lecture and demonstration at the Boston Athenaeum for the American Academy of Arts and Sciences. That day the Centennial Exposition opened in Philadelphia. Gardiner Hubbard, on the committee for the Massachusetts education and science exhibit, arranged for space for Bell to display his telephone and multiple telegraph, since the deadline for entering in the electrical section had passed. Meanwhile on May 24 Bell gave his first demonstration for the general public at M.I.T. with a clock-spring transmitter telephone in the auditorium communicating with another in a neighboring house.

On June 14, picturesque Emperor Pedro II of Brazil visited Boston and called on Bell at the Boston School for the Deaf to observe the Visible Speech method. Dom Pedro was due back at the Centennial in a few days for the judging of the electrical entries, yet modest Bell never mentioned the telephone. Hubbard, already in Philadelphia, was soon importuning Bell by telegraph to get his exhibit ready. Sir William Thomson (later Lord Kelvin) and other experts were arriving to act as judges, and Elisha Gray had his exhibit all set up.

Bell protested that he had exam papers to grade, but Mabel firmly intervened and got him and his apparatus aboard the train. Once in Philadelphia he began to enjoy himself. The exhibition was "prodigious and so wonderful that it absolutely staggers one," he wrote Mabel. He was innocently thrilled to meet Sir William and the other distinguished scientists.

The judges had chosen June 25, a Sunday—when Philadelphia's blue laws closed the Centennial to the general public—to judge the exhibits that depended on sound. Dom Pedro, his empress, and his retinue drove up to the Main Building in open carriages as the electrical judges strolled over from their hotel. Bell

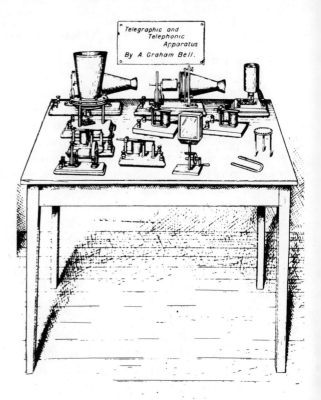

Bell's exhibit at the Philadelphia Centennial. (American Telephone and Telegraph)

joined the party at Elisha Gray's exhibit, under the aegis of Western Union, near one of the main aisles. Listening to Gray's lecture, he thought the Ohioan's demonstration of multiple telegraphy a failure, but the others seemed impressed by the novel transmission of musical tones. As the presentation ended, Dom Pedro recognized Bell and came over to shake hands. According to Bell's later account, which doubtless owed something to his enjoyment of the dramatic, the judges were ready to call it quits—the day was stifling—but Dom Pedro insisted on everyone trudging to the end of the vast Main Building and up a flight of stairs to the Massachusetts education exhibit at the south end of the East Gallery. Here Bell had set up on a small table his multiple telegraph, a manometric flame to show an undulating current in visible form, and, finally, the "Centennial iron-box receiver."

Wires ran along the railing of the gallery to Bell's transmitters a hundred yards away at the northeast corner: a liquid variable-resistance transmitter, and two electromagnetic transmitters. Bell explained the principles of his harmonic telegraph, and Dom Pedro and Sir William successfully transmitted signals both singly and simultaneously. "I then explained the 'Undulatory Theory' and offered to test the transmission of the human voice," Bell later wrote his parents. He withdrew to the end of the gallery and began singing into one of the membrane telephones. Sir William sitting at the table heard the song faintly in the iron-box receiver pressed against his ear, and then, far away but with startling distinctness, the words, "Do you understand what I say?" He clapped the cylinder to his ear again. "Yes! Do you understand what I say!" Sir William shouted. "Where is Mr.

Bell? I must see Mr. Bell!" He rushed to the gallery where Bell was still shouting, "Do you understand what I say?" The emperor in turn pressed his ear to the receiver, cried out, "I hear, I hear!" and repeated the words, "To be or not to be," and presently Bell, still declaiming Hamlet's soliloquy, heard feet pounding down the gallery and saw portly Dom Pedro trotting toward him "at a very un-emperor-like gait," followed by half the crowd. The other half was jostling for a chance to hear at the receiver end, among them Elisha Gray, who later testified, "I listened intently for some moments, hearing a very faint, ghostly, ringing sort of a sound; but finally I thought I caught the words, 'Aye, there's the rub.' I turned to the audience, repeating these words, and they cheered."

That afternoon Elisha Gray called on Bell in his hotel room. The two inventors had a long friendly talk about the multiple telegraph—the issue in dispute at the moment rather than the telephone. The litigation that developed later was painful to Bell and probably to Gray, too. The powerful Western Union Telegraph Company sought to use Gray's and other inventions and claims as a means of getting around Bell's patent rights and operating its own telephone companies. The infant Bell Company sued and throughout the interminable courtroom battles that followed, Bell was invariably vindicated on the basis of the originality of the application of his undulatory current principle.

Gray went on inventing, taking out some seventy patents in all and earning large sums of money—more, in fact, than Bell ever got from the telephone. When the Ohioan died in 1901 while experimenting with underwater signaling to vessels at sea, a friend and partner neatly summarized his telephone research: "Of all the men who didn't invent the telephone, Gray was the nearest."

From a historical point of view, Gray's chief interest lies in the fact that even had Bell not succeeded, the telephone would have been invented in America. That the dawning electrical age was off to an American start was a presage of the future of technology's new marriage with science. Britain and continental Europe were scarcely finished as technological innovators, in electricity-electronics any more than in other fields. Yet with the telephone America seemed to become the technological *primus inter pares.*

In at least a sense, Bell's Centennial triumph was the climax of his life. Further improvements resulted in a second basic patent in early 1877. A few months later the first regular telephone line was installed, fittingly enough, to connect Charles Williams's Boston shop with his home in Somerville. The Bell Telephone Company was founded July 9, and two days later Bell and Mabel Hubbard were married.

Soon after, in 1881, Bell virtually severed his connection with the company, and for the remaining forty-one years of his life (he died in 1922) experienced the pleasure of doing whatever he wanted, which, in Bell's case, consisted of an astonishing variety of zestful intellectual hobbies. There were a succession of inspired experiments, most of which he left to others to complete: a wireless telephone operated by light waves, which he called the "photophone"; heavier-than-air flight; the tetrahedral (triangular pyramid) construction component, anticipating the "space frame" system; hydrofoils (one of Bell's did 70 miles per hour in 1919); an artificial respiration "vacuum jacket" that was the forerunner of the iron lung; an electrical surgical probe invented in an attempt to locate the assassin's bullet lodged in President Garfield's body, and later universally used until the development of the X ray; an "audiometer" for measuring acuity of hearing. His interest in the deaf never flagged. He campaigned for the oral method of teaching and for public day schools, helping many victims personally, and finding his most celebrated protégée in the gifted Helen Keller. Work with the deaf led to studies of heredity in deafness, and the use of census returns in statistical work to a hand in shaping United States census policy. At his Cape Breton, Nova Scotia, summer home, he studied heredity by raising sheep. Through Gilbert Grosvenor, whom he persuaded in 1899 to become editor of the National Geographic Society's periodical (the following year Grosvenor married the Bells' daughter Elsie), he helped build a modest publication into a significant mass-subscription educational magazine. With Mabel he sponsored the Montessori Method of education and enthusiastically supported women's suffrage.

In his later years Bell retold the story of the invention of the telephone a thousand times in interviews, lectures, and writing, and never ceased to enjoy it. To the stately and imposing middle-aged man with the patriarchal beard and increasing stoutness, long separated from his invention, the events of those exciting years seemed almost to have happened to someone else, a tall thin, intense, impetuous youth with jet-black hair and side whiskers. Once he ruefully observed to a reporter, "I have become so detached from it that I often wonder if I really did invent the telephone, or was it someone else I read about?"

25

Edison Invents the Industrial Research Laboratory

In 1847, THE SAME YEAR Alexander Graham Bell was born in Edinburgh, Thomas Alva Edison was born in Milan, Ohio. Edison's parents had arrived ten years earlier, his carpenter father Sam Edison fleeing Canada after taking part in the Mackenzie-Papineau insurrection of 1837. It was the second time that Edisons had taken refuge across the United States-Canada border, Sam's grandfather John Edison having been a New Jersey Tory who spied for General Howe and fled to Canada to escape a Yankee noose.

Tom Edison thus came honestly by his own quirky, thorny, maverick individualism, because in this last of seven children, four of whom survived to adulthood, Nancy Edison had hatched an odd chick indeed. Fragile in body, with a very large head, the child was hard to manage and harder to understand, full of curiosity, a born experimenter, feeding a friend Seidlitz powders (an effervescent laxative) to make him fly, sitting on eggs to hatch them, wiring the tails of two tomcats together and rubbing their fur to produce electricity, mixing explosive chemicals in the cellar, setting fire to his father's barn "just to see what it would do." Many of his experiments ended in disaster; some, like the burning of the barn, in a public thrashing (by his father). Investigating the sawmills, the warehouses, the village streets, he had one narrow escape after another, falling into a grain elevator and nearly smothering in wheat, half-drowning in the canal, getting butted by a ram while investigating a bee's nest. His father reflected later, "He did not share to any extent the sports of his neighborhood. He never knew a real boyhood like other boys."

Tom Edison was seven when the family moved to Port Huron, Michigan, quitting a declining Milan that had been bypassed by the new railways its canal capitalists had foolishly refused to let into town. In Port Huron, Sam Edison became a dealer in feed, grain, and lumber, and Tom had his first and only venture into formal schooling, lasting three months. Dreamy and intractable, he declined to answer the teacher's questions and drew on his slate instead of doing his assignments.

Diagnosis at long distance is suspect, but on the basis of what is known of Edison's school problems, and other evidence, modern medical science suggests that he may have suffered from dyslexia, a still-little-understood affliction that interferes with reading and writing, in which Edison had the company of Einstein, Woodrow Wilson, Nelson Rockefeller, and several million others. Both the boy and his mother were wounded when he overheard the teacher describe him to a school inspector as "addled," and declare that he was not worth keeping in school. Nancy Edison indignantly set to educating him herself, perhaps partly to save the school fee, American education being as yet neither free nor compulsory. Edison later accurately described his education in *Who's Who* as "Received some instruction from his mother." The Edison front porch was the schoolroom. A childhood friend recalled a summer day when "a few of us boys were playing in front of the house [Edison's father's recollection was apparently not wholly accurate], when a lady appeared on the porch, a nice, friendly looking one, plainly dressed and wearing a lace cap. . . . She called out in a pleasant voice: 'Thomas Alva, come in now for your lessons.' The boy obeyed without a word. . . ." Nancy exposed him to Shakespeare, Dickens, Gibbon, and Hume, and turned him, dyslexic or not, into a rapid and enthusiastic reader. An elementary treatise on science captivated him, and he began to squander his pocket money on chemicals and wire.

In 1859 the Grand Trunk Railway opened between Port Huron and Detroit. Tom, now twelve, got a job as a newsboy and candy butcher on the train that left Port Huron at 7 A.M. and reached Detroit at 10. Before the return trip, he had several midday hours, which he improved as one of the earliest members (card number 33) of the newly opened Detroit Public Library. He described his procedure: "I started with the first book on the bottom shelf and went through the lot, one by one." Among them were such ponderous masterpieces as Burton's *Anatomy of Melancholy* and Hugo's *Les Misérables,* and at fifteen he even made a heroic assault on Newton's *Principia,* but confessed later that it gave him "a distaste for mathematics from which I have never recovered." A book which made a favorable impression on him was Andrew Ure's *Arts, Manufactures and Mines,* which dispraised the "academical philosophers" like Newton, with their "barren syllogisms" and "equational theorems," and extolled the practical artisan-inventors like Newcomen, Watt, and Arkwright.

After his daily visit to the library, Edison ran to catch the train and return to Port Huron at 9:30 P.M. The train consisted of two passenger cars and a combination baggage and smoking car. In the latter the young entrepreneur kept his stock of newspapers and candy, and, in the course of time, his chemical laboratory, transferred from the home cellar. One day a lurch of the train ignited some phosphorus and set the car on fire. Conductor Alexander Stevenson ejected the labora-

Thomas A. Edison in 1861, at fourteen. (U.S. Department of the Interior, National Park Service, Edison National Historic Site)

tory from the train, and, according to an apocryphal story, boxed the experimenter's ears, causing his lifelong deafness. Edison himself attributed the handicap to an incident two years earlier when a trainman helped him scramble into a car with his arms full of newspapers by grabbing him by the ears: "I felt something snap inside my head, and the deafness started from that time and has progressed ever since." In reality, his deafness seems to have originated in childhood scarlatina, aggravated by the later injury.

It was not long before Edison had newsboys on two other trains, and branched out into the produce business, shipping fresh vegetables from Detroit to Port Huron, picking up butter at stations on the way to sell in Detroit, along with berries in season. He also bought a little secondhand printing press and once a week printed his own paper, the *Weekly Herald*, which he sold to passengers. The only edition that has survived, that of February 3, 1862, contains railway news items—a Haitian government agent who filed a fraudulent baggage claim, the birth of a child in the Detroit Grand Trunk station—along with notices of stagecoach connections, lost-and-found items, advertisements, a homily ("Reason Justice and Equity, never had weight enough on the face of the earth to govern the councils of men"), an international news item ("The thousandth birthday of the Empire of Russia will be celebrated at Novgorod in august"); a joke (" 'Let me collect myself,' as the man said when he was blown up by a powder mill"); and a list of wholesale food prices:

> Butter at 10 to 12 cents per lb.
> Eggs at 12 cents per dozen.
> Lard at 7 to 9 cents per lb.
> Dressed hogs at 3.00 to 3.25 per 100 lbs.

Mutton at 4 to 5 cents per lb.
Flour at 4.50 to 4.75 per 100 lbs.
Beans at 1.00 to 1.20 per bush. . . .

The *Weekly Herald* brought Edison a monthly profit of about $45, but he abandoned the project after a friend persuaded him to turn it into a gossip sheet, *Paul Pry,* and the subject of one of his stories threw him into the St. Clair River.

With the idea that he could sell more newspapers if he learned of news events in advance, Edison hung around the composing room of the *Detroit Free Press* to read the headlines while type was being set. A great opportunity came when dispatches arrived from the Battle of Shiloh. After hastily scanning the proofs, Edison ran to the station and, in return for some subscriptions, induced the telegraph operator to wire word of the battle ahead, to be chalked up on the bulletin boards in all the stations, promising details in the newspapers. The next problem was to get an extra supply of newspapers on credit—a thousand instead of his usual three hundred. Undiscouraged by the circulation manager's refusal, the boy appealed to editor Wilbur F. Storey, who gave his approval. At the first stop, where he usually sold two papers, a crowd was waiting on the platform; he sold thirty-five. At Mt. Clemens he raised his price from a nickel to ten cents a copy, selling about 150 to a "howling mob" that was waiting for him. By the time he had reached Port Huron the price was twenty-five cents and he had made "what was to me then an immense sum of money."

Through his railroad experience, the boy had become interested in telegraphy, and had rigged a line of stovepipe wire between his house and that of a friend a half-mile away, nailed to trees, with bottle-insulators. That summer of 1862, he turned from amateur to professional telegrapher. He was waiting on the Mt. Clemens platform while his train switched freight cars when he saw the stationmaster's little boy playing in the gravel ballast in the path of a shunted box car, and snatched the child to safety. As a reward, the stationmaster offered to teach him train telegraphy. Giving up his newsboy-candy-butcher job, the boy appeared in Mt. Clemens the first day with a set of telegraph instruments that he had made himself from bits of scrap in a Detroit gun shop. He spent five months boarding with the stationmaster and learning his trade, then applied for and got a job as night operator at the Port Huron station.

The Port Huron job was the beginning of a six-year career as one of the army of tramp telegraphers that traveled from city to city serving the ever-expanding empire of Western Union. In the spring of 1864 Edison moved on to Stratford Junction, Ontario, where he became a dispatcher and created his first invention—a clockwork mechanism that automatically sent his check-in signals during the night, allowing him to sleep. The device was a success until the main office replied to the signal and got no answer. Reprimanded, he continued to nap, but engaged a yardman to awaken him periodically. One night the yardman was late, and a head-on collision was narrowly averted on the single track line. The next day Edison resigned before he could be fired, or possibly even jailed, and slipped back into the United States to look for a job.

Moving restlessly from one city to another, Toledo, Fort Wayne, Indianapolis, Cincinnati, he became a skillful operator, able to send and receive at a rapid pace, though not yet at the dazzling speed of the virtuosos of the profession who "took press," i.e. news dispatches. He was inspired to a fresh invention. Each telegraph receiver was equipped with a register that recorded the messages in dots and dashes on a strip of paper; Edison built a second register that recorded from the first at a slower pace. He showed a fellow apprentice the device, and the two impressed the station manager by their apparent skill, not revealing that the register from which they were reading was moving more slowly than normal. But on the night of Lincoln's reelection in 1864, returns poured in for hours, and when the operator at the other end signed off, Edison and his friend had an hour and a half's work to catch up on. The newspapers complained, the second register was discovered, and Edison was ordered to dismantle it.

He was almost as difficult an employee as he had been a scholar—absentminded, balky, quarrelsome, self-absorbed, awkward, slovenly. His deafness and lack of social graces tended to isolate him from his colleagues. Milton Adams, a Cincinnati telegrapher, described him at eighteen as "decidedly unprepossessing in dress, and rather uncouth in manner. . . . His nose was very prominent, giving a Napoleonic look to his face. . . . The boys did not take to him cheerfully, and he was *lonesome*." But at nineteen he was an operator with "no superiors, and very few equals," who had developed a legible and uniform copperplate handwriting with which he could effortlessly "take press" with the best in the profession, winning several intercity contests. Off the job his time was spent on batteries and circuits. He was already experimenting with a "duplex" telegraph, to transmit two messages over a single wire. Most of his wages went for books and equipment. A fellow-operator described him as "strolling in [to] blandly ask some of us to lend him half a dollar with which to get his supper. When reminded that he had received half a month's salary that day, he would smile, and taking a brown, paper-covered parcel from under his arm, he would display a Ruhmkorff coil, an expensive set of helices, or something equally useless to the eyes of his comrades. . . ." If there was little money left for food, there was none for clothing, and one winter he went without an overcoat and "nearly froze."

From Cincinnati he went on to Memphis, Nashville, and then Louisville, where he defied the office manager's order that he cease experimenting, and one day spilled a carboy (large glass bottle used for corrosive liquids) of sulfuric acid, which seeped through the floor to the manager's room below and ate through his desk and carpet. Once more he was out of a job. Early in 1867 he joined two other telegraphers on a trip to New Orleans, intending to sail for Brazil, where the government was offering high salaries to telegraphers; but in New Orleans he abandoned the project, on the advice of a Brazilian. His friends went on as far as Vera Cruz, where they died of yellow fever.

At twenty-one, after visiting Port Huron, Edison boarded a Grand Trunk train for Boston, with the promise of a Western Union job with his Memphis friend, Milton Adams. He arrived looking his seediest, in ill-fitting and none-too-clean clothes, a battered broad-brimmed hat, down-at-heels shoes. He was well aware of the eccentricity of his own dress: "My peculiar appearance caused much mirth," he candidly recorded. The other operators planned a hazing, arranging to have his first message sent by one of the fastest men on the New York line. The New York man began slowly, gradually increasing to top speed; Edison effortlessly kept pace, and finally opened the key to advise the operator, "Young man, change off and send with your other foot."

In Boston, Edison browsed through the secondhand bookshops along Cornhill Street. His prize find was a two-volume edition of Faraday's *Experimental Researches in Electricity,* which opened a new world. "His explanations were simple," Edison wrote later. "He used no mathematics. He was the master experimenter." On quitting the night shift at 4 A.M. he began reading Faraday and read until it was time to go back to work. He tried Faraday's experiments, and told Milt Adams, "I am now twenty-one. I may live to be fifty. Can I get as much done as he did? I have got so much to do and life is so short, I am going to hustle."

With the discovery of Faraday, experimentation began to crowd everything else out of Edison's life. Bored with his favorite task of "taking press," he amused himself by crowding hundreds of words on one page, in a hand so minute that it had to be recopied before the newspaper compositors could use it; rebuked, he countered by centering a single word on each sheet of paper. He was asked to resign, which suited him.

He had already discovered Charles Williams's electrical shop on Court Street where Thomas Watson went to work a few years later, and where Bell had his instruments made. Advertising in a trade journal that "T.A. Edison has resigned his situation in the Western Union office, Boston, and will hereafter devote his full time to bringing out his inventions," Edison set up his workshop in a corner of the Williams establishment, where he produced his first patentable invention, a voting machine for legislatures, which registered "ayes" and "nays" on a roll of chemically-treated paper. Borrowing money for the trip to Washington, he demonstrated the device before a congressional committee. It worked perfectly, but the congressmen pronounced it "the last thing on earth that we want here. Filibustering and delay in the counting of the votes are often the only means we have for defeating bad legislation. . . . Take the thing away." Edison returned to Boston swearing never to invent anything "which was not wanted, or which was not necessary to the community at large."

His next venture was an improved stock ticker; again the device worked well, but this time he neglected to safeguard his patent rights and saw his unguarded intellectual property picked off by the privateers of free enterprise. Another effort, an improved duplex telegraph, was a technical failure, and he suddenly found himself in debt. Boston had proved unlucky, and leaving behind his instruments, books, and personal belongings, he borrowed the fare for a night steamboat trip to New York.

Edison made the rounds of the New York telegraph offices, borrowing from an operator a dollar that, beginning with a supper of apple dumplings and coffee, fed him for three days. Calling at the office of the Gold Indicator Company, central bureau of the stock ticker that relayed price changes from the floor of the Gold Exchange to brokerage houses, he obtained permission to sleep on a cot in the battery room.

Three days later, in the midst of a market crisis, the central stock ticker broke down. The financial district was in pandemonium, with hundreds of messengers storming the Gold Indicator Company. Just as the president of the company, S. S. Laws, arrived, Edison succeeded in diagnosing the problem: a contact spring had broken off and fallen between two gear wheels. Laws importuned, "Fix it! Fix it! Be quick, for God's sake." Edison replaced the spring and reset the indicator dial, while clerks hastened off to restart the receivers in the brokerage houses.

Next day Laws sent for Edison and hired him as assistant to the company's chief electrical engineer, Franklin Pope. A month later Pope left to start his own firm, and Edison inherited his job, at $300 a month. He was in charge of the indicator on September 24, 1869, "Black Friday," when financial manipulators Jay Gould and Jim Fiske attempted to corner the gold market. As prices first rocketed upward and then, on President Grant's order to the Treasury to sell gold, plummeted, Edison and his crew struggled to keep the indicator in touch with fluctuations. "I sat on top of the Western Union telegraph booth to watch the surging, crazy crowd," he wrote later. ". . . Amid great excitement, Speyer, the banker, went crazy and it took five men to hold him; and everybody lost their head. . . . The Western Union operator came to me and said, 'Shake, Edison, we are O.K. We haven't a cent.' I felt happy because we were poor."

A week later Laws sold out to Western Union. Edison left the company to form a partnership with Franklin Pope to develop another improvement on the stock ticker, a device every day more revered in Wall Street. They also took in a silent parner, J. W. Ashley, editor of *The Telegrapher,* who contributed advertising space to the partnership. When Western Union bought their improvement for $15,000, Edison, who had done all the work, got only $5,000. After a few similar transactions, he terminated the partnership.

Shortly after, Marshall Lefferts, president of Western Union, engaged him to add further refinements to the stock ticker. Three weeks later Edison brought a model to Lefferts's office for a demonstration. According to one of his favorite stories of later years, when Lefferts asked him to put a price on his rights, and on certain other work he had done for Western Union, Edison demurred, afraid to ask for the $5,000 that he thought would be "about right," and ready to settle for $3,000. "General, suppose you make me an offer." Lefferts stunned him with an offer of $40,000. The check—the first he had ever handled—made another good story: When the bank teller handed it back to him for endorsement, Edison ran to Lefferts's office with it thinking he had been cheated. Lefferts sent his secretary to help cash the check, but that only created another problem. The teller counted out $10 and $20 bills in a cubic-foot stack which the inventor sat up all night to guard. Next day he found out about bank accounts.

All his life Edison had spent every dollar, or nickel, he could spare on books and apparatus for his research. Now he suddenly had $40,000 and a commission from Lefferts to manufacture the new improved stock ticker. With some of his capital he set up in a loft in Newark (4–6 Ward Street) and as his work force grew to fifty and then 250 hands, he wrote his parents in Port Huron, "I am now what you Democrats call a 'Bloated Eastern Manufacturer'!"

He was indeed a manufacturer, but the role was too constricting for his bursting intellectual energy. Ideas were tumbling out of his head every day, and in the crowded Newark loft he launched one new research project after another until he had forty-five going simultaneously. He averaged a patent a month.

As his chief assistants he hired a nucleus of outstanding men, each of whom had his own specialty to contribute to the team: John Ott, a mechanic who became his chief draftsman; a Swiss clockmaker named John Kruesi, who superintended the laboratory; an Englishman, Charles Batchelor, who transformed Ott's drawings into working models; Will Carman, who kept the accounts and managed the machine shop.

In 1871 Edison took time out to fall in love with and marry sixteen-year-old Mary Stilwell, an employee of his Newark shop. Time out, but not much; an hour after the ceremony he remembered a production problem and was back in the shop in his shirtsleeves. A family tradition had it that at midnight someone reminded him of the time and he exclaimed, "Midnight! By George, I must go home then! I was married today!"

In 1873 his headlong work schedule was interrupted by another kind of adventure. His first experience with big business, the $40,000 deal with Marshall Lefferts, had been a pleasure. Now he discovered another side to Wall Street. A rather mysterious firm called the Automatic Telegraph Company commissioned him to produce an automatic printing telegraph, a marriage of telegraph and stock ticker, which would both receive and type out messages. After four months of intensive research and systematic testing whose results he graded in his daybook in his own code as "N.G." (no good), "D.B." (damned bad), "N.B." (no better), "L.B." (little better), "E." (encouraging), and "V.E." (very encouraging), he produced a successful working model. At the same time Edison was also working on a revolutionary development for Western Union, a quadruplex that could carry four messages simultaneously, two in either direction. In April 1873 Edison sailed for England to demonstrate his quadruplex, and returned home to find New York in the grip of a financial panic. His own business was threatened by the failure of Western Union to meet payments due for his work—to avoid paying him, president William Orton, Lefferts's successor, had simply decamped for an "extended tour."

The slippery financier Jay Gould now revealed himself as the power behind the Automatic Telegraph Company, and offered to buy the inventions Edison was working on for Western Union. Edison agreed, and was promptly double-crossed. Gould used his anticipated control of the patents to force mergers with the Atlantic and Pacific Telegraph Company and Western Union, then turned around and discarded the patents without ever paying Edison anything. Having achieved his object of winning a telegraph monopoly, Gould had no interest in improved technology, as Edison perceived at once: "I knew no further progress in telegraphy was possible, and I went into other lines."

In the fall of 1875 he made an accidental discovery in pure science that put his name permanently into the science vocabulary. The "Edison effect"—bright sparks produced by a vibrator magnet—indicated the passage of energy through space, suggesting the possibility of communication without wires. Similar sparks had been observed by Joseph Henry and Faraday, and James Clerk Maxwell had

Edison printing telegraph. (Smithsonian Photograph No. 34,993)

theorized about the electromagnetic waves that caused them. Edison's report aroused great interest among scientists, but the world was not quite ready, and for the time being the "Edison effect," with its near uncovering of electronics, remained a tantalizing mystery.

That same fall Edison reached a momentous decision. It amounted in a way to no more than a logical extension of his already established working arrangements. Though the basic idea of the Newark company was manufacturing, and invention theoretically a sideline, Edison in his own mind had from the beginning reversed the priorities, regarding the manufacturing operation as a more or less distracting bore. The Panic of '73 even showed it to be an unprofitable bore, at least part of the time, and he now resolved to drop it completely and concentrate on invention.

Consequently the Newark loft no longer served his purpose, and he looked around the neighboring countryside for a place where he could build the kind of plant he needed. On the Pennsylvania Railroad between Elizabeth and Metuchen, rural and secluded and yet only twenty-five miles from New York, he found a whistle stop that he thought would do. The name of the place was Menlo Park.

There on a hilltop, like the founder of a new religion building his church, he constructed a white two-story structure (it even looked like a church) that was completed early in 1876. On the first floor, inside the door, was a small office. Behind it was a workroom, one of whose features was a galvanometer emplaced on masonry pedestals that reached the ground under the floor, to protect against vibration. Behind the workroom was a machine shop with an array of belt-driven metal-cutting lathes. The second floor was an immense laboratory lined on all sides with shelves laden with riches—thousands of bottles of chemicals, copper wire, storage batteries, induction coils, magnets, telegraph components—an inventory the Charles Williams shop in Boston might have envied. Down the center of the room were work tables, a storage chest, and a sink. The laboratory was equipped with the most up-to-date metering devices and other electrical apparatus, as well as photographic equipment and a small steam engine as a power source. A pot-bellied stove supplied heat. Later, a separate library building was added to house all the current scientific publications.

LEFT Mary Stilwell, whom Edison married in 1871. (Department of the Interior)

RIGHT Edison at the time of the Menlo Park venture. (Department of the Interior)

Edison bought a house two blocks from the laboratory for his family, which in the 1870s was enlarged by three children who, despite the proximity, saw none too much of their father. Now and then he made trick toys for them, such as a glass swan that sprayed water when a child blew into it. Edison's subordinates perforce imitated the life-style of their chief. "My children grew up without knowing their father," John Ott recalled. Why did he put up with such interminable working hours, he was asked, and replied, "[Edison] made me feel that I *was making something with him. I wasn't just a workman.*" Another veteran of Menlo Park, Francis Jehl, wrote, "In those halcyon days of youth and enthusiasm, when sentiments were magnified almost to the verge of hallucination, the laboratory appeared to the writer . . . like an alchemist's den of yore, the place where nature's elements were [transmuted]."

At the far end of the lab stood an improbable piece of equipment: a pipe organ, used in testing sound. In the middle of the long evening work session, the night watchman was sent out for midnight snacks of crackers, cheese, and ham from the village store; everyone took turns telling stories, and finally "a song would start, in which the lot of us would join," as Francis Jehl wrote later. "This midnight pause was always welcome, and no one enjoyed it more than Edison." Among the chemicals on the shelves were a selection of common medications, from which

Menlo Park laboratory, spring 1876, shortly after its completion, with the Edison staff on the front porch. (Collections of Greenfield Village and the Henry Ford Museum, Dearborn, Michigan)

Edison was fond of prescribing for his assistants when they complained of feeling ill, taking down a bottle or two, mixing a dose, and handing it to the sufferer with the words, "Here, take this."

When work was slack Edison sometimes laid men off, but Monday morning they came back anyway. Edison smiled and shrugged and told his superintendent to try to find them work.

Edison's procedures were always methodical and painstaking, seldom leaping a theoretical gap without trying every intermediate possibility one by one—his "needle in the haystack" method, according to Nikola Tesla, future inventor of the induction motor, another veteran of Menlo Park. Sometimes the haystack numbered straws in the thousands before the needle was found—as in his famous fourteen-month search for the filament for the incandescent lamp, which ended with a carbon-coated length of the cotton thread Hannah Wilkinson Slater had invented.

Fabulous Menlo Park produced hundreds of inventions besides the electric light, including such spectaculars as the phonograph, the carbon-button telephone transmitter, the electric power station, and the original ancestor of the electron (vacuum) tube, which made possible the electronics industry. Menlo Park's successor, the Edison Laboratory in West Orange, whither Edison moved his operation when it outgrew its birthplace in 1887, added the dictating machine, a practical motion-picture camera and projector, a more efficient cement kiln, poured-concrete construction, and many more.

Through his years in Menlo Park Edison was a legendary but homely figure, walking from home to laboratory in the morning and back at night in wide-brimmed straw hat, hands thrust into pockets, eyes fixed on the plank sidewalk, sunk in thought, but sometimes stopping to chat with some of his men on the stoop of Mrs. Jordan's boarding house, or with Mrs. Jordan herself. However neglectful he seemed of his family, the death of Mary Edison of typhoid fever in 1884 was a blow from which he never really recovered. His second wife, Mina Miller, daughter of a founder of the Chautauqua educational show-business circuit, undertook to spruce him up for presentation in polite society, and more or less succeeded, though he still preferred clothes that looked as if he had slept in them—as he so often had. His later decades (he lived to 1931) were financially unburdened, though he never got rich out of the inventions that made billions for others (when his electric company was merged into General Electric in 1892, he was finessed out of the electric light business), and the $4 million he had made he lost in a disastrous magnetic ore-separating venture, over which his only comment was a cheerful, "Well, it's all gone, but we had a hell of a good time spending it!"

Arriving on the technological stage at the end of the era of the shirtsleeve tinkerer, he was the last and greatest of the tinkerers, his name becoming the very synonym for inventor, his tousled looks the very image. His quizzical brand of individualism, in some ways reminiscent of John Fitch, heightened the aura of folk hero that grew up around him. American schoolteachers quoted such aphorisms as "Genius is ten per cent inspiration and ninety per cent perspiration," as they taught generations of American schoolchildren about his seventy-two-hours-at-a-stretch labors to produce the great technological commonplaces of the new life: electric light, phonograph, motion pictures.

Yet of all Edison's inventions the most significant was Menlo Park itself. The world's first industrial research laboratory, prototype of all modern research centers, Menlo Park consummated the marriage of technology and science while it institutionalized the future of research. With it, the greatest of the Yankee tinkerers put an end to a century of Yankee tinkering.

AMERICA 1876

America 1876

WITH EDISON'S INVENTION of Menlo Park, America began seriously to pay the world back for all the technology the world had given America. To inheritance from prehistory (fire, tool-making, agriculture), from ancient Asia and Africa (the wheel, spinning and weaving, metallurgy), from classical Europe (the screw, the waterwheel), from medieval Eurasia (the crank, paper, printing, gunpowder), had been added the smuggling and pirating of Sam Slater and Francis Cabot Lowell from the British Industrial Revolution, and all the nineteenth-century borrowings, ranging from Volta's battery to Fourneyron's water turbine. The account between America and the world could not easily be squared, and in fact a hundred years after 1876 it would be reasonable to say that all America can hope to do is to keep up interest payments on a borrowed principal too vast to amortize.

Nevertheless, when the world unwittingly invested its stock of technology in America, it made a first-rate investment, even if in 1876 the profits seemed still to be accruing mostly to America. In its first century the country had accomplished an expansion in every dimension without historic parallel. What Hamilton's friend Tench Coxe called "a nation of moderate numbers dwelling in a country of redundant soil" rose in population from 2 million to 50 million, its urban fraction simultaneously shifting from a twentieth to a fourth, while consumer goods rose from a handicraft trickle to a mass-production torrent, lifting standards of living from insecure, hazard-ridden poverty to slightly more secure, slightly less hazardous, unevenly distributed affluence. There were American writers and artists whose names were known in Europe, and the Washington government did not hesitate to address peremptory messages to all the other capitals in the world.

The transformation had come about in part through political and military means—Louisiana Purchase, Mexican War—but infinitely more important was the manipulation of the continent by the powerful hand of technology. So swift, incessant, and even accelerating had been the changes that Rip Van Winkle was probably well advised to take his twenty-year nap at the very outset of the period, when he could come back and find his native town practically unchanged. Had Rip slept for two decades in the early or middle nineteenth century in western New York State, the Ohio-Mississippi valley, or Chicago, he would have thought himself awakening on another planet.

By 1876 the medieval European agricultural technique that had sufficed to crowd the Stone Age natives out of their hunting and gathering grounds, even while scandalizing European visitors with its wastefulness, had been supplanted by Obed Hussey, Cyrus McCormick, John Deere, and their successors with a mechanized, high-speed, low-cost, large-scale cultivation of the Midwest prairie that amounted to a revolution.

It was one of several. Starting with textile manufacturing (destined long to remain the classic takeoff base for an underdeveloped country) under Slater and Lowell, ably abetted by David Wilkinson and Paul Moody, and in a second stream of development from Eli Whitney and John Hall, the "American System of Manufacturing" assembled accurately machined interchangeable parts in unheard-of volume to win the unstinted admiration of the most advanced nations of the Old World.

The transportation revolution of the nineteenth century was by no means wholly made in America. But John Fitch, the Stevenses, and many others had made substantial contributions. Most were inextricably interrelated to British and European technology—like George Westinghouse's revolutionary railroad brake, displayed at the Centennial, derived from the compressed-air machinery invented by Daniel Colladon for the Mont-Cenis Alpine tunnel. The American-European tradeoff was certainly not so disproportionate as to be unreasonable. The steam-power inventions of Fitch and Oliver Evans were independently arrived at, and the steamboat that grew out of them was one more typically American technological expression, in effect the imposition of mass production on transportation. In the communications revolution accomplished by telegraph and telephone, Joseph Henry, Samuel Morse, Alexander Graham Bell, Elisha Gray, and Thomas Edison played the most conspicuous roles (without forgetting Faraday, Ampère, and Oersted).

Some of the American achievements displayed at the Philadelphia Exposition had a long future ahead of them. Roebling's web-trussed suspension bridge was the ideal long-span crossing for the traffic to be created by descendants of Oliver Evans's *Orukter Amphibolos* when powered by the internal-combustion engine John Stevens (among others) had conceived, and shod by Charles Goodyear's rubber. The automobile in turn would add a major new refinement to the "American System" in the form of Henry Ford's moving assembly line, improbably adapted from the Cincinnati and Chicago meat packers whose expeditious carcass handling had fascinated British traveler William Chambers in 1854. The assembly line in turn would be improved on by the introduction of automation, reviving the historic principle of Oliver Evans's flour mill. The basic physical component of automation, the transfer machine, by which the workpiece is automatically repositioned in a sequence of operations, was pioneered by the Waltham Watch Company in 1888 in the town where Francis Cabot Lowell and Paul Moody had sixty years earlier built their machine shop.

William Kelly's mass-produced steel, demonstrated as a structural material by Captain Eads's bridge, found its great métier in the "skyscraper," a characteristically American word for the most characteristic of American buildings, pioneered by James Bogardus, and made practical by Elisha Otis.

The inventions of Bell and Edison pointed the way to the vast future of electronics, including the immense family of descendants of the mechanical computer, represented at the Philadelphia Exhibition by George Grant's mechanical monster. The research laboratory descendants of Menlo Park—General Electric, DuPont, Bell Labs, and many others at home and abroad—contributed signally to the flood of innovation of the twentieth century.

The shortcomings of triumphant technology were not overlooked in America, 1876. Quite the contrary; they were glaringly visible in the smoky, filthy, crime-ridden city working-class districts. The middle class was far better off than either the urban or rural lower classes, who still far outnumbered it, but it too suffered many hazards and inconveniences, from transportation disasters through urban epidemics to summer heat and flies (though the air-conditioning principle had been demonstrated, rather amazingly, in a Florida fever hospital by Dr. John Gorrie in 1842).

One of the most prevalent problems was pollution, known in 1876 as dirt. The rural countryside had its familiar dirt, but the new dirt of the city established records in its variety and abundance. Help was on the way in the form of sewage systems, garbage collection, and other city services, and in the "laborsaving" devices in the Philadelphia Exposition's Women's Pavilion, which, several decades of their history ultimately showed, did not so much save housewives time as produce cleaner houses and cleaner families.

The American working class in 1876 had a hard row to hoe before it could surpass the working and living conditions—the more idyllic as they receded into the past—of Lucy Larcom and her Lowell mill mates of the 1830s and 1840s. Uninhibited exploitation of labor—man, woman, and child—was now the order of the day (and the moving assembly line, miracle of production efficiency, would presently add a subtly powerful means of tyranny). The enlightened interest taken in the welfare of his employees by Francis Cabot Lowell was forgotten until twentieth-century industrial sociologists rediscovered its value and tried to persuade indifferent corporate management. Meantime strikes, lockouts, blacklists, sabotage, and violence colored the industrial scene, while the usual financial panics continued to be followed by the usual depressions, periodically reducing crowds of working-class families to the usual begging and crime. Farm families were no better off with their intermittent droughts, floods, price collapses, and foreclosures.

Add in national problems that seemed to be getting worse instead of better—political corruption (Tweed Ring, Grant scandals), oppression of minorities (Ku Klux Klan, the Indian wars—Custer's misadventure occurred this very year), and no one would claim that on the American Centennial the American millennium was near.

But the successive solutions to technical and material problems, so brilliant and startling in their novelty, so familiar and commonplace after their acceptance, that had carried the country to 1876 had by no means exhausted their career. They offered a persuasive if little heeded argument against the national passion for argument over an endless succession of issues that proved one after the other to be futile or irrelevant. Perhaps the most important message Evans, Hall, McCormick, Eads, and the other makers of the American Industrial Revolution should have for their descendants today is that democratic rationalism calls for turning issues into problems, not problems into issues.

Bibliography

A Note on the Bibliography

The traditional vocabulary of technological history—"inventors" and "inventions"—has long been out of date and never had more than a qualified validity, since strictly speaking no single person has ever invented anything all by himself, and nearly all inventions are the product of scores, hundreds, or thousands of mostly anonymous craftsmen, mechanics, and other tinkerers. Nevertheless, writers and researchers in the history of American technology cannot fail to be appalled by the contrast in our historical and biographical literature between the political, military, and cultural heroes on the one hand and the engineers, technicians, and scientists on the other. The political Founding Fathers have had their due, or perhaps a little more, while most of the industrial-economic Founding Fathers are callously neglected.

Few inventors are undeservedly famous—Morse, who invented little, was a gifted man, and Fulton, who invented little more, was a hero as well as a genius—while many are undeservedly obscure. Despite his place of distinction in world technological history, Oliver Evans is the subject of only one biography, a scholarly work available only in a few university libraries. John Fitch has been given a competent popular biography (long out of print) but his own fascinating memoir remains unpublished. Samuel Slater, John Stevens, Robert Stevens, Obed Hussey, John Ericsson, and Joseph Henry deserve better biographies than presently exist, but are at least in better case than Walter Hunt, Paul Moody, David Wilkinson, Elisha Root, Thomas Blanchard, Frederick Howe, Theodore Burr, James Geddes, Benjamin Wright, and many other engineers and inventors who still await biographies of any description, and most of whom pass unmentioned even in encyclopedias. (But a splendid example of what can be done if a writer gets some research backing is Richard Sanders Allen's classic series on covered bridges and their builders.)

Apart from biographical data, controversies demand resolution, or at least illumination—some modern scholars, the Patent Office to the contrary notwithstanding, have questioned whether William Kelly does, after all, deserve to be credited with inventing the Bessemer process, and the precise value of Eli Whitney's mass-production pioneering remains in debate.

Similar fine questions can be raised about the inventors of the sewing machine, typewriter, and other devices that emerged from successful assemblage of multiple contributions.

Finally, there is the matter of emphasis in American history as it is written and taught. Admitting that men do not make history, Oliver Evans any more than Thomas Jefferson, the traditional emphasis is defective. The contributions of our technological heroes need to be weighed more intelligently against those of the statesmen, generals, explorers, jurists, and social reformers, something that cannot be done adequately until they have received appropriate individual study.

General

America Through British Eyes, ed. Allan Nevins. New York, 1948.

Bidwell, Percy Wells, *History of Agriculture in the Northern United States, 1620–1860.* Washington, D.C., 1925.

Bogart, Ernest L., *Economic History of American Agriculture.* Wilmington, Delaware, 1973.

Burlingame, Roger, *Backgrounds of Power.* New York, 1949.

———, *Engines of Democracy.* New York, 1940.

———, *Inventors Behind the Inventor.* New York, 1966.

———, *Machines that Built America.* New York, 1965.

———, *March of the Iron Men, a Social History of Union through Invention.* New York, 1937.

Burstall, Audrey, *A History of Mechanical Engineering.* London, 1963.

Clark, Dan Elbert, *The West in American History.* New York, 1937.

Clark, Victor S., *History of the Manufactures of the United States.* 3 vols. Washington, D.C., 1929.

Dahnhof, Clarence H., *Change in Agriculture: the Northern United States, 1820–1870.* Cambridge, Massachusetts, 1969.

DeCamp, L. Sprague, *The Heroic Age of American Invention.* New York, 1961.

Early Engineering Reminiscences (1815–40) of George Escol Sellers, ed. Eugene Ferguson (U.S. National Museum Bulletin 238). Washington, D.C., 1964.

Farming in the New Nation (1790–1840), ed. Darwin P. Kelsey. Washington, D.C., 1972.

Faulkner, Harold U., *American Economic History.* New York, 1943.

Ferguson, Eugene, *Bibliography of the History of Technology.* Cambridge, Massachusetts, 1968.

Finch, James Kip, "A Century of American Civil Engineering." *Transactions of the American Society of Civil Engineers,* 1953.

Forbes, R. J., *Man the Maker, a History of Technology and Engineering.* London, 1958.

Fuller, Edmund, *Tinkers and Genius, the Story of the Yankee Inventors.* New York, 1955.

Gates, Paul W., *The Farmer's Age: Agriculture 1815–1868.* New York, 1960.

Giedion, Siegfried, *Mechanization Takes Command, a Contribution to Anonymous History.* New York, 1948.

Gilfillan, S. C., *The Sociology of Invention.* Chicago, 1935.

Habakkuk, H. J., *American and British Technology in the Nineteenth Century.* Cambridge, England, 1962.

Hindle, Brooke, *Technology in Early America.* Chapel Hill, North Carolina, 1966.

Iles, George, *Leading American Inventors*. Freeport, New York, 1968. (Reprint of 1912 publication.)

Jewkes, John, Sawers, David, and Sillerman, Richard, *The Sources of Invention*. New York, 1958.

Kouwenhoven, John A., *Made in America: the Arts in Modern Civilization*. Garden City, New York, 1962.

Kranzberg, Melvin, and Pursell, Carroll W., Jr., eds., *Technology in Western Civilization*. 2 vols. New York, 1967.

Merritt, Raymond H., *Engineering in American Society, 1850–1875*. Lexington, Kentucky, 1969.

A Mirror for Americans, Life and Manners in the United States, 1790–1870, as Recorded by American Travelers, ed. Warren S. Tryon. 3 vols. Chicago, 1952.

National Geographic Society, *Those Inventive Americans*. Washington, D.C., 1971.

Nettels, Curtis P., *The Emergence of a National Economy, 1775–1815*. Vol. II, The Economic History of the United States. New York, 1962.

Oliver, John W., *History of American Technology*. New York, 1956.

Popular Culture and Industrialism, 1865–1890, ed. Henry Nash Smith. Garden City, New York, 1967.

A Popular History of American Invention, ed. Waldemar Kaempfert. 2 vols. New York, 1924.

Readings in the History of American Agriculture, ed. Wayne D. Rasmussen. Urbana, Illinois, 1960.

Schumpeter, Joseph, *The Theory of Economic Development*. Cambridge, Massachusetts, 1934.

Shannon, Fred A., *The Farmer's Last Frontier: Agriculture, 1860–97*. New York, 1945.

Strassman, W. Paul, *Risk and Technological Innovation: American Manufacturing Methods during the Nineteenth Century*. Ithaca, New York, 1959.

Taylor, George Rogers, *The Transportation Revolution, 1815–1860*. Vol. IV, The Economic History of the United States. New York, 1951.

Thompson, Holland, *The Age of Invention, a Chronicle of Mechanical Conquest*. New Haven, 1921.

Tuckerman, Henry T., *America and Her Commentators*. New York, 1864.

Usher, Abbott Payson, *A History of Mechanical Inventions*. Boston, 1959.

Whitworth, Joseph and Wallis, George, *The Industry of the United States in Machinery, Manufactures and Useful and Ornamental Arts*. London, 1854.

Woodward, W. E., *The Way Our People Lived, an Intimate American History*. New York, 1944.

Wright, Louis B., *Everyday Life on the American Frontier*. New York, 1968.

Wright, Louis B., and Fowler, Elaine W., *Life in the New Nation, 1787–1860*. New York, 1974.

By Chapter

Philadelphia 1876

Leng, John, *America in 1876, Pencillings during a Tour in the Centennial Year*. Dundee, Scotland, 1877.

Maass, John, *The Glorious Enterprise, the Centennial Exhibition of 1876 and H. J. Schwarzmann, Architect-in-Chief.* Watkins Glen, New York, 1973.

McCabe, James D., *The Illustrated History of the Centennial Exhibition Held in Commemoration of the One Hundredth Anniversary of American Independence.* Philadelphia, 1876.

Magee's Illustrated Guide of Philadelphia and the Centennial Exhibition. Philadelphia, 1876.

*Popular Culture and Industrialism.

Rae W. Fraser, *Columbia and Canada, the Eastern States in the Centennial Year.* New York, 1879.

Sandhurst, Phillip T. and others, *The Great Centennial Exhibition, Critically Described and Illustrated.* Philadelphia, 1876.

Visitors' Guide to the Centennial Exhibition and Philadelphia, May 10 to November 10, 1876. Authorized by the Centennial Board of Finance. Philadelphia, 1876.

1. AMERICA 1776

Abbott, Wilbur C., *New York in the American Revolution.* New York, 1929.

American Husbandry, ed. Harry J. Carman. 2 vols. Port Washington, New York, 1964 (reprint; originally published in London, 1775).

*America Through British Eyes.

*Bidwell, History of Agriculture.

*Bogart, Economic History of American Agriculture.

Boucher, Jack E., *Of Batsto and Bog Iron.* Batsto, New Jersey, 1973.

Butler, David F., *United States Firearms, the First Century, 1776–1875.* New York, 1971.

Clarke, Mary Stetson, *Pioneer Iron Works.* Philadelphia, 1968.

Farming in the New Nation, ed. Kelsey.

*Faulkner, American Economic History.

Fisher, Douglas A., *The Epic of Steel.* New York, 1963.

Hadfield, Joseph, *An Englishman in America, 1785.* Toronto, 1933.

*Hindle, Technology in Early America.

Kurjack, Dennis C., *Hopewell Village.* Washington, D.C., 1961.

Lewis, Berkeley R., *Small Arms and Ammunition in the United States Service, 1776–1865.* Washington, D.C., 1968.

Lyman, Susan Elizabeth, *The Story of New York, an Informal History of the City.* New York, 1964.

McRobert, Patrick, *A Tour Through Part of the North Provinces of America.* Edinburgh, 1776.

*A Mirror for Americans.

*Nettels, The Emergence of a National Economy.

Pierce, Arthur D., *Iron in the Pines, the Story of New Jersey's Ghost Towns and Bog Iron.* New Brunswick, New Jersey, 1957.

*Readings in the History of American Agriculture.

Rosebush, Waldo, *American Firearms and the Changing Frontier.* Spokane, Washington, 1962.

Russell, Carl P., *Guns on the Early Frontiers, a History of Firearms from Colonial Times Through the Years of the Western Fur Trade.* Berkeley, California, 1962.

Sloane, Eric, *A Museum of Early American Tools.* New York, 1973.

* See earlier citation.

Warden, G. B., *Boston, 1689–1776*. Boston, 1970.

Weld, Isaac, Jr., *Travels Through the States of North America and the Provinces of Upper and Lower Canada During the Years 1795, 1796 and 1797*. 2 vols. London, 1800.

Whitehill, Walter Muir, *Boston, A Topographical History*. Cambridge, Massachusetts, 1968.

*Woodward, The Way Our People Lived.

*Wright, Everyday Life on the American Frontier.

*Wright and Fowler, Life in the New Nation.

2. The adventures of John Fitch

Bathe, Greville, *Three Essays, a Dissertation on the Genesis of Mechanical Transport in America*. St. Augustine, Florida, 1960.

Boyd, Thomas, *Poor John Fitch, Inventor of the Steamboat*. New York, 1935.

Fitch, John, *The Original Steamboat Supported, or a Reply to James Rumsey's Pamphlets*. Philadelphia, 1788.

Fitch, John, *Papers* (unpublished: Autobiography and History of the Steamboat, November 12, 1790—Library Company of Philadelphia).

———, *Papers* (unpublished: diary, surveyor's notebook, letters, accounts, will, and miscellaneous, in the Library of Congress).

Flexner, James T., *Steamboats Come True: American Inventors in Action*. New York, 1944.

Parsons, Mira Clarke, "John Fitch, Inventor of Steamboats," *Ohio Archaeological and Historical Publications*, Vol. VIII, IX, Columbus, Ohio, 1900.

Richardson, William H., "John Fitch, Patriot, Martyr, Pioneer Steamboat Inventor, *Mechanical Engineering,* June 9, 1932.

3. Oliver Evans invents the Automated Factory

Anderson, Oscar, *Refrigeration in America*. Princeton, New Jersey, 1957.

Bathe, Greville and Bathe, Dorothy, *Oliver Evans, a Chronicle of Early American Engineering*. Philadelphia, 1935.

*Early Engineering Reminiscences of George Escol Sellers.

Evans, Oliver, *The Young Mill-Wright and Miller's Guide*. Philadelphia, 1795.

———, *A Trip Made by a Small Man in a Wrestle with a Very Great Man*. Washington, D.C., 1814.

———, *The Abortion of the Young Steam Engineer's Guide*. Philadelphia, 1805.

*Flexner, Steamboats Come True.

*Giedion, Mechanization Takes Command.

Hamilton, Edward P., *The Village Mill in Early New England*. Sturbridge, Massachusetts, 1964.

Memorial to Congress of Sundry Citizens of the United States Praying Relief from the Oppressive Operation of Oliver Evans' Patent. Baltimore, 1813.

Oliver Evans to His Counsel, in Defence of His Patent Rights. Washington, D.C. (?), 1817.

Zimiles, Martha and Zimiles, Murray, *Early American Mills*. New York, 1973.

* See earlier citation.

4. SAM SLATER DISCOVERS AMERICA

Bagnall, William R., *The Textile Industries of the United States.* 1893. (Reprints of Economic Classics, New York, 1971.)

Cameron, E. H., *Samuel Slater, Father of American Manufactures.* Portland, Maine, 1960.

David Wilkinson's Reminiscences. Providence, 1861 (Rhode Island Society for the Encouragement of Domestic Industry).

Fennelly, Catherine, *Textiles in New England, 1790–1840.* Sturbridge, Massachusetts, 1961.

Lewton, Frederick A., "Samuel Slater and the Oldest Cotton Machinery in America," *Annual Report of the Board of Regents of the Smithsonian Institution.* Washington, D.C., 1926.

Lincoln, Jonathan T., "The Beginning of the Machine Age in New England: David Wilkinson of Pawtucket." *New England Quarterly,* 1933.

Merrimack Valley Textile Museum, *Wool Technology and the Industrial Revolution.* Andover, Massachusetts, 1965.

Rivard, Paul E., *Samuel Slater, Father of American Manufactures.* Pawtucket, Rhode Island, 1974.

Rolt, L. T. C., *A Short History of Machine Tools.* Cambridge, Massachusetts, 1965.

Ware, Caroline F., *Early New England Cotton Manufacturing, a Study in Industrial Beginnings.* New York, 1966.

White, George S., *Memoir of Samuel Slater, the Father of American Manufacturers.* New York, 1967.

Woodbury, Robert S., *History of the Lathe to 1850.* Cambridge, Massachusetts, 1964.

*Zimiles and Zimiles, *Early American Mills.*

5. ELI WHITNEY: THE COTTON GIN AND INTERCHANGEABLE PARTS

Battison, Edwin A., "Eli Whitney and the Milling Machine." *Smithsonian Journal of History,* Vol. 1, No. 2, 1972.

——, "A New Look at the 'Whitney' Milling Machine." *Technology and Culture,* Vol. 14, No. 4, 1966.

David Wilkinson's Reminiscences.

Fuller, Claud E., *The Whitney Firearms.* Huntington, West Virginia, 1946.

Green, Constance McL., *Eli Whitney and the Birth of American Technology.* Boston, 1956.

*Lincoln, "The Beginning of the Machine Age in New England."

Mirsky, Jeanette, and Nevins, Allan, *The World of Eli Whitney.* New York, 1952.

Olmstead, Denison, *Memoir of Eli Whitney, Esq.* New Haven, 1846.

*Rolt, *Machine Tools.*

White, Edward Hartwell, *The Development of Interchangeable Mass Manufacturing in Selected American Industries from 1795 to 1825.* (Unpublished doctoral thesis, University of Maryland, 1973.)

Woodbury, Robert S., *History of the Grinding Machine.* Cambridge, Massachusetts, 1964.

——, *History of the Gear-Cutting Machine.* Cambridge, Massachusetts, 1958.

*——, *History of the Lathe.*

——, "The Legend of Eli Whitney and Interchangeable Parts." *Technology and Culture,* I (Summer 1960).

* See earlier citation.

6. AMERICA 1801

America Through British Eyes.
Baily, Francis, *Journal of a Tour in North America, 1796–97.* London, 1856.
Bernard, John, *Retrospections of America, 1789–1814.* New York, 1887.
Bidwell, History of Agriculture.
Daley, Robert, *The World Beneath the City.* Philadelphia, 1959.
Faulkner, American Economic History.
Gates, The Farmer's Age.
Hulbert, Archer Butler, *Pioneer Roads and Experiences of Travelers.* Historic Highways of America, Vol. 12. Cleveland, Ohio, 1904.
Lyman, The Story of New York.
A Mirror for Americans.
Nettels, The Emergence of a National Economy.
Taylor, The Transportation Revolution.

7. THE STEAMBOAT RACE

Bathe and Bathe, Oliver Evans.
Dickinson, H. W., *Robert Fulton, Engineer and Artist, His Life and Works.* London, 1913.
Finch, James Kip, *Early Columbia Engineers.* New York, 1929.
Flexner, Steamboats Come True.
Sutcliffe, Alice Crary, *Robert Fulton and the Clermont.* New York, 1948.
Taylor, The Transportation Revolution.
Thurston, Robert H., *The Messrs. Stevens of Hoboken as Engineers, Naval Architects and Philanthropists.* Philadelphia, 1874.
———, *Robert Fulton.* New York, 1891.
Turnbull, Archibald Douglas, *John Stevens, an American Record.* New York, 1928.
Watkins, J. Elfreth, *John Stevens and His Sons, Early American Engineers.* Washington, D.C., 1892.

8. THE COVERED BRIDGE BUILDERS

Allen, Richard Sanders, *Covered Bridges of the Middle Atlantic States.* Brattleboro, Vermont, 1959.
———, *Covered Bridges of the Middle West.* Brattleboro, Vermont, 1970.
———, *Covered Bridges of the Northeast.* Brattleboro, Vermont, 1974.
———, *Covered Bridges of the South.* Brattleboro, Vermont, 1970.
Billings, Henry, *Bridges.* New York, 1956.
Black, Archibald, *The Story of Bridges.* New York, 1936.
Description of Ithiel Town's Improvement in the Construction of Wood and Iron Bridges. New Haven, n.d.
Edwards, Llewellyn N., *A Record of the History and Evolution of Early American Bridges.* Orono, Maine, 1959.
Fletcher, Robert and Snow, J. P., *History of the Development of Wooden Bridges.* (Papers in the Engineering Center Library, New York.)
Gies, Joseph, *Bridges and Men.* Garden City, New York, 1963.

* See earlier citation.

Jakeman, Adelbert M., *Old Covered Bridges*. Brattleboro, Vermont, 1963.
Life and Works of Thomas Paine, ed. William M. van der Weyde, Vol. I. New Rochelle, New York, 1925.
Sloane, Eric, *American Barns and Covered Bridges*. New York, 1954.
Steinman, David B. and Sara Ruth Watson, *Bridges and Their Builders*. New York, 1957.
*Weld, *Travels Through the States of North America*.

9. FRANCIS CABOT LOWELL, BOSTON PIRATE

America Through British Eyes.
Appleton, Nathan, *Introduction of the Power Loom and Origin of Lowell*. Lowell, Massachusetts, 1858.
*Bagnall, *Textile Industries*.
Coburn, Frederick W., *History of Lowell and Its People*. New York, 1920.
Coolidge, John, *Mill and Mansion, a Study of Architecture and Society in Lowell, Massachusetts, 1820–1865*. New York, 1967.
Dickens, Charles, *American Notes*. New York, 1884.
*Fennelly, *Textiles in New England*.
Gibb, George Sweet, *The Saco-Lowell Shops, Textile Machinery Building in New England, 1813–1849*. Cambridge, Massachusetts, 1950.
Larcom, Lucy, *A New England Girlhood, Outlined from Memory*. Boston, 1889.
———, *An Idyl of Work*. Boston, 1875.
Josephson, Hannah, *The Golden Threads, New England's Mill Girls and Magnates*. New York, 1949.
Miles, Henry A., *Lowell, As It Was, and As It Is*. New York, 1972 (Reprint; originally printed 1846).
Mirror for Americans.
Robinson, H. J. H., *Loom and Spindle, or Life Among the Early Mill Girls*. New York, 1898.
Scoresby, William, *American Factories and Their Female Operatives*. New York, 1968 (Reprint; originally printed 1845).
Tharp, Louise Hall, *The Appletons of Beacon Hill*. Boston, 1973.
*Ware, *Early New England Cotton Manufacturing*.
Ware, Norman R., *The Industrial Worker, 1840–1860*. Boston, 1924.
*Zimiles and Zimiles, *Early American Mills*.

10. "THE EIGHTH WONDER OF THE WORLD"

America Through British Eyes.
Calhoun, Daniel H., *The American Civil Engineer: Origins and Conflict*. Cambridge, Massachusetts, 1960.
Chalmers, Harvey II, *The Birth of the Erie Canal*, New York, 1960.
Condon, George E., *Stars in the Water, the Story of the Erie Canal*. Garden City, New York, 1974.
40' x 28' x 4', The Erie Canal—One Hundred and Fifty Years, ed. Lionel D. Wyld. Rome, New York, 1967.
Hulbert, Archer B., *The Great American Canals*, Vol. II, *The Erie Canal*. Cleveland, Ohio, 1904.
Miller, Nathan, *The Enterprise of a Free People: Aspects of Economic Development in New York State During the Canal Period, 1792–1838*. Ithaca, New York, 1962.

* See earlier citation.

Mirror for Americans.
Shaw, Ronald E., *Erie Water West, a History of the Erie Canal, 1792–1854.* Lexington, Kentucky, 1966.
Tanner, H. S., *A Description of the Canals and Railroads of the United States.* New York, 1840.
*Taylor, *Transportation Revolution.**
Wyld, Lionel D., *Low Bridge! Folklore and the Erie Canal.* Syracuse, 1962.

11. AMERICA 1826: FIFTY YEARS OF INDEPENDENCE

America Through British Eyes.
Blane, William Newnham, *An Excursion Through the United States and Canada During the Years 1822–23, by an English Gentleman.* London, 1824.
*Calhoun, *The American Civil Engineer.**
Chapelle, Howard I., "The Pioneer Steamship Savannah: A Study for a Scale Model," *Contributions from the Museum of History and Technology,* Bulletin 228. Washington, D.C., 1961.
Faux, W., *Memorable Days in America, Being a Journal of a Tour in the United States.* London, 1823 (Reprinted in *Early Western Travels, 1748–1846,* ed. Reuben Gold Thwaites, Cleveland, Ohio, 1905).
*Hulbert, *The Great American Canals.**
Hunter, Louis C., *Steamboats on the Western Rivers, an Economic and Technological History.* New York, 1969.
Mirror for Americans, ed. Tryon.
*Taylor, *Transportation Revolution.**
Tocqueville, Alexis de, *Journey to America,* trans. George Lawrence, ed. J. P. Mayer. London, 1959.
Trollope, Frances, *Domestic Manners of the Americans,* ed. Donald Smalley. New York, 1949.
*Woodward, *The Way Our People Lived.**
*Wright and Fowler, *Life in the New Nation.**

12. THE STEVENSES, PETER COOPER, AND THE AMERICAN RAILROAD

Dunn, Gano, *Peter Cooper, 1791–1883—a Mechanic of New York.* New York, 1949.
*Finch, *Early Columbia Engineers.**
Hewitt, Edward R., *Those Were the Days.* New York, 1943.
Mack, Edward C., *Peter Cooper, Citizen of New York.* New York, 1949.
Smiles, Samuel, *The Life of George Stephenson and of His Son Robert Stephenson.* New York, 1868.
*Taylor, *Transportation Revolution.**
*Thurston, *The Messrs. Stevens.**
*Turnbull, *John Stevens.**
*Watkins, *John Stevens and His Sons.**

13. JOHN HALL AND SAM COLT: THE BIRTH OF THE "AMERICAN SYSTEM"

Brown, Stuart E., Jr., *The Guns of Harper's Ferry.* Berryville, Virginia, 1968.
*Butler, *United States Firearms.**

* See earlier citation.

Edwards, William B., *The Story of Colt's Revolver, the Biography of Colonel Samuel Colt.* New York, 1957.

Haven, Charles Tower, *A History of the Colt Revolver.* New York, 1940.

Huntington, R. T., *Hall's Breechloaders.* York, Pennsylvania, 1972.

Mitchell, James L., *Colt.* Harrisburg, Pennsylvania, 1959.

Peterson, Harold L., ed., *Encyclopedia of Firearms.* New York, 1964.

Rohan, Jack, *Yankee Arms Maker, the Story of Sam Colt and His Six-shot Peacemaker.* New York, 1948.

*Rolt, *A Short History of Machine Tools.*

*Rosebush, *American Firearms.*

*Russell, *Guns on the Early Frontiers.*

Rywell, Martin, *Samuel Colt, a Man and an Epoch.* Harriman, Tennessee, 1952.

*White, Edward Hartwell, *Development of Interchangeable Mass Manufacturing.*

*Woodbury, "Legend of Eli Whitney and Interchangeable Parts."

14. Obed Hussey and Cyrus McCormick: Mechanization of Agriculture

Barclay-Allardice, Robert, *Agricultural Tour in the United States and Upper Canada.* Edinburgh, 1842.

Bare, Margaret, *John Deere, Blacksmith Boy.* Indianapolis, 1964.

*Bidwell, *History of Agriculture.*

*Bogart, *Economic History of American Agriculture.*

Clark, Neil McCullough, *John Deere: He Gave to the World the Steel Plow.* Moline, Illinois, 1937.

Farming in the New Nation.

*Gates, *The Farmer's Age.*

Greeno, Follett L., *Obed Hussey, Who, of All Inventors, Made Bread Cheap.* Rochester, New York, 1912.

Holbrook, Stewart, *Machines of Plenty: Pioneering in American Agriculture.* New York, 1955.

Hutchinson, W. T., *Cyrus Hall McCormick.* 2 vols. New York, 1930.

Kendall, Edward C., "John Deere's Steel Plow." *Contributions from the Museum of History and Technology,* Bulletin 218. Washington, D.C., 1959.

McCormick, Cyrus III, *The Century of the Reaper.* Boston, 1931.

Readings in the History of American Agriculture.

Rogin, Leo, *The Introduction of Farm Machinery in Its Relation to the Productivity of Labor in the Agriculture of the United States in the Nineteenth Century.* Berkeley, California, 1931.

15. Charles Goodyear, Gentle Lunatic

Barker, Preston W., *Charles Goodyear, Connecticut Yankee and Rubber Pioneer.* Boston, 1940.

Goodyear, Charles, *Gum-Elastic and Its Varieties, with a Detailed Account of Its Applications and Uses and of the Discovery of Vulcanization.* 2 vols. New Haven, 1853.

Goodyear Tire and Rubber Company, *Life of Charles Goodyear.* Akron, Ohio, 1900.

Regli, Adolph C., *Rubber's Goodyear, the Story of a Man's Perseverance.* New York, 1941.

Wolf, Howard and Ralph, *Rubber, a Story of Glory and Greed.* New York, 1936.

* See earlier citation.

Wolf, Ralph F., *India Rubber Man, the Story of Charles Goodyear.* Caldwell, Idaho, 1939.

16. JOSEPH HENRY, SAMUEL MORSE (AND SEVERAL OTHERS) INVENT THE TELEGRAPH

Coulson, Thomas, *Joseph Henry, His Life and Work.* Princeton, 1950.
Davenport, Walter R., *Biography of Thomas Davenport, the "Brandon Blacksmith," Inventor of the Electric Motor.* Montpelier, Vermont, 1929.
Davenport, Willard G., "Work and Inventions of Thomas Davenport, Inventor and Prophet of the Use of Electro-Magnetism as a Motive Power," *Proceedings of the Vermont Historical Society,* Burlington, Vermont, October 1 and November 7, 1900.
Mabee, Carleton, *The American Leonardo, a Life of Samuel F. B. Morse.* New York, 1943.
The Papers of Joseph Henry, Vol. I, Dec. 1797–1832, The Albany Years, ed. Nathan Reingold. Washington, D.C., 1972.
Sharlin, Harold I., *The Making of the Electrical Age.* New York, 1963.
Thompson, Robert L., *Wiring a Continent: The History of the Telegraph Industry in the United States, 1832–1866.* Princeton, 1947.

17. THE SEWING MACHINE COMPLETES THE TEXTILE REVOLUTION

Caulon, J. J., *Genius Rewarded, or the Story of the Sewing Machine.* New York, 1880.
Cooper, Grace Rogers, *The Invention of the Sewing Machine.* Smithsonian Bulletin 254, Washington, D.C., 1968.
Ewers, William and Baylor, H. W., *Sincere's History of the Sewing Machine.* Phoenix, Arizona, 1970.
Gilbert, Keith R., *Sewing Machines.* London, 1970.
Lewton, Frederick I., "The Servant in the House: a Brief History of the Sewing Machine," *Smithsonian Annual Report,* 1929.
Parton, James, "The History of the Sewing Machine," *Atlantic Monthly,* May 1867.

18. AMERICA 1851

Beaver, Patrick, *The Crystal Palace, 1851, 1936.* London, 1970.
*Bidwell, *History of Agriculture.*
*Bogart, *Economic History of American Agriculture.*
Carter, Samuel III, *Cyrus Field, Man of Two Worlds.* New York, 1968.
Chambers, William, *Things as They Are in America.* New York, 1854.
Condit, Carl W., *American Building Art: the Nineteenth Century.* New York, 1960.
*Dahnhof, *Change in Agriculture.*
Dibner, Bern, *The Atlantic Cable.* Norwalk, Connecticut, 1959.
Ferguson, Eugene S., "John Ericsson and the Age of Caloric," *Contributions from the Museum of History and Technology,* Bulletin 228. Washington, D.C., 1960.
*Gates, *The Farmer's Age.*
*Gies, *Bridges and Men.*
Hamilton, Gail (pseudonym for Mary Abigail Dodge), *Wool-Gathering.* Boston, 1867.
Hobhouse, Christopher, *1851 and the Crystal Palace.* London, 1950.
*Holbrook, *Machines of Plenty.*

* See earlier citation.

*Hunter, *Steamboats on the Western Rivers.*

Petersen, L. A., *Elisha Graves Otis, 1811–1861, and His Influence Upon Vertical Transportation.* New York, 1945.

Rae, W. Fraser, *Westward by Rail, the New Route to the East.* New York, 1871.

*Rogin, *Introduction of Farm Machinery.*

*Taylor, *Transportation Revolution.*

Trollope, Anthony, *North America,* ed. Donald Smalley and Bradford Allen Booth. New York, 1951.

*Ware, Norman R., *The Industrial Worker.*

19. JOHN ROEBLING BRIDGES THE NIAGARA GORGE

*Billings, *Bridges.*

*Black, *Story of Bridges.*

Dempsey, G. Drysdale, *Tubular and Other Iron Girder Bridges.* London, 1850.

*Gies, *Bridges and Men.*

Harrod, Kathryn, *Master Bridge Builders: the Story of the Roeblings.* New York, 1958.

Schuyler, Hamilton, *The Roeblings: a Century of Engineers, Bridge Builders and Industrialists, 1831–1931.* Princeton, New Jersey, 1931.

Smith, H. Shirley, *The World's Great Bridges.* New York, 1953.

Steinman, David B., *The Builders of the Bridge, the Story of John Roebling and His Son.* New York, 1950.

*Steinman and Watson, *Bridges and Their Builders.*

Vose, George L., *Bridge Disasters in America.* Boston, 1887.

20. WILLIAM KELLY AND MASS-PRODUCED STEEL

Bessemer, Sir Henry, *Autobiography.* London, 1905.

Bishop, Philip, "The Beginnings of Cheap Steel." *Contributions from the Museum of History and Technology,* Bulletin 218, Washington, D.C., 1959.

Boucher, John N., *William Kelly, a True History of the So-Called Bessemer Process.* Greensburg, Pennsylvania, 1924.

Casson, Herbert N., *The Romance of Steel.* New York, 1907.

Fisher, Douglas A., *The Epic of Steel.* New York, 1963.

Jeans, William T., *The Creators of the Age of Steel.* London, 1884.

Wertime, T. A., *The Coming of the Age of Steel.* Chicago, 1962.

21. THE TECHNOLOGY OF CIVIL WAR

Bruce, Robert V., *Lincoln and the Tools of War.* Indianapolis, 1956.

*Butler, *United States Firearms.*

Canfield, Eugene B., *Notes on Naval Ordnance of the American Civil War, 1861–1865.* Washington, D.C., 1960.

Coggins, Jack, *Arms and Equipment of the Civil War.* New York, 1962.

Dorsey, Florence, *Road to the Sea.* New York, 1947.

Eaton, Clement, *A History of the Southern Confederacy.* New York, 1954.

Fuller, Claud E. and Steuart, Richard D., *Firearms of the Confederacy.* Huntington, West Virginia, 1944.

* See earlier citation.

Johnson, Robert U., and Buel, Clarence Clough, *Battles and Leaders of the Civil War.* 4 vols. New York, 1956.

*Lewis, *Small Arms and Ammunition in the United States Service.*

Lord, Francis A., *Civil War Collector's Encyclopedia.* New York, 1965.

Parsons, John E., *Smith & Wesson Revolvers, the Pioneer Single Action Models.* New York, 1957.

Ripley, Warren, *Artillery and Ammunition of the Civil War.* New York, 1970.

Weber, Thomas, *The Northern Railroads in the Civil War, 1861–65.* New York, 1952.

Winchester, Harold F., *Winchester, the Gun that Won the West.* Washington, D.C., 1952.

22. CAPTAIN EADS BUILDS THE ST. LOUIS BRIDGE

Carnegie, Andrew, *Autobiography.* Boston, 1920.

*Dorsey, *Road to the Sea.*

*Gies, *Bridges and Men.*

How, Louis, *James B. Eads.* Freeport, New York, 1970 (reprinted from edition of 1900).

Woodward, C. M., *A History of the St. Louis Bridge.* St. Louis, 1881.

Yager, Rosemary, *James Buchanan Eads: Master of the Great River,* Princeton, 1968.

23. CHRISTOPHER SHOLES AND THE TYPEWRITER

Drouin, F., *Les machines à écrire.* Paris, 1890.

Foulke, Arthur T., *Mr. Typewriter, a Biography of Christopher Latham Sholes.* Boston, 1961.

Richards, G. Tilghman, *The History and Development of Typewriters.* London, 1964.

Roby, H. W., *Story of the Invention of the Typewriter.* Menasha, Wisconsin, 1925.

Twain, Mark, "The First Writing Machines," *The $30,000 Bequest and Other Stories.* New York, 1906.

Weller, Charles E., *Early History of the Typewriter.* La Porte, Indiana, 1918.

Zellers, John A., *The Typewriter, a Short History on Its 75th Anniversary.* New York, 1948.

24. ALEXANDER GRAHAM BELL INVENTS THE TELEPHONE

Aitken, William, *Who Invented the Telephone?* London, 1939.

American Telephone and Telegraph, *The Career of Alexander Graham Bell.* New York, 1946.

The Bell Telephone: the Deposition of Alexander Graham Bell in the Suit Brought by the United States to Annul the Bell Patents. Boston, 1908.

Bruce, Robert V., *Bell: Alexander Graham Bell and the Conquest of Solitude.* Boston, 1973.

Casson, Herbert N., *The History of the Telephone.* Chicago, 1910.

Kingsbury, J. E., *The Telephone and Telephone Exchanges, Their Invention and Development.* New York, 1972.

Mackenzie, Catherine, *Alexander Graham Bell.* Boston, 1928.

Waite, Helen E., *Make a Joyful Sound.* Philadelphia, 1961.

Watson, Thomas A., *Exploring Life.* New York, 1926.

* See earlier citation.

25. EDISON INVENTS THE INDUSTRIAL RESEARCH LABORATORY

Beasley, Rex, *Edison*. Philadelphia, 1964.

Bryan, George S., *Edison, the Man and His Work*. Garden City, New York, 1926.

Dyer, Frank L., and Martin, Thomas C., *Edison, His Life and Inventions*. 2 vols. New York, 1910.

Edison, Thomas A., *Diary*. New York, 1948.

Jehl, Francis, *Menlo Park Reminiscences*. Dearborn, Michigan, 1937.

Josephson, Matthew, *Edison*. New York, 1959.

Miller, Francis T., *Thomas A. Edison, Benefactor of Mankind*. Philadelphia, 1931.

Passer, Harold C., *The Electrical Manufacturers, 1875–1900*. Cambridge, Massachusetts, 1953.

*Sharlin, *Making of the Electrical Age*.

Silverberg, Robert, *Light for the World: Edison and the Power Industry*. Princeton, 1967.

Simonds, William A., *Edison, His Life, His Work, His Genius*. New York, 1940.

* See earlier citation.

INDEX